THE RISE OF MESO GOVERNMENT
IN EUROPE

THE RISE OF MESO GOVERNMENT IN EUROPE

edited by
L. J. Sharpe

SAGE Modern Politics Series Volume 32
Sponsored by the European Consortium for
Political Research/ECPR

SAGE Publications
London · Newbury Park · New Delhi

First published 1993
Reprinted 1996

SAGE Publications Ltd
6 Bonhill Street
London EC2A 4PU

SAGE Publications Inc
2455 Teller Road
Thousand Oaks, California 91320

SAGE Publications India Pvt Ltd
32, M-Block Market
Greater Kailash – I
New Delhi 110 048

British Library Cataloguing in Publication data

Rise of Meso Government in Europe. – (Sage Modern Politics
Series; Vol. 32)
I. Sharpe, L. J. II. Series 321.9
ISBN 0–8039–8776–5

Library of Congress catalog card number 92–56383

Typeset by Type Study, Scarborough
Printed in Great Britain by Antony Rowe Ltd, Chippenham, Wiltshire

Contents

The Contributors

Sabino Cassese, Faculty of Law, University of Rome, Italy
Montserrat Cuchillo, Faculty of Law, Pompeu Fabra University, Barcelona, Spain
Frank Delmartino, Department of Political Science, Katholieke Universiteit Leuven, Belgium
Tore Hansen, Institute for Political Science, University of Oslo, Norway
Michael Keating, Department of Political Science, University of Western Ontario, London, Ontario, Canada
Antoni Kukliński, European Institute of Local and Regional Development, University of Warsaw, Poland
Sonia Mazey, Faculty of Social and Political Sciences and Churchill College, Cambridge, UK
L. J. Sharpe, Nuffield College, Oxford, UK
Paweł Swianiewicz, European Institute of Local and Regional Development, University of Warsaw, Poland
Theo A. J. Toonen, Department of Public Administration, University of Leiden, Netherlands
Luisa Torchia, Regional Studies Institute, Rome, Italy

Preface and Acknowledgements

The project of which this book is the main product was conceived at a research conference organized by the European Consortium for Political Research held in Mannheim in 1986. In 1987 the Volkswagen Stiftung very generously agreed to fund the project, we owe a special debt of gratitude to the Stiftung for its support. Among other things, it enabled us to meet over an extended period so as to maximize interchange and discussion, thus ensuring a higher level of comparability in our endeavours than is normally possible and, we hope, improving their general quality. But that, of course, is for the reader to judge. We had originally intended to include Germany in the list of countries covered but, although a chapter was prepared by Joachim Jens Hesse from which we all benefited, it was rapidly overtaken by the massive changes that accompanied the amalgamation of East and West Germany and so, regrettably, had to be omitted.

The Volkswagen grant enabled us to enjoy the benefit of the skills of Peter John, whose tireless efforts as research assistant for a year are very much appreciated. We would like to thank the management of IAFE (a division of ENI), who through the good of offices of Sabino Cassese were our hosts for a memorable meeting at their centre at Castel Gondolfo. Equal thanks are due to the Rector of Warsaw University, who through Antoni Kukliński made the splendid Radziejowicach Palace available to us for another research meeting. We owe special thanks to the Warden and Fellows of Nuffield College, Oxford, who provided the venue for the first and the last of our meetings. Last but by no means least the editor wishes to acknowledge the invaluable secretarial assistance provided by Elaine Herman.

1

The European Meso: An Appraisal

L. J. Sharpe

This book is concerned with what seems to be a near-universal phenomenon over the last twenty years or so in the Western European state, namely the emergence of an intermediate level of government between the centre and the basic municipal or communal level. This new institutional type either takes the form of an entirely new system of *regional* elected government exercising executive, and sometimes legislative, powers (Italy, France, Spain, Belgium, Portugal in part and possibly Greece), or it is a strengthened and refurbished *county* level of local government (Norway, Sweden, Denmark, the UK and some *Länder* in West Germany). The Netherlands, as Theo Toonen explains, is a kind of halfway house between the two types. In a few cases, such as France (the *département*) and Germany (the *Regierungsbezirk*), an essentially administrative meso level, has also taken on a new lease of life. Such is the tendency of institutional political science to generate neologisms, and its corresponding incapacity to build up a basic and lasting nomenclature, that all should hesitate before inflicting, or perpetuating, yet another relatively new term on the reader. But in this case it is a reasonable infliction, if only to avoid any confusion with 'region', for the institution we are to scrutinize is both much more and to some extent less than regional; hence the chosen title, 'meso' (from the Greek, *mesos* for middle). It is perhaps best described in abstract terms as a 'decision space' rather than a level of government. That is to say, it may be seen as a level within the government structure that is more appropriate for certain kinds of decisions and policies than either central or local government.

The first question that arises is, why devote a whole book to the meso? Any answer to such a question must emphasize, first, that the meso constitutes one of the most important institutional changes in the modern Western state that has occurred over the past couple of decades. Important not simply in terms of the power that it wields in some countries, but also because in its extreme form the meso not only has changed the character of the state, but can pose critical questions about the very nature of the unitary state and its continuing utility or relevance as a concept in political science (King, 1982; Bennett, 1989a; Leonardi and Nanetti, 1990). The struggle for the creation of the meso has also been important in the politics of some European states. This has obviously been the case for Belgium where, as Frank Delmartino's chapter demonstrates, the meso has reflected the central fact of Belgian political life for at least the past two decades. In Spain, too, it is inconceivable that the new democratic state could have been launched in 1979 without the creation of at least the three Autonomous Communities. In France it was de Gaulle's abortive attempt to create a new meso via the 1969 referendum that finally brought him down, thus ending the most vital era in post-war French politics. Although no British regional meso was in fact launched, it was the Labour government's decision in 1979 to stick by the 40 per cent rule in the Scottish referendum which led to its defeat, sponsored by the Scottish Nationalists, in a vote of confidence in the House of Commons and the subsequent election of Mrs Thatcher. This was a momentous change that has since led to one of the most significant, not to say revolutionary, administrations in modern British political history, and one that has had policy ramifications throughout the West.

The meso has also figured at the supra-national level in Western Europe, partly because since the early 1970s it has become an object of EC funding, and partly because other EC policies have enhanced regional consciousness in peripheral regions by favouring heartland interests either directly, as in the case of the Common Agricultural Policy, or indirectly by integrating and concentrating the internal market in manufactures, a process that will accelerate after 1992. Meso development is, then, inextricably bound up with EC development in those states that are members of the Community. Indeed, some see the rise of the meso as an inevitable concomitant of EC growth and expansion. In its extreme form this prediction becomes the 'Europe of the regions' thesis which sees the meso as being in a symbiotic relationship with Brussels, with the nation state slowly wasting away in redundancy. While the burgeoning meso, as the beneficiary of the *subsidiarity* principle (Adonis and Jones, 1991), balances the centralization of power in Brussels. Whatever the accuracy of the 'Europe of the regions' thesis – and we will return to it later – there can be little doubt that the regional meso is going to be an increasingly important element in the evolution of the EC. The meso, then, is prima facie a subject which needs little justification for book-length treatment. But more than that, the emergence of the meso signals perhaps an even more important change of the post-war Western state which reopens key questions concerning the territorial dimension of representative politics that have been quiescent during the early phase of the development of that state.

The second question that a study of the Western European meso prompts is, why did it emerge when it did? If the meso is such a widespread phenomenon and in some cases has attained a significant political salience, what are the aspects common to the Western European state that have precipitated such a comparatively uniform institutional response of this kind? Or, is its near-universality merely an accident? Undoubtedly its origins are both complex and varied and national political traditions in Western Europe vary enormously in form and process. Teasing out uniformities, therefore, is a hazardous exercise fraught with pitfalls for even the most know-ledgeable and intrepid of comparativists. Nevertheless, that is no excuse for not trying, since the prima-facie evidence clearly suggests that something universal may be at work. It is for others to judge whether this exercise succeeds in demonstrating the existence of such universality. But, of course, that would not be the only, or indeed the most important, test of the rationale for this collection; for there is the need to gather in a manageable form a reasonably up-to-date account of the meso as a political and administrative phenomenon, quite apart from any requirement to uncover its causes or rationale.

Regional ethnic nationalism

Bearing such thoughts in mind, the first causal factor associated with the meso in terms of its importance for the nation state itself is the rise of regional ethnic nationalism beginning in the early 1960s.[1] Its key importance is best seen in the cases of Belgium and Spain where the extent of the transformation of the unitary state has gone furthest to accommodate the aspirations of the strongest regional subcultures within the respective territories of the two countries.

Regional nationalism also seems to have played a part in the establishment of regional government in Italy in the late 1940s, under the regional clause of the new democratic constitution of 1948. For regional governments were created only in the five special regions, all of them peripheral, whose allegiance to the state at the time could be deemed to be, in varying degrees, problematic: Sicily, Sardinia, Valle d'Aosta, Trento-Alto Adige, Friuli-Venezia-Giulia. In France, too, a regional nationalist element, but no more, may be said to have contributed to the legislation that finally created fully fledged regional government in the early 1980s. The UK provides the final example of the direct influence of regional nationalism on the creation of the meso. But in this case the birth of the meso was aborted, although, as the British chapter in this volume suggests, the chances of a meso government at least for Scotland and Wales are now perhaps stronger than they have ever been.

Important as regional nationalism is as a reason for the creation of meso government, and perhaps even more for sustaining it once created, it has to be recognized, first, that the conditions for the emergence of such nationalism vary considerably from state to state. There can be no better way of illustrating such variation than by comparing Italy and Spain, two countries which at the broadest level share some socio-cultural characteristics. In Italy there are no regional nationalist movements of any consequence, since the final pattern of the special regions was settled with the *proporz paket* of the 1970s for the Bolzano province in the Trento-Alto Adige region. It could be claimed that the appearance of regional *leghe*, or parties, in the late 1980s in some of the Italian regions where they have attracted a sizeable proportion of the vote at regional elections reflects the emergence of regional movements comparable to those operating in Spain. But as Sabino Cassese and Luisa Torchia's chapter emphasizes, this phenomenon has much more to do with anti-southern and anti-foreign immigration sentiment than it does with regionalism. However, the conditions which elsewhere might be thought to be the key conditions for regional nationalism abound in Italy. For example, two highly peripheral regions, Sicily and Sardinia, which speak a dialect of standard Italian that in both cases could be defined as a separate language are also islands. In other peripheries in the north actual foreign languages and comparably strong dialects predominate. The wide variations in the relative prosperity of the different segments of the Italian state, which are among the most striking in Western Europe and certainly match those in Spain, might also be seen as a stimulator of regional consciousness. Above all, Italy itself is one of the youngest states in Western Europe, achieving its present unity only in 1860 – prior to which, San Marino apart, it was divided into eight separate, often antagonistic and ancient sovereign states and principalities. Most surprising of all, the Italian regional boundaries, finally completed with the creation of Molise in 1973, bear no relationship to these former states, with the exception of Tuscany, which, if we ignore the Grand Duchy of Lucca, does broadly follow the boundary of the old Tuscan Grand Duchy.

The contrast with Spain could not be greater, for not only is Spain one of the oldest European states, being founded with broadly its present boundaries in 1492, it was also a major imperial power including in its empire colonies in Italy itself. Yet some of the older kingdoms and principalities that formed the present state have lived on for five centuries after unification with a strong sense of regional identity such that it was inconceivable that the aspirations these feelings fed were not reflected in the new post-Franco constitution. It must also be recognized that the strength and character of regional nationalism varies as much as its causes. In terms of its strength, it runs from the almost implacable demands of the two major language groups in Belgium – which seem to have no limit short of rendering nugatory the Belgian unitary state – to the desire for some institutional recognition of a sense of difference from the core, or majority, culture of the kind that seems to inform those French and Italian regions where there is any sense of cultural difference in the first place. It need hardly be added that such differences in regional consciousness render the possible consequences of creating a meso to be vastly different. The extreme regional nationalist movements which often include hatred of the core culture as part of their ideological repertoire seek ultimately some form of separation from the host state, so meso government becomes the thin end of a wedge. The moderate regional nationalists at the other end of the spectrum may, by contrast, become more loyal to the central state as a consequence of getting their own meso government.

Extreme separatist regional movements, as the following chapters indicate, are in a small minority among Western European states and where they do exist the separatist aspiration may be publicly downplayed. Where it is not, as in the Basque and the Scottish cases, it is dressed up in the modernizing rhetoric of European integration. As the Basque ETA (Euzkadi Ta Askatasoma) movement has it, the aim is not simply to leave the Spanish state, but to become the thirteenth star in the EC flag. Nor should extremism be identified with violence. The Scottish nationalist movement is one of the strongest in Western Europe, but it has always rigidly eschewed any violence, especially assassination or bombing. It has always pursued its aims in an impeccably democratic manner. Equally, extremism does not necessarily imply secession, for such an association breaks down in the case of Belgium. The primary actor in the emergence of what is perhaps the most extreme form of meso government, the Flanders region, has sought to correct the disparity between its superiority in numbers and later in economic power and its second-class status within the Belgian state, especially in relation to its language (Mughan, 1979). Broadly speaking, as Frank Delmartino's chapter emphasizes, it has achieved its aims and the Flemish language now has parity of esteem and Flemings commensurate political power. Only the problem of the continuing expansion of the Brussels agglomeration (and thus the French language) remains as a perceived threat to Flemish interests. It follows that the Flemish nationalist movement, although one of the most virulent in Western Europe, is now reconciled to the new minimal Belgian state and certainly does not seek separation.

The Flemish example is, as we shall see, a special case, but it does point to the wider question: to what extent does the emergence of the meso in the ethnically heterogeneous European states put the integrity of such states at risk? One way of answering that question is to conceptualize the range of regional aspirations in economic terms. This approach may be justified because economic effects are usually assumed to be vital in modern, high-consumption Western European societies, such that almost all major political issues have to have an economic referent in order to be regarded as salient. In such terms, we may distinguish extremist nationalist movements as being those which are prepared to countenance a fundamental change in the allocatory order – that is to say, some form of separation from the core state – thus creating a new national economy. We may call this extremist type of movement *investment* regional nationalism (Green, 1982), and in the nature of the case it is the minority among Western European regional movements. The majority of regional nationalist movements do not seek separation but, rather, some institutional and symbolic recognition of their sense of difference from the core culture. We may call this form *consumption* regional nationalism; not conforming to the norms of the core culture becomes a collective consumption good (Johnson, 1968: 14–15). Not for the consumption nationalist the high risks of putting the existing allocatory order in jeopardy; rather, the prudential motivation of improving that system in their favour by extracting more resources from the centre and pursuing more vigorous economic development policies. Such a tactic will, paradoxically, probably increase the power of the central state. Hence the question that dogged the regional debate, especially in relation to regional planning throughout Western Europe in the late 1960s: was regionalism a centralist or decentralist process?

If such an economic approach to categorizing the strength and character of regional nationalist movements has any validity, it follows that we may expect that investment nationalist movements will tend to be at their strongest during periods of prosperity when the risks involved in separation are lower. Conversely, periods of economic recession will tend to have the reverse effect. Defining regional nationalism in this way, it must be emphasized, is not to imply that regional nationalist movements are exclusively, or even mainly, economic in origin. Some clearly are, but it is impossible to fit all various manifestations of regional nationalism into either an economic deprivation mould – Languedoc and Galicia – or an economic superiority one – Flanders and Catalonia. In so far as it is possible to generalize about origins, the majority of manifestations of regional nationalism seem to have a socio-cultural origin. There are exceptional cases such as the quasi-separatist movement in Alberta in Canada and that of Western Australia in Australia, but there seems to be no equivalent in Europe to these, what may be called purely territorial regional nationalisms. The socio-cultural trigger is, in the broadest terms, a consciousness of difference from the majority culture that goes beyond mere localized variation and involves a difference in language, religion or ethnicity, or all three. It is such prior conditions which may enhance an economic difference, but regional nationalism is rarely simply determined by economic factors. In some cases the prior conditions may be largely institutional in origin, rather than cultural or economic, as in the case of Scotland or Catalonia; here the peripheral area has existed in the past as a distinctive sovereign political entity – the reverse, as it were, of Engels's *geschichtlosen Völker*, that is, those ethnic regional groups that have never enjoyed autonomy. In essence, regional nationalism is the nationalism of 'secondary' nations which in the past succumbed to, and were absorbed for various reasons by, 'primary nations' but which now seek some recognition of their national status usually short of separate nation-statehood (Connor, 1973; Smith, 1979).

So much for describing regional nationalism. There remains to be answered the question, why, since it has existed presumably since the host state was formed, did it give rise to political movements when it did almost universally in the early 1960s? Obviously in a world of almost instant communication one factor is emulation, but that does not account for the initiators who were emulated. We argue later in this chapter that regional nationalism is part of the process of democratic maturation, and there can be little doubt that in the case of Spain and to some extent Italy the emergence of regional nationalism was a direct consequence of the ending of authoritarian rule through the establishment of democracy. In other Western European countries the trigger was not democracy but the ending of the Second World War and the return to freedom of expression. But for some regions there had to be some delay before the movement could 'come out', since their aspirations had been tainted with collaboration, or accusations of it, with the German occupying power. Such was the position of the Flemish nationalist movement, as it was of the Breton, the Corsican and, of course, the Alsatian.

There was also the fact of uneven development itself, highlighted by regional economic planning doctrines, as we shall see, which meant that some peripheries did not share in the increased prosperity of the core state. The battle for equality was territorialized. In yet other peripheries the very consequences of growth – industrialization and cultural homogenization – far from unifying the political systems as orthodox theory predicted, generated a *reaction* of cultural defence. The rise of regional identity in this case was an attack on the consequences of growth (Sharpe, 1979: ch. 1).

Additional explanations

Decisive as regional nationalism has certainly been in the emergence of meso government in some countries and in sustaining it once established, especially in Spain and Belgium, it is not in any sense the only reason for the rise of the meso. Still less it is likely to be the most important influence on how the meso has been flourishing since its creation in those countries where regional nationalism has been relatively weak, such as France and especially Italy. There are, however, likely to be a host of possible additional determining factors associated with the emergence of the meso; the problem is selecting those that have the greatest degree of plausibility and universality. Bearing this in mind, there seem to be four distinct groups of factors which the chapters that follow suggest have had the most impact. They may be called *rational-functional*, *ideological*, *sectional* interest and *central advantage*.

Rational-functional
The rational-functional set of motives or reasons for establishing a meso has to do with two key socio-economic changes at the local level of the modern advanced industrial state. The first is geographical and may be called the suburban (or second urban) revolution. If the first urban revolution is the centripetal movement of the surplus agricultural labour generated by higher agricultural productivity and lower mortality in rural areas to the burgeoning industry in the towns, the second urban revolution is the centrifugal movement of population and industry from the core of the urban centres to their outer margins largely as a consequence of industrial congestion, economic growth and rising living standards. There is a third and subsequent migratory process from suburbia to largely rural settings. This is the so-called counter-urbanization process and we will come to it later (Berry, 1976). The urban growth consequent upon the suburban revolution means that the old pre-industrial local government structure is under-bounded and no longer corresponds to socio-geographic reality. The requirement is for geographically larger areas. At the extreme such under-boundedness may require the designation of new jurisdictions of meso proportions: in a metropolitan area, for example.

The second key change under the rational-functional head is

functional in origin; as the Western state has expanded its activities during the twentieth century an increasing proportion of that expansion as measured by expenditure has taken place at the sub-national level.[2] The modern state, at least up until the early 1980s, in short, has been growing at the sub-national level at a faster rate than at the centre (Sharpe, 1988). At the local level one of the characteristics of these new sub-national tasks is that they may entail large, expensive and indivisible capital investments that require a high throughput if costs are to be kept within manageable limits. Large indivisible capital and large throughputs demand large base populations; so, like suburbanization, this functional change also required larger local government units, but larger in population terms. A similar need also arose in relation to the much higher externalities of the new functions, so local government units needed to be enlarged geographically as well if benefits received were to match local tax obligations.

To summarize, the rational-functional set of factors is all to do with enlarging the local government structure in order to cope with urbanization and new service responsibilities. The creation of the meso, whether it be a new-style county or a new regional government, forms part of the restructuring process in the sense that it attempts to deal with extreme cases, that is, those where the need for enlargement both geographically and in population terms is at its greatest. There is another sense in which such restructuring is linked to the creation of the meso. In those countries where for various reasons it is difficult to modernize the local government system, since it will among other things involve the abolition of some municipalities, the creation of the meso may be seen as a convenient alternative method of achieving the necessary increase in scale. Here lies one possible reason why Northern European states have not created entirely new regional governments, since they were able to modernize their local government systems. In Southern Europe, by contrast, where the resistance of the local government system to modernization was compounded by other factors peculiar to the Napoleonic, or fused-hierarchy, mode of central–local relations (France, Italy, Spain, Belgium, Portugal), the region became an attractive option. We will return to this possible source of meso variation later.

This is probably the most convenient point to add an additional linked regionalizing factor, namely changing public attitudes. Whereas the onward march of urbanization may be seen as an *objective* determinant of enlarged sub-national governments, the changing 'mental maps' of the some inhabitants of the spread city, especially those involved in the third urban revolution mentioned earlier, may constitute an increasingly important *subjective* determinant. Such outer suburbanities may travel 30 or 40 miles to their place of work and think nothing of driving 10 miles to shop for groceries. With such extended movement patterns, it seems likely that their sense of localness and its importance may have diminished. In short, more citizens than in the past may be willing to tolerate units of sub-national government of a territorial scale that matches their own movement patterns.

Before turning to the second set of additional causes of the meso it may be helpful to conceptualize those origins that may be loosely described as functional: to locate the meso, that is, in the longer-term functional evolution of the modern Western unitary state; and, indeed, of federal states, for a meso is also discernible within the larger German *Länder*. Broadly speaking, up until the 1920s it would be possible to posit two basic levels of government in unitary states, the *local* and the *central*, each with its complement of tasks loosely based on two distinct rationales. At the local, or communal, level the rationale was a simple *externality* rule; the communal government should be responsible for those collective consumption tasks that had few, or no, externalities beyond the boundary of the community on behalf of which the tasks are performed. In that way benefits received and tax obligations are congruent – those who consume the service pay for it. Such self-contained services may include primary and secondary education, refuse collection, sewage disposal, local roads, street lighting, recreation space, meeting halls and so forth. In Napoleonic systems the local government itself might not undertake these low-externality functions, but it was accountable to its electorate for them.

The rationale for the allocation of public functions to the *centre* may be said to be essentially that of *indivisibility*. The core tasks are largely pure public goods such as public order, enforcement of the law, defence, foreign relations, maintenance of the currency, the judicial system, economic management, nationwide communications and so forth. Via these two rules – the communal externality rule and the national indivisibility rule – most of the major governmental tasks of the pre-welfare unitary state were allocated. The arrival of the post-Second World War welfare state, plus the prolonged economic boom and the rapid urbanization that accompanied it, meant that a new set of public functions were created some of which could not be easily fitted into this duality. For some of them, what may be called the SHEW (social, health, education and welfare) group of services, the externalities were usually too great for communal government. Their cost was often too great as well, given the almost universal inelastic local tax base of local government. Moreover, the onward march of urbanization rendered the simple dichotomy of national and communal levels outdated in major urban areas.

As we have noted, local government was modernized or enlarged in the Northern European dual or split hierarchy systems (Norway, Denmark, Sweden, Finland, the UK), and this meant that some externalities attributable to the new functions, such as new-style secondary and vocational education and land use planning, could be internalized. In the Napoleonic fused hierarchy states the pressure to change communal boundaries was less, since the centre was the service provider, thus rendering externality and economies-of-scale problems less important; it was not constrained, in short, by communal boundaries. In any case, in such systems the capacity to provide local functions is not a necessary attribute of local government as it is in the dual or split hierarchy systems of Northern Europe.

Other SHEW functions were taken on by the centre. As in all things, countries varied as to which these were, but certain practices seem to have been common to most countries. For example, the centre has usually retained responsibility for the disbursement of transfers, that is, cash payments for ameliorating income inequalities derived from either the trade or the life cycle. This was partly a consequence of all central governments retaining progressive income tax, but it is also no doubt related to the relative ease of centralizing transfer payments because only low levels of discretion at the point of payment are required and there are measurable outputs.

The fiscal dominance of the centre and the extent to which it has taken a wide-ranging role of economic management, derived from Keynesian demand management plus the pressure for equality, have tended to extend the role of the centre. Such extension was in terms not so much of exclusive competence – horizontalism – but of establishing vertical operating partnerships with non-central governmental, quasi-governmental and private institutions. One such partnership is of critical importance to the evolution of the meso: that of economic planning at the regional level, which we will come to in a moment. This new style of vertical intervention has put a premium on the establishment of complex co-operative relationships between the centre and its non-central partners in which both its control and its dependency are extremely difficult to disentangle (Hanf, 1978; Rhodes, 1986).

Not only has the extension of the centre's role become more complex and difficult to map; the centre has also been careful not to overload itself with all of the new SHEW functions. In 12 of the 22 so-called advanced industrial democracies, such has been the centre's reluctance that the sub-national system had by the early 1970s grown beyond the point of overtaking the centre in terms of its share of total public expenditure. The 12 include, as might be expected, all the federal systems except Australia, but also 8 unitary states. The reasons for the centre's resistance to outright centralization are no doubt many and almost certainly have included, as we shall see, the tendency for the centre to off-load to the periphery functions it did not wish to undertake for various reasons and to shed some financial responsibility. Also a technocratic desire for autonomy in some sectors may have played a part, as we shall see.

Regional planning   One very important aspect of the rational-functional root of the meso is regional planning. State planning since the Second World War in the West tended to follow the French indicative model, particularly in Belgium, Italy and the UK (Hayward and Watson, 1975). There was also a form of indicative planning in Spain (Richardson, 1975). The distinctive feature of the indicative model that is relevant concerns its departure from the sectoral Gosplan style adopted originally by the USSR in favour of a spatially structured plan based on regions. This fundamental change was in recognition of the vastly different economic conditions that may obtain from region to region within the national economy. In order to achieve the overall growth objective the essence of the planning exercise was to have a planning system which would make it possible to vary policy and aims on a regional basis in recognition of such varying conditions. This mode entailed among other things the creation of a regional structure of deconcentrated government where central planning staffs, or *missions*, linked up with representative elements of the region from local government, industry, trade unions and so forth. Together the two sides formulated a regional plan, within the parameters set by the centre, which then formed part of the national plan. This process and structure had a number of effects on the political system. In the first place, they introduced, or re-enforced, a regional dimension by giving the region official recognition, especially in terms of highlighting the degree of variation in the fortunes of regions despite the post-war economic boom. Above all, they seemed to provide a rationale for channelling central aid to the poorer regions and damping down growth in the boom regions. For this reason alone it would be wrong to view regional planning simply as an example of rational-institutional design. In a very real sense it was also an attempt by the centre to be seen to be responding to the plight of the poorer regions. It did not matter that its intentions were not in fact redistributional, but, rather, the need to reduce the wage-push inflationary effects of the very high growth regions on the economy as a whole. By giving a redistributional patina to regional policy, the centre hoped to recruit supporters for the planning process and enhance its own political support.

This was not the only sense in which the regional planning phase became entangled in issues that were not really part of its purpose; for, as the Italian and UK chapters emphasize, the regional machinery came to be seen by some as embryo governments which could be the engine for, among other things, the decentralization of the state, the enhancement of popular participation and the modernization of the economy. However, in reality it was intended to be none of these things, for its purpose was simply to make central planning more efficient and was thus an extension of the central state's power and had no necessary connection with decentralization or popular participation (Sharpe, 1972). But such misinterpretations helped form the foundations for regional government.

There is another sense in which the regional planning phase was something more than a rational-functional institutional change. In the quasi-clientilist systems of Southern Europe both its representative institutions and its redistributive consequences meant that regional planning encroached on the preserves of the *notables* and seemed to offer new sources of patronage, so that it became invested with a political importance that went to the heart of central–local relations. In this way regional planning was drawn into the national party battle in France throughout the late 1960s and 1980s (Mény, 1982a). In some countries regional planning was given added lustre by being associated with the case for local government modernization in the sense that the economic planning region was seen as the crucial link between national and local planning. It was the link that joined national economic planning – planning investment over time – with local land use planning – the planning of investment in space.

Although by the anti-statist 1990s regional planning had long ceased to be important, the whole regional planning episode was an extremely important phase in the evolution of the meso in those countries where it has evolved at the regional level. In the first place, it provided an established task for the new governments which was extremely important, especially in Italy, since it raised the meso's public visibility (Selan and Donnini, 1975). Second, it provided, or re-enforced, a given spatial structure in which the meso could be firmly rooted, thus avoiding a lengthy wrangle over boundaries. The regional planning phase also sparked off ideas and concepts which still persist in the politics of meso government, the most important of which is the notion of the meso level as its own economic saviour in the sense of both tapping into the international system for, say, foreign investment, and also defending its interests where, for example, the unevenness of economic growth means that it does not share in national growth. The fact that the first strategy seeks to bypass the centre while the second seeks its assistance should not blind us to the possibility that this economic role of the meso may be one of its enduring functions (Hebbert and Machin, 1984). Most sub-national policy-making is, in the nature of the case, a blend of dependency and autonomy.

To summarize the rational-functional root of the meso, the emergence after the Second World War of the urbanized, affluent, unitary welfare state has transformed the public sector such that the traditional basis for the distribution of state functions between centre and locality was no longer satisfactory. Given the limitations on increasing the scale of the local level, the less urgent necessity to do so in Napoleonic states and the various restrictions on outright centralization, either a new meso level of government had to be created, or the upper tier of local government refurbished, to cope with the new tasks and at the same time avoid the drawbacks, perceived or real, of both the centre and the traditional communal level. In the case of France, as Sonia Mazey's chapter reveals, the functional component of meso growth is discernible not only in the creation of the region but in the growth in power of the *département* as well (Bernier, 1991). In short, whereas the causal relationship may have been very much stronger for other factors, particularly ethnic heterogeneity in Southern Europe, and, as we shall see, ideological factors, functional pressures could have independently led to the creation of some sort of meso in the long run. The regional planning element in the evolution of the meso was extremely important, especially for those countries where it takes the form of regional government, for it provided a lasting basis for the new meso in terms of a basic set of boundaries. It is significant, too, that land use master planning remains a core function of virtually all meso governments, regional or county. It is this broadly functional origin of the meso that may also partly explain the differences between the form the meso takes in Southern as compared with Northern states in Western Europe.

Ideological
We may deal with the ideological aspect of the meso's origins fairly briefly. There are two strands to it, and the first is the inevitable identification of decentralization with democracy in those states that endured the long night of fascist centralization. It was this association which strongly influenced the federal character of the post-war West German Constitution. More decisively, the assumption that

decentralization is inherently democratic accounts for one of the most distinctive characteristics of the post-Franco Spanish state, the Autonomous Community, as Montserrat Cuchillo's chapter emphasizes. Similar associations of democracy with decentralization were also responsible for the regional clause of the post-war Italian Constitution.

Reaction to fascist centralization, however, is not the only sense in which it is possible to argue that there are ideological underpinnings of the European meso. Tore Hansen's chapter on Norway makes it clear that the refurbishment of the county (*fylke*) was strongly influenced by a widely shared desire emerging in the 1970s to decentralize the Norwegian state. A similar motivation is even more apparent in the rejuvenation of the Danish county (Kjellberg, 1988; Norton, 1988b). As the 1958 commission on local government reform in Denmark put the matter: 'The explicit intention with this reform proposal has been to create the basis for a rational decision of functions within public administration such that the concept of democracy expressed in the institution of local government can be more firmly entrenched' (Kjellberg, 1988: 59). Some association between the promotion of democracy, in particular public participation, and the strengthening of local government is apparent in the Swedish county reforms (Gustafsson, 1983; Norton, 1988a; Elander and Montin, 1990). There is some academic disagreement as to how far subsequent developments in central–local relations ostensibly aimed at decentralizing power, such as the 'free county' and 'free commune' experiments in Denmark, Norway and Finland, as well as in Sweden, have in fact done so or were intended to do so (Elander and Montin, 1990; Rose, 1990; Etherington and Paddon, 1991). But it cannot be denied that one of the stated aims of the experiment in all four countries was that of enhancing public participation in government by decentralization (Stewart and Stoker, 1989; Lodden, 1991) and that is why it received public support. Moreover, the experiments did actually decentralize power. Even Rose, the most penetrating and most sceptical observer, concedes this much (Rose, 1990: 228).

Nor is the explicit decentralization-equals-democracy policy aim in creating or strengthening the meso merely yet another example of Scandinavian avant-gardism, for a similar relatively low-key decentralist aim is discernible in Germany in the later 1960s (Hrbek, 1986). It was also an explicit major policy aim of the French Socialists, formerly a bastion of the Jacobin state, when they came to power in the early 1980s. Although lacking the drama of the French volte-face, conceiving the new regions as a way of rejuvenating the well-springs of Italian democracy was also a contributory thread in the belated

implementation of the regional clause of the constitution in 1970.
Both the French and the Italian decentralizing processes were to
some extent also the products of severe social disruption in both
countries during the late 1960s (*les événements* in France and the
autunno caldo in Italy), although it must be readily conceded, as we
shall see, that party interests were much to the fore in both countries
as well. At a somewhat broader level, the relative success of the meso
must also be seen against what seems to be a clear change in public
attitudes towards the state, in particular a sense of dissatisfaction
throughout the West with the strong, though perhaps largely
unintended, inclination of the post-war welfare state towards bureaucratization and centralization (Walker, 1991).

At risk of excessive speculation, the origin of such centralization
and bureaucratization may be seen as an initial preoccupation during
the early stages with the need to ensure greater interpersonal equality
and to establish minimum standards of welfare and income maintenance throughout the national territory. The emphasis was, then,
mainly on the creation of the most efficient instrumentalities for
achieving such aims – for achieving, that is, production efficiency in
service delivery as defined largely by those providing the service, to a
receptive but largely inert set of recipients. Such preoccupations with
production efficiency became increasingly less acceptable to the
majority, it may be surmised, since, in the nature of the case, it took
too little account of consumer preferences and perhaps rising living
standards and expectations. This part of the decentralizing and
de-bureaucratizing movement is associated with consumers attempt-
ing to wrest control from technocrats and change the direction of the
welfare state towards consumption rather than production efficiency.
This is a process Coombes has called 'layering' (Coombes, 1979: 6).

Decentralization of the state apparatus may not be the only
manifestation of the push for consumption efficiency, for it is also
linked to the demand for privatization. Privatization in this context
may be seen merely as another form of decentralization which its
proponents would claim is a much better mode for ensuring
consumption efficiency, since it allegedly renders the service subject
to the market test. It is of some interest in this connection that one of
the Western European states that has resisted the decentralization
trend we are discussing – indeed has embarked on a centralization of
the state sometimes on a heroic scale – the UK, is also the same
country where privatization has been embraced with the greatest
enthusiasm.

There is another, possibly related change in the broad character of
welfare state politics that has effected not so much the emergence of
meso government as its successful operation once created. It is

derived from the enhanced role of the state in the post-war period in managing the economy which has entailed a growth in the power of producer groups to bargain with the central state over economic policy. Only be gaining the acquiescence of such groups could the new activist state wield the demand management policies which ensured the economic stability and growth to finance redistribution. This, broadly speaking, is the origin of 'tripartism' and 'corporatism', which tend to characterize the economic policy-making process of the Western state (Lehmbruch and Schmitter, 1982). The enhancement of the power of producer groups (trade unions, professional associations, employer and trade associations) over non-producers that corporatism generated may be said to be offset to some extent by redistribution and welfare to non-producers (unemployed, senior citizens, the indigent) in the sense that it enhanced their individual autonomy. However, sectoral producer-dominated corporatism and individual universalistic welfare both tend to squeeze out territorial politics based on *communal* interests: that is to say, the collective interests of consumers generated by territorial propinquity and the corresponding interests of industry derived not from sectoral or occupational solidarity, but from geographical location.

For example, the creation of minimum welfare standards has to assume a probably false degree of uniformity of conditions throughout the national territory. Thus in the implementation of national standards new inequalities could be unwittingly generated. Such inequalities would be not necessarily between individual consumers but also between locationally specific collectivities such as local labour markets, or affect industry which is peripheral to major production centres. More seriously, the centralized welfare-disbursing institutions have no automatic incentive to combat the complex problem of communal inequality and may, indeed, enhance it simply because going with the societal grain is always easier administratively than positive intervention over time designed to redress inequalities. Similar collective geographical inequalities may be generated by corporatism, since it will tend to be dominated by the leading echelons of the core sectoral groups, and thus bargaining tends to be shaped around their interests and not those of the periphery. The key point is that the creation of the meso provides a new bargaining arena based on territory rather than sector, where non-producer groups via communal institutions at the meso level may correct some of the distortions generated by universalistic egalitarianism and corporatism alike (Mény, 1986). Something very much like this counterbalancing territorial bargaining seems to have emerged in the quasi-meso of the three Offices for Scotland, Wales and Northern Ireland in the UK. It is also clearly evident in the national organization of the Italian regions, as Sabino Cassese and Luisa Torchia make clear, which has created a new resource bargaining arena with the centre. Such a territorially based counter-weight to corporatism and universalism is also likely to emerge in Spain and possibly France as well. It is, of course, a built-in feature of German federalism. In a more diluted form, promoting territorial bargaining with the centre for more resources as a reaction to the effects of universalistic egalitarianism and corporatism was woven into the regional planning movement of the 1960s, discussed earlier. There may be another link between corporatism and the meso. Victor Pérez-Diaz in his analysis of the evolution of the post-Franco Spanish state argues that corporatism is another form of meso in the sense that it creates an intermediate forum between central government and the industrial sectors. He sees the creation of the territorial meso and the economic or sectoral meso as part of a necessary tactic by the nascent Spanish democratic state, bereft as it was of normal legitimacy, to generate its own legitimacy by delegating extensive authority to the two types of meso, thus creating 'instrumental consent' in relation to two critical and potentially destabilizing issues – regional nationalism and industrial unrest (Pérez-Diaz, 1990).

There is an additional sense in which it may be claimed that ideological factors have played a part in meso formation and perhaps even more in sustaining meso-style government since its inception. This sense is directly linked to the rational-functional set of causal factors to the extent that it, too, links larger local government units to better functional performance, but seeks that improvement in terms not so much of superior cost effectiveness as of superior outputs. For example, only by enlarging local government units in rural areas, so this argument runs, can the quality of teaching and ancillary equipment be sufficient to ensure that the life chances of rural pupils approach equality with those of their urban counterparts. Thus the ideology involved in this case is one of territorial equality and the object of the exercise is that interpersonal equality can be achieved, or improved, despite decentralization, if the decentralized service delivery units are functionally capable. The best illustration of this ideological root of meso evolution – and evidence that it may have achieved its aims – is given in Tore Hansen's chapter on Norway.

This root of the meso pre-dates the post-welfare-state, anti-centralization aim and seems to have been a lively issue in the immediate post-war years in Scandinavia (Kjellberg, 1988), when local government was regarded by egalitarians as a hang-over from nineteenth-century liberalism that sought to perpetuate territorial inequality and therefore was a barrier to the establishment of the welfare state. Conservatives, by contrast, saw it as a bastion of liberty against the depredations of the centralist modern state. Similar ideological battles are discernible about the role of local government in other Western European states, especially France and the UK,[3] and stand in sharp contrast to the decentralization-equals-democracy assumption so prevalent, as we have noted, among the Western European states that succumbed to fascism.

Sectional
We now come to the third group of factors that have played a part in the evolution of the meso. We may call this group *sectional* interests and the first are those of political party. The establishment of a meso government involves some redistribution of state power exercised by representative institutions, so political party interest in the meso is almost axiomatic. Even in a one-party system this party advantage effect can operate, as Antoni Kukliński and Pawel Swianiewicz's chapter on Poland underlines. The Polish meso structure, itself of very ancient origins, was simply brushed aside in favour of much smaller units in 1975 when Gierek feared that the power of the central Communist Party was under threat from party cabals at the old meso level.

But the party effect is perhaps most clearly evident, as Gourevitch has pointed out, when parties are in opposition. His 'decision rule' for French parties is to varying degrees probably universal in all bipolar party systems: 'When in the opposition, support decentralization; when in power, hang on to all the instruments centralization provides' (Gourevitch, 1980: 49). This is not a recipe for decentralization to flourish, and fierce bipolar party competition is almost certainly an important factor in the strong centralist tradition of British politics. However, where, as in the French case, one party languishes for an extended period in opposition then it may be tempted (or forced) into making decentralization not just a matter of tactics but a cornerstone of party policy, as the French Socialists did in 1982 despite a long history of Jacobinism. As the chapter on the UK suggests, a similar Pauline conversion seems to be occurring in the British Labour Party as a result of its long sojourn in the wilderness for what in 1992 was thirteen years.

In multi-party systems no such built-in barrier to decentralization exists, since there is no comparable threat of an all-dominant rival, nor has the governing coalition a single party interest to defend. Hence a bargain had to be struck between the Christian Democrats and the Left in Italy in 1970 before the regional clause of the Constitution could be activated. Party interest can then be the catalyst which creates the meso, and in this case one of the beneficiaries was the opposition party; for the creation of regional government enabled the Communists (the PCI) to shine in a non-municipal arena, thus providing an additional shop window where it could demonstrate that it was ready for national power. The Christian Democrats saw their advantage in the creation of the regions, it has been claimed, in the following terms:

> devolution shifted the focus of social discontent away from the centre, transferred responsibility for the most sensitive sectors (public services such as schools, hospitals, housing, transport) to new bodies, and involved the left wing (and especially the PCI) in managing the crisis and those areas worst affected by internal migration and industrialization and uncontrolled urbanization of the cities of the North. (Mény, 1986: 17)

So both the hegemonic and the opposition party had a stake in the creation of the new meso and, according to Berti, sought 'to maintain at all events an operational consensus for protecting the power base and preserving the role of the party system'.[4]

Explicit party bargaining did not play such a direct part in the creation of the Spanish meso, since there were powerful regional forces already in the field setting severe limits on the scope of any deal. Nevertheless, the LOAPA, the Law for the Harmonization of the Devolution Process, could not have been achieved without the agreement of the two major parties – the Spanish Socialist Party (PSOE) and the Unión del Centro Democrático (UCD) – which hastily negotiated the *pacto autonómico* following the abortive rightist coup of 1981. It is also possible to see the Spanish meso, as in Italy, providing a consolation prize for the opposition parties as the PSOE seems to be assuming the mantle of the Spanish hegemonic party on the model of the Christian Democrats in Italy.

The second sectional interest that the meso may serve is not so much the party as the individual politician. This is especially so where the accumulation of offices is usually sought for its own sake – as an emblem of political status, as in France – or as a means of extending the personal power of a patron seeking support in a more strongly clientelist system. Even where neither of these objectives is consciously sought, it seems reasonable to presume that the new political offices that are available as a consequence of creating a new level of government will tend to be favoured rather than resisted by the political class.

The third sectional interest that the meso may be said to serve is that of the state bureaucracy in fused hierarchical or Napoleonic systems. Based originally on a notion of the indivisible nation state, but today sustained much more on the functional requirements of a highly fragmented local government system, one of the Napoleonic model's key characteristics is centre-to-periphery service delivery hierarchies whose task is to provide local services that cannot be provided by the local government system itself. It follows that such bureaucracies have a strong interest in the maintenance of the status quo and resist the kind of structural modernization that the said fragmented local system may be thought to require in order to meet the service requirements of an advanced industrial society. These outstationed bureaucrats have powerful allies in their resistance to reorganization in the form of national local government pressure groups, such as a national federation of mayors, which have a direct stake in the retention of all local units, however small. Together these two groups constitute an unbeatable alliance, especially when re-enforced by those *notables* who enter national politics, where they are able to exert even more crucial resistance to local government structural change. In France, for example, they regularly colonize the Cabinet itself. But whereas the central field services may continue to make good the economies-of-scale deficiencies of the local government structure, the *territorial*-scale needs of local services (mainly derived from high levels of externalities) still constitute a defect of the system unless met by some form of joint action between local governments.

An alternative solution is to create a meso that will meet such externality and scale requirements but at the same time leave the local government structure largely intact. This procedure of achieving functional objectives for local government, but avoiding all the political problems of changing its structure, was taken one stage further in Italy. The Italian regions not only assumed tasks which had outgrown the archaic local government system, but took a hand themselves in creating a new joint institution comprising several municipalities – the *comprensori* – for planning, urban development and waste disposal. As Sabino Cassese and Luisa Torchia point out, it was an abortive experiment but that it was attempted indicates the link between the creation of the meso and local government modernization, a link that seems to have been reforged under the terms of the Legge no. 142 of 1990 for transforming some provinces into metropolitan governments. This conception of the meso as a more feasible alternative to local government structural reorganization in the Napoleonic states is further illustrated in the Spanish case. During the very high economic growth years of the 1960s the archaic system of local government found it difficult to cope. Moreover, vital infrastructural investment was not undertaken by the Franco government. It also proved difficult to effect the necessary co-ordination between the outstationed central field services at the level of the *diputación*. One of the tasks of the new Spanish meso has been to attempt to make good this Francoist legacy and in some

Autonomous Communities the regional government itself has embarked on local government modernization.

As Sonia Mazey's chapter on France makes clear, the regional solution to local government's scale deficiencies has had the added attraction for central field service bureaucrats of providing new job opportunities and career structures for some without at the same time disturbing the entrenched position in local government of the remaining field services. Bureaucratic advantage finds expression in the non-Napoleonic systems, by contrast, not in the resistance to local government structural modernization, but, rather, in *support* of change, since the local bureaucracies which are directly employed by local government have no comparable stake in the status quo. In short, the local public bureaucracies in Northern Europe will tend, on balance, to favour the enlargement of local units, since it will mean better career structures and higher salaries. Again the effect is to make local structural reform easier than in Southern Europe.

More tentatively, there may be additional public bureaucratic interest in the creation of the meso for certain types of technocracy throughout Western Europe. There is some evidence that, as the Western state has progressively sought to demarketize health care services since the Second World War – part of the emergence of the SHEW group of services – the new governmental tasks this change has entailed have often been undertaken neither by the centre itself nor by the local government but by the meso level. Examples include the regions of Italy, the county in Norway and Sweden and the quasi-meso of the regional bodies of the National Health Service in the UK. Bureaucratic, or rather technocratic, preference for the meso in these cases is not so much the desire to achieve job protection, or better career structures, but, rather, that degree of professional autonomy which the meso as a 'decision space' offers that is of sufficient scale but may be relatively free from the constrictions of general government operating both below (local) and above (central). This desire for professional autonomy may be especially important precisely for those public services like health care where it is regarded as being crucial to task performance – clinical freedom – especially tasks, that is, which may be construed in life-or-death terms. The public health services have a built-in tendency to explosive cost expansion, partly as a consequence of derived demand – government-induced lower mortality rates mean more children of school age – partly because of high rates of technical innovation and partly because of demographic changes – the old and the young 'consume' more health expenditure. The centre may therefore also prefer to acquiesce in the technocratic desire to operate at the meso level so as to insulate itself from the perennial problem of ever-increasing expenditure.

Central advantage

This conflict-avoidance decentralization strategy leads us neatly to the final aspect of the Western European state which we will consider that seems to have links with the near-universal emergence of the meso. We may call it *central advantage*, by which is meant the extent to which central government has favoured the meso in order to promote its own interests, and we begin with taxation. One of the most important political developments in the Western state in the post-war period is the huge increase in taxation. At the turn of the century the public sector accounted for less than 10 per cent of gross national product (GNP) in most countries. By 1986, by contrast, in no less than seven Western European states – Belgium, Austria, the Netherlands, France, Norway, Sweden and Denmark – taxes (including social security payments) comprised over 50 per cent of GNP. In Denmark and Sweden the percentage was over 60. In most cases government growth has been far faster than the growth of the economy. Government growth has also exceeded, even, the rate of growth of the fiscal dividend which a growing economy generates because of the progressiveness of its income tax. For example, over the period 1950–76 the public sector grew five times as much as individual take-home pay in Sweden, in Italy by four and a half times and in the USA, Britain and France by almost three times (Rose and Peters, 1978: 62). In order to meet this growth of public expenditure, there has been a corresponding increase in the proportion of the electorate in the income tax system, which is still the largest source of revenue in many Western states. In 1950 a British head of household, for example, did not pay any income tax until his earnings reached the national average wage. By 1975, however, he began paying income tax at less than half the average national wage (Rose and Peters, 1978: 98).

The major consequence of this growth in the taxed electorate is that governments have come increasingly under pressure to reduce expenditure, or at least to moderate its growth. Reducing the 'tax burden', in short, has long ceased to be largely a middle- and upper-class issue but has become a mass issue. In order to respond to it, central governments have, broadly speaking, three strategies they can adopt. The first and most obvious is simply to cut their own expenditure. Here lies one of the primary causes of the monetarist and cut-back politics that emerged following the onset of the post-oil-shock recession of the mid-1970s, whether it be Glistrupism, Thatcherism or Reaganism. However, this strategy is more easily advocated than undertaken, since, among other things, the deflationary effect of such governmental cuts is simply to increase state commitments to meet unemployment and personal income loss thus generated. Moreover, the political forces most in support of cuts usually prove in reality to be less in favour of cuts *pe se* than of cuts in certain public services and *increases* in others: for example, less welfare expenditure but more on defence or more on the police. Those voters who support expenditure cuts *in principle* (that is, irrespective of what the expenditure is for) are by no means as numerous as the generalized resistance to taxes would suggest. Discrete benefits (lower taxes), it seems, will always be preferred if they lead to generalized rather than discrete disbenefits, that is, a cut in someone else's state-provided benefit. In addition, part of the attraction to voters of the monetarist package was that it also promised tax reduction as a consequence of public expenditure cuts. But in practice tax cuts (because implemented on incentive grounds) have tended to benefit the rich, and the general tax level has not changed and may even have increased. The long and short of the matter is that cutting public expenditure has not been an easy governmental option.

As a consequence, a second strategy has been very popular and this is the lowering of tax visibility by increasing the level of existing non-income taxes, creating new ones or by devising new taxes but calling them something else. For example, in Britain the proportion of total taxation raised by income fell between 1979 and 1989 from 36.4 per cent to 28.1 per cent, whereas value added tax (VAT) almost doubled over the period and corporation tax exactly doubled (*Reform of Direct Taxation*, 1990). Increasing indirect rather than direct taxation does probably lessen voter resistance, particularly if the indirect tax is disguised as a kind of payment for a benefit received such as a car, or television licence, or a health insurance 'contribution'. None the less there must be limits to this ploy and that brings us to the third strategy which is open to governments for ameliorating the problem of the insatiable public demand of governmental services but an increasing unwillingness by the same public to pay for them. It also brings us back to the main thread of our discussion. This is the 'off-loading' strategy; that is to say, the centre avoids public resistance to increased taxation by divesting itself of service responsibility. It has two elements; the first is to transfer the service to the private sector. This privatization off-loading strategy lies outside our ambit, although it is worth noting that it has been occurring throughout Western states with perhaps greatest enthusiasm in New Zealand in the late 1980s. This is 'Rogernomics', so named after a former New Zealand Finance Minister, Roger Douglas. Privatization, however, may have limitations. It tends to be limited, for example, to those public services that have fairly low public goods characteristics, that is, services that can be 'packaged' for market sale. Moreover, it has to be a service which will attract private capital, or entail costly market rigging by government before the sale can be effected.

A second off-loading possibility for government is, then, 'off-loading to the periphery', that is, either the transfer of a service responsibility, and thus its costs, to a lower level of government, or the reduction in central contributions to the cost of locally produced services. That is what Mény and Wright have called 'decentralizing penury' (Mény and Wright, 1985: 7) and Hirsch 'conflict-diversification strategy' (Hirsch, 1981: 603). Off-loading to the periphery may have the added advantage for the centre of forcing the non-central institutions to act more responsibly by becoming active participants in the cut-back process rather than disgruntled but passive victims (Elander and Montin, 1990; Rose, 1990). A relatively moderate example of this kind of off-loading is a switch from earmarked or specific central grants to block grants. Above all, off-loading can be presented by the centre as an act of self-denial in the interests of greater public participation, or democracy, or whatever. The consequence of the off-loading strategy is that the sub-national or peripheral level of government is forced either to reduce expenditure itself, or to raise more revenue via its own taxation system. Again Britain must be our example and the UK chapter in this volume reveals that, in pursuance of vigorous off-loading policies, the total of central grants to local government was reduced by a remarkable 18 per cent over the period 1979–89.

The most widespread and generalized example of the off-loading strategy has been the abolition of the large and highly expensive nineteenth-century 'total institutions' for the care of, for example, the mentally ill and the handicapped throughout the West in favour of catering for their needs by means of various forms of 'community care', which usually means some form of local government. A similar shift may be discerned in the treatment of children in need of care and of the very elderly by domiciliary or quasi-domiciliary services at the local level rather than in institutions (Lerman, 1982). Precisely what the criteria for the off-loading strategy will be in relation to the meso level is difficult to specify, but there is some evidence that there has been a widespread movement in favour of sub-national levels for some health and welfare services in the evolution of the welfare state. That is the conclusion of one major study covering Italy, Switzerland, Sweden, Israel, France, Japan, West Germany and the USA (Ashford, 1990). It was probably evident, as we have noted, in the case of Italy when the ordinary regions were created in 1970. Another possible example is the transfer of social assistance to the French *département* in 1982 and it is also evident in the growth of the role of the meso in public health and hospital services in Norway, Italy and Sweden. In the UK, such services have been located at the quasi-meso level for over forty years.

This brings us to the end of the answer to the questions posed at the outset, namely, why was the meso created and why has it survived? We now turn to the final questions posed at the outset to be considered, which are, what are the implications of the meso for the unitary state and what is the meso's future.

Implications of the meso

At the broadest level of explanation the emergence and re-enforcement of the meso level among European unitary states may be characterized as the necessary adjustment in its internal structure in order to accommodate new responsibilities. Each public function, this explanation asserts, has both an optimum scale and an optimum territorial jurisdiction. Given the wide range of new public responsibilities the state acquires as it is required to cope with new problems – economic, demographic, ideological – a perennial problem confronts it. How are these two scale desiderata – optimum size and optimum area – to be met within the necessarily rigid limits set by the traditional structure of accountable government? Here lies another reason for the increasing institutional complexity of the modern state's service delivery system, ranging from the almost purely private, through various degrees of para-statal agencies and public corporations, to the traditional sub-national institutions. The constant emphasis in the literature about intergovernmental relations on flexibility, complementarity and interdependence (Mény and Wright, 1985) and the growing importance of networks, or linkage systems, generally (Hanf, 1978; Rhodes, 1988) reflect the complex nature of modern service delivery systems as they strive to devise appropriate institutional arrangements for new tasks. As Richard Rose has put it: 'The growth of the welfare state has transformed a system of government which did little and then at separate levels of government in isolation from one another to a system in which interdependence is now the norm so that "policy unites which constitutions divide"' (Rose, 1985: 21).

It would be an error to see the need to fit scale and jurisdiction to the multifarious functions of the modern state as the sole origin of the new intergovernmental complexity. The nature of the policy, especially where government seeks to influence what it does not control, and the fiscal incapacity of sub-national government are also important, and there are no doubt other considerations. However, it is a major factor, and the emergence of the meso is one of its most significant expressions, since it extends the institutional range of formal accountable government, thus offering a greater chance of matching function to its scale or territorial optima and also, perhaps, introducing an element of greater coherence.

The meso and democratic maturation
The emergence of the meso may also mark another fundamental point in the evolution of the modern Western state. We have already referred to the possibility that it may strengthen the territorial dimension of the state's representative politics, thus to some extent counteracting the effects of universalism and the sectional politics of corporatism. This notion of the meso as an instrument for the reassertion of territoriality in the political system can be further refined by dividing the egalitarian thrust of modern democratic politics into two different forms of equality: *individualistic* and *communalistic*. Individualistic equality asserts that 'if no individual is discriminated against then no group can be'. Communalistic equality is achieved by measures that will improve the position of the group as a whole (Barry, 1972). When discussing the origins of regional movements in Western Europe, Urwin defines the same duality somewhat differently: the modern citizen of a democracy has two basic rights. The first, communalistic, is the 'right to roots', that is, to have the right to chose his or her ethnic identity. The second, individualistic, right Urwin calls the 'right to options', that is, the right to opportunities to make full use of his or her abilities (Rokkan and Urwin, 1983: 191).

The problem is that these two rights, or egalitarian concepts, may be in conflict. For example, the right to options must entail population mobility and such mobility may denude the peripheral region of its youngest and brightest. So the right to roots may require state subsidies to all in a peripheral community irrespective of the income of its inhabitants who enjoy the benefits of such subsidies. The rich in the region may indeed get the lion's share of such subsidies. In other words, communalistic equality in a unitary state may mean relaxing the egalitarian imperatives of common citizenship which are derived from the universal franchise. The communalistic equality principle may be even more subversive of interpersonal equality, since it can mean, and in federal states almost always does mean, that the formal one-person-one-vote-of-equal-value rule is relaxed in favour of granting sub-national communities (that is, the constituent states of the federation) some equality of political power irrespective of the size of their electorates. The communalistic equality rule recognizes that the national state may not be the sole repository of the sense of identity of all citizens. The emergence of the meso reflects an assertion of that communalistic principle; and since it seems to be based on sectional, perhaps even atavistic, values of ethnicity and race that are in direct conflict with the universalistic, common citizenship values that dominated the first phase of the post-war welfare state, the demand for roots was thought by some to be a kind of anti-democratic regression (Sharpe, 1989). However, if we view it in historical terms, and in particular in terms of the evolution of democracy in the European state, it becomes clear that rather than being regressive, communalistic egalitarianism and thus the meso can be seen as a natural progression in the evolution of representative democracy in a multicultural unitary state. The universal adult franchise and its concomitant common citizenship which together form the foundation of individualistic egalitarianism are of relatively recent origin. Most Western states did not grant the vote to 18-year-olds until the 1960s, and, give or take a few years, votes for all adult women until three decades earlier.

Not only is the universalistic franchise recent, its emergence in some Western states was severely interrupted. For no sooner was it achieved than it was suspended, sometimes for a extended period, by internal anti-democratic revolutions (Portugal, Italy, Germany, Spain, Austria, Vichy France and Greece); or it came to an end by external invasion by a foreign anti-democratic power (Czechoslovakia, Belgium, Netherlands, France, Denmark, Norway). In short, stable representative democracy in the sense in which it is known and understood today is in historical terms still a relatively novel phenomenon and, it may be safely asserted, has yet to reveal all of its consequences and implications for the working of the political system. One of the most important of these implications is derived from the theory of individual equality itself, for as a truly revolutionary doctrine these implications have necessarily been very slow in emerging. It is a revolutionary doctrine in the sense that it runs counter to almost all other forms of decision-making in modern society, which are still essentially hierarchical. This is not the place the explore the consequences of this revolutionary – not to say subversive – quality of representative democracy, except to note that the disjunction between the political sector and other sectors will always pose the question as to why equality is confined to the former. It could be said that the response to this question provides a vital dynamic to the political process in all Western democracies, and it takes the form of democratic 'leakage' from the political sector to the social and economic sectors. But this leakage is a long-term process and can only arise where the citizenry exercise their rights without interruption and generations emerge who have no other experience but the democratic. In other words, provided there is a continuity the other sectors will slowly, sometimes very slowly, be democratized. Slowly because it is a process based on persuasion and not force, for it will be resisted if only on efficiency grounds. Be that as it may, of more relevance to the present discussion is not so much a leakage of the egalitarian virus into the economic and social orders, but, rather, the more rapid process of its extension *within* the political system from the right to choose leaders and influence the conduct of government to choosing the entity in which such choices will take place. If the individual as a citizen of the polity has the right to choose leaders and influence government, there is a no logical reason why that right to choose stops short of deciding, by the normal democratic processes of persuasion, debate and voting, *in which polity* the citizen will make such choices.

So the right to roots can be defined as being a logical extension of what may be called a process of democratic maturation. And, since most Western states are in territorial terms the product of a decidedly non-democratic past, such as war, dynastic alliances and religious conflict, the potential for boundary change in multicultural democracies is potentially considerable. In Western Europe, as we have seen, this form of instability is not widespread, although it must not be forgotten that it is a dynamic that is, none the less, still active as the number of new breakaway states and proto-states that have emerged since the end of the Second World War testifies: Iceland, Algeria, Malta, Faroes, Greenland, North Cyprus and South Cyprus (Sharpe, 1989). In Eastern Europe since 1989 the link between democratization and the right to roots has manifested itself in the most dramatic and accelerated form conceivable. It has not been a maturation process so much as an explosion of ethnic unrest, especially in the most heterogeneous Eastern European state, Yugoslavia. Even the democratization of the former Soviet Union has released an upsurge of sometimes violent regional nationalism. But this instability is partly a function of the much higher level of heterogeneity in many Eastern European states as compared with Western Europe. Also, the vital but peculiarly problematic role of Communist hegemony must not be discounted, for it very effectively held down, but in no sense apparently diminished, the extent of ethnic consciousness. On the analogy of the boiling saucepan, the larger the pan and the more securely the lid is held down, the greater the explosion when the lid breaks. But it seems likely that the key factor in the Eastern European revolution is the link between the right to choose leaders and a new economic order, and the right to choose the preferred polity in which the first two choices are to take place. The very suddenness of the inter-ethnic conflict does not deny the maturation thesis; rather, its sometimes brutal violence demonstrates the absence of a preceding democratic maturation process.

In Western Europe, by contrast, the right to choose roots has evolved much more slowly, because in the democratic canon violence is ruled out by definition. Yet evolve it has as a natural progression, rather than retrogression, in the non-homogeneous states. It has expressed itself in the creation of a new level of sub-national government, and only in exceptional circumstances has it involved the creation of new states. In a nutshell, the meso signals one form of democratic maturation.

The arrival of the meso may also signal another form of democratic maturation as well, for it provides additional opportunities for the citizen to exercise his or her democratic rights in terms both of voting and of affecting the conduct of government by being elected. A meso government can thus be seen as an addition to the 'democraticness' of the state. If, as we have argued, the democratic right feeds on itself – if, that is, it is a learning process – it is reasonable to presume that the disparity between the formal power it accords the individual and his or her power in reality will sooner or later be realized. For although the rhetoric of democracy casts the individual in the star role in the democratic drama, in reality – given the scale of even the smallest Western state – the average citizen's normal capacity to influence government is infinitesimal. If such disparities between promise and performance are gradually recognized as the democratic regime persists, we may further presume that pressure will be exerted, sooner or later, to enhance the individual's capacity to influence government. It is not claimed that such corrective actions will automatically occur, or that our average citizen is always thirsting to exercise his or her democratic rights; yet if the assumption of growing participatory dissatisfaction with the gap between promise and reality as a function of democratic evolution is broadly correct, then one major avenue for ameliorating it is the decentralization of the state. Here perhaps lies part of the underlying explanation of the various decentralizing movements we have already discussed, such as the free commune movement in Scandinavia and the social disruptions in the late 1960s on behalf of greater public participation in Southern Europe. It may also partly explain the long-term trend, also noted earlier, among Western states for public expenditure to rise at a faster rate at the sub-national as compared with the national level of government, at least up until the 1980s.

The future

In what direction can we expect the meso to evolve in Western Europe in the future? This is a difficult question to answer with any finality, but the experience of Italy, where the meso is now firmly established and rooted in the politico-administrative system, despite its unpropitious birth in 1970 as the result of a party-political deal, suggests that the meso does have a role to fulfil. In some Italian regions, so it is claimed, the regional councils have not merely demonstrated their efficacy, they presage a new political order and in some cases have made a decisive difference to their own economies (Nanetti, 1988; Leonardi and Nanetti, 1990). However, as Sabino Cassese and Luisa Torchia's chapter in this volume suggests, it is important not to exaggerate the success of the Italian regions by taking the most dynamic Red Belt examples as typical. Not only do the Italian regions vary considerably in the extent to which they exploit their formal power (they tend to be most slothful in the south); those that do exercise their full powers are then constrained by the constitutional court. Some regions, far from ushering in a new order, are tainted with the excessive bureaucracy that often characterizes the central administration (Freddi, 1980; King, 1987). But whatever the performance of the Italian meso, there can be little doubt that, viewed overall, the palm must go to the Belgian regions, which now occupy a more important place in the Belgian power structure than the central state itself. Second place must go to the Spanish Autonomous Communities, which within three years of their creation were spending a proportion of total state expenditure which approached that of the *Länder* in the Austrian federal system (Castells Oliveres, 1987: 258). Moreover, the full potential implications of the Spanish decentralizing legislation inaugurated in the early 1980s have yet to be reached.

In any assessment of the European meso the refurbished county of Northern Europe must not be forgotten. Although the subject of relatively little academic interest, since it neither is an entirely new institution nor was the product of national political convulsions, it remains, nevertheless, a key player in the politico-administrative system. If present trends in the decentralization of the welfare state continue, it clearly has a very resilient future.

All things considered, this volume undeniably demonstrates that the Western European unitary state has evolved a new level in its governmental structure which seems to form part of a genuinely decentralist impetus. Whether this means that we now need to devise a new category of 'quasi-federal' (Bennett, 1989b) or 'devolutionary' (Leonardi and Nanetti, 1990) in addition to federal and unitary remains to be seen. Obviously, as Frank Delmartino's chapter makes clear, Belgium has evolved well beyond the textbook limits that conventionally denote a unitary state. Belgium, as he puts it, is 'a federal state in *statu nascendi*', and in terms of decentralization has perhaps gone beyond even what is normally regarded as appropriate in a federal state as well. For it is a paradox that a decentralizing unitary state on the heroic scale of Belgium lacks any limit to the transfer of power to its constituent parts; whereas a federalizing process, by definition, always has a centralizing impetus. The essence of the federal exercise is the coming together of what was formerly separate so that the primary purpose is to create a new central element, the federal power. Unlimited decentralization in a unitary state has no such necessary limit on the power of the constituent units. Belgium is, then, very much a special case: the first Western state to go into voluntary semi-liquidation, as it were, without a shot being fired. Although Spain's decentralizing process has yet to run its full course, it seems highly unlikely that, whatever the aspirations of its more militant peripheral nationalists, it will follow the Belgian pattern. The primary aim of the 1978 Constitution was, after all, to preserve the unitary state. Spain has also demonstrated that it can tolerate a remarkably high level of asymmetry under this formula, including not only the considerably greater power of the 'historical' regions, but, equally, the special tax-raising privileges of the 'foral' regions of the Basque Country and Navarra, plus the formal right of the localities to opt out of the regional system altogether. Conceivably such elasticity could be further exploited if need be without sacrificing unitariness. It is idle to haggle over terminology, however. The key conclusion is that the Western European unitary state is now a different kind of unitary state (Bogdanor, 1987). What it is to be called is of secondary importance. It now encompasses a new sub-national dimension, so that, as Hebbert has argued, 'sovereignty is devolved but not divided. The subdivisions of the state are reconstructed rather than the state itself' (Hebbert, 1987: 242). Predictions about political institutions are always risky, but all the indications are that this new institution will grow in importance, for, as we have argued, it meets a vital political need, especially in the multicultural states, and a functional need as well.

One important factor in any assessment of the future of the meso in the EC states is the impact of the EC itself. The EC affects the regional meso in member states in two indirect ways and one direct way. Indirectly the internal common market leads to market concentration, thus rendering more peripheral the peripheral member states (Ireland, Portugal, Greece, for example) and even more *their* peripheries. Some of the peripheries of the heartland states (the French Midi, the Italian Mezzogiorno, the former East German *Länder*) are also affected. This peripheralization process will accelerate after the creation of an unimpeded market after 1992. The second indirect impact of the EC is derived from the operation of the Common Agricultural Policy, which in 1991 still constituted the overwhelmingly dominant function of the EC, absorbing some 70 per cent of its expenditure, including bureaucracy costs. The vast expenditures involved enhance the peripheralization of the periphery, since they tend to favour the larger arable and less labour-intensive farms of the heartland and discriminate against the small labour-intensive peripheral farms (Mény, 1982b; Molle and Cappelin, 1988). Some idea of the unevenness of the CAP subsidy distribution, but not its geographical distribution, can be gleaned from the fact that about 80 per cent of EC farm support goes to only 20 per cent of its farmers (*Economist*, 1991). Negotiations were under way in 1991 to change the character of the CAP away from price support to income maintenance. This change if effected will, over the long term, shift the balance in favour of the smaller farms, but in early 1992 it had not got majority backing. Even if it does, however, the long-term future still lies with the larger specialized, more efficient farms in monetary cost terms on the superior soils of the EC heartland. In short, both of the indirect effects of the EC will be to stimulate the predominantly agricultural peripheral regional movements to resist their relative economic decline. They now have numerous collective organizations which could enhance such resistance (Anderson, 1982), including the EC's own Committee of the Regions and Local Communities which since 1988 has had a consultative role in the formation of EC regional policy and following the 1991 Maastricht Treaty is now firmly established as a consultative part of the decision-making process under article 198a of the treaty. The third and direct EC impact on the regions is the European Regional Development Fund (ERDF) and its associated initiatives. The ERDF was set up precisely to meet the problem of regional peripheralization after the accession of the UK, Ireland and Denmark in 1972 which were all on the rim of the original EC core. The fund has been considerably expanded both in scale and scope since then, and, as Michael Keating emphasizes in his chapter on EC regional policy, the Community's interest in the regions has increased as a consequence of 1992, such that it will be buttressed by a planned tripling of the ERDF funds.

Such enhancement of EC direct initiatives on behalf of regions, the steady erosion of member-state autonomy as a consequence of EC legislative expansion and the decline of member states' ability to control their own economies, especially after 1992, has led to a renewal of the prediction by some of a very rosy future for the regions. This future, so the prediction runs, will culminate in the regions becoming the dominant unit of government below the EC institutions, thus superseding the national states, which will gradually atrophy as the principle of *subsidiarity* renders them obsolete (Adonis and Jones, 1991). This is the 'Europe of the regions' thesis (Rhodes, 1978). Such a prediction cannot be dismissed out of hand, given the example of Belgium. Nevertheless, it does not seem a very likely outcome for the foreseeable future, given the most minimal requirements that such an outcome would demand. In the first place, for a Europe of the regions to come into being, there have to be both regional consciousness and regional institutions in *all* member states. But no such prior conditions exist in, say, Denmark or Ireland, and although the Netherlands is busy drawing up 'Euroregions' (see Theo Toonen's chapter) they are, as yet, purely paper constructs. Secondly, there is as yet no central capability in terms of a bureaucratic machine in Brussels able to bring it about. As Michael Keating points out in his chapter, the Brussels bureaucracy is quite small and so far has lacked the capacity even to monitor its own rather modest regional aid policy adequately. It has also failed so far to bypass national governments, which still control the disbursement of the ERDF and, as Keating also illustrates, manipulate it to their own advantage. Moreover, if the ERDF is increased to 25 per cent of the Community budget, as planned, it will still be only a small part of nationally based regional aid, so that its impact will still be marginal. Experience so far does not suggest either that there has been any increase in the power and status of regions, even where, as in the case of the German *Lander*, they have been given direct access to Community institutions and a consultative status. There may even have been a decline in their influence, according to Gerstenlauer, who sees the *Länder* links with Brussels not as enhancing their independence from Bonn, but, rather, as hastening the trend towards 'the unitary federal state' in Germany (Gerstenlauer, 1985). This is a conclusion shared by Hebbert, who also cites in support the experience of the Spanish and Italian meso with Brussels (Hebbert, 1987).

In any assessment of the EC regional aid policy it has to be remembered also that the regions are usually lumped together with local government in EC funding arrangements, and this tends to blunt the extent to which the regions can exploit the EC aid system to their advantage. The future of the meso, in any case, will always be to some extent bound up with the future of local government; for, in the last analysis, the latter is always in competition with and not an ally of the meso. Moreover, the localities have allies in those member states' central governments that are apprehensive about the rise of the meso. What evidence there is suggests that local government has been considerably more successful up to the mid-1980s in attracting Community aid than the regions (Jones, 1985; Rhodes, 1986).

What may be of critical importance in the relationship between the EC and the regions is the extent to which the more advanced regional movements have strongly identified with the Community. In Spain this is a natural outcome, since an aspect of regionalist propaganda in the Basque Country and Catalonia alike is that they are the advance guard of European modernity as compared with laggardly Castile and Andalucia. It is therefore entirely appropriate that they should embrace Brussels in preference to Madrid. But even in Scotland, which has no sense of cultural or technological one-upmanship over the rest of the UK, the Scottish National Party's switch to favouring 'independence for Scotland but within Europe' has improved its following, especially with the young but also with its marginal supporters – the consumption nationalists, as we have defined them – who require precisely the reassurance that independence will not ruin the economy that the 'within Europe' caveat provides. According to a 1992 Scottish poll, some 31 per cent of all Scots favour Scottish independence within the EC (*Sunday Times*, 1992).

One final and perhaps the most telling point needs to be made against the 'Europe of the regions' thesis, and that is the almost complete absence of any regional ambition to replace the national state in most member countries. As we have emphasized, Belgium is very much a special case, and strong regional movements that seek the kind of status the thesis implies are very few indeed – Scotland, Catalonia, the Basque Country and, possibly, Corsica. Thus *if* the member states of the Community are to break up under regional pressure, this is likely to be confined to very few of them; and the outcome is unlikely to be a division into regions, but, rather, into a small handful of new member *states*. Although such a fragmentation process will be fraught with difficulties, not least the resistance of the region's host state, new states, as we have noted, are not a novel phenomenon even in Western Europe. So this very limited form of fragmentation cannot be ruled out. One possibility that could overcome host-state resistance is the solution that has been tentatively discussed in relation to Gibraltar, which is now a British territory but to which Spain lays claim. The solution is that Gibraltar would cease to be a UK colony but would not be returned to Spain. Instead it would become a kind of ward of the EC itself but not a new member state (*Observer*, 1991). Caution about such a solution is in order, since the two parties to it – Spain and the UK – are themselves the most susceptible to regional secession among EC members. The last thing either government will welcome, it may be presumed, is a formula that would undoubtedly ease the process of secession of their more recalcitrant regions.

Two further factors could have a key influence on such a change.

The first is the example of Ireland, for not only was it part of an EC member state within living memory – the UK – but it is also smaller and poorer than most of the potential secessionist regions. Yet it enjoys all of the advantages of full EC membership (including being designated as a region as well as a member state), such that transfers from Brussels constitute some 6 per cent of the Irish GDP.

Perhaps a more telling example that could influence such secession is the emergence of constituent polities in Russia and Yugoslavia as independent states. When Slovenia, Croatia, and the three Baltic countries can become fully fledged states virtually overnight, it seems likely that the more advanced regional movements will be emboldened to push for secession. It is, perhaps, too early to discern the full impact of the whole dramatic transformation of the state system in Eastern Europe and European Russia on the rest of Europe. It has been in essence the final act in the long process of decolonization throughout the world which began after 1945. Yet it is worth emphasizing that it has also been a process of disintegration which has been fired by national self-assertion of groups which see themselves as being trapped in another state – which is precisely one of the primary determinants, as we have emphasized, of the creation of the meso in Western Europe.

So much for speculation. The emergence of the meso in Europe, it may be safely concluded, is a very important change, perhaps even 'one of the most radical institutional innovations ever seen in some European states' (Mény, 1986).

Notes

1 The literature on regional ethnic nationalism in Europe is large, but see, for example: Esman, 1977; Sharpe, 1979; Rokkan and Urwin, 1983; Hebbert and Machin, 1984; Tiriakin and Rogowski, 1985; Keating, 1988.

2 See Blair, 1991, which suggests that since the early 1980s sub-national expenditure has been declining as a proportion of total public sector expenditure at least at the local government level.

3 See, for example, the running debate that was conducted by Leo Moulin and others over several issues of *Public Administration* in the 1950s and which is reproduced in Feldman, 1986.

4 Berti, 1979: 482; quoted and translated in Mény, 1986.

References

Adonis, Andrew and Jones, Stuart (1991) *Subsidiarity: History, Policy and the Community's Constitutional Future*. Oxford: Nuffield College.

Anderson, M. (1982) 'The political problems of frontier regions', *West European Politics*, 5 (4).

Ashford, D. (1990) 'Intergovernmental social transfers and welfare state: menace or promise?', *Government and Policy*, 8 (2).

Barry, B. (1972) 'Reflections on conflict', *Sociology*, 6 (4).

Bennett, Robert (1989a) 'Territory and administration', in Robert Bennett (ed.), *Territory and Administration in Europe*. London: Pinter.

Bennett, Robert (1989b) 'European economy, society, politics and administration', in R. Bennett (ed.), *Territory and Administration in Europe*. London: Pinter.

Bernier, L. L. (1991) 'Decentralization and its effects: a test hypothesis in the French case', paper to American Political Science Association annual meeting, Washington, DC.

Berry, B. L. (1976) 'The counter-urbanization process: urban America since 1970', in B. L. Berry (ed.), *Urbanization and Counter-Urbanization*. London: Sage.

Berti, B. (1979) 'La reforma dello stato – la vicenda regionale', in L. Graziano and S. Tarrow (eds), *La crisi italiana*. Turin: Enaudi.

Blair, P. (1991) 'Trends in local autonomy and democracy: reflections from a European perspective', in R. Batley and G. Stoker (eds), *Local Government in Europe*. London: Macmillan.

Bogdanor, V. (1987) 'Federalism and devolution: some juridical and political problems', in Roger Morgan (ed.), *Regionalism in European Politics*. London: Policy Studies Institute.

Castells Oliveres, A. (1987) 'Financing regional government in Spain: main trends and a comparative perspective', *Government and Policy*, 5 (3).

Connor, W. (1973) 'The politics of ethnonationalism', *Journal of International Affairs*, 27 (1).

Coombes, David (1979) 'Introduction', in David Coombes, Hrbek, R., Schuttemeyer, S., Condorelli, L. and Parsons, W., *European Integration, Regional Devolution and National Parliaments*. London: Policy Studies Institute.

Economist (1991) 23 February.

Elander, Ingemar and Montin, Stig (1990) 'Decentralization and control: central–local government relations in Sweden', *Policy and Politics*, 18 (3).

Esman, M. J. (ed.) (1977) *Ethnic Conflict in the Western World*. Ithaca: Cornell University Press.

Etherington, D. and Paddon, M. (1991) 'The free local government initiative in Denmark – modernization, innovation or control', *Local Government Studies*, 17 (4).

Feldman, L. (ed.) (1986) *The Government and Politics of Urban Canada*. Toronto: Methuen.

Freddi, G. (1980) 'Regional devolution, administrative decentralization and bureaucratic performance in Italy', *Policy and Politics*, 8 (3).

Gerstenlauer, H.-G. (1985) 'German *Länder* in the European Community', in M. Keating and B. Jones (eds), *Regions in the European Community*. Oxford: Clarendon.

Gourevitch, Peter (1980) *Paris and the Provinces*. Berkeley: University of California Press.

Green, L. (1982) 'Rational nationalists', *Political Studies*, 30 (2): 238.

Gustafsson, Agne (1983) *Local Government in Sweden*. Stockholm: Swedish Institute.

Hanf, K. (1978) 'Introduction', in K. Hanf and F. W. Scharpf (eds), *Interorganizational Policy Making*. London: Sage.

Hayward, J. E. and Watson, M. (eds) (1975) *Politics, Planning and Policy Making*. London: Cambridge University Press.

Hebbert, M. (1987) 'Regionalism: a reform concept and its application to Spain', *Government and Policy*, 5 (3).

Hebbert, M. and Machin, H. (eds) (1984) *Regionalization in France, Italy and Spain*. London: London School of Economics.

Hirsch, J. (1981) 'The relative autonomy of the state: the reproduction of capital and urban conflicts', in M. Dear and A. J. Scott (eds), *Urbanization and Urban Planning in Capitalist Society*. London: Methuen.

Hrbek, R. (1986) 'The political dynamics of regionalism: FRG, Austria, Switzerland', in R. Morgan (ed.), *Regionalism in European Politics*. London: Policy Studies Institute.

Johnson, H. G. (1968) 'A theoretical model of economic nationalism in new and developing states', in H. G. Johnson (ed.), *Economic Nationalism in Old and New States*. London: Allen & Unwin.

Jones, B. (1985) 'Conclusion', in M. Keating and B. Jones (eds), *Regions in the European Community*. Oxford: Clarendon.

Keating, M. (1988) *State and Regional Nationalism: Territorial Politics and the European State*. Hemel Hempstead: Harvester.

King, Preston (1982) *Federalism and Federation*. London: Croom Helm.

King, R. L. (1987) 'Regional government: the Italian experience', *Government and Policy*, 5 (3).

Kjellberg, F. (1988) 'Local government and the welfare state: reorganization in Scandinavia', in Brune Dente and Francesco Kjellberg (eds), *The Dynamics of Institutional Change*. London: Sage.

Lehmbruch, G. and Schmitter, P. C. (eds) (1982) *Patterns of Corporatist Policy-making*. London: Sage.

Leonardi, R. and Nanetti, R. Y. (eds) (1990) *The Regions and European Integration*. London: Pinter.

Lerman, P. (1982) *Deinstitutionalization and the Welfare State*. New Brunswick: Rutgers University Press.

Lodden, Peter (1991) 'The "free local government" experiment in Norway', in R. Batley and G. Stoker (eds), *Local Government in Europe*. London: Macmillan.

Mény, Y. (ed.) (1982a) *Dix ans de régionalization en Europe: bilan et perspectives*. Paris: Cujas.

Mény, Y. (1982b) 'Should the Community regional policy be scrapped?', *Common Market Law Review*, 4 (2).

Mény, Y. (1986) 'The political dynamics of regionalism: Italy, France, Spain', in R. Morgan (ed.), *Regionalism in European Politics*. London: Policy Studies Institute.

Mény, Y. and Wright, V. (1985) 'General introduction', in Y. Mény and V. Wright (eds), *Centre–Periphery Relations in Western Europe*. London: Allen & Unwin.

Molle, W. and Cappelin, R. (eds) (1988) *Regional Impact of Community Policies in Europe*. Aldershot: Gower.

Mughan, Anthony (1979) 'Modernization and regional relative deprivation: towards a theory of ethnic conflict', in L. J. Sharpe (ed.), *Decentralist Trends in Western Democracies*. London: Sage.

Nanetti, R. Y. (1988) *Growth and Territorial Politics: The Italian Model of Social Capitalism*. London: Pinter.

Norton, Alan (1988a) *Sweden*. Birmingham: Birmingham University, Institute of Local Government Studies.

Norton, Alan (1988b) *Denmark*. Birmingham: Birmingham University, Institute of Local Government Studies.

Observer (1991) 8 August.

Pérez-Diaz, Victor (1990) *Governability and the Scale of Governance: Meso-governments in Spain*. Madrid: Instituto Juan March.

Reform of Direct Taxation (1990) London: Fabian Society.

Rhodes, R. A. W. (1978) 'Regional policy and a "Europe of the regions"', in D. Gillingwater and D. A. Hart (eds), *The Regional Planning Process*. Farnborough: Saxon House.

Rhodes, R. A. W. (1986) *European Policy Making, Implementation and Sub-Central Governments*. Maastricht: European Institute of Public Administration.

Rhodes, R. A. W. (1988) *Beyond Westminster and Whitehall*. London: Unwin-Hyman.

Richardson, H. N. (1975) *Regional Development Policy and Planning in Spain*. Farnborough: Saxon House.

Rokkan, S. and Urwin, D. (eds) (1983) *Economy, Territory, Identity*. London: Sage.

Rose, L. E. (1990) 'Nordic free-commune experiments: increased local autonomy or continued central control?', in D. S. King and J. Pierre (eds), *Challenges to Local Government*. London: Sage.

Rose, R. (1985) 'From government at the centre to nationwide government', in Y. Mény and V. Wright (eds), *Centre–Periphery Relations in Western Europe*. London: Allen & Unwin.

Rose, R. and Peters, G. (1978) *Can Governments Go Bankrupt?*. London: Macmillan.

Selan, V. and Donnini, R. (1975) 'Regional planning in Italy', in J. Hayward and M. Watson (eds), *Planning, Politics and Public Policy*. Cambridge: Cambridge University Press.

Sharpe, L. J. (1972) 'British politics and the two regionalisms', in W. Wright and D. Stewart (eds), *The Exploding City*. Edinburgh: Edinburgh University Press.

Sharpe, L. J. (1979) *Decentralist Trends in Western Democracies*. London: Sage.

Sharpe, L. J. (1988) 'The growth and decentralization of the modern democratic state', *European Journal of Political Research*, 16 (3).

Sharpe, L. J. (1989) 'Fragmentation and territoriality in the European state system', *International Political Science Review*, 10 (3).

Smith, A. D. S. (1979) *Nationalism in the Twentieth Century*. London: Martin Robertson.

Stewart, J. and Stoker, G. (1989) 'The "free government" experiments and the programme of public services reform in Scandinavia', in C. Crouch and D. Marquand (eds), *The New Centralism*. Oxford: Basil Blackwell.

Sunday Times (1992) 26 January.

Tiriakin, E. A. and Rogowski, R. (eds) (1985) *The New Nationalism of the Developed West*. Boston: Allen & Unwin.

Walker, D. B. (1991) 'Decentralization: recent trends and prospects from a comparative governmental perspective', *International Review of Administrative Sciences*, 57 (1).

2

Belgium: In Search of the Meso Level

Frank Delmartino

Studies published on Belgium over the last few years have been almost exclusively devoted to the theme of reforms at the top of the institutional pyramid. Within the period of practically a quarter of a century the unitary state has rebuilt itself into a quasi-federal entity. The most striking innovation involved has been the introduction of Cultural Communities and Social-Economic Regions at the sub-national level. In retrospect, the constitutional amendment of 1970, which became fully operational only ten years later, turned out to be the initial impetus towards the creation of the new federal construction.

Anyone who is interested in the meso level in Belgium is therefore faced with the difficult task of identifying it. Should he or she be focusing on the traditional provinces that have had an intermediate position between the local level of government and the state for ages? Or should he or she choose the recent regions that, for their territorial scale, are formally situated between the provinces and the state, but are politically constituting themselves more and more as constituent states in a federal system?

Our choice might be motivated by the enormous interest existing even abroad in the federalizing Belgian state reform. The provinces, on the contrary, have led a slumbering life. Nevertheless, exclusive attention to the regional level would be scientifically unjustified. The Belgian regions are increasingly distancing themselves from an intermediary position in order to impose themselves as separate entities within the Belgian state and the European Community. The actual meso level, as a consequence, is left out in the cold. The role of bringing into harmony central policy options and local implementation is barely provided. And the management of supra-local tasks has not yet been clearly regulated. In short, Belgium is in search of a fully fledged intermediary or meso governmental level.

The first section of this chapter seeks to put the issue mentioned above in its historical context. Subsequent sections elaborate the main characteristics of the provincial institutions as well as those of the new governmental structure. The chapter concludes by placing the Belgian meso experience in the context of growing European unification.

From administrative and economic decentralization to regionalization

For many observers the Belgian state reforms started in 1970, when cultural autonomy (articles 3 *ter* and 59 *bis*) as well as the principle of the regionalization (art. 107 *quater*) were entered into the Constitution. However, this has only been a provisional end in an institutional transformation process that initially aimed at administrative and economic decentralization rather than true regionalization. The roots of the problem stretch back into the history of Belgium. Belgium has characterized itself from its independence in 1830 onwards as a unitary state, without taking into account its historical diversity. The differentiation is of a twofold nature. The most striking cleavage is of a *linguistic-cultural* nature. In the north of the country, in Flanders, Dutch used to be the everyday speech, but because of the separation from the Northern Netherlands in the sixteenth century this colloquial language has drawn apart from standard Dutch. The spoken variant usually only existed as a series of dialects. During the Spanish and Austrian domination, and *a fortiori* under French rule, the French language gained importance, not only being used in the south of Belgium, the Walloon provinces, but at the same time serving as the lingua franca throughout Western Europe. The upper class all over the country, as a consequence, used the language and thus helped to unify the newly organized state. French became the official state language and was to keep that status until the beginning of this century.

In still another aspect the historical inheritance was neglected in 1830 as well as in the next century. As in the whole of the Low Countries, the central state was of very recent origins. Previously the Netherlands had always been known as the 'United Provinces', each province being strongly aware of its identity and with a well-developed internal government. Even at the time of the 'Brabantine revolution' against the Austrian regime (1789) and during the revolutionary days of September 1830, Belgium was referred to as the United Belgian Provinces. But as soon as the new state was able to impose its authority the conception changed radically. In the Constitution of 1831 it is already mentioned that Belgium is to be 'divided' into provinces and communes. The traditional decentralization after the French model has made its entry. Belgium has become a French-speaking, French-style unitary state.

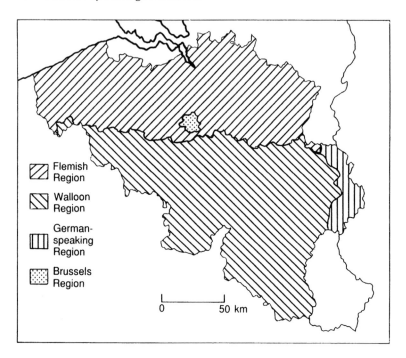

Figure 1   *The Belgian regions*

In the nineteenth century Belgium endured this twofold suppression of its differentiated past rather well. The upper class in
Flanders was, after all, imbued with the French standard language
through the educational system, the governmental and judicial
apparatus and the army – in short, all official manifestations of the
state authority. Also there was free movement of labour and such
emigration was a unifying factor as workmen from the rural north
emigrated or commuted in large numbers to the more industrialized
south. It was especially important in Brussels, where the immigrants
from Flanders were assimilated by generally adopting the language of
the upper class in power. Despite its Flemish historical roots,
Brussels became in this way a mainly French-speaking city. This
relatively smooth process of transformation was only interrupted in
this century. With regard to the *language problem* the First World
War was a major turning point. The Romantic movement for the
recognition of the Dutch mother-tongue and Flemish cultural
autonomy, which had until then mainly found support among the
intellectual groups in society, spread to become a large popular
movement. The soldiers at the front became conscious of the

anomaly of having to fight for a country that discriminated against their own language. The Belgian government with the King as its spokesman was forced to promise reforms. The most important of these was the full manhood suffrage that allowed the numerical majority of Flemings to become politically completely emancipated. Legislation followed that gave Dutch equal status with French in phases, culminating in 1963 when the language barrier was permanently defined. This had the effect of making Dutch the official language in the region to the north of the country and confirming French in its exclusive position in the south (see Figure 1). The later issue of cultural autonomy in 1970 is but a logical consequence of this historical evolution.

As a result of this striking evolution, in studies of the decentralization of Belgium too little attention has been paid to the local government dimension. As the state in the earlier part of the century allocated new functions such as water supply, electricity, gas and waste disposal to the 2,663 communes, so the local government structure had to be adjusted in order to cope with these new tasks. In 1922 the communes were authorized to create *intercommunal associations*, thus enabling them to effect better service delivery. Later, in the 1930s, because of the need to plan, in both economic and land-use terms, the creation of agglomerations was considered. Some mergers were indeed achieved during the period of the war but were abandoned in 1944, linked as they were with foreign rule. By the end of the 1950s the state had taken up the task of regional economic development and the communes started joining in *intercommunal associations for regional development* that actively promoted industrial expansion. The provinces also took responsibility for the stimulation and co-ordination of regional economic development and became the conduit for foreign (in this era mainly American) investment. Out of these efforts the *Regional Development* Boards would emerge (1970), regulated by public laws and, in Flanders at least, on a provincial territorial basis. Summarizing, it may be stated that the state as well as provinces and communes in this way contributed to the remarkable welfare boom of the 1960s.

Offshoots of this process were institutional innovations such as the 'agglomerations and federations of communes' (1971) and the systematic merger of the communes (1975-7). Agglomerations and federations are one expression of compulsory intercommunal co-operation, with well-defined assignments (mainly planning and development) and with directly elected councils. They met, however, with heavy resistance in the traditional communal setting and in 1975 were finally rejected as alien to the basic administrative structure. The communes preferred enlarged communes to a double structure of communes and federations. Since 1977 Belgium has had only 589 communes with an average area of 52 sq km and an average population of 16,678 inhabitants. These larger communes have undoubtedly been better equipped than before to meet contemporary local tasks.

In parallel with these changes at the provincial and communal level, the reform fever also affected the state in its totality. It was a double challenge. On the one hand, there was a manifest desire for *decentralization* as a means of modernizing governmental policy-making. The creation of the welfare state has indeed led to a certain degree of centralization in Belgium which was felt to be dysfunctional. The solution was seen as being the decentralization of decision-making, and even of power. This was an ever-recurring theme in the conclusions of various commissions (such as the Centre Harmel in 1958) and government statements.

The administrative decentralization to provinces and communes was, however, always looked upon in connection with economic decentralization through institutions created *ad hoc*, such as the Regional Development Boards mentioned above and the Regional Economic Councils for Flanders, the Walloon provinces and Brabant, which are charged with general policy counselling. This indicates the impact of planning in economic thinking in the 1960s, but it also reveals the second challenge for the Belgian state, that is, the sub-national regions increasingly stressing their distinctive features.

The Walloon provinces in particular combined the demand for greater administrative autonomy with more economic self-governing. These demands were derived not only from the determined socialist majority in the south of the country, but also from the sharp economic recession. The Walloon provinces got ever more involved in the crisis of the traditional industries of coal and steel. From being the core of industrial development, Wallonia steadily declined while Flanders was flourishing and attracting (foreign) investors. The national government, with its Flemish dominance, was accused of a lack of interest in this decline. Thus emerged a true crisis of legitimacy for the Belgian state, which was accused by the extreme Walloon political groups of being 'l'état belgo-flamand'.

Thus an administrative reform developed into a state reform. Decentralization into provinces and communes was no longer sufficient. The power was to be spread to entities that were identifiable in a larger political context: Wallonia, Flanders, Brussels. The administrative and economic reform was thus linked with the language demarcation and the cultural communities. The foundations for the later emergence of a federal entity were, in our opinion, laid during this period of 'crystallization' from 1968 to 1969.

In the Eyskens–Merlot government policy statement in 1968 the 'modernization' of the provincial institutions is still mentioned, together with a long list of competences that were to be transferred to these provinces. One year later the so-called 'Taskforce of 28', an official parliamentary commission with representatives of all political parties, decided in principle in favour of the regions. This option was inscribed in the Constitution in 1970 (art. 107 *quater*), but only became operational during the next decade. The provinces had obviously lost the battle and were completely bypassed. Nine years after the government had promised to strengthen them a political agreement emerged to abolish the directly elected Provincial Councils (Egmont Agreement, 1977) and to reduce the provinces to mere administrative organs. Their survival is to be attributed to the fact that the said political agreement was revoked for completely different reasons.

The modernization of the sub-national system therefore did not entail a reinforcement of the traditional types of government but, rather, the creation of a totally new level. Our analysis of the provincial and the regional institutions will show that this did not solve the intermediary, or meso, problem.

The traditional meso level: the provinces

The institutions

For 150 years the organizational structure of the provinces has remained nearly unchanged. The intermediate position of the province in the three-tier governmental structure was never up for discussion. Its task was established in the Constitution: the promotion of provincial interests, with the key actors being defined by the Provincial Law of 1836: the Provincial Council, the Permanent Deputation and the Provincial Governor, assisted by a provincial administration under the direction of a Provincial Registrar. We will briefly describe the essential tasks of those actors before going into the provincial responsibilities as such.

The Provincial Council (Provincieraad, Conseil Provincial)   As with most local government in democracies, great importance is assigned to the elected representatives of the people. Indeed, promoting the provincial interests implies choices of policy and these must finally be legitimated by a 'parliamentary assembly'. The direct election of the Provincial Council highlights its political character; a policy must be outlined and not merely carried out administratively according to guidelines established at higher levels.

It was precisely this characteristic of the provinces that proved to be sensitive both at the time of Belgian independence and in the Egmont Agreement in 1977. In the first period, political activity was feared that would go beyond the promotion of specifically provincial interests, for it was feared that the confederal idea of the United Provinces would rise again. Political contact between Provincial Councils was therefore explicitly forbidden; but, moreover, the councils also had their meetings curtailed and were strictly supervised.

By 1977, however, the political significance of the province was so diminished that it was suggested they be simply eliminated. Thus the province would be reduced solely to an administrative organ under the direction of a governor as a governmental commissioner.

However, this proposal did not become reality. The Provincial Councils are still directly elected. They consist of 50 to 90 members – according to the size of the province – and, in principle, new elections are held every four years. However, these elections coincide with those for the national Parliament, the latter not always sitting out a full legislative term. This linking of the two elections is subject to some debate because it tends to nullify provincial issues, which get overwhelmed by national ones in the election.

Once assembled, the Provincial Council chooses among its members a chairperson to preside over the meetings. The main duties of the Provincial Council may be summarized as follows:

- The annual voting of the budget, including the expenditure for the next year, and of the revenues needed to balance the books. This also implies the levying of taxes. The discussion of the budget, of course, always involves a general discussion on past and future policy.
- The annual balance of the books for the past year.
- Taking the necessary measures on public works such as loans to be taken out and the purchase of properties.
- Appointing the provincial officials (unless the matter is delegated to the Permanent Deputation), determining their wages and pensions with regard to the limits of the general provisions concerned.
- Establishing institutions for dealing with provincial matters.

A significant reform of the functioning of the Provincial Council was carried out early in 1984. The law of 6 January repeals the limiting provisions of 1836, noted earlier, and the councils now can meet freely, that is, as often as the matters under their authority require.

The assembly is convened by the chairperson, who also draws up the agenda. Whenever one-third of the council members so request, the chairperson has to convene the assembly, on the basis of the agenda drawn up by these members and on the day and hour they request. Moreover, the council members may add items to the agenda, on the condition, however, that their motions are turned in to the chairperson in writing at least two (working) days in advance. The item added to the agenda must be accompanied by an explanatory note or some other informative document. An item that does not appear on the agenda may not be brought up for discussion, except in the case of an emergency, recognized by at least two-thirds of the members present. A Provincial Council cannot be validly in session unless more than half of the members are present. Each decision taken must be supported by an absolute majority. In case of a tie, the proposal is rejected.

The Permanent Deputation (Bestendige Deputatie, Députation Permanente)   Six members of the Provincial Council are permanently delegated – deputized – to assume, in collaboration with the governor, the responsibility for the daily administration of the province. These 'permanent delegates' are elected for the full duration of the Provincial Council's mandate. According to law, the Provincial Governor is the chairperson, with voting rights, of the Permanent Deputation. Again, decisions are taken by an absolute majority of the members present.

The daily administration of the province involves, among other things, the following responsibilities:

- The preparation of the budget drafts and of the accounts to be presented to the Provincial Council.
- The preparation of other proposals and plans concerning provincial policy that are to be presented to the Provincial Council.
- The supervision of the provincial accounting: the paying of warrants, the endorsement of the estimated costs of public works approved by the Provincial Council and so on.
- The protection of the rights of the province, particularly in legal disputes.
- Numerous other decisions related to the day-to-day management of the province, its institutions and personnel.

In addition, the Permanent Deputation is charged with important duties as a fellow administrative organ of the central government, including the settlement of administrative disputes. It serves, in other words, as a kind of administrative court where one can lodge an appeal against certain decisions of lower administrations.

The Provincial Governor (Gouverneur)   The Provincial Governor is the representative in the province of the central government as well as the chairperson of the Permanent Deputation who is qualified to vote. Hence, he or she is undeniably a key figure, even if we take the dual character of his or her function into consideration. As chairperson of the Permanent Deputation, the governor is charged with the implementation of the decisions made by the Provincial Council and the delegation itself. As a representative of the central government, however, he or she may distance him- or herself from these same decisions and, for example, suspend them pending a ministerial order. Even though this extreme situation rarely occurs, it nevertheless illustrates the remarkable position of the governor. Besides his or her duties as member and chair of a collegiate decision-making body with an overall political character, he or she also is an official legally carrying out central government instructions. Besides, numerous laws, decrees and general administrative decisions provide for an intervention of the Provincial Governor in his or her own name. In this act he or she is not answerable to the Permanent Deputation nor to the Provincial Council. It is evident that, however great the personal prestige that the Provincial Governors enjoy, this combination of the functions of governmental commissioner and head of the decentralized administration raises questions.

As the Belgian state evolved, centralization was slowly relaxed, although key figures such as the mayor are still centrally appointed as this is the usual procedure in the Netherlands. In Belgium today, however, the central appointment of the mayor is only formal. It tends to confirm the political balance of power expressed in the election of the communal council. The mayor, in fact, reflects in the first instance the result of the elections and afterwards power is entrusted to him or her by the central government.

As for the Provincial Governor, however, nothing has changed. Despite his or her significant impact on the determination and implementation of provincial policy, he or she functions independently from the political balance of power in the Provincial Council. Even in France, the 'motherland' of administrative centralization, such a situation is considered to be outdated. Since 1982 the French prefect saw his or her function reduced to the role of a governmental commissioner and the leadership in *départemental* as in regional affairs has been entrusted to directly elected politicians.

Likewise, the double function of the Provincial Governor is reflected in the *provincial administration*. Officials from the Ministry of the Interior work side by side with provincial officials. In principle, the officials appointed on the provincial level only take up tasks in the field of the administrative decentralization. The civil servants, on the contrary, assist the governor in the tasks he or she performs on behalf of the central government. In practice, however, this distinction cannot be held and causes organizational problems. For example, ambiguity surrounds the function of the *provincial registrar* as the immediate assistant of the governor who is also the highest-ranking civil servant.

For the sake of completeness, we mention that in Brabant, besides the governor, a vice-governor is also appointed. This person assists the governor in performing his or her duties in the whole of the province and replaces him or her when absent. However, he or she is best known as supervisor of the application of the laws and ordinances relating to the use of the languages in administrative matters and in education. Recently, the Flemish community has also entrusted the vice-governor with the administrative supervision of the communes in Flemish Brabant. If, however, the vice-governor does not belong to the Dutch language group this task is taken over by the governor him- or herself.

District Commissioners   In conclusion, the District Commissioners (Arrondissementscommissarissen, Commissaires d'Arrondissement) have to be mentioned. Their main task used to be directing and supervising the communes under tutelage, that is, the communes with less than 5,000 inhabitants. Since the merger of the communes (1977) this guidance and supervisory task has largely disappeared. Nevertheless, a re-evaluation of this function is being considered. The redefinition pictures them rather as the direct assistants to the governor for particular assignments. For this reason they figure in this survey.

A typology of the responsibilities at the intermediate or meso level

Supervisory tasks   Viewed in its entirety and not simply in terms of its legal duties, the role of the province is diverse. Perhaps its authoritative position over local government is not the most essential task, but certainly the most striking in the eyes of the outside world. Although a relationship based on supple advising, consulting and co-ordination may be achieved with the communes in many areas, it remains obvious to all concerned that the provinces, governor and Permanent Deputation ultimately play the part of the judge. It is, indeed, a matter not only of checking the communal decisions in terms of laws and decrees applied, of determining their legality, but moreover of weighing them against the so-called public interest, of checking their political suitability. This public interest can adopt many different faces, since it concerns matters not only of vital interest to the nation, but of any interest higher than the commune's.

Hence, the supervising authorities may intervene (by denying an approval, by suspending or annulling) whenever, in their opinion, the requirements for healthy financial or good personnel management are not being met, or simply when the decision is considered to lack adequate preparation.

Even though interventions on grounds of content rarely occur, they nevertheless demonstrate the extent of administrative supervision which the province as the most directly involved governmental agent is authorized to exercise. This role of the ultimate judge threatens to overshadow a series of other relations, recently developed. Indeed, the planning, promoting, co-ordinating and other duties cannot be detached from the fundamental relation of supervision.

Co-ordinating tasks   The compass of responsibility in question is situated at the cutting edge between implementing policy, initiated from above, and the acknowledge of the dossiers passed up from the lower levels. Here the province is the 'intermediary' agent *par excellence* which can detach itself from the diversity of local situations in order to elaborate an optimal arrangement for a larger territory, without, however, losing touch with the local characteristics of the problems formulated.

The central government has fully recognized this critical characteristic and charges the province – that is, the governor – with the organization of the fire departments, the emergency services and the general contingency plan. It is, indeed, at this level that one can get the best overall view of the needs, co-ordinate the measures to be taken and, if necessary, act as the authority issuing by-laws. This role of go-between is also appreciated outside the realm of urgent interventions, for instance in giving public administration (province and commune) a lead in the right direction in the use and application of information technology, in organizing police training or, though only recently, in co-ordinating crime prevention.

Planning tasks   Since the breakthrough of regional economic policies, the provinces have taken measures to stimulate and direct regional development. These were new tasks and the provinces decided upon the formula of the non-profit organization, after the example of the 'provincial economic councils', and upon a form of intercommunal co-operation in order to involve the communal administrations.

In 1970 the central government thought it necessary to fit this undeniable provincial dynamism into a nationally structured planning organization. These Regional Development Organizations

(Gewestelijke Ontwikkelingsmaatschappijen or GOM, Sociétés de Développement Régional or SDR), which are in Flanders tailor-made to the provincial scale, have continued the existing traditions to the best of their ability, but are institutionally cut off from the specific formulation of a provincial policy. Indeed, it is not sufficient to include a significant number of Provincial Council members in the management board of a GOM, or even to entrust the chair to a member of the Permanent Deputation, in order to ensure a good fit with provincial policy. In the first instance, the GOMs are the antennae of an unsatisfactorily functioning central planning organization. These are, in other words, decentralized central services, whereas the provincial economic councils originated as a part of territorially decentralized task management. Even though it is clear to all insiders that in Flanders co-ordination with provincial decision-making is still realized on a personal level, nevertheless from an institutional viewpoint it is to be regretted that the provincial authorities did not have such a policy instrument at their immediate disposal in the crucial socio-economic domain. In Wallonia this instrument was completely detached from the provincial sphere and transferred to the region.

Stimulative and initiating tasks The provincial framework seems to fulfil *par excellence* not only the requirement of instituting a dialogue between representatives of the government and the private sector and to promote binding agreements, but also that of dynamic innovation. It enjoys the ideal position of keeping in touch with new management insights and developments, as well as with the specific needs on the local and supra-local levels. The possibilities contained in the new policy measures of the central authorities can be evaluated on the spot and translated concretely into opportunities in the field.

This stimulative activity should, however, not be interpreted as a mere 'selling' of the central government's options. Precisely because of their intermediate position, the provincial authorities are able to see gaps very quickly, and even dysfunctions, in the central government's measures. Whenever possible, they have pointed out these inadequacies, though most of the time without getting much of a hearing. Since the 1970s, the provinces have indeed barely been 'heard' in the central decision-making process. They are not the only victims of this centralist trend. The same applies to the local authorities which are being confronted with norms that are unsuited to local situations.

Sometimes stimulating an active policy in various areas has motivated the provinces to initiate certain developments themselves. The distinction between this and the 'executive tasks' mentioned below is, of course, subtle. We would, however, like to reserve this latter category for provincial task completion under own management. By taking the initiative, we mean rather the realization of an initiative as co-executant, together with others. In this way the provinces are involved in the founding of intercommunal associations and non-profit organizations of all kinds. They cover a great variety of activities, ranging from socio-economic development to environmental protection and the care for the disabled. Financial and managerial intervention by the province can take different forms, from (quasi-) total financial support to (modest) participation in the provision of capital.

Executive tasks   The provinces have pursued 'provincial interests' in a creative way during the past 150 years. They not only have stimulated and supported, co-ordinated and planned; in many cases they have set their hand to the plough themselves. Numerous public services have thus come into being and still thrive under provincial direction. Most familiar are the schools, that is, technical schools and secondary education. A manifest shortage of these institutions clearly existed. Moreover, they also inaugurated recreation parks, (socio-cultural) training centres, libraries, swimming pools and so on.

Financial means   Taxes constitute the most important income source for the provinces (40 per cent). Primarily (77 per cent), they

Table 1   *The principal categories of provincial resources, 1988–90 (in million Belgian francs)*

	1988	%	1989	%	1990	%
According to the budget						
Provincial fund	7,554	17.2	7,399	16.5	7,716	16.5
Taxes	17,708	40.3	17,986	40.2	18,538	39.8
Education	12,491	28.5	13,703	30.6	14,458	31.0
Other income sources	6,163	14.0	6,696	12.7	6,911	12.7
Total	43,916	100.0	44,783	100.0	46,620	100.0
According to the accounts						
Provincial fund	7,619	16.1	7,482	17.6		
Taxes	18,852	39.9	17,747	41.6		
Education	10,559	22.4	9,802	23.0		
Other income sources	10,229	21.6	7,591	17.8		
Total	47,259	100.0	42,623	100.0		

Table 2   *Provincial expenditure, 1988–90 (in million Belgian francs)*

	1988	%	1989	%	1990	%
Total expenditure	43,940	100	45,089	100	47,288	100
Economic classification						
Staff	23,993	54.6	25,071	55.6	27,658	58.5
Operating expenditure	5,418	12.3	5,515	12.2	5,715	12.1
Transfers	4,208	9.6	4,643	10.3	4,067	8.6
Debt	10,321	23.5	9,860	21.9	9,848	20.8
Functional classification						
General debt	412	0.9	377	0.8	327	0.8
General administration	4,124	9.4	4,343	9.6	4,709	10.0
Private assets	305	0.7	303	0.7	309	0.6
Central services	1,286	2.9	1,374	3.1	1,373	2.9
Police, judiciary	101	0.2	99	0.2	112	0.2
Road transport	2,612	5.9	2,560	5.7	2,603	5.5
Waterways	501	1.1	527	1.2	571	1.2
Industry, commerce	1,377	3.1	1,428	3.2	1,478	3.1
Agriculture, fishery	538	1.2	543	1.2	600	1.3
Education	19,147	43.7	19,580	43.4	21,618	45.7
Recreation	999	2.3	1,059	2.3	1,122	2.4
Youth	319	0.7	300	0.7	326	0.7
Culture	1,371	3.1	1,456	3.2	1,571	3.3
Sports	532	1.2	552	1.2	580	1.2
Arts	610	1.4	624	1.4	698	1.5
Church fabric	110	0.3	104	0.2	110	0.2
Social welfare	1,999	4.6	1,971	4.4	1,919	4.1
Health care	2,582	5.6	2,591	5.7	2,394	5.1
Public health	1,821	4.1	1,969	4.4	1,718	3.6
Housing, town planning	2,330	5.3	2,099	4.7	2,102	4.5
Various	864	2.0	1,230	2.7	1,000	2.1

are provincial surtaxes on a property-based state tax. Next, there is a grant from the central government that makes up 16.5 per cent of income. Thirdly, a high percentage is linked to the educational services provided by the provinces. The numerous provincial education institutions are indeed heavily financed by the communities, and one should take this into account when interpreting Tables 1 and 2. Against a big share of the item 'education' on the expenses side (45 per cent) stands the subsidy from the central authorities of 31 per cent of the total income of the provinces. Nevertheless, it is precisely the educational facilities that have contributed the most to shaping the public's image of the provinces at the services level.

Out of this brief survey of institutions and tasks arises a final impression of unfulfilled possibilities. The provinces are democratically legitimated and have functionally been perfectly equipped to pursue a supra-local policy, for they have a professional official apparatus and a powerful management (governor). But they have not been grafted onto the political-ethnic cleavages characterizing the country. Therefore they do not qualify for the redefinition in the new federal pattern.

Since the regional level with regard to its size fits in very closely with the provinces (4½ provinces for each region), the traditional intermediate level has since 1969 been considered by many to be superfluous: not because of any failure in the performance of the provinces, but because they got squeezed between the enlarged local administrations and the expansive regions.

The new meso level: the regions

Anyone who dared describe the recently created Belgian Social-Economic Regions as a kind of intermediate government would immediately provoke incensed reactions from both constitutionalists and politicians. From a juridicial-political point of view, they would, moreover, be in the right. The regions – for convenience's sake we also put the Cultural Communities in this category – are rather to be characterized as constituent states in a federal system, with all the features connected with such a status – namely, parliamentary assembly, government and above all, powers and legal standards that are not subordinate to the national Parliament nor to the national government.

We first want to put this very particular form of Belgian regionalism and federalism in a historical context – that is, developments since 1980 – and subsequently to state some essentials as to their governmental character. Very important in terms of the theme of this book, finally, is how we interpret the role of the regions. That is to say, are they new central governments or are they partly also higher-level intermediate bodies?

Reform in three stages

To the foreign observer and to the majority of the Belgian people alike, the state reform appears to be a never-ending story. For over a quarter of a century negotiations and measures have been succeeding one another, and still the end is not in view. Almost every government, however, declares at its inauguration that it will take care of the 'final' structure. In the meantime, it has become evident that the reason for the long-lasting life of this issue has nothing to do with the inability to make decisions. After all, many fundamental decisions were taken and were implemented both in the articles of the Constitution and in operational reform laws. In the course of this process, however, the objective of the reform and even the state concept itself have undergone change. In a period of twenty-five years, the Belgian state has developed from a decentralized unitary state, through a regional state, into a federal state *in statu nascendi*. In order to get a better understanding of the position of the traditional and new meso level we would like to indicate only a few outlines of this evolution.

As was mentioned above, the *first constitutional revision* of 1970 provided both for *Cultural Communities* and *Social-Economic Regions*, but only the cultural dimension has been fully executed. A parliamentary assembly (a *council*) was established for the Dutch-speaking as well as for the French-speaking Cultural Community (later also for the German-speaking Community), consisting of the directly elected members of the national Parliament from the language regions concerned. These councils received full legislative competence. Their 'decrees' have the same status as national laws, but only within the restrictively defined cultural field of policy. This constituted an impressive degree of autonomy, but it was restricted in its scope, since it was confined to cultural matters in the narrow sense, that is, it excluded education, training and welfare. How important are legislative powers, if the executive power – government as well as administration – remains on a national level?

However, 1970 was the starting point of a considerable political dynamic, especially in Flanders which had insisted most explicitly on this cultural autonomy so that the entire legislation in the cultural sphere was fundamentally rewritten. The issue was not the regional specification of the national basic laws, but an independently functioning legal system comparable to the legislation in the various German *Bundesländer*. In short, 1970 was a modest start but contained from the early beginnings an orientation towards a federal order. The *regions*, on the other hand, only existed on paper. Article 107 *quater* of the Constitution could not be operationalized because the 'special' majority required was lacking in Parliament. And yet, Minister Perin did not wish to postpone the mainly Walloon desire for regional autonomy *sine die*.

In 1974 a regular law carrying his name was established providing for regional ministerial committees within the national government charged with 'regional matters'. This was an important innovation with regard to organization and contents, since an embryonic executive power for the regions arose, and at the same time it was decided which matters of policy might be considered as belonging to the regional sphere. From a juridical point of view this was no harrowing event, but on the political-psychological level it was one of the utmost importance. The reform of 1980 would elaborate on these experiences. After the unsuccessful attempt to come to an all-round settlement (Egmont Agreement, 1977) due to the tricky matter of Brussels and its suburbs, the bright idea was to put Brussels into the institutional 'refrigerator' for a while and to concentrate on the new structures for Flanders and Wallonia. In the summer of 1980 the die was cast. The communities received additional powers (training, welfare, public health services) and, moreover, a real government, the *exécutif*, functioning outside the national government this time. The *regions*, on the other hand, for the first time enjoyed full civil rights: a parliamentary assembly with full decree authority, an *exécutif* and a number of territory-related tasks lying within the scope of the Law Perin.

The communities and regions were thus launched, even when a lot of uncertainties remained in circumscribing their powers. An extraordinary law court, the Arbitral Tribunal, was created in order to settle in an authoritative way conflicts over powers on the model of the constitutional courts in federal states. On the Flemish side the community and region were also amalgamated. In this way one sole institution arose, the Flemish Community, combining all transferred powers, consisting of one parliament and one government: in short, the embryo of a Flemish state. On the French-speaking – Walloon – side an identical tendency towards fusing the community and the region was present, but the antagonisms between Brussels and Wallonia still thwarted a merger.

However innovatory and far-reaching the reforms in 1980 were, they have never completely satisfied their proponents. Unease existed about the ambiguous and often barely operational allocation of authority. Equally, there was dissatisfaction about the financial autonomy of the communities and regions, for they were only licensed to spend those financial means distributed to them from the central kitty. During the 1980s it can be said that the concept of the state itself underwent change. The top priority was not regional autonomy, but the reform of the state in a federal sense – that is, the creation of two fully fledged constituent states and a metropolitan region with comparable powers.

It followed that the next reform therefore ought to be comprehensive, and include a radical transfer of power, no longer concerning separate topics but, rather, consistent terrains of policy. It should create fully fledged regional parliaments and offer a full financial basis to independently operating states within a federal system. Change of this type would be fundamental and a considerable part of it has already been implemented. In 1988–9 the powers of the communities

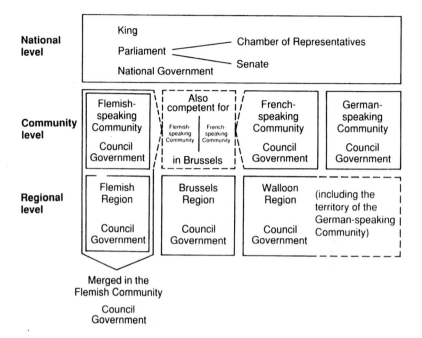

National level

King
Parliament — Chamber of Representatives
National Government — Senate

Community level

Flemish-speaking Community
Council
Government

Also competent for
Flemish-speaking Community | French-speaking Community
in Brussels

French-speaking Community
Council
Government

German-speaking Community
Council
Government

Regional level

Flemish Region
Council
Government

Brussels Region
Council
Government

Walloon Region
Council
Government

(including the territory of the German-speaking Community)

Merged in the
Flemish Community
Council
Government

Figure 2   *Organigram of Belgian political institutions*

and regions were radically enlarged, with education going to the communities, infrastructure and sectoral economic policy to the regions.

In 1989, at last, the metropolitan Region of Brussels became operational, a regulation for finances was finally worked out, and the authority of the Arbitral Court was increased. Three hot issues are at present up for discussion: the so-called *residual* (that is, remaining) powers, the presence on the international scene of communities and regions, and finally the reform of the national Parliament.

This last issue unlocks deep emotions. Belgium has a traditional bicameral system (Parliament and Senate), so the obvious solution seems to be to transform the Senate into a 'Chamber of Communities and Regions' and to provide for directly elected councils for those communities and regions. The problem is especially delicate, however because the existing Senate would have to be prepared to abolish itself in the present form. Moreover, political parties in Belgium no longer operate on a national basis. Hence, out of consultations between a multitude of 'regional' parties, a national consensus has to emerge; and yet the general feeling prevails that again the barrier will be surmounted before long. Belgium will thus prove its ability to deal with its internal political chasms, but the price to be paid is a rather complex and sometimes asymmetric structure and a complicated segmentation of powers. Both elements will be briefly dealt with and the present status questions will be explained.

It should be kept in mind that since 1990 a striking evolution has been taking place, that is, the shift of political weight from the French-speaking Community to the Walloon Region. As mentioned above, on the Flemish side both institutions have been virtually amalgamated since 1980. With the Brussels Region being independent, and co-operation between the French- and Dutch-speaking population progressing more smoothly, the purpose of a French-speaking Community separately functioning in the south of the country is being questioned. Clearly there is a movement towards a merger of the French-speaking Community and the Walloon Region: not so much as a fusion between equal partners (as formerly in Flanders) but, rather, as an absorption of the former by the latter. The severe lack of funds in the French-speaking Community, responsible as it is for money-consuming education, is just another reason to push forward on this course. This amalgamation would both simplify the structure of the Belgian state (see Figure 2) and accentuate more clearly the reorganization of Belgium into two equal constituent states together with an autonomous metropolitan region. Despite the fact that the community and region are becoming assimilated it is still relevant to distinguish between their respective legal powers.

The competences of the communities

Cultural matters, such as fine arts and cultural heritage, broadcast and television, permanent education, leisure and tourism, professional training

Education: the school system, from kindergarten to university

Health care, although the social security system remains a national competence

Social aid, especially the Centres for Public Aid, youth care, care for the elderly, integration of immigrants

The competences of the regions

Economic policy, although with important exceptions, such as the monetary and financial policy and the legal framework (commercial law, labour law, social security, etc.)

The exploitation of *natural resources* (except for the continental plateau) and the distribution of energy

Employment policy

Public works and transport: highways, roads, waterways, ports, coastal protection, dikes, urban transport, etc.

Urban planning, monuments and sites

Housing

Environment and protection of nature, except for the treatment of nuclear waste

Water: production, distribution, purification

Provincial and municipal institutions: the regions control and supervise (*tutelle administrative*) provinces and communes, including the intercommunal societies. They are competent for the financing of the local governments and assign subsidies for their public works.

The reader interested in further details can consult Alen (1990, 1992).

The meso level under pressure

The enumeration of competences abundantly illustrates that the communities and regions have been charged with tasks that in most states rest with the central government, as well as with specific sub-national missions. Hence, what may be regarded as the traditional meso level – the province – has been reduced to local government, merely administrating a larger territory than the commune. The specificity of the provincial level – that is, its supervising, co-ordinating and planning duties – is no longer emphasized. The provinces have become mere decentralized administration, with mainly executive tasks.

In a country like Belgium, in the long run this status is nothing less than a death sentence. The size of the regions makes every intermediate body between them and the communes totally redundant. At best the provinces can be used as a geographical and administrative frame for implementing national and regional policies; but as an independent policy body, their role is over. This development is to be regretted; for along with the disappearance of the provinces vanishes the acknowledgement of specifically intermediary tasks. The regions no longer function as intermediary governments, but fully exploit the recently gained right to determine their policy independently. The adaption of national policy to local circumstances, the outstanding task of an intermediary body, is lost. Such a process can only result in increasing centralization, a phenomenon observed in both Flanders and Wallonia.

And yet, the final word has not been said. Paradoxically enough, in the growing EC the regions might in the long run become *de facto* the new intermediary level between a federal Europe and local government. For, together with the member states, they have to translate the federal directives into operational regulations for the implementation of local policy. Regardless of the far-reaching legislative competences of the region, it is to be expected that the setting of standards in many vital, policy areas will become the exclusive right of the highest, European level, while the implementation of these policies may mainly become a regional matter. Belgium, after all, may have contributed to the new European institutional system by establishing this new type of meso level.

Further reading and references

Alen, A. (1990) *Belgium: Bipolar and Centrifugal Federalism*. Brussels: Ministry for Foreign Affairs.

Alen, A. (1992) *Treatise on Belgian Constitutional Law*. Dordrecht: Kluwer.

Dunn, J. A. (1974) 'The revision of the constitution in Belgium: a study of the institutionalization of ethnic conflict', *Western Political Quarterly*, 27 (1).

Frognier, A. P., Quevit, M. and Stenback, M. (1982) 'Regional imbalances and centre–periphery relationships in Belgium', in S. Rokkan and D. W. Urwin (eds), *The Politics of Territorial Identity*. London: Sage.

Kossman, E. H. (1978) *The Low Countries, 1780–1940*. Oxford: Oxford University Press.

Lejeune, Y. (1990) 'Belgium', in H. J. Michelmann and P. Soldatos (eds), *Federalism and International Relations – the Role of Sub-National Units*. Oxford: Clarendon.

Lorwin, V. R. (1966) 'Belgium: religion, class and language and national politics', in R. A. Dahl (ed.), *Political Oppositions in Western Democracies*. New Haven: Yale University Press.

Maes, R. (1985) *La Décentralisation Territoriale*. Brussels: Imbel.

Maes, R. (1992) *De Intercommunales*. Bruges: Vanden Broele.

Mughan, A. (1979) 'Modernization and regional relative deprivation: towards a theory of ethnic conflict', in L. J. Sharpe (ed.), *Decentralist Trends in Western Democracies*. London: Sage.

Mughan, A. (1985) 'Belgium: all periphery and no centre', in Y. Mény and V. Wright (eds), *Centre–Periphery Relations in Western Europe*. London: Allen & Unwin.

Senelle, R. (1978) *The Reform of the Belgian State*. Brussels: Ministry of Foreign Affairs.

Zolberg, A. (1977) 'Splitting the difference: federalization without federalism in Belgium', in M. J. Esman (ed.), *Ethnic Conflict in the Western World*, Ithaca: Cornell University Press.

3
Developments at the French Meso Level: Modernizing the French State

Sonia Mazey

Meso government in France

Technically speaking, the meso level of government in France includes the 100 departments (*départements*), 6 urban communities, districts, numerous intercommunal groupings and 26 regions which lie between the 36,394 communes and the central state (see Figure 1).[1] While the departments date from Napoleon I, the rest are administrative creations of the Fifth Republic. Since 1958, territorial reform has rarely been absent from the political agenda as successive governments have attempted to reform and rationalize the legendary 'one and indivisible' Republic. Yet, in contrast to other European countries where territorial reform has entailed radical changes, French local government reform has been minimal and incremental in nature, each initiative adjusting slightly the existing arrangement. Even the more ambitious decentralization programme implemented by the Socialist government between 1982 and 1986 left intact the traditional units of local government – the departments and communes. Nevertheless, the cumulative impact of these piecemeal changes has been a significant increase in the importance of the meso level. Here, two parallel trends can be clearly identified: the progressive extension of the financial and political autonomy of the departmental councils; and the piecemeal establishment of elected regional governments.

The growing importance of the departmental level is, in large part, due to the inability of most communes (71 per cent of which contain fewer than 700 inhabitants) to provide even the most basic amenities. Departments have thus – in functional terms at least – become the primary providers of non-central services, and in that sense the most important element at the French meso level. The increased financial and functional importance of French departmental authorities is clearly relevant to any discussion of the changing nature of centre–periphery relations in France. However, the following discussion focuses upon the development and performance of the newly created

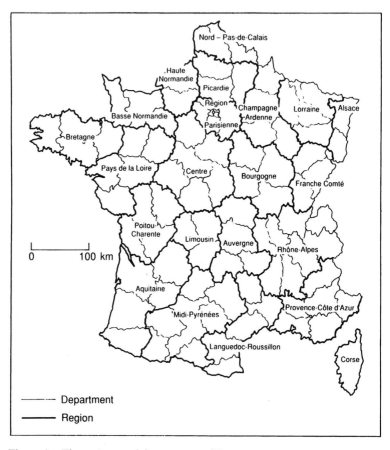

Figure 1   *The regions and departments of France*

regional authorities, which in many respects may be regarded as the principal meso level. Whereas the departments perform a range of 'traditional' local authority functions, the regional authorities were established to carry out a specific task: the promotion and co-ordination of socio-economic development. Since their inception French regional authorities have been primarily responsible for the co-ordination of local authority investment, regional planning and fostering partnerships with local and nationalized industries. Though regionalist pressures undoubtedly contributed to the post-war development of the region and in certain parts of France (for example, Bretagne, Occitania and the Basque region) remain politically and socially influential, the meso was not established to satisfy these pressures. Indeed, care was taken to ensure that the administrative boundaries of the regional authorities did not coincide with historic regions. Rather, regional structures were imposed upon localities by a *dirigiste* state concerned primarily with administrative and economic modernization; and despite its subsequent political development, the French meso remains essentially functional in its role.

This chapter begins by outlining the gradual development of the regional politico-administrative structures since 1958, focusing upon the impact of the 1982 decentralization programme. Particular attention is paid here to the organization and financial and functional importance of the new meso. The second section of the chapter discusses the causes of the growing importance of the meso and highlights those factors which have determined the nature of centre–periphery relations. In general terms, this analysis demonstrates that while functional considerations – notably linked to economic modernization and administrative rationalization – have consistently persuaded governments of the need to strengthen the meso level of government and administration, the precise nature of the changes proposed has been shaped by ideology, political considerations, financial pressures and public opinion. In addition, all governments have had to accommodate the resistance of administrative and political elites to any restructuring which might reduce their own power. The chapter concludes with a tentative assessment of the present economic and political importance of the French meso.

Developments at the meso level

The emergence of the region, 1958–81

The early development of the region in France was unquestionably prompted by the exigencies of national economic planning. Administrative reforms introduced in 1964 consolidated the twenty-two planning regions which had been created in 1959 and established a rudimentary institutional framework at the regional level. The prefect of the principal department in each region became the official regional prefect with authority over the other prefects in the region. An advisory Regional Administrative Conference was established in each region, bringing together under the chairmanship of the regional prefect the heads of the ministerial field services and the other departmental prefects in the region in an attempt to co-ordinate public investment decisions within the framework of the National Economic Plan. In addition, two further institutions were created in each region: the Regional Mission and the Commission for Regional Economic Development (CODER). The former comprised a small group of senior administrative and technical officials, appointed by the Prime Minister and intended to act as the personal 'brains trust' of the regional prefect. The CODER was a corporatist, consultative body comprising 'experts' (appointed by the Prime Minister), local politicians and socio-economic elites within the region. Members were consulted on the regional section of the National Economic Plan and informed of forthcoming state investment in the region (Machin, 1974). Despite their essentially administrative nature, the above reforms nevertheless added momentum to a wider political debate in the 1960s on centre–periphery relations which was accompanied by growing demands for further decentralization. Moreover, the issue was no longer simply one of administrative efficiency; the events of May 1968 gave fresh impetus to disparate regionalist movements and prompted widespread public support for greater participation and *autogestion*.

Unable to ignore these developments, President Pompidou's Gaullist government reluctantly introduced the 1972 regional reform (the loi Frey) which granted the region the legal status of a territorial public establishment – a corporate body with legal authority within a functionally defined area. The official role of the new regional establishment was to contribute to the economic and social development of the region. More specifically, the region could contribute financially to public works programmes of regional importance, or projects undertaken by the constituent local authorities and/or the state. The reform also granted regions a consultative role in the formulation of the regional section of the Plan. The institutional framework of the region was strengthened slightly with the creation of two new regional assemblies: the Regional Council, which enjoyed deliberative power over the regional budget (see below); and a consultative Economic and Social Committee. The former comprised all national politicians within the region – who were ex-officio members – together with an equal number of locally elected politicians (that is, municipal and general councillors). The Economic and Social Committee, which replaced the CODER, brought together representatives from various socio-economic organizations and technical experts. The regional prefect remained as the regional executive (Wright, 1979).

The 1972 reform also provided the region with its first budget, the size of which was, however, strictly limited by the imposition of a fiscal ceiling determined by the government (set at 15 francs per capita in 1974). From the state, the regional authority received the fiscal revenue raised from the issue of driving licences in the region. In addition, the region could add supplements to two national taxes (vehicle registration and property transactions) and local direct taxes. In addition to fiscal revenue, regions could borrow money for specific projects of a regional nature (subject to the approval of the Conseil d'Etat). In fact, regional budgets were and still are derisory compared to those of other local authorities; in 1975 the budget of a single department, the Nord, slightly exceeded the sum total of the twenty-two regional budgets. Regional expenditure was also subject to several legal constraints. Since the regional authorities were not permitted to employ independent administrative personnel, the budget was primarily an investment budget. Moreover, the reform specified that regional investment had to be channelled into projects which were to be undertaken by the constituent local authorities and/or the state.

Despite the decentralist rhetoric surrounding the 1972 reform, there was little in it to please regionalists. Inserted between the mosaic of local authorities and the state, the official role of the region was to co-ordinate local expenditure within the framework of national priorities as defined in the Plan. Essentially, the regional public establishments were departmental federations. Departmental and communal rivalries dominated the Regional Councils while local interests shaped regional expenditure. Nevertheless, between 1974 and 1981 the regional public establishments gradually assumed an institutional identity and began to play a more significant role in sub-national economic development. The early pattern of numerous, uncoordinated and piecemeal investments gave way to more coherent, medium-term investment programmes which were increasingly based upon clearly defined regional priorities. Projects typically financed by the regions included communications (road, rail and waterways), telecommunications development, agricultural modernization, industrial aid (after 1977) and rural development.

Several factors contributed to this shift. Regional councillors became more confident of their role; regions began to assume a political identity which often helped to define regional priorities (left-wing regions, in particular, were keen to establish alternative economic strategies); and regional revenue steadily increased during this period. Pressure from the regional prefect also meant that regional investment was increasingly channelled into nationally defined priority programmes within the framework of the decentralized seventh Plan. Finally, the budgetary and policy-making powers of the region were increased after 1977. In particular, the regions were accorded new powers to set up regional transport schemes, administer regional parks, help new and ailing industries and allocate category III (departmental) state investments in the region. Thus, by the time the Socialists came to power in 1981 regions were already playing an interventionist role in the regional economy and had in most cases acquired significant *de facto* political importance. Indeed, several regional presidents had (illegally) established advisory *cabinets* (Sadran, 1982; Mény, 1983).

The introduction of regional government, 1982–8

The Defferre reforms implemented by the Socialist government between 1982 and 1986 transformed the regional public establishments into regional governments. In March 1982 executive power at the regional level was transferred from the appointed regional prefect to the elected regional president (of the Regional Council). The prefectoral staff and ministerial field agencies were placed at the disposal of the president, who is also free to appoint additional political and technical advisers. The regional prefects were abolished and replaced by *commissaires de la République* (who in several instances were one and the same person!). Though lacking the regional executive powers of their predecessors, the *commissaires* (who are once again called prefects) are now formally responsible for the co-ordination of all ministerial field services and the preparation of the regional plan. All forms of *a priori* administrative, technical and financial control over regional authority decisions were also abolished in 1982; regional authority actions are now subject to *a posteriori* legal and financial control by the administrative tribunals and the newly created regional Cours des Comptes. Following the first ever direct regional elections in March 1986 the twenty-two metropolitan regions and the four overseas territories became fully fledged local authorities with full revenue-raising powers. The major concession made to autonomists and regionalists was the Special Statute granted to Corsica in 1982 which set the island apart legally from the other regions and granted it additional state subsidies and greater autonomy over educational, cultural and social policies (Keating and Hainsworth, 1986; Mazey, 1987).

French regional government: profile and performance

The Defferre reforms left intact the regional administrative boundaries established in 1959 and added to these the four overseas territories (see Table 1).

The average size of the metropolitan region (that is, including Corsica, but excluding the overseas territories) is 24,723 sq km, though as Table 1 shows they vary in size from 8,280 sq km (Alsace) to 45,348 sq km (Midi-Pyrénées region). The average regional population size is 2,512,700 inhabitants (102 sq km). Once again, however, there is considerable variation between the Ile de France region (Région Parisienne, containing the capital city), which has a population of 10,073,200 (839 sq km), and Corsica (Corse), which has just 240,200 inhabitants (28 sq km) (INSEE, 1988).

Table 1   *Size and population of the French regions*

Region	No. of departments	Area (sq km)	Population 1982[1] (000s)	Inhabitants per sq km (1982)	Population (1986)[2]
Alsace	2	8,280	1,566.0	189	1,599.6
Aquitaine	5	41,308	2,656.5	64	2,718.2
Auvergne	4	26,013	1,332.7	51	1,334.4
Bourgogne	4	31,582	1,596.1	51	1,606.9
Bretagne	4	27,209	2,707.9	100	2,763.8
Centre	6	39,151	2,264.2	58	2,324.4
Champagne-Ardenne	4	25,606	1,345.9	53	1,352.2
Corse	2	8,680	240.2	28	248.7
Franche Comté	4	16,202	1,084.0	67	1,085.9
Ile de France	8	12,012	10,073.2	839	10,249.7
Languedoc-Roussillon	5	27,376	1,926.5	70	2,011.9
Limousin	3	16,942	737.2	44	735.8
Lorraine	4	23,547	2,319.9	99	2,312.7
Midi-Pyrénées	8	45,348	2,325.3	51	2,355.1
Nord-Pas-de-Calais	2	12,414	3,932.9	317	3,927.2
Basse Normandie	3	17,589	1,351.0	77	1,372.9
Haute Normandie	2	12,317	1,655.4	134	1,692.8
Pays de la Loire	5	32,082	2,930.4	91	3,017.7
Picardie	3	19,399	1,740.3	90	1,773.5
Poitou-Charentes	4	25,810	1,568.2	61	1,583.6
Provence-Alpes-Côte-d'Azur	6	31,400	3,965.2	126	4,058.8
Rhône-Alpes	8	43,698	5,015.9	115	5,153.6
Metropolitan regions	96	543,965	54,334.9	100	55,279.4
Guadeloupe	1	1,780	328.4	184	333.0
Guyane	1	91,000	73.0	1	84.0
Martinique	1	1,100	328.6	299	328.0
Réunion	1	2,510	515.8	205	551.0
Overseas regions	4	96,390	1,245.8	13	1,296.0
France	100	640,355	55,580.7	87	56,575.4

[1] 1982 Census figures.
[2] Estimate.
Source: 'Les Collectivités territoriales', *Les Cahiers français*, 239, Jan./Feb. 1989: 27.

In each region there are two representative assemblies (both of which were created by the 1972 regional reform), the Economic and Social Committee and the Regional Council. The former is a consultative body comprising between 40 and 110 members which is indirectly elected every six years and which brings together representatives from:

- professional and business associations (at least 35 per cent of seats);
- trade unions (at least 35 per cent of seats);
- welfare, cultural and consumers' organizations (25 per cent of seats);
- experts in fields pertinent to regional development, nominated by the Prime Minister (5 per cent of seats).

Each committee elects its own president, determines its own rules of procedure and gives its opinion on all proposed regional policies. In addition, the committee's president may convene extraordinary sessions to discuss any issue affecting the region, though not more than once every three months.

The Regional Council – which, depending upon the size of the regional population, is composed of between 31 (Guyane) and 197 (Ile de France) representatives – is the deliberative assembly. Between 1972 and 1986 the councils existed as indirectly elected bodies comprising all national politicians within the region together with an equal number of departmental and municipal councillors from within the region. As part of the Defferre programme, regional elections were initially scheduled to take place in 1983, but were for various reasons repeatedly postponed by the Socialist government. The election of the 1,840 regional councillors in metropolitan and overseas France finally took place alongside the legislative elections of 16 March 1986, with the same electoral system used for both contests. Electors voted in a single ballot for departmental lists and the 'highest averaging' method was then used to allocate seats to lists. In order to obtain any seats a list must win at least 5 per cent of the departmental vote. Regional councillors, elected for a six-year period, in turn elect their own regional president (for a six-year period), who as the regional executive heads an executive bureau (also elected for six years) in which all political parties must be represented in proportion to their weight within the Regional Council.

As indicated in Table 2, the results of the 1986 regional elections closely mirrored those of the legislative ballot held the same day. This was hardly surprising given the circumstances; regional election campaigns had everywhere been dominated by national issues and parties while prominent national figures and traditional *notables* had been generously represented on the regional lists. The political composition of the Regional Councils is illustrated in Table 3. The

Table 2   *The results of the French legislative and regional elections of 16 March 86*

Lists	Legislative elections % vote	Seats	Regional elections % vote	Seats
Extreme Left	1.53	—	1.13	—
PCF	9.78	35	10.35	178
PS	31.04	206	29.13	552
MRG	0.38	2	0.58	17
Other Left	1.05	7	2.42	59
Ecologists	1.21	—	2.40	4
Regionalists	0.10	—	0.31	6
RPR	11.21	76	10.09	182
UDF	8.31	53	8.82	157
RPR-UDF	21.46	147	20.41	451
Other Right	3.90	14	5.38	93
FN	9.65	35	9.56	137
Other extreme Right	0.20	—	0.08	—
Total valid votes	28,036,678		27,789,101	

The table does not include the results of two overseas constituencies, Saint Pierre et Miquelon and Wallis et Futuna. In each case one deputy was elected under the old double ballot, simple majority system.

PCF   Parti Communiste Française (French Communist Party)
PS   Parti Socialiste (Socialist Party)
MRG   Mouvement des Radicaux de Gauche (Left-wing Radical Movement)
RPR   Rassemblement pour la République (Rally for the Republic (Gaullists))
UDF   Union pour la Démocratie Française (French Democratic Union)
RPR-UDF   Coalition list
FN   Front National (National Front)

Sources: figures from the Ministry of the Interior, *Le Monde*, 20 March 86; Mazey, 1986: 299

right-wing RPR and UDF parties controlled all but two metropolitan regions (Limousin and Nord-Pas-de-Calais) which were controlled by the Socialists. However, five right-wing presidents owed their position to the support of Jean-Marie Le Pen's extreme right-wing party, the FN, which holds the balance of power in five regions (Aquitaine, Languedoc-Roussillon, Franche Comté, Haute Normandie and Picardie). Proportional representation also entitled the FN to a number of seats in regional bureaux (Mazey, 1986). In sociological terms, regional councillors are not very different from their departmental and municipal counterparts. Indeed, due to the widespread practice of *cumul des mandats* (multiple office-holding) they are in many cases the same person. Among the 577 deputies elected to the National Assembly in June 1988, for instance, there

Table 3   *Percentage of Regional Council seats won by each party, 1986*

Region	PCF	PS	MRG and other Left	Reg.	Ecol.	RPR-UDF	CNIP and other Right	FN	Total no. of seats	President
Alsace	—	21	2	—	4	57	—	15	47	Marcel Rudloff (CDS-UDF)
Aquitaine	10	36	2	—	—	42	5	5	83	J. Chaban-Delmas (RPR)
Auvergne	9	32	—	—	—	53	2	4	47	V. Giscard d'Estaing (UDF-PR)
Bourgogne	9	31	2	—	—	42	9	5	55	Marcel Lucotte (UDF-PR)
Bretagne	5	37	—	—	—	46	10	2	81	Yvon Bourges (RPR)
Centre	11	31	4	—	—	37	13	4	75	Marcel Dousset (UDF-PR)
Champagne-Ardenne	9	32	—	—	—	43	6	11	47	Bernard Scasi (UDF-CDS)
Corse	11	10	20	10	—	30	16	3	61	J.-P. de Rocca Serra (RPR)
Franche Comté	5	37	5	—	—	44	—	9	43	Edgar Faure (UDF-Rad.)
Ile de France	10	31	2	—	—	41	5	12	197	Michel Giraud (RPR)
Languedoc-Roussillon	14	32	2	—	—	31	9	12	65	Jacques Blanc (UDF-PR)
Limousin	20	37	—	—	—	41	2	—	41	Robert Savy (PS)
Lorraine	5	33	—	—	—	48	4	10	73	Jean-Marie Rausch (UDF-CDS)
Midi-Pyrénées	6	30	11	—	—	37	11	5	87	Dominique Baudis (app. UDF)
Nord-Pas-de-Calais	17	32	3	—	2	34	4	11	113	Noel Joseph (PS)
Basse Normandie	2	22	11	—	—	44	13	4	45	René Garrec (UDF)
Haute Normandie	11	36	2	—	—	40	6	6	53	Roger Fosse (RPR)
Pays de la Loire	5	32	4ª	—	—	42	13	3	93	Olivier Guichard (RPR)
Picardie	15	33	—	—	—	38	7	7	55	Charles Baur (UDF-PSD)
Poitou-Charentes	6	36	4	—	—	43	9	2	53	Louis Fruchard (UDF-CDS)
Provence-Alpes-Côte-d'Azur	12	26	1	—	—	34	6	21	117	Jean-Claude Gaudin (UDF-PR)
Rhône-Alpes	9	30	1	—	—	38	13	9	151	Charles Béraudier (UDF)
Guadeloupe	24	29	—	—	—	46	—	—	41	Felix Proto (PS)
Martinique	—	51	—	—	—	49	—	—	41	Aimé Césaire (PS)
Guyane	—	—	61	—	—	29	10	—	31	Georges Othily (PS app.)
Réunion	30	13	—	—	—	40	18	—	45	Pierre Lagourgue (ind. Right)

ª Includes two PSU representatives.

Additional abbreviations to those listed for Table 2:

CNIP   Centre National des Indépendants et Paysans
CDS   Centre des Démocrates Sociaux (Social Democratic Centrists)
CDS-UDF   Coalition list
PR   Parti Républicain (Republican Party)
PSD   Parti Social-Démocrate (Social Democratic Party)
Rad.   Parti Radical (Radical Party)

Sources: compiled from 'La France des régions', *Le Monde – Dossiers et documents*, April 1986; Macy, 1986: 300

were 130 regional councillors. Moreover, of these 130 deputies/regional councillors, 57 were mayors, 39 were municipal councillors, 51 were general (that is, departmental) councillors, and 4 were general council presidents (Mabileau, 1989: 75). Legislation introduced in 1985 has recently restricted the number of 'significant' offices an individual may hold to two.[2] The impact of this reform which was implemented only gradually between 1986 and 1992, was greatest at the regional level. Several *grands notables* have already chosen to give up their regional mandate in preference to other local elective offices, a factor which might clear the way in future years for the emergence of a 'new' regional political elite (Mabileau, 1989). (For results of the 1992 election see Appendix.)

The regional executive determines the dates of plenary assembly meetings and fixes the policy agenda. Both assemblies contain a number of standing committees which scrutinize legislative proposals. All decisions taken by the Regional Council must be transmitted to the state representative (the Commissaire de la République) within two weeks. If he or she believes the decision to be financially or administratively irregular, the commissaire must refer the decision to either the regional administrative tribunal or the regional Cours des Comptes. Technically speaking, regional decisions become legally binding from the moment they reach the prefecture. In practice, there is considerable liaison between regional presidents and the commissaire before publication of regional legislation in order to ensure that regional proposals meet legal and financial requirements. In 1988, for example, just 902 financial decisions were referred to the regional Cours des Comptes from *all* local authorities, a figure which represented less than 0.4 per cent of all local authority budgetary decisions (Paugam, 1989: 47).

Until 1982 the regional assemblies were totally dependent upon the administrative services of the general prefecture. In April 1982, however, the regional administrative services were placed under the personal control of the regional presidents, who may also appoint additional administrative, political and technical advisers. In order to attract high-quality local and regional administrators, a series of administrative reforms were introduced between 1984 and 1987 integrating national and local civil service career structures and salary scales. Generally speaking, regional presidents were quick to make use of their new powers of appointment; between 1981 and 1984 the number of officials employed by the regional authorities rose from just 413 to 2,278.

The average number of administrative staff employed by the regional authority in 1984 was 102, though numbers varied from 30 in Limousin to 323 in Nord-Pas-de-Calais (Rondin, 1985: 254). One

Table 4   *Local authority administrative personnel, 1.1.87*

Organization	No. of administrators[1]
Regions	3,337
Departments	168,813
Departmental public establishments	8,051
Communes	748,964
Communal social welfare centres	54,659
Education offices	11,798
Intercommunal groupings	42,994
Districts	6,948
Urban communities	22,141
Public housing	33,846
Municipal banks	1,101
Total[2]	1,102,652

[1] Converted into full-time equivalent.
[2] Metropolitan and overseas France.
Source: 'Les Collectivités territoriales', 1989: 66

consequence of this development has been a steep increase in the proportion of the regional budget which is now devoted to administrative costs. However, as indicated in Table 4, regional bureaucracies are modest in size compared to those of other local authorities.

Regional finances
Prior to 1982, the financial resources of the regional authorities were strictly controlled by the central government. Of particular importance in this respect was the fact that regional tax revenue (the regions' principal source of revenue) was subject to an annual fiscal ceiling determined by the government (set at 15 francs per person in 1974, reaching 67.68 francs in 1981 and 169 francs in 1986). Furthermore, the maximum amount of money regional authorities could borrow from the Caisse des Dêpots et Consignations before 1982 was directly linked to the size of their fiscal income. However, since 1982, regional expenditure has risen sharply for three major reasons. First, the fiscal ceiling on regional revenue was increased significantly after 1981, and following the 1986 regional elections the ceiling was abolished on the grounds that directly elected assemblies should be free to determine their own taxation levels. Secondly, the 1982 reforms transferred to the regions a number of new responsibilities for which they now receive financial compensation from the state in the form of grants and fiscal transfers (see below). Thirdly, the rules governing regional authority borrowing have been relaxed

since 1982 and several regions have taken advantage of this fact. The principal sources of regional revenue are threefold: regional taxes, central government grants and loans.

In practice, there are considerable variations between regions in terms of resources. In 1987, for instance, the two smallest regional budgets were those of Corsica and the Franche Comté region, which totalled 329.4 million francs and 411.1 million francs respectively. At the other end of the scale in that year were the Ile de France and Nord-Pas-de-Calais regions with budgets of 5,513 million francs and 2,013.9 million francs. In this year the average-size metropolitan regional budget was 1,172.5 million francs (the twenty-two metropolitan regional budgets totalled 25,797 million francs) (*Le Monde – Dossiers et documents*, 1988). Though no single factor accounts for this diversity it is possible to identify two apparently important variables. First, the revenue base of a region is strongly linked to population size. Since 1982, the regions have been free to levy a regional tax on the issue of driving licences (*permis de conduire*) and on vehicle registration (*carte grise*) in the region. In addition, they may add regional supplements to the property sales tax and the four local taxes (that is, the land and property sales taxes, residency tax and business tax). Predominantly urban regions with a high population density thus have a clear fiscal advantage over their rural counterparts, since fiscal income accounts for (on average) just over 56 per cent of regional revenue. The other relevant criterion in determining regional budgets is political allegiance. Generally speaking, left-wing-controlled regions have tended to impose higher taxes and to borrow more heavily than ring-wing regional authorities.

French local authority expenditure generally increased significantly during the 1980s as new responsibilities were devolved to all levels of local government (rising from 9 per cent of GDP and 40.8 per cent of the state budget in 1981 to 10.3 per cent of GDP and 53 per cent of the state budget by 1987 – see Table 5. During this period regional budgets rose faster than those of the departments and communes. Notwithstanding this development, region authorities remain very much the poor relation among French local authorities. In 1987, regional budgets accounted for 20.6 per cent of the departmental budgets (compared to just 7.1 per cent in 1981), 9.8 per cent of those of the communes (compared with 3.8 per cent in 1981), less than 3 per cent of the state budget (as opposed to less than 1 per cent in 1981) and just 0.6 per cent of French GDP (compared with 0.2 per cent in 1981).

The 1982–6 decentralization programme produced sharp increases in local taxation levels generally. Between 1981 and 1984 the fiscal income of the communes increased by 55 per cent from 63,390 million

Table 5   *Local authority budgets, 1981–7 (in milliard francs)*[1]

Public expenditure	1981	1987
Communes	157.0	300.0
Communal groupings[2]	38.7	76.4
Departments	84.0	143.0
Regions	6.0	29.5
Total local authorities	285.7	548.9
State budget	700.5	1,033.1
Gross national product	3,164.8	5,301.3

[1] All figures in current prices.
[2] This includes urban communities, districts, communal syndicats, public establishments.

Source: Démocratie locale, 1989

francs to 98,054 million francs), and that of the departments by 100 per cent (from 24,974 million francs to 49,961 million francs), while the fiscal income of the regions rose by 135 per cent (from 3,662 million francs to 8,590 million francs) (Caisse des Dêpots et Consignations, 1986: 80). Whereas in 1980, 43 per cent of tax revenue went to the state and 11 per cent to local authorities, by 1987 these figures were 39 per cent and 14 per cent respectively (*Le Monde*, 10.8.88). Generally speaking, all local authority taxes have risen more sharply since 1981 than national ones. However, regional taxes have risen most steeply of all following the removal of restrictions on their revenue-raising powers. Nevertheless, it is important to remember that regional fiscal revenue in 1988 accounted for just 20 per cent of departmental fiscal income and 12 per cent of communal tax revenue (*Le Monde*, 6.10.88). Moreover, as illustrated in Figure 2, fiscal income is by far the largest source of regional revenue, accounting for some 50 per cent of total income.

Functions of the French meso
In contrast to the departmental and communal budgets, those of the regions – despite the sharp increase in regional authority administrative costs since 1982 – are primarily investment budgets. The specific *raison d'être* of the region is socio-economic development and economic planning. Successive governments since 1981 have also publicly declared that the regional authorities are expected to play a leading role in the fight against unemployment. More specifically, French regional governments are now formally responsible for:

● *Urbanism* – co-ordination of, and support for, urban development, including public housing.

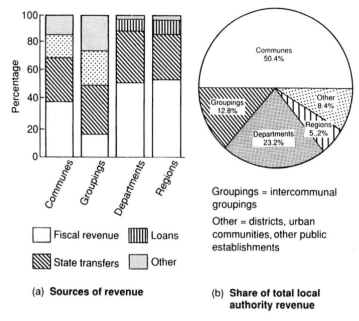

(a) Sources of revenue

Fiscal revenue

State transfers

Loans

Other

Groupings = intercommunal groupings

Other = districts, urban communities, other public establishments

(b) Share of total local authority revenue

Figure 2　*Local authority finances, France, 1988* (Démocratie locale, *1989*)

- *Transport* – the organization of regional public transport schemes, improvements in road and rail networks, development of coastal fishing fleets, port industries and inland waterways.
- *Education* – construction, equipment and maintenance of the buildings of secondary schools, agricultural colleges and cultural/ sports centres.
- *Vocational training* – the establishment and administration of professional/vocational/youth training programmes.
- *Economic planning* – the formulation (and implementation) of a regional plan and negotiation of *contrat de plan* with the state, local authorities, industries and banks.
- *Environmental/cultural action* – preservation of regional sites/ parks and maintenance of regional archives and museums.

While regions may intervene in any of the above areas in a piecemeal fashion, all regional administrations have co-ordinated the bulk of their investment within the framework of the *contrats de plan* which, since 1984, have formed the basis of French economic planning. Each Regional Council, in consultation with the regional prefect, prepared a five-year regional plan (1984–8) outlining medium-term investment priorities. This document formed the basis for a contractual agreement (*contrat de plan*) between the region and the state, committing the signatories to the financing of regional programmes. These operations also involved the participation of the constituent local authorities and private and nationalized industries in the region and were often funded in part by local and regional credit institutions. By 1985 all regions including Corsica had signed such an agreement and the total amount of money allocated to over one thousand projects totalled some 63,000 million francs (37 million francs on the part of the government and 25,581 million francs on the part of regions).

The introduction of decentralized planning was justified by the Socialists in 1981 in terms of greater local democracy and participation. Between 1986 and 1988, when Jacques Chirac's neo-liberal coalition government was in power, decentralized planning was encouraged as a means of promoting local enterprise and public/private sector partnerships. The ideological change thus brought little change in practice; preparations for the tenth Plan (1989–93) followed the same pattern as those for the ninth Plan. The Socialists' return to power in June 1988 confirmed the trend away from centralized planning in favour of local- and regional-level partnerships between industries and local authorities.

Primary among the projects financed in this manner are industrial, technical and professional training, industrial development, development of information technology, communications improvements and agricultural modernization. In addition, regional authorities (often acting in conjunction with constituent local authorities) may grant subsidies, loans and/or tax concessions to ailing companies, new firms locating in the region or firms which take on new employees. All regions have also established agencies to advise local employers on investment, marketing and export strategies.

In practice, the extent to which the regional authorities have made use of their powers of economic intervention has varied considerably depending on the level of resources available, political affiliation, the response and attitudes of constituent local authorities and employers in the region, national government investment priorities and so forth. Regional investment strategies have also been influenced by the specific features and problems of the regional economy. The regional government of Nord-Pas-de-Calais, for instance, has played a major role in the renovation of the port industries, cross-Channel ferry services and the Channel Tunnel project. The Midi-Pyrénées regional authority has funded several projects related to the wine industry, while Bretagne Regional Council has devoted a considerable proportion of its resources to promoting agricultural modernization.

Explaining the development of the meso
Clearly, there was no single cause of the developments outlined above. The aim in this section is to highlight the various factors which together help to explain how and why the meso has been strengthened. The following discussion also reveals the extent to which various factors have at different times limited the extent of this process. For analytical purposes these variables are considered in isolation; in reality, of course, a whole constellation of factors – some favourable to the growth of the meso and others limiting its development – were operating at any one time. Where possible these links will be highlighted.

Economic planning
The commitment of the planning agency, DATAR and successive Gaullist governments to indicative economic planning was probably the single most important, immediate cause of the development of functional regionalism in the 1960s. But support for the establishment of regional planning structures did not signify any enthusiasm on the part of these administrations for *political* decentralization. On the contrary, the new regional structures established in 1964 and 1972 were intended primarily to strengthen the central state by increasing administrative control over local political activity at the local and regional levels. And, as Hayward (1969) and Gourevitch (1980) have argued, the government also hoped that the establishment of regional representative assemblies – however limited and undemocratic in nature – would actually defuse mounting regionalist pressure in areas such as Bretagne and Corsica for more substantive decentralization.

In the 1970s official thinking on planning changed: centralized planning went out of fashion. Growing economic disparities between regions – notably between Paris and the provinces – prompted planners and politicians alike to question the efficacy of centralized economic planning. Paradoxically, this development gave a further boost to the region. Beset by financial problems and ideologically opposed to centralized planning the Barre government (1976–81) looked to local authorities to share the financial burden of economic recovery. Regions, in particular, were expected to play a much greater role in the formulation and implementation of the seventh Plan (within the framework of regional priority programmes and *contrats de pays*) than had previously been the case (Hayward, 1984). This development was welcomed by many Regional Councils – particularly those controlled by the Socialists – which were keen to develop alternative economic strategies to those of the government.

The commitment of the Socialist government elected in 1981 to decentralized economic planning based upon regional development plans further enhanced the importance of the region after 1982. Moreover, whereas other Socialist policies were either halted or reversed with the coming to power of a right-wing government in 1986, the decentralized planning mechanisms were left intact. Beneath the change in political rhetoric (less emphasis on the need for local participation and more on the need to stimulate local private enterprise), the planning role of the French meso was further strengthened.

Economic modernization
A closely related factor which has contributed to the development of the meso has been the commitment of all governments to economic modernization. The Napoleonic model of centre–periphery relations based upon some 37,000 communes and 96 departments was designed for a rural nation and had by the 1960s become ill suited to the needs of an industrialized, urban society. The departments were simply too small to serve as viable economic planning units, while demographic change had rendered the communal structure function-ally obsolete. (In 1975, 73 per cent of the 36,394 remaining communes had fewer than 700 inhabitants and only 767 had more than 10,000 inhabitants.) In consequence, many communes were unable to provide even the most basic of amenities and were totally dependent upon state financial and technical assistance. In the 1970s, however, criticism of the centralized state mounted amid complaints of inefficiency and excessive bureaucratization. Governments thus sought to devolve responsibility for local service provision to the regions and departments. As outlined earlier in the chapter, regions (and departments) have thus come to play a more important role in the provision of financial assistance and technical advice for small communes as well as the organization of public transport, health care and social services.

A more recent development which looks likely to increase still further the economic significance of the regional authorities is the completion of the European internal market by January 1993. Unlike the German *Länder*, French regional authorities are not formally involved in the formulation of Community policies. However, French regional and local authorities have for several years been actively involved in a number of European organizations and lobbies including the Association of European Frontier Regions (ARFE), established in 1971, the Conference of EC Maritime Regions, which was established in 1973 and whose headquarters are in Rennes, the Council of Communes and Regions of Europe (CCRE), set up in

1984, and the Council of Regions, established in 1985, renamed the Assembly of Regions (ARE) in 1987 and based in Strasbourg. The latter organization has a membership of 107 regional authorities (including 11 from non-EC countries) and was accorded formal consultative status by the European Commission in 1986 (Chauvet, 1989: 10). In addition, several regions have set up their own office in Brussels. In fact, most French regions are in receipt of EC funding (that is, from the European Social Fund and European Regional Development Fund). In particular, the Community has been keen to support inter-regional projects such as the Integrated Mediterranean Programme, the Rhine–Rhône Waterway project and the Channel Tunnel project (for which both the Nord-Pas-de-Calais region and Kent County Council receive EC funding).

Completion of the internal market will entail the free circulation of capital (notably investment) within the EC, the opening up of hitherto closed markets for goods and services provided by public (including local and regional) authorities and free mobility of labour within the EC, including open access to many public sector jobs previously reserved for nationals. Clearly, these changes will affect local and regional authorities throughout the Community, which will be competing with each other for EC funding, investment, service contracts and jobs. Thus, in February 1989 the Socialist government declared the need for further territorial reform involving a reduction in the number of regions to ensure that French regional authorities would be able to compete with their European counterparts after 1992 (*Le Monde*, 3.2.89). Although nothing came of this text (which was adopted by the Socialist Party), the debate surrounding the capacity of French local and regional authorities (which are so much more numerous and smaller than other European sub-national authorities) to compete with other EC local authorities for EC funding, contracts and investment after 1992 is unlikely to disappear. Meanwhile, the much wider debate on a 'Europe of the regions' and the principle of 'subsidiarity' has given fresh impetus to French regionalism.

Ideological pressures
As outlined above, the *étatiste* nature of Gaullist ideology effectively ruled out the possibility of *political* decentralization during the 1960s and early 1970s. Equally, as Mény has pointed out, until the late 1960s the Socialist and Communist parties were also united in their support for a centralized administrative state, which they regarded as the principal guarantee of democratic equality and essential for socialist economic planning (Mény, 1974). During the 1960s, how- ever, several left-wing intellectuals, many of whom were later to join

the rejuvenated Parti Socialiste, became vocal supporters of regional decentralization – notably the Breton regionalist Michel Philipponneau and Michel Rocard, leader of the intellectual left-wing Parti Socialiste Unifié and author of the provocative *Décoloniser la Province*. The Communist Party, prompted into action by these initiatives, declared its support for substantive decentralization in 1971.

The ideological shift towards decentralization in general and the region in particular on the part of the Left was prompted partly by the need to present a democratic alternative to the Gaullist regional reforms. It was also a response to growing disillusionment with centralized economic planning (see above). Added to these pressures was the fact that the 1960s and 1970s were in France – as in other European countries – characterized by the revival of regional nationalist movements (spurred on by the 1972 regional reform) which campaigned for further and more far-reaching regional reform. Meanwhile, economic and industrial disputes also tended to assume the character of regional protests against a capitalist centralized state. As a broad coalition movement the Parti Socialiste, established in 1969, attracted the support of diverse groups which were committed to some form of decentralization – regionalists, environmentalists, technocrats (in favour of decentralized planning) and *autogestionnaires* who advocated greater citizen participation. The presence of these groups served to revive the ideological debate within the party on decentralization and a consensus quickly emerged in favour of decentralization (albeit somewhat variously defined). By 1972 the Socialist Party was thus publicly committed (along with the Communist Party) to the abolition of the prefects, the creation of elected regional governments and the introduction of decentralized economic planning.

Political considerations
The pace of decentralization in France has to a considerable extent been determined by changes in the national political configuration. The electoral strength of left-wing opposition parties at local levels throughout the 1960s and 1970s constituted a brake on the development of the meso, since Gaullist and right-wing governments were, understandably, reluctant to devolve power to left-wing-controlled authorities. There was also a further complication. Both President Pompidou and President Giscard d'Estaing were dependent at the parliamentary level upon the support of centrist and conservative local *notables* who as *cumulards* were strategically placed within the Senate and National Assembly to resist any reform which might undermine their local power base. Opposition from these groups was

undoubtedly a major reason for President Giscard d'Estaing's sudden loss of enthusiasm for further regional decentralization after his election in 1974. On the other hand, his desire to appease these groups undoubtedly facilitated the introduction of the Bonnet laws (see above), which contributed to the increased financial autonomy of the departments.

The election of the Socialist government in 1981 made further decentralization politically possible. In contrast to its right-wing predecessors, the Socialist government came to power with a long-standing commitment to decentralization and a large parliamentary majority. Though well established in local politics, Socialist and Communist politicians did not fear the introduction of elected regional governments. Indeed, having been out of power at the national level since 1958, left-wing local politicians – particularly the younger ones – were keen to maximize the autonomy and financial weight of local and regional councils. Ironically, the increasing unpopularity of the Socialist government after 1982 brought heavy local electoral losses for the Left after 1983 and the Socialists were to end up devolving power to right-wing opposition-controlled authorities. Needless to say, by this time the latter had become firm advocates of decentralization.

Local political and administrative elites
The pace of decentralization and the shape which the meso has taken in France – that is, the strengthening of the departments and the piecemeal establishment of an additional regional level of government – owes much to the political influence of local political and administrative elites. More specifically, these groups have effectively resisted the introduction of any major reform, such as the replacement of departments by regions, which might undermine their own power, which rests, to a considerable extent, upon the centralized state. While the formal relationship between state officials and local politicians is a straightforward one of administrative control, the reality is more complex. As numerous sociological studies have revealed, local politicians are often more powerful, and their relationships with local officials less antagonistic, than theory would suggest. In practice, local *élus* and prefects often join forces in order to defend the interests of 'their' department or commune at the national level (Grémion, 1976). The horizontal integration of the politico-administrative system (which exists at all levels of the hierarchy) creates a degree of local autonomy which has, in practice, made effective local government reform an extremely difficult task (Dupuy and Thoenig, 1983, 1985). The resilience of the Napoleonic local government structures can to a large extent be explained by the

strategic location of powerful administrators and politicians who have colluded in defending the departmental and communal structures.

Many local politicians have also been able to influence government policy by more direct means. Most national politicians in France hold at least one local office. In 1980, 42 per cent of senators held two local offices; 246 of the 491 deputies elected to the National Assembly in 1981 were mayors, 249 were general councillors, and 19 were members of the Paris city council. The origins of the *cumul des mandats* lie in the localized nature of nineteenth-century French parliamentary politics, but the practice has been sustained by the electoral benefits to be gained by national politicians from maintaining a local power base. The presence of local *élus* at the national political level (in government and Parliament) is a central feature of French politics and means that local interests cannot (as they may in Britain, for instance) be easily overridden. In particular, local politicians have been anxious to ensure that the region does not kill off the department.

The combined pressures of local politicians and administrators has been an important factor in determining, and constraining, the growth of the region. For evidence of this influence one has only to refer to the departmentalized nature of the regional structures established in the 1960s (the CODER were dominated by local politicians while the prefects defended the interests of their department within the Regional Administrative Conferences); to the endemic departmental cleavages within the Regional Councils between 1974 and 1981 (rotating presidencies, allocation of budgets); to the preservation of the Napoleonic structures in the 1982–6 reforms; and finally to the prominence of traditional local *notables* within the newly elected Regional Councils.

An assessment and implications

The growth in the importance of the French meso in recent years means that the French state is – in formal terms at least – more decentralized and more democratic than it was in 1958. However, it is important to end this discussion with a critical appraisal of these developments. In particular, to what extent have these changes really transformed the notorious 'one and indivisible' Republic? Does the increasing financial and political importance of the meso signify a weakening of the unitary state? Or is it simply a case of old wine in new bottles – a functional devolution of responsibilities within a modernized and refurbished state.

Clearly, important changes have occurred. The introduction of directly elected regional governments endowed with revenue-raising and legislative powers is a potentially important development and *grands notables* such as Olivier Guichard, regional president of Pays de la Loire, have lost little time in exercising their powers, not simply over constituent local authorities but also in relation to national government. Polls also indicate that a majority of French people believe and hope that the region will in the future become the most important level of sub-national government (Percheron, 1987). The introduction of regional government has not, however, been accompanied by any reduction in the powers, functions and financial importance of the department, whose functional responsibilities, financial and administrative resources far outweigh those of the regions. Indeed, the development of the region has been accompanied by a significant increase in the responsibilities and resources of both the departmental and communal authorities. The departments, for instance, are now responsible for the provision of most welfare and health care services whilst the communes are now responsible for urban development and town planning. Thus, the development of the region has definitely not resulted in any reduction in the powers of the traditional levels of local government.

In terms of the functions they perform, French regions are concerned primarily with the co-ordination of national and local investment strategies. In short, their role is to act as a catalyst for economic modernization and industrial development. In order to be effective, regional authorities must co-operate with the state and/or constituent local authorities when it comes to urban transport schemes, the formulation of regional economic plans and so on. Thus, in functional terms, the regional authorities enjoy only limited autonomy and have fewer responsibilities for service provision than the departments.

In terms of access (that is, the extent to which the meso has informal links with the centre) the regions are, in terms of political personnel, enmeshed with both the national and local levels of government. Despite the 1985 legislation limiting the number of elective offices an individual may hold to two, the practice of *cumul des mandats* remains a central feature of French political life. Percheron's study of seventeen regional authorities revealed that 61 per cent of regional councillors held one or two additional elective offices, while 16 per cent held three or more additional mandates (Percheron, 1987: 92). In accordance with the 1985 anti-*cumul* legislation, politicians were obliged to reduce the number of *significant* elective offices they held to two by 1992. The main effect of this legislation to date has been to force traditional *grands notables* such as Raymond Marcellin, Michel d'Ornano, Jacques Chaban-Delmas and Michel Giraud to give up either the regional or the departmental presidency. In practice, all have chosen to renounce the regional post in favour of the latter. Given the much greater financial and functional importance of the department and its traditional political importance, the choice is not surprising. In socio-political terms also, regional political elites are generally similar to their departmental and communal counterparts. There is also considerable informal integration between the regional and national administrative systems. One reason for this is that the regional administrative services comprise many former members of the state civil service who are integrated into the national administrative elite through the *grands corps*.

In formal terms, the regions enjoy 'general powers' of competence and may therefore pass legislation on any issue which falls within their jurisdiction. Many issues, however, lie beyond the regions' sphere of competence. Furthermore, most regional legislation is, in practice, prepared jointly by the region, the relevant ministerial field services and the regional *commissaire*. The continuing financial links between the meso and the national levels of government further inhibit local autonomy. The Socialist decentralization programme did not include comprehensive financial reform. Instead, the reform specified that any responsibility devolved to a local authority would be accompanied by a corresponding financial transfer. This means that regions and departments remain financially dependent upon the central government. Whether or not such financial dependence subtracts from local autonomy is, of course, a subject of long-standing debate. Many local politicians have certainly complained that state grants have been made conditional upon local investment in national priority sectors. Another frequent complaint from local politicians is the inadequacy of state financial transfers, which they claim has led to the recent sharp increases in local taxation.

It thus seems reasonable to conclude that while the French meso has undoubtedly become more important in recent years, this development should be viewed as a pragmatic response to the urgent need to modernize the Napoleonic state. This said, it should be added that the French regional governments have only enjoyed full local authority status since 1986; it is, therefore, still too early to pass a definitive judgement on their performance and prospects. Their future development will depend upon a number of variables, including: (a) the extent to which the restrictions upon *cumul des mandats* and political developments (such as environmental and regionalist movements) facilitate the emergence of a qualitatively new regional political elite; (b) the future status of economic planning; (c) the level of regional finances; (d) the capacity of the departments to meet their increased responsibilities; and (e) the attitude of national political elites towards the region.

Appendix: Results in metropolitan France of the French regional elections, 1992

This chapter was written in 1990. Regional elections were subsequently held on 22 March 1992. The results of these elections are summarized below.

	Number	% vote
Registered voters	37,344,864	
Votes cast	25,652,385	68.7
Valid votes cast	24,431,676	65.4
Abstentions		31.3
Extreme left	298,643	1.2
PC	1,963,562	8.0
PS	4,468,849	18.3
Other Left	523,070	2.1
GE	1,744,350	7.1
Verts (Greens)	1,659,798	6.8
Other ecologists	184,916	0.8
Other regionalists	108,549	0.4
Catég.	942,217	3.9
UPF	8,071,623	33.0
Other Right	1,021,079	4.2
FN	3,396,141	13.9
Extreme Right	48,879	0.2

Additional abbreviations to those listed for Tables 2 and 3

GE   Génération Ecologie (Ecology Generation)
Catég. RPR and UDF separate lists
UPF   Union pour la France (Union for France – RPF-UDF coalition list)

Source: Figures from the Ministry of the Interior, in *La France dans ses Régions*, *Le Monde*, April, 1992, p. 90.

Table: The number of Regional Council seats won by parties in the 1992 and 1986 regional elections

Region	pc	Ext. PC	PS	Other Left	Total Pres. Maj.	GE	Verts	Other ecol.	UDF	RPR	Other Right	Total Right	FN	Other ext. Right	Other
Alsace	–	–	6	–	6	3	6	–	11	8	1	20	9	2	1
	–	–	10	1	11	–	2	–	15	10	2	27	7	–	1
Aquitaine	6	–	19	1	20	7	2	–	15	14	3	32	8	–	1
	8	–	30	2	32	–	–	–	17	18	4	39	4	–	10
Auvergne	4	–	9	–	9	2	3	–	11	10	3	24	4	–	–
	4	–	15	–	15	–	–	–	15	10	1	26	2	–	1
Bourgogne	3	–	10	4	14	2	5	–	11	12	1	24	8	–	–
	5	–	17	2	19	–	–	–	11	12	5	28	3	–	1
Bretagne	3	–	19	–	19	6	6	–	18	17	6	41	7	–	1
	4	–	30	–	30	–	–	–	24	13	8	45	2	–	–
Centre	8	–	17	1	18	5	3	–	17	11	4	32	11	–	–
	8	–	23	3	26	–	–	–	15	13	10	38	3	–	4
Champagne-Ardenne	3	–	9	–	9	2	2	–	10	10	2	22	8	–	–
	4	–	15	–	15	–	–	–	9	11	3	23	5	–	6
Corse[a]	6	–	6	6	18	–	–	–	6	12	9	27	4	–	–
Franche Comté	–	1	10	12	10	2	3	–	10	9	2	21	5	1	6
	2	–	16	–	18	–	–	–	10	9	–	19	4	–	–
Ile de France	17	–	32	1	33	22	15	–	30	53	2	85	37	–	–
	20	–	61	4	65	–	–	–	25	55	9	89	23	–	–
Languedoc-Roussillon	8	–	14	–	14	4	3	–	–	–	9	24	13	–	1
	9	–	21	1	22	–	–	–	11	10	5	26	8	–	–
Limousin	4	3	13	–	13	1	2	–	6	12	–	18	1	–	–
	8	–	15	–	15	–	–	–	5	12	1	18	–	–	1
Lorraine	3	–	10	6	16	6	5	–	11	13	8	32	10	–	1
	4	–	24	–	24	–	–	–	17	18	3	38	7	–	–

Region	PC	Ext. PC	PS	Other Left	Total Pres. Maj.	GE	Verts	Other ecol.	UDF	RPR	Other Right	Total Right	FN	Other ext. Right	Other
Midi-Pyrénées	5	–	23	4	27	1	6	–	16	19	8	43	6	–	3
	5	–	26	10	36	–	–	–	18	14	10	42	3	–	1
Nord-Pas-de-Calais	15	–	25	2	27	6	8	–	13	14	–	30	15	–	15
	19	–	36	3	39	–	–	–	16	22	5	43	12	–	–
Basse Normandie	1	–	8	1	9	4	4	–	10	10	4	24	5	–	–
	1	–	10	5	15	–	1	–	10	10	6	26	2	–	–
Haute Normandie	5	–	13	1	14	4	4	–	9	9	1	19	8	–	1
	6	–	19	1	20	–	–	–	10	11	3	24	3	–	–
Pays de la Loire	–	3	16	4	20	6	6	1	20	20	8	48	8	–	1
	5	–	30	4	34	–	5	–	22	17	12	51	3	–	–
Picardie	6	–	9	–	9	4	5	–	10	11	1	22	8	–	3
	8	–	18	–	18	–	–	–	12	9	4	25	4	–	–
Poitou-Charentes	3	–	13	–	13	3	4	–	13	11	1	25	5	–	2
	3	–	19	2	21	–	–	–	13	10	5	28	1	–	–
Provence-Alpes-Côte-d'Azur	10	–	20	10	30	3	3	–	24	17	2	43	34	–	–
	14	–	30	1	31	–	–	–	23	17	7	47	25	–	–
Rhône-Alpes	11	1	23	6	29	10	11	–	29	26	10	65	29	–	1
	13	–	45	2	47	–	–	–	30	27	20	77	14	–	–

For each region the first row shows seats in 1992; the second row shows seats in 1986.

[a] These figures include the results of the 16 March 1986 elections in Corse Sud and those of 22 March 1987 for Haute Corse, following the annulment of those of 1986.

Additional abbreviations to those listed in Tables 2, 3 and above:

Total Pres. Maj.: Total number of left-wing regional councillors favourable to the Mitterrand presidential Majority.
Total Right: Total number of Right-wing Opposition regional councillors excluding National Front and extreme Right-wing councillors.

Source: Le Monde, 24 March 1992

Notes

1 *Districts*, established by decree in 1959, are public establishments comprising several communes which voluntarily unite for development purposes. *Urban communities* were created by legislation in 1966 and are administrative public establishments with financial and planning responsibilities in major urban areas. *Intercommunal groupings* are voluntary associations of communes for the provision of municipal services such as public transport and refuse collection.
2 An individual may only hold two 'significant' elective offices. 'Significant' offices include those of Member of the European Parliament, deputy, senator, regional councillor, mayor of a commune with more than 20,000 inhabitants or assistant mayor of a commune with a population of more than 100,000. In addition, it is no longer possible for an individual to be president of both a departmental and a regional council.

Select further reading

Dayries, J.-J. and Dayries, M. (1986) *La Régionalisation*. Paris: Presses Universitaires de France.
Dupuy, F. and Thoenig, J.-C. (1983) *Sociologie de l'administration française*. Paris: Armand Colin.
Dupuy, F. and Thoenig, J.-C. (1985) *L'Administration en miettes*. Paris: Fayard.
'L'Europe des Régions' (1989) special issue of *Après-demain*. 314–15 (May–June).
Giard, J. and Schiebling, J. (1981) *L'Enjeu régional*. Paris: Messidor/Editions Sociales.
Grémion, P. (1976) *Le Pouvoir périphérique*. Paris: Editions du Seuil.
INSEE (1988) *La France et ses régions*. Paris: Collections INSEE.
'Les Collectivités territoriales' (1989) *Les Cahiers français*, 239 (Jan.–Feb.) Paris: Documentation Française.
Ministère de l'Intérieur (1989) *Les Collectivités en chiffres*. Paris: La Documentation Française.
Muret, J.-P., Fournier, D., Peyré, S. and Pian, F. (1986) *Le Conseil régional*. Paris: Syros.
Percheron, A. (ed.) (1987) *La Région: an 1*. Paris: Presses Universitaires de France.
Rondin, J. (1985) *Le Sacre des notables*. Paris: Fayard.
Tenzer, N. (1986) *La Région en quête d'avenir*. Paris: La Documentation Française.
Terrazoni, A. (1987) *La Décentralisation à l'épreuve des faits*. Paris: Librairie Générale de Droit et de Jurisprudence.

References

Caisse de Dêpots et Consignations (1986) *Tableau de bord des finances locales 1970–1984*. Paris: Editions du Moniteur.
Chauvet, J.-P. (1989) 'Participation des collectivités territoriales aux décisions européennes: le rôle des lobbies locaux et régionaux', *Après-demain*, 314–15, May/June: 9–12.
Démocratie locale (1989) 'Bulletin d'informations statistiques de la DGCL', supplement, 56, July/Aug.

Dupuy, F. and Thoenig, J.-C. (1983) *Sociologie de l'administration française*. Paris: Armand Colin.

Dupuy, F. and Thoenig, J.-C. (1985) *L'Administration en miettes*. Paris: Fayard.

Grémion, P. (1976) *Le Pouvoir périphérique*. Paris: Editions de Seuil.

Gourevitch, P. (1980) *Paris and the Provinces*. London: Allen & Unwin.

Hayward, J. (1969) 'From functional regionalism to functional representation in France', *Political Studies*, 17: 48–75.

Hayward, J. (1984) 'From planning the French economy to planning the French state: the theory and practice of the priority action programmes', in V. Wright (ed.), *Continuity and Change in France*. London: Allen & Unwin.

INSEE (1988) *La France et ses régions*. Paris: Collections INSEE.

Keating, M. and Hainsworth, P. (1986) *Decentralisation and Change in Contemporary France*. Aldershot: Gower.

Le Monde – Dossiers et documents (1988) '1981–1988: Bilan du septennat'.

'Les Collectivités territoriales' (1989) *Les Cahiers français*, 239, Jan./Feb. Paris: Documentation Française.

Mabileau, A. (1989) 'La Limitation du cumul des mandats: premiers effets à retardement', *Les Cahiers*, 28, July.

Machin, H. (1974) 'Local government change in France; the case of the 1964 reforms', *Policy and Politics*, 2: 249–65.

Mazey, S. (1986) 'The French regional elections of 16 March 1986', *Electoral Studies*, 5: 297–312.

Mazey, S. (1987) 'Decentralization: la grande affaire du septennat?', in S. Mazey and M. Newman (eds), *Mitterrand's France*. London: Croom Helm.

Mény, Y. (1974) *Centralisation et décentralisation dans le débat politique française 1945–69*. Paris: Fondation Nationale des Sciences Politiques.

Mény, Y. (1983) *Centres et périphéries: le partage du pouvoir*. Paris: Economica.

Ministère de l'Intérieur (1989) *Guide budgétaire communal, départementale et régional*. Paris: Documentation Française.

Muret, J.-P., Fournier, D., Peyré, S., Pian, F. (1986) *Le Conseil régional*. Paris: Syros.

Page, E. and Goldsmith, M. (1988) *Central and Local Relations*. London: Sage.

Paugam, P. (1989) 'Six ans de contrôle budgétaire: un bilan globalement positif', *Les Cahiers*, 28, July.

Percheron, A. (ed.) (1987) *La Région: an I*. Paris: Presses Universitaires de France.

Rondin, J. (1985) *Le Sacre des notables*. Paris: Fayard.

Sadran, P. (1982) 'La régionalisation française: esquisse d'un bilan (1972–1980)', in Y. Mény (ed.), *Dix ans de régionalisation en Europe*. Paris: Editions Cujas.

Wright, V. (1979) 'Regionalization under the French Fifth Republic: the triumph of the functionalist approach', in L. J. Sharpe (ed.), *Decentralist Trends in Western Democracies*. London: Sage.

4

The Meso Level in Italy

Sabino Cassese and Luisa Torchia

The Italian meso experience falls within the Southern European 'structural' category, since the main meso developments can be identified in the successful establishment of a new level of elected regional government all over the country.

The history of Italian regions is not, nevertheless, exempt from contradictions and drawbacks. The regional reform was a reform from above. It had a long period of gestation (1861–1970) but a rapid process of implementation (1970–7), and regions have met a number of problems as far as legitimization and institutionalization of the new level of government are concerned.

The well-established tradition of a binary administrative system, based on the two tiers of central administration and local government, has worked against the implementation of a pure 'territorial' model. Vertical, functional links between levels of government (central, regional and local) are as important as the structural division of tasks and functions.

Italian regions have the two main features of a territorial meso level; they are an intermediate level of government between national government and local authorities, and they enjoy political autonomy. We will try to describe in the following pages the process through which Italian regions were set up, their constitutional status and their performance over the last twenty years.

Original features of the Italian system

The history of Italian political and administrative institutions during the last 120 years can be described in very general terms as a continual effort to reduce asymmetries and create uniform conditions throughout the country.

The basic models (functional to this purpose) designed to achieve the political and administrative unification of the new state in the second half of the last century were imported from France. The Napoleonic occupation, on the one hand, and the French influence on both Piedmont and the Kingdom of the Two Sicilies, on the other, led to the transplanting of institutions and rules inspired by principles of centralization and uniformity.

Italy belongs only partly, though, to the 'Napoleonic' group. The main differences as compared to the French model are basically attributable to two factors: the conditions of unequal development within the country, which are due particularly to the social, economic and political backwardness of the south and some areas of the centre and north, and the lack of homogeneity of the ruling class. The northern industrialists and the rich southern landowners had differing interests which were settled by means of an economic and political compromise only towards the end of the last century, when the country passed from a *laissez-faire* economic policy to a protectionist one.

The imitation of certain distinct features of the French system did not produce homogeneity between the French and the Italian experience. This is proved, for example, by the different role played by the prefect in the two systems and by the different effects brought about by the introduction of administrative law as special law. It has in fact already been observed (Cassese, 1987) that, whereas the uniformity of French administration was a product of centralized government, the uniformity of Italian administrative law had another purpose, as it was the product of the will to overcome or, at least, attenuate differentiation. A highly centralized system was in France a starting condition, while in Italy it was an aim to pursue.

The social, economic and political backwardness of the south and some areas of the centre and north, covering the Alpine and the Apennine mountain ranges, was considered to be the result of backward institutions. The regular and uniform application of the (more advanced) Piedmontese institutions would, it was assumed, ensure the comparable development of these areas. This attempt was, however, abandoned twenty years after Italian unity, thanks to the special laws (benefiting Naples, Sicily, Sardinia and Basilicata), which introduced special bodies and procedures applying only to specific areas of national territory.

As far as the intellectual debate is concerned, there is still another important difference compared to countries belonging to the Napoleonic group. Part of the (small) ruling class at the time considered the British model, based on self-government, to be more advanced and modern than the French model and compared the liberal tradition of self-government with the authoritarian tradition of centralization. This debate on self-government had, however, only a marginal effect on modifying the effective functioning of political and administrative institutions.

One may add another typical feature of the Italian system to the aforementioned differences from the pure Napoleonic model: a preference for negotiated rules as opposed to imposed rules. Even though the latter appear to prevail, they are always camouflaged by a more or less informal negotiation, which recently has acquired its own institutional forms. Preference for 'negotiated law' as opposed to 'imposed law' may once more be explained by the extremely varying conditions existing in different parts of the country (Cassese, 1987).

In fact, the several interest groups that have dominated Italian political and social life have very few common interests. As a consequence, it has always been difficult to define a general interest, equally important for everybody, to which generally accepted rules and institutions might attach. The political process and the legislative process are, in fact, encumbered with negotiations among the different groups, so that the rules and the laws produced by the same process are, usually, a compromise among different priorities.

Regions in the Italian Constitution

Setting up the Italian regions was a complex and tortuous process requiring a long period of preparation (1861–1970) but was rapidly carried into effect, so much so that the expression 'regionalism without regions' has been used (Pastori, 1980). The 'regional problem' has been a topic subjected to proposals and political contrasts right from the unification of the Italian state; its evolution has proceeded, however, in the framework of the history of ideas, without adding anything to the history of the institutions, until the constitutional charter was promulgated after the Second World War (Rotelli, 1967; Ruffilli, 1971).

The lack of 'regional communities' deprives regionalism of its prime dynamic, so that this territorial dimension is especially novel in the context of the Italian experience. Moreover, it is an experience in which municipalities, viewed as bodies endowed with original legitimacy, have always played an important role.

The boundaries of regions established in the Constitution are, in fact, the boundaries of the ancient 'statistical departments' set up almost a century earlier (see Figure 1). The attempt to draw and establish new boundaries was rapidly ruled out by sharp disagreement on the constitutive elements of regional identity and by the bias against differentiation and particularism which has been an underlying Italian institutional experience since unification in 1861.[1]

The regions were not therefore set up until the 1948 Constitution and even then only on paper. The main reason motivating the members of the constituent assembly was the desire to react against

Figure 1   *Italy: regional boundaries*

the centralization enforced by fascism (which had abolished the election of local representatives). Centralization was considered to be a typical product of fascist authoritarianism, and the distribution of power which regionalism would have brought about appeared to be the most effective solution for safeguarding the democratic system.

Three basic reasons may be singled out in the constituent assembly debate on the regional clause. These were:

1 The need to distribute power in such a way as to prevent a single power taking over. It is for this reason that the Christian Democrats

(DC) were in favour of the regions at the time, whereas the Communists (PCI), who were still under the influence of Leninist thinking, were against. Moreover, the two parties were not sure about their respective strengths, and the political climate created by the cold war did not allow bipartisan decisions on such sensitive topics.

2 The need to bring rulers and ruled closer together. For example, the creation of points of access and consultation and bringing the institutions closer to citizens were the *pièce de résistance* of a certain wing of Italian regionalism, which was aware of the low level of representative, administrative and political institutions at the time. This theme of the gap between institutions and the people is a recurring one in post-war Italian politics.

3 Of lesser importance, the need to increase the rate of citizens' participation in public life.

The constitutional status of Italian regions can be described as follows. Regions have legislative powers concerning functions which are listed in article 117 of the Constitution[2] and they carry out the administrative tasks connected to those functions. Their powers are limited both by the 'national interest' and by other regions' interests. Regional finance is conceived as a part of public finance as a whole and it must be co-ordinated with state finance and municipal finance (art. 119). Regions are political bodies, entrusted with legislative and administrative powers, operating within boundaries that at the time seemed very clear (Paladin, 1985). The distance between constitutional provisions and the actual setting up of Italian regions is, however, not only temporal (this part of the constitution was enforced only after twenty-five years) but also cultural and political, as we will try to demonstrate later.

Failure to enforce the Constitution

Constitutional rules relating to the regions were not enforced, furthermore, until the 1970s, except for the special statute regions (Sicily, Sardinia, Val d'Aosta, Trentino-Alto Adige, Friuli-Venezia-Giulia). These regions were created because of specific situations such as the presence of ethnic minorities and conditions of social and economic backwardness. The statutes of these special regions were promulgated between the 1950s and the 1960s in the form of constitutional laws, but the experience of the special regions has not been relevant until the setting up of the ordinary regions (Bartole et al., 1985). They were an exception in a highly centralized and uniform system, and even their powers were limited, while after the 1970s they lost, at least partially, their distinctive features and became part of a uniform regionalized system.

There are several reasons for the failure to enforce the regional element of the Constitution. First of all, there were political reasons; the party with a relative majority nationally – the DC – has altered its original position and feared that setting up the regions would have strengthened the opposition in some parts of the country. In particular it was felt that the creation of regions would favour the Communist opposition, which had in the meantime also altered its position towards favouring political decentralization. Secondly, the markedly authoritarian and centralist mentality of bureaucracy, which had moved from the fascist regime to the democratic system without undergoing significant changes, was hostile to the setting up of the regions. The continuity between fascist and post-fascist years has been a relevant feature of the Italian administrative system; the bureaucrats (and their fundamental values) were changed only marginally with the advent of the democratic regime.

Thirdly, the underdeveloped conditions of some of the country areas and the process of economic reconstruction in progress during the whole of the 1950s and part of the 1960s were used as an excuse to justify the need to centralize and to maintain unitary control of economic policies.

Regionalization

At the end of the 1960s two important changes occurred, one at an economic level and the other at a cultural level. Economic growth was such as to make more resources available for use not simply in terms of accumulation, but also in terms of distribution. As in other European countries, pluralism and institutional polycentrism in Italy depends strongly on the availability of economic and financial resources; redistribution cannot be enforced simply by diminishing resources for one group in favour of another group, but only by giving more to every group, or at least maintaining the previous allocations. Similar considerations apply to decentralization, which is usually seen by the ruling class as a costly operation that can be achieved only when the general level of growth is steadily rising. As we shall see later, when a financial crisis struck in the 1970s, regional autonomy and power shrank.

The second important change was occurring in the cultural realm. The authoritarian culture, which prevailed during the fascist period and persisted into the years immediately following the Second World War, gave way to widespread acceptance of democratic and pluralistic values. A new generation of bureaucrats, who were not compromised with the fascist regime, entered into central administrations. They considered democracy not as a novelty which could undermine their status, but as a set of principles which should, at least in some degree, rule their behaviour.

Thus, economic development and the emergence of a non-fascist national identity were the two main conditions required for speeding up and in a certain way forcing through the process of regionalization, which was carried into effect in a fairly short time, as compared, say, with France, where the process took over twenty years.

In less than ten years (from 1970 to 1977) the regions were set up and endowed with administrative powers, personnel and financial resources. At the end of the 1970s the regions had substantial powers in terms of social services (excluding education) and territory planning, as well as more restricted powers, not to be underestimated, in the realm of economic intervention.[3] Private law and penal law were, however, and still are, strictly reserved to the national Parliament.

One of the reasons explaining the speed of the regionalization process was the convergence in the 1970s of different political and cultural tendencies, which viewed the setting up of the regions as a fundamental step in the reform and modernization of the administrative and political system as a whole, even though they had different objectives: for example, 'the regions as a reform of the state', or 'the regions for the benefit of planning', or 'the regions for greater participation'.[4] An additional reason put forward in some studies was the attempt to use the regions as a political instrument to relieve social, political and other pressures on the centre, by defusing the tensions that were so typical of Italy in the 1970s (Rotelli, 1979).

A crucial factor in the creation of a widespread consensus about the regional reform was, in any case, the need for the political class as a whole to gain more influence and more leverage *vis-à-vis* the traditional administrative apparatus. The central apparatus had grown to enormous dimensions since the 1950s and it was endowed with more and more powers. As a consequence, the influence of the political class shrank. It shrank still further simply because policy formulation and implementation require more and more technical skills.

The regional reform aroused great expectations. As we have noted, different groups expected different things from regions, but almost everybody in the 'regionalist front' valued the regional reform as a great occasion to modernize the Italian state, to reorder its administrative apparatus and to strengthen its democratic features.[5]

This explains why many leading scholars of regionalism, who were involved directly in the process of reform, were very firm in declaring that regions should have been political bodies and not administrative bodies.[6] Making them political was seen as a guarantee of autonomy and differentiation, while administrative regions were seen as being in the realm of uniformity and subordination to central directives. An echo of the old distinction between politics and administration, so clear in the nineteenth century, can be discerned in this debate. In fact, as we shall see later, the administrative weakness of the regions has probably played an important role in the stagnation of Italian regional experience.

Weakness of Italian regions

By the end of the 1970s, however, this speeded-up process had lost its momentum. Unfavourable appraisals of the (short) regional experience multiplied; the regions were accused of not producing the positive effects that had been hoped for; and the low efficiency and functionality of regional bodies were emphasized (Sorace, 1979).

At the end of the 1970s the regions were the weak point of a system and constituted in a sense a kind of foreign body within the Italian system. The reform of central administration and local government, which was meant to complement the regional reform, quickly turned out to be politically impracticable.[7] The role meant for the regions has therefore been continually threatened by administrative political bodies from above and below that are endowed with vast powers and have a much longer tradition behind them.

Attempts to implement a territorial reorganization by introducing a new intermediate level of government between the region and the municipality have also failed. Many regions tried to set up such *comprensori*, which were conceived as administrative units larger than municipalities. Most of the latter are, in Italy, very small and unable to carry out administrative tasks and services that require the larger scale necessary for modern personal service delivery, and the *comprensori* were seen as a way of overcoming this deficiency. Existing provinces, on the other hand, have boundaries drawn up according to very ancient criteria, so that they also are inadequate for planning and related services. The *comprensori* disappeared after a few years, and it is now the common opinion that it is impossible to impose any territorial reorganization on local government. The resistance of local government is, therefore, a crucial factor in slowing down and weakening the evolution of any meso other than the regions.

What the French call the *découpage* of the territory is highly irrational. Local offices, regional offices and central field services operate on the same territory without any clear distinction of tasks and functions. Overlapping of functions and responsibility is normal and a fair amount of time and resources are expended in co-ordinating the activity of different bodies, each with different priorities.

In addition to this the regions have encountered difficulties in inserting themselves into a political system, the basic cell of which is formed by the municipality (and, partly, by the provinces), and which consists of parties with strong centralized organizations (on the distribution of votes, see Tables 1, 2 and 3). Regional constituencies do not coincide with electoral constituencies (Cazzola et al., 1986). The result of this is that by the end of the 1970s the regions were no longer included in the 'political agenda'; regionalization was no longer a priority for the political class.

After this chapter was largely completed, regional elections were held in 1990, and the so-called 'regional parties' (in Italian, *leghe*) gained a significant share of the vote. It is too early to judge whether this denotes a long-term regionalization of Italian politics; similar phenomena are not new in Italian politics, but they do not usually last for more than one election. The growing weakness of the Communist Party is probably a prominent factor of the *leghe* success, because the right-wing electorate was no longer afraid of weakening the Christian Democrats in casting their vote for the *leghe*. The *leghe* attitude has been so far so racist as to be politically unacceptable to national parties and so far they have refused to take responsibilities in regional government even if this attitude will probably change in the future, as a consequence of the large share of votes (80 seats in the national Parliament) the *leghe* obtained in the last national election (spring 1992). The *leghe* are probably more a renewed signal of the north–south cleavage than a signal of emerging regional identities.

Relations between government levels: interdependence, regional functions and regional finance

The evolution of Italian regionalization may be described as a process of growing interdependence between the centre and the periphery.

The 1948 Constitution referred to the principle of the separation between state and regional administration; each level of government was to have (or should have had) a separate, independent and well-defined area of responsibility. This separation was intended to ensure regional autonomy and to prevent interference and conditioning by the centre. The regions were, moreover, assigned only policy sectors and matters considered at the time to be of minor importance. The regional institution was thus conceived as a sort of giant municipality, but also endowed with legislative power (Giannini, 1963). However, the laws enforcing the regional clause of the Constitution have followed different principles, and have established an often disorderly division of responsibilities in such a way as to abandon the separation principle completely.

Table 1 *Percentage party share of the vote by region for Chamber of Deputies election, 1987*

Region	Democrazia Cristiana (DC)	Partito Comunista Italiano (PCI)	Partito Socialista Italiano (PSI)	Movimento Sociale Italiano Destra Nazionale (MSI-DN)	Partito Republicano Italiano (PRI)	Partito Socialista Democratico Italiano (PSDI)	Partito Liberale Italiano (PLI)	Partito Radicale (P Rad.)	Lista Verde	Others
Piemonte	28.2	25.2	13.2	4.8	5.1	3.9	4.1	4.1	3.5	7.9
Valle d'Aosta	—	—	—	5.3	—	—	—	—	—	94.7[1]
Lombardia	33.5	23.6	16.9	4.8	4.1	2.2	2.2	2.9	3.3	6.5
Trentino-A. Adige	26.0	8.1	9.6	7.1	2.8	1.0	1.1	2.1	4.6	37.6[2]
Veneto[3]	43.9	18.3	14.0	3.9	3.0	2.4	2.0	2.9	3.7	5.9
Friuli-V-Giulia[4]	33.6	19.2	18.5	6.2	3.6	4.2	2.7	3.5	3.5	5.0
Liguria	28.4	32.3	13.8	5.4	4.1	1.9	3.0	3.2	4.0	3.9
Emilia-Romagna	24.0	44.3	12.4	3.8	4.7	1.9	1.6	2.0	2.5	2.8
Toscana	25.8	43.4	12.9	4.4	3.3	1.3	1.1	2.0	2.7	3.1
Umbria[5]	29.2	40.2	14.3	6.4	2.4	1.2	0.8	1.5	1.8	2.2
Marche	34.5	34.6	12.1	5.4	3.6	2.3	1.0	1.8	2.6	2.1
Lazio[6]	34.4	25.9	12.9	8.2	3.4	3.1	1.9	3.4	3.0	3.8
Abruzzi	42.2	27.4	12.0	5.8	2.1	3.7	1.1	2.1	1.9	1.7
Molise	57.3	20.1	8.3	4.3	2.0	2.1	1.8	1.2	1.1	1.8

Table 1 *cont.*

Region	Democrazia Cristiana (DC)	Partito Comunista Italiano (PCI)	Partito Socialista Italiano (PSI)	Movimento Sociale Italiano Destra Nazionale (MSI-DN)	Partito Republicano Italiano (PRI)	Partito Socialista Democratico Italiano (PSDI)	Partito Liberale Italiano (PLI)	Partito Radicale (P Rad.)	Lista Verde	Others
Campania	41.9	21.0	14.9	7.4	3.0	4.4	2.1	2.0	0.9	2.4
Puglia	37.8	23.3	15.3	8.3	4.1	4.0	2.3	1.8	1.7	1.4
Basilicata	46.1	25.5	13.5	5.0	1.3	4.2	0.9	1.0	1.0	1.5
Calabria	37.1	25.3	16.9	6.5	2.6	4.6	1.2	1.2	0.8	3.8
Sicilia	38.8	19.8	14.9	8.9	4.8	4.1	3.0	2.3	1.2	2.2
Sardegna	34.2	25.3	11.4	4.7	2.3	3.1	1.0	2.6	—	15.4[7]
Italy	34.3	26.6	14.3	5.9	3.7	3.0	2.1	2.6	2.5	5.0
North–centre	31.7	28.6	14.1	5.2	3.8	2.4	2.1	2.9	3.2	6.0
South	39.7	22.5	14.5	7.4	3.4	4.1	2.0	2.0	1.1	3.3

[1] Of which 55.1% for UV-MADP-PRI (Union Valdotaine – Movimento Autonomista Democratici Progressisti – PRI).
[2] Of which 33.09% for PPST (Partito popolare del Sud Tirolo).
[3] Belluno province excluded.
[4] Belluno province excluded.
[5] Rieti province included.
[6] Rieti province excluded.
[7] Of which 12.0% PSd'Az (Partito Sardo d'Azione).

Source: ISTAT, 1988b

Table 2   *Percentage party share of the vote by region for Senate election, 1987*

Region	Democrazia Cristiana (DC)	Partito Comunista Italiano (PCI)	Partito Socialista Italiano (PSI)	Movimento Sociale Italiano Destra Nazionale (MSI-DN)	Partito Republicano Italiano (PRI)	Partito Socialista Democratico Italiano (PSDI)	Partito Liberale Italiano (PLI)	Partito Radicale (P Rad.)	Lista Verde	Others
Piemonte	28.4	26.4	12.9	4.7	5.2	4.2	4.5	3.7	2.6	7.4
Valle d'Aosta	–	–	–	4.0	–	–	–	–	–	96.0[1]
Lombardia	34.4	24.6	16.8	4.7	4.0	2.4	2.3	2.5	2.6	5.7
Trentino-A. Adige	28.3	9.2	–	7.5	2.9	–	1.2	–	–	50.2[2]
Veneto	44.0	19.2	14.4	4.0	3.1	2.8	2.1	2.4	3.0	5.0
Friuli-V-Giulia	36.1	21.3	19.8	6.6	3.9	–	2.9	–	3.5	5.9
Liguria	30.3	34.4	–	5.7	4.4	–	3.0	–	3.8	18.4
Emilia-Romagna	24.9	46.1	–	4.0	4.7	–	1.7	–	2.3	16.3
Toscana	27.0	45.1	–	4.5	3.3	–	1.2	–	2.5	16.4
Umbria	26.9	43.6	15.5	5.5	2.3	0.9	0.7	1.2	1.5	1.9
Marche	35.1	36.0	12.1	5.4	3.3	2.0	0.9	1.5	1.9	1.8
Lazio	33.4	27.7	12.9	9.2	3.5	2.7	2.0	3.1	2.4	3.1
Abruzzi	41.3	29.7	12.7	6.2	1.6	2.4	1.1	1.8	1.6	1.6
Molise	56.9	–	–	6.9	2.5	–	–	–	–	33.7[3]

Table 2 *cont.*

Region	Democrazia Cristiana (DC)	Partito Comunista Italiano (PCI)	Partito Socialista Italiano (PSI)	Movimento Sociale Italiano Destra Nazionale (MSI-DN)	Partito Republicano Italiano (PRI)	Partito Socialista Democratico Italiano (PSDI)	Partito Liberale Italiano (PLI)	Partito Radicale (P Rad.)	Lista Verde	Others
Campania	36.1	23.5	14.5	9.6	4.3	4.6	2.4	1.9	0.8	2.3
Puglia	35.6	25.1	14.7	10.2	3.9	4.6	1.5	1.7	1.5	1.2
Basilicata	42.6	28.1	14.3	5.7	1.4	4.1	0.7	0.9	0.9	1.3
Calabria	36.0	30.5	—	10.5	1.8	—	0.9	—	—	20.3
Sicilia	34.1	21.6	15.3	10.2	5.9	4.3	3.8	2.7	—	2.1
Sardegna	36.3	28.2	—	6.1	—	—	—	—	—	29.4[4]
Italy	33.6	28.3	10.9	6.5	3.8	2.4	2.2	1.8	2.0	8.5
North-centre	32.3	30.0	10.5	5.3	3.9	1.9	2.2	1.8	2.6	9.5
South	36.5	24.6	11.8	9.2	3.7	3.5	2.0	1.6	0.6	6.5

[1] Of which 54.6% for UV-MADP-PRI.
[2] Of which 34.4% for PPST.
[3] Of which 28.0% for All. Dem. Mol.
[4] Of which 14.2% for PSd'Az.

Source: ISTAT, 1988b

Table 3   Percentage party share of the vote for regional councils

Region	DC	PCI	PSI	Lega Lom-barda	Liste Verdi	MSI-DN	PRI	PSDI	PLI	Other
Regions with ordinary statute (6–5–90)										
Piemonte	27.9	22.8	15.3	5.1	6.7	3.6	4.0	3.2	4.1	7.3
Lombardia	28.6	18.8	14.3	18.9	5.2	2.5	2.6	1.7	1.4	6.0
Veneto	42.4	15.6	13.7	5.9	7.1	2.7	2.6	2.1	1.6	6.3
Liguria	27.5	28.4	14.1	6.1	5.7	3.4	4.1	2.3	3.0	5.4
Emilia-Romagna	23.4	42.1	12.4	2.9	4.9	3.0	4.8	1.9	1.5	3.1
Toscana	25.9	39.8	13.6	0.8	3.8	3.3	3.5	1.6	1.1	6.6
Umbria	27.5	38.3	16.1	0.2	3.6	4.4	2.8	1.2	0.8	5.1
Marche	36.3	30.0	12.7	0.2	4.9	3.9	3.7	2.5	1.7	4.1
Lazio	34.4	23.8	14.3	0.2	6.3	6.5	4.8	2.8	1.8	5.1
Abruzzi	46.6	20.5	14.7	0.2	3.0	3.8	3.4	2.8	2.3	2.7
Molise	58.8	14.3	12.0	0.2	1.4	3.3	3.0	3.5	2.6	0.9
Campania	40.8	16.7	19.0	0.2	4.0	4.9	4.8	5.0	2.5	2.1
Puglia	40.7	18.7	19.7	0.3	3.3	6.2	3.0	4.3	2.2	1.6
Basilicata	47.1	19.2	18.0	0.2	1.4	3.4	2.0	6.1	1.5	1.1
Calabria	38.2	19.4	22.3	0.3	2.0	4.3	2.9	5.8	2.0	2.8
Total	33.4	24.0	15.3	5.4	5.0	3.9	3.6	2.8	2.0	4.6
Regions with special statute										
Valle d'Aosta (26–6–88)	19.4	13.9	8.3	—	0.9	1.8	2.2	1.6	1.6	50.3
Trentino-Alto Adige (20–11–88)	27.0	5.7	8.3	—	7.1	6.5	2.5	1.0	0.9	41.0
Bolzano-Bozen	9.1	3.0	4.0	—	6.7	10.3	1.1	—	—	65.8
Trento	45.3	8.4	12.6	—	7.4	2.6	4.0	2.0	1.8	15.9
Friuli-Venezia-Giulia (26–6–88)	37.2	17.6	17.7	—	6.0	5.5	2.6	4.0	1.6	7.8
Sicilia (16–6–91)	42.3	11.4	13.1	—	1.2	4.8	3.6	5.3	2.7	15.6
Sardegna (11–6–89)	35.0	23.2	14.0	—	2.8	3.5	3.9	4.6	—	13.0

Source: ISTAT, 1988b

The initial transfer of responsibilities to the regions in the early 1970s was restricted in two different ways. First, functions were assigned only partly to the regions and partly to the state administration, so that each task required the joint intervention of the two bodies if it were to be carried out. Secondly, at the same time as this transfer of responsibilities, a manoeuvre aimed at centralizing financial resources was carried into effect by means of a tax reform (Serrani, 1972). This reform centralized tax-levying powers in favour

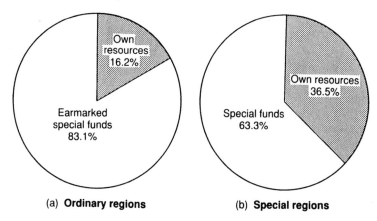

Figure 2 *Main composition of Italian regional revenues, 1980 (ISTAT, 1988a)*

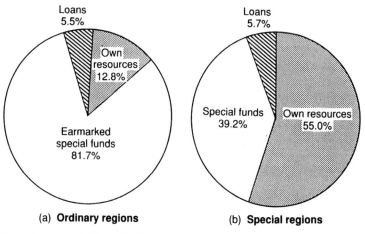

Figure 3 *Composition of Italian regional revenues, 1987 (Department for the Budget, 1988)*

of central government, thus drastically reducing the regions' (and the municipalities') powers. Regional financing was therefore derived from state assignments; the regions thus became partly responsible for spending but not for levying revenue.

During the second half of the 1970s the responsibilities transferred to the regions were considerably expanded to the extent that their autonomy increased in functional terms. Increasingly stricter limits were, however, imposed on regional autonomy as far as the availability of financial resources was concerned. The so-called special funds (for agriculture, health, transportation and so on) were added to the transfers of generally allocated resources. In order to be entitled to these funds it was necessary to comply with rules imposed by the centre; regional finance was thus conditioned by restraints as well as originating from the centre (Cassese, 1987) (see Figures 2 and 3).

The contradiction between extending regional functions and reducing regional financial autonomy is a typical example of the continuous tension characteristic of the Italian situation – that is, tension between the political and administrative system's centrifugal tendencies and the recurrent attempt to reconstruct the cohesion and uniformity of the system itself (Dente, 1985a, 1985b). One important consequence of this contradiction was in fact the development, which has gathered pace especially during the last few years, of forms of interlinking between state and regional administrations.

Functional and structural interlinking between levels

In sectors where the regionalization of functions has been most widely exercised (agriculture, health, public residential building, transportation, tourism, local crafts and environment), a model based on the joint action of state and regional administrations has been applied. For each sector, in fact, the drafting of a plan containing relevant general rules and policies was established as well as the existence of a special financial fund to be divided between the regions for carrying interventions into effect. Both the functions involving financial planning and those involving the planning of intervention had, moreover, to be jointly exercised by the state and the regions. Joint committees and mixed procedures were therefore set up, by means of which the central administrations of the state and regions together defined the fundamental lines of public intervention in a specific sector.

Participation by the regions and state administration in joint committees and mixed procedures was often established by laws passed during the 1970s, but was generally restricted to a single state administration and a single region. The aforesaid sector planning established, on the other hand, the contemporaneous participation of all the regions and several central departments. The aim was to make the decisions taken binding, to some extent, on all the parties involved in a committee or procedure (Desideri and Torchia, 1986).

Setting up a committee or a mixed procedure nevertheless produced a dual effect. One effect was to concentrate the exercise of a number of state or regional functions in a specific place on a permanent basis; we are therefore talking about an effect producing centralization. On the other hand, this was not a reappropriation by the state of regional functions. Both regional and state functions involving planning were exercised jointly by a committee, or by means of procedure, in which all the interested parties were represented. The concentration of functions therefore brought about an alteration in the nature of the centre, which no longer consisted exclusively of state administrations, but was open to other parties and thus became representative (Torchia, 1988).

The experience and functioning of these forms of interlinking have been the subject of much criticism because of the restriction of regional autonomy and confusion of responsibilities. The existence of such bodies is, however, proof of the high degree of interdependence marking intergovernmental relations in Italy; if it is true that the regions depend on the state for the allocation of resources, it is also true that the state administrations depend on the regions for the implementation of their decisions on programmes. The main effect of this interdependence is the multiplication of cases in which a system of formal or informal negotiation is applied, as opposed to imposition from the centre.

The 'association' of regions

As a result of the high rate of interdependence marking inter-governmental relations, a process of 'association' of the regions has been taking place. The regions have set up their own Presidents' Conference expressing positions shared by what may be described as the 'regional front'. This conference has its own back-up structure, Centro di informazione, studi e documentazione (CINSEDO), responsible for co-ordinating common initiatives by the regions. Furthermore, a State–Regions Conference chaired by the Prime Minister has been set up, in which the presidents of all the regions take part in order to express the regional point of view on general policy that affects the regions. The regions have thus lost part of their 'individual' autonomy to which they are entitled, but they have obtained greater contractual power as a group.

This reflects the experience of local authorities (municipalities and provinces), which by tradition have always had their own associations for bargaining and negotiating with the centre on a field basis. This at least partly confirms the hypothesis that the regions must, if they want to count in the political process and to strengthen their autonomy, negotiate with the centre.

There are in Italy, as we have noted, different versions of regionalism, based mainly on the ideas of the reformers at the beginning of the 1970s, each with a different set of priorities, although all have something in common. The regions, for example, were seen by some as an instrument for extending democracy, by others as an instrument for channelling and dispelling social tensions. Even those keener on modernizing the central apparatus adopted a slogan – the regions as a reform of the state. All of these various objectives have meant that the regions were historically moulded into a reform more dependent on the often contradictory transformation processes of the social and political system that the regions were supposed to perform rather than a straightforward emancipation of the periphery.

It is important to emphasize that the association of regions is different from the association of provinces and municipalities in the sense that the regions have legislative powers and their association is both a territorial and a functional association. Regions bargain, therefore, not only about the interests they represent but also about the use they can make of their powers.

Conflicts between regions are, moreover, a normal event: special regions against ordinary regions, southern regions against northern regions, rich regions against poor regions. The cleavages within the regional front are clear and always manifest. On the other hand, regions have an interest in accommodating their conflicts so as to present a common front against the central government. This means that collaboration among regions is somewhat diminished by the necessity to negotiate with the centre.

Performance of Italian regions

Regional studies are dominated in Italy by the legal approach. It is thus not surprising that the performance of the regions have received scant attention (Freddi, 1980; Putnam et al., 1984). Most analysis dedicated to this subject deals with only one region, or with specific tasks, and does not make clear the parameters of evaluation.

The regions themselves have not been interested, till recently, in collecting and analysing data on their own performance. In the last few years, however, some regions have set up committees and offices with the task of collecting data on regional expenditure and regional personnel (Leonardi, 1987).

However, a detailed appraisal of regional performance is made impossible by the lack of significant criteria. There is sharp disagreement, for example, among scholars and practitioners on the parameters to use (see Santantonio, 1987). The data given below refer to regional legislation, regional personnel and regional finance.

Regional legislation
Regional legislation varies considerably from region to region in terms of both quantity and quality. Generally speaking, however, it

may be said that the better-quality legislation has been undertaken by the northern regions, as compared with the southern, except for the odd isolated exception. The number of laws passed during the first eighteen years covering three terms ranges from 500 in regions making the least use of their legislative powers to 1,000 in the more prolific regions.

Regional legislation is often legislation disciplining micro-interventions, distributing financing flows or repeating year after year financing and interventions which have already been decided. Few regions have paid attention to problems concerning drafting or feasibility, even though some improvement has been accomplished in the most recent period.

It should, however, be remembered that laws passed by some regions have served as a foundation on which national laws have been promulgated. A good example is in the professional training sector. Thus new rules and bodies tried out experimentally in the periphery have been extended to the entire national territory.

Regional personnel

As Table 4 shows, regional personnel make up a relatively modest proportion of total public employment: a mere 2 per cent of the total. The conditions of service of regional personnel are defined by collective labour contracts which are incorporated in, and promulgated by, state laws.

Table 4   *Civil servants by category of institution, 1986–90*

						Percentage variance			
Institution	1986	1987	1988	1989	1990	$\frac{1987}{1986}$	$\frac{1988}{1987}$	$\frac{1989}{1988}$	$\frac{1990}{1989}$
Central ministries	1,885	1,885	1,934	1,944	2,008	—	+2.6	+0.5	+3.3
Regions	77	78	79	79	81	+1.3	+1.3	—	+2.5
Provinces	64	66	67	69	69	+3.1	+1.5	+3.0	—
Communes	554	570	584	589	593	+2.9	+2.5	+0.9	+0.7
Local health units	614	620	620	626	629	+0.9	—	+0.9	+0.5
Social security offices	63	63	63	63	63	—	—	—	—
Other public bodies	130	127	130	130	131	−2.3	+2.4	—	+0.8
Autonomous public enterprises	507	283	281	286	281	−44.2	−0.7	+1.8	−1.7
Municipal agencies	156	156	158	158	158	—	+1.3	—	—
ENEL (national electricity)	115	116	115	114	113	+0.9	−0.9	−0.9	−0.9

Source: ISTAT, 1991

Table 5   *Revenues and expenditures of regions and special provinces, 1986 (in million lire)*

Region	Revenue			Expenditure		
	Current	Capital	Total	Current	Capital	Total
Piemonte	3,941.7	613.9	4,555.6	4,060.2	686.4	4,746.6
Valle d'Aosta	721.6	70.1	791.7	341.5	610.2	951.7
Lombardia	8,323.6	668.9	8,992.5	8,196.1	957.6	9,153.7
Trentino-Alto Adige	65.1	n.a.	65.1	60.9	1.9	62.8
Bolzano-Bozen	1,381.8	234.6	1,616.4	885.0	776.7	1,661.7
Trento	1,307.3	202.2	1,509.5	935.4	567.5	1,502.9
Veneto	4,035.7	732.7	4,768.4	4,391.8	988.3	5,380.1
Friuli-Venezia-Giulia	1,734.8	847.8	2,582.6	1,333.6	1,298.4	2,632.0
Liguria	1,861.4	260.6	2,122.0	1,861.1	333.6	2,194.7
Emilia-Romagna	3,840.2	615.7	4,455.9	3,790.0	766.6	4,556.6
Toscana	3,551.3	443.6	3,994.9	3,576.4	534.0	4,110.4
Umbria	847.7	286.9	1,134.6	805.5	262.9	1,068.4
Marche	1,395.1	300.7	1,695.8	1,399.4	305.8	1,705.2
Lazio	5,396.9	385.6	5,782.5	5,894.0	521.6	6,415.6
Abruzzi	1,256.0	260.9	1,516.9	1,064.1	494.3	1,558.4
Molise	352.0	173.6	525.6	363.3	214.8	578.1
Campania	5,437.8	880.6	6,318.4	5,618.1	994.5	6,612.6
Puglia	3,775.7	446.5	4,222.2	3,543.2	1,469.5	5,012.7
Basilicata	616.0	297.6	913.6	655.5	330.5	966.0
Calabria	2,058.2	896.4	2,954.6	1,718.8	783.0	2,501.8
Sicilia	9,132.1	2,603.6	11,735.7	7,736.5	7,394.5	15,131.0
Sardegna	2,721.4	782.0	3,503.4	1,866.9	1,806.0	3,672.9
Italy	63,753.4	12,004.5	75,757.9	60,097.3	22,096.6	82,195.9

Source: ISTAT, 1988b

Regional finance

The salient features of regional finance have been set out earlier. Tables 5, 6 and 7 demonstrate the dimensions of regional finance and its subdivision into main categories. As Figure 4 reveals, regional spending constitutes 21 per cent of total public expenditure.

Regions have often been accused of being unable to spend and use financial resources. Especially during the early years the amount of so-called *residui passivi* (money allocated but not spent) was huge, especially in southern regions. Most regions lack the kind of technical expertise which is necessary to make full use of their planning powers and even the drafting of regional budgets is often of poor quality.

It must be remembered that the weakest and poorest regions, in the south, find an additional source of money in the Department for the Mezzogiorno and in the connected agencies. These are central offices which operate (or should operate) in strict co-ordination with southern regions.

Table 6   Expenditure by sectors, absolute values (in million lire) and percentages, 1981 and 1986

Sector	Special regions	1981 %	1986 %	Ordinary regions	1981 %	1986 %	Ord. reg. north	Ord. reg. centre	Ord. reg. south
General expenses	2,014.585	7.9	7.0	2,398.726	3.6	3.9	929.192	621.628	847.906
Education	1,093.541	3.4	3.8	998.484	2.9	1.6	284.867	277.106	436.511
Professional training	971.802	2.1	3.4	1,295.257	2.1	2.1	497.654	205.631	591.972
Social security	657.293	2.2	2.3	1,141.236	2.1	1.8	479.998	247.568	413.670
Health	7,045.708	41.8	24.3	37,673.337	62.7	60.5	18,805.983	9,206.943	9,660.411
Agriculture	2,181.493	10.0	7.5	4,035.333	6.8	6.6	1,109.108	771.696	2,154.529
Forests	337.079	1.9	1.2	264.015	1.1	0.4	101.521	57.620	104.874
Hunting and fishing	45,753	0.2	0.2	86.878	0.2	0.1	49.487	16.128	21.263
Fairs and markets	103.589	0.2	0.4	50.937	0.1	0.1	26.927	5.905	18.105
Local crafts	1,222.129	2.6	4.2	422.262	0.8	0.7	88.145	138.243	195.874
Tourism	342.909	1.2	1.2	456.914	0.6	0.7	74.509	97.884	284.521
Transport	1,306.050	3.1	4.5	5,369.684	2.7	8.6	2,362.135	1,702.731	1,304.818
Land use planning	1,328.146	7.0	4.6	2,439.569	3.5	3.9	707.880	931.217	800.472
Housing	1,107.868	4.9	3.8	1,991.563	5.5	3.2	531.951	584.451	875.161
Others	9,223.945	11.5	31.8	3,667.507	5.3	5.8	1,067.808	910.923	1,688.776
Total	28,981.890	100.0	100.0	62,291.702	100.0	100.0	27,117.165	15,775.674	19,398.863

Source: Rapporto sulle regione 1988, 1989

Table 7   *Expenditure by sector per capita (in thousand lire), 1988*

Sector	Special regions	Ordinary regions	North reg.	Centre reg.	South reg.
General expenses	225	50	40	57	61
Education	122	21	12	25	31
Professional training	109	27	21	19	42
Social security	74	24	21	23	30
Health	789	781	805	843	691
Agriculture	244	84	47	71	154
Forests	38	5	4	5	7
Hunting and fishing	5	2	2	1	2
Fairs and markets	12	1	1	1	1
Local crafts	137	9	4	13	14
Tourism	38	9	3	9	20
Transport	146	111	101	156	93
Land use planning	149	51	30	85	57
Housing	124	41	23	54	63
Others	1,032	76	46	83	121
Total	3,244	1,291	1,161	1,445	1,387

Source: *Rapporto sulle regione 1988*, 1989

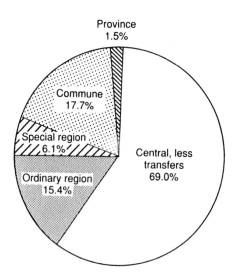

Figure 4   *Italian public expenditure by level of government, 1985 (Berglione, 1989)*

Conclusions

Hypotheses on Italian regionalization

In conclusion, a number of hypotheses on Italian regionalization may be formulated.

First, regional reform may be defined as a simultaneous cause and effect of the expansion process of the 'political class'. This hypothesis would also be confirmed by other changes connected to regional reform, such as the institution of the national health service. The critical consideration is that the new institutions generate an increase in the number of positions reserved for people through some form of election who are essentially appointed by political parties.

The main reason for expanding the number of posts available to the political class has been attributed in some studies to the difficulties that politicians meet when they need to impose their priorities and policies on the state bureaucracy and public agencies. The easiest and most painless way of overcoming the resistance of bureaucrats is, therefore, to increase one's own importance and manoeuvring space by creating new political bodies providing additional offices (Cassese, 1986).

Secondly, regionalization has been made possible by economic growth, for it is such growth that has made possible the distribution of policies the regions perform. These redistributed processes are partly directed towards activities typical of the welfare state (in relation to which the regions have fairly wide powers), and partly make it possible for politicians to manage a quota of public spending directly without intermediaries. This means, though, that the role of the regions is to an extent linked to the availability of economic resources; whenever resources diminish, the role of the regions is also affected, especially in relation to the social services. A reduction in available resources may, moreover, lead to an attempt to discharge the burden of unpopular policies into the regions; recent proposals to confer limited powers to levy taxes to the regions may indeed be interpreted in this context.

Thirdly, regionalization may be considered to be an attempt on the part of certain groups belonging to the political class to compensate for the low degree of territorial representation which in some ways is typical of the Italian situation. This explains the attraction and passion of the discussion about the region as a political versus administrative body; here politics was seen as a guarantee of democracy and participation, whereas administration was a synonym for bureaucracy, centralization and the rejection of 'civil society' demands. This comparison turned out to be at least partially false and abstract. The regions' capacity to work out autonomous and innovative policies and carry them into effect depends to a large degree on the extent of the assigned administrative functions, and on the efficient functioning of regional administration.

The meso level in Italy: dislocation of the centre

The Italian meso experience can be interpreted as a good example of a mixed approach. Structural reform and functional links between levels of government have interreacted, producing an interesting, if somewhat confused, situation. More recently, functional links have become more and more important, shaping the activity and the priorities of both regional and central administration.

On a more general level of discussion, it can be argued that the Italian meso experience has produced a dislocation of the centre within the political and administrative system (Cassese, 1986; Torchia, 1988). The state administration is no longer as pervasive as it was before regionalization. Moreover, most important planning decisions and priorities must be taken jointly by state administration and regions. The central state has no way to impose its own will; it has to negotiate with the regions. These new partners, on the other hand, are dependent on the state, especially as far as financial resources are concerned. The way in which this interdependence is taking shape and its institutional forms are probably the most prominent and interesting features of the Italian meso experience.

Notes

1 The fact of Italy being a 'late-comer' among nation states explains, at least partly, why unity and uniformity have been, and partially still are, so important and relevant within the political realm. It is not surprising, given the country's history, that the strenuous defence of particularism (*municipalismo*) and strenuous efforts to implement uniformity have both been significant features of the Italian system. The existence of a strong Communist Party has, in more recent times, restrengthened the bias in favour of uniformity and against differentiation (see p. 123). It must be noted, also, that the different traditions of pre-unification states were almost never allowed to survive, because they were often linked with domination by foreign powers, this being the main reason why pre-unification differentiation has never emerged as an important feature of sub-national politics in the modern Italian state.

2 The list contains the following: organization of regional administrative apparatus, sub-municipal boundaries, fairs and markets, health, professional training, municipal museums and libraries, territorial planning, tourism, regional transportation, regional roads, water, lakes, mineral and thermal waters, mines, hunting, fishing in internal waters, agriculture and local crafts. This list could be radically altered and enlarged in the near future, if the amendments proposed by the Parliamentary Commission for Constitutional Reform, set up in 1992, are passed by Parliament.

3 The main law on regionalization, d.P.R. (decreto del Presidente della Repubblica) no. 616/1977, contains provisions about regional powers in four large fields:

administrative organization, social services, economic development and territorial planning. For every field are listed the regional functions and their content.

4 See *Le regioni: politica o amministrazione?*, 1973.

5 See *Dalla parte delle regioni*, 1975.

6 See *Le regioni: politica o amministrazione?*, 1973.

7 Both reforms require a very high political cost and there is no political party which could clearly and surely gain from them. Moreover, municipal authorities are the basis of party organization, while regions are not an important level within the electoral system.

Select further reading

Annuario delle autonomie (Rome), periodical.

Baldassarre, A. (1983) *Rapporti fra regioni e governo: i dilemmi del regionalismo*, in *L'autonomia regionale nel rapporto con il Parlamento e il Governo: Bollettino di legislazione e documentazione regionale*, 5 (suppl.), Rome, Camera dei Deputati.

Baldassarre, A. (1984) 'I raccordi istituzionali fra Stato e regioni speciali', *Le Regioni*, 4.

Barbera, A. and Bassanini, F. (eds) (1979) *I nuovi poteri delle regioni e degli enti locali*. Bologna: Il Mulino.

Bartole, S., Vandelli, L., Mastragostino, F. (1984) *Le autonomie territoriali: ordinamento delle regioni e degli enti locali*. Bologna: Il Mulino.

Bertolissi, M. (1983) *L'autonomia finanziaria regionale: lineamenti costituzionali*. Padua: Cedam.

Cassese, S. (1984) 'La regionalizzazione economica in Italia: un sistema alla ricerca di un equilibrio', *Le Regioni*, 2.

D'Atena, A. (1988) 'Regione', in *Enciclopedia del diritto*. Milan: Giuffre.

Giannini, M. S. (1984) 'Regioni e riforme istituzionali: note introduttive', *Quaderni regionali*, 2–3.

'L'accordo nella cooperazione fra Stato e Regioni e fra Regioni' (1985) *Quaderni Formez*, Rome.

'Le regioni nella realtà sociale e politica di oggi', *Bollettino di legislazione e documentazione regionale*, 7 (suppl.), 4 vols, Rome: Camera dei Deputati.

Martines, T. and Ruggeri, A. (1987) *Lineamenti di diritto regionale*. Milan: Giuffrè.

Osservatorio finanziario regionale (Milan), periodical.

Rapporto sulle regioni 1988 (1989) Milan: Franco Angeli.

References

Bartole, S., Falcon, G., Vandelli, L., Allegretti, U. and Pubusa, A. (1985) *Le regioni, le province, i comuni*, Vol. I, *Commentario della Costituzione*, ed. G. Branca, art. 114–20. Bologna: Zanichelli.

Berglione, E. (1989) 'La fimenta regionale', in *Rapporto sulle regioni 1988*. Milan: CINSEDO/Franco Angeli.

Cassese, S. (1984) 'Italy: a system in search of an equilibrium', in M. Hebbert and H. Machin (eds), *Regionalization in France, Italy and Spain*. London: International Centre for Economics and Related Disciplines.

Cassese, S. (1986) 'Centro e periferia. I grandi tornanti della loro storia', *Rivista trimestrale di diritto pubblico*, 1.

116   *The rise of meso government*

Cassese, S. (1987) 'I caratteri originari e gli sviluppi attuali dell'amministrazione pubblica', *Quaderni costituzionali*, 3.
Cazzola, F., Ilardi, M., Martines, T., Priulla, G. and Scarrocchia, S. (1986) *Autonomia politica regionale e sistema dei partiti*. Milan: Giuffre.
Dalla parte delle regioni (1975) Milan: Quaderni della Fondazione Olivetti.
Dente, B. (1985a) *Governare la frammentazione*. *Stato regioni ed enti locali in Italia*. Bologna: Il Mulino.
Dente, B. (1985b) 'Intergovernmental relations as central control policies: the case of Italian local finance', *Government and Policy*, 3.
Department for the Budget (1988) *Relazione previsionale e programmatica per il 1988*.
Desideri, C. and Torchia, L. (1986) *I raccordi fra stato e regioni*. Milan: Giuffre.
Freddi, G. (1980) 'Regional devolution, administrative decentralization and bureaucratic performance in Italy', *Policy and Politics*, 8.
Giannini, M. S. (1963) 'Le regioni: rettifica e prospettive'. *Nord e Sud*, 42–3.
ISTAT (Istituto Nazionale di Statistica) (1987) *Anumario statistico*. Rome: ISTAT.
ISTAT (1988a) *Bilanci consuntivi delle regioni e delle province autonome anno 1985*. Rome: ISTAT.
ISTAT (1988b) *Le regioni in cifri*. Rome: ISTAT.
Leonardi, R. (1987) *La regione Basilicata*. Bologna: Il Mulino.
Le regioni: politica o amministrazione? (1973) Milan: Quaderni della Fondazione Olivetti.
Paladin, L. (1985) *Diritto regionale*. Padua: Cedam.
Pastori, G. (1980) 'Le regioni senza regionalism', *Il Mulino*, XXIX.
Putnam, R., Leonardi, R. and Nanetti, R. (1984) *La pianta e le radici*. Bologna: Il Mulino.
Rapporto sulle regione 1988 (1989) Milan: Franco Angeli.
Rotelli, E. (1967) *L'avvento della regioni in Italia*. *Dalla caduta del regime fascista alla costituzione repubblicana (1943–1947)*. Milan: Giuffre.
Rotelli, E. (1979) 'Le regioni dalla partecipazione al partito', in L. Graziano and S. Tarrow (eds), *La crisi italiana*. Turin: Einaudi.
Ruffilli, R. (1971) *La questione regionale dall'unificazione alla dittatura*. Milan: Giuffre.
Santantonio, E. (1987) 'Italy', in E. Page and M. Goldsmith (eds), *Central and Local Government Relations*. London: Sage.
Serrani, D. (ed.) (1972) *La via italiana alle regioni*. Milan: Fondazione Olivetti.
Sorace, D. (1979) 'Le regioni italiane alle fine degli anni '70', *Le Regioni*, 4.
Torchia, L. (1988) *Le amministrazioni nazionali*. Padua: Cedam.

5

Dutch Provinces and the Struggle for the Meso

Theo A. J. Toonen

The struggle for the meso in the Netherlands

It is crowded if not overpopulated at the Dutch meso level. A working definition of the meso level of government would be: the administrative level which has public authority in a territory that is smaller than the national territory, but at the same time exceeds that of the municipalities. In the Dutch case, this definition embraces a vast multitude of representative and administrative units: provinces, water control boards, municipal joint provisions, national deconcentrated services, inspectorates, national government field organizations, a vast variety of forms of functional decentralization and quasi- or non-governmental organizations (NGOs), and a plural and constantly changing system of districts in which the different policy sectors (police, fire brigade, social policy, economic affairs, environmental enforcement agencies and so on) are administratively organized. In the Netherlands, meso government is pre-eminently an example of multi-organizational governance and administration.

In this chapter we restrict ourselves to the territorial, general-purpose government organization. This makes the institutional landscape at the meso somewhat more surveyable. It also means, however, that the meso governance of substantial parts of notable policy areas such as health care, welfare, cultural affairs, education and water management will largely fall outside the scope of this presentation. Substantial parts of public policy in these areas are, particularly at the meso level of government, carried out by functionally organized public, semi-public and non-profit 'third sector' institutions. These occupy the relatively vast and diverse institutional area between 'core' public sector and private market arrangements and are quite deliberately retained to perform tasks within the Dutch state system.

Given this restriction to the territorial state organization, and seen from within, the picture at the meso level of the Dutch governmental system is still complicated. Over the past fifty years, the evolution of the structure of the Dutch territorial government system, between the national and the municipal levels of government, reflects a so far inconclusive struggle of at least three different kinds of meso government: the historical, the local and the European.

The historical meso can be defined as the formal, constitutionally recognized intermediate level of government between municipal and national governments. In the Netherlands this is the province (*provincie*). The province is a constitutionally defined and legally independent, territorial general-purpose government unit. It is constitutionally entrusted with a general competence (autonomy) and among other things is charged with the general supervision of Dutch municipalities. The Dutch province is a fully fledged layer of government with its own constitutional, legal and democratic legitimation and a directly elected representative body.

The local meso can be defined as the form of intermediate government which is actually perceived as such by the actors within the intergovernmental and administrative system themselves. A local meso might coincide with the historical meso. Up until the end of the 1980s, however, the local Dutch meso was perceived as the administrative arrangements at the level between the municipal and provincial levels of government: the urban agglomeration and the rural region. In the Dutch administrative jargon of the 1970s and 1980s the word 'region' almost exclusively referred to the functional space at the level between provinces and municipalities. The concept of regional government in the Netherlands primarily refers to inter- or supra-municipal forms of organization. At the beginning of this decade these definitions are shifting and this reflects the growing importance of the third type of meso.

This third type, the European meso, can be defined as the interrelated cultural and socio-economic spatial entities which can be identified and distinguished from a broader European perspective. In the Netherlands the relevant European meso has not yet been clearly defined and incontrovertibly identified. Some will prefer to perceive the Netherlands as just one region in Europe, if not merely as a constituent part of an even larger regional entity: North-Western Europe. Any other effort to demarcate a European region will not lead to the identification of many more than three to four of them within the current national borders of the Netherlands: the international and the trade-oriented urbanized western part; the somewhat peripheral, agricultural and dairy-farming-oriented north-eastern part; and the rural, more residential and more and more continentally oriented south and south-eastern parts of the country. In short, the concept of the European meso refers to structures and processes on a scale somewhere between the current provincial and national levels of government.

Figure 1   *The Dutch provinces: the historical meso*

The historical meso in the Netherlands is constituted by the twelve Dutch *provincies* (see Figure 1). As of old the province occupies the formal, constitutional level of intermediate government between the national and the municipal levels. Thus, foreign observers will readily identify the Dutch *provincie* as the primary locus for a study which deals with meso or intermediate levels of government. As a point of departure we will take this view too.

The province is – also within the Netherlands itself – the least studied form of territorial general-purpose government within the Dutch (inter)governmental system. This relative neglect is indicative. By the end of the 1980s, the most probable reaction by Dutch observers, laypeople and professionals alike was to overlook, ignore or even renounce provinces as of little or no importance in conducting Dutch public affairs.[1]

In so far as the meso has been studied in the Netherlands attention has usually focused on the administrative level between provinces and municipalities. More specifically this meso level has often been identified as the 'regional gap' and has dominated the political and academic debate on the reorganization of the Dutch sub-national administrative system over the past forty years. This debate has recently been revitalized (Commissie Montijn, 1989; RBB, 1989b). This regained interest is prompted by the 'discovery' of the European dimension of urban and regional management. The issue is whether a fragmented, functionally organized intermunicipal governance of the Dutch urbanized areas will allow the bigger Dutch cities (Amsterdam and Rotterdam and, somewhat aside, The Hague, Utrecht and a dozen regional urban municipalities) to effectively compete with their European rivals or counterparts. Putting regional or meso government into a European perspective, however, creates a highly dynamic situation. While using the same words one implicitly changes the definition and content of the concepts of 'meso' and 'region' (Dente, 1990). Thus, an intriguing situation arises.

This chapter presents an overview. The second section proceeds with a brief description of the historical development of the Dutch provinces and of their contemporary multi-organizational meso context. In the third section a description will be provided of some general socio-economic, political and administrative characteristics of the contemporary Dutch provinces. The fourth section provides an analysis of the position of the province in the overall administrative system of the Netherlands. The question to be considered is whether the historical meso in the Netherlands will finally become the local meso or whether the province as a meso will finally become history.

Developments at the meso level in the Netherlands

The contemporary Dutch provinces, largely with their current boundaries, have a long and rich history. Once, they were the constituent and powerful elements of the federal Dutch Republic. The unification of the Netherlands occurred under French domination at the end of the eighteenth century. It has partly been the fear of the resurrection of the pre-Napoleonic Dutch federalism which contributed to the containment of the power of the provinces after the centralized French regime was relaxed. Since the establishment of the Dutch decentralized unitary state in 1848–51, which still characterizes the constitutional framework of the Dutch sub-national administration of today, the municipalities – and not the provinces – have been the most important institutions for sub-national, decentralized government in the Netherlands (Toonen, 1987, 1990).

The period before 1579

By about the year 1000, the Netherlands – part of the 'Middle Kingdom' which was the result of the division of Charlemagne's empire (843) – was split up into several virtually autonomous regions. These were governed by the bishop of Utrecht, the dukes of Brabant and Gelderland, the counts of Holland, Zeeland and Flanders and various barons. Friesland had already managed to regain its freedom.

The Dutch name for the current provincial council – which is the representative body at the provincial level, dates from this time (1464). The word *staten* refers to the three orders – the nobility, the clergy and the burgers (citizens) – who gathered to decide about tax proposals and other charges on their 'privilege' by the regional ruler (Geersing, 1987).

In the fourteenth century, the dukes of Burgundy became influential and tried to establish a certain unity among the Dutch provinces. A Grand Council was designated to represent all of the provinces collectively. This attempted centralization did not succeed. Under Charles V, who became ruler of all the seventeen northern and southern provinces in 1543, the provinces were ruled by a Governor. He was assisted by a 'Council of State'. Each province was headed by a *Stadhouder*. They had their own 'provincial estate'. The provinces had their representatives in the States-General – Staten Generaal – which is nowadays in Dutch still the official designation of the joint meeting of the Second (Parliament) and First Chamber (Senate) in the Netherlands.

The period 1579–1795

Alva's conquest in 1568 began the Eighty Years War against Spain which ended in 1648. In 1579 the seven northern provinces concluded the Union of Utrecht to remain united in their struggle against Spain. This led in 1581 to the declaration of independence from Philip II, the King of Spain. The provinces called themselves the United Provinces of the Netherlands, also known as the 'Dutch Republic', or simply 'Holland'.

Until 1795 the main power remained vested with the sovereign provinces. In the confederation of 'the Republic of the Seven United Provinces' the binding elements were: the external threat of Spain (until 1648); the States-General, composed of provincial representatives; and the Council of State (the still existing Raad van Staten), which at the time was composed of the Stadholder(s) and twelve other members.

Besides these binding elements provincial autonomy was limited by some other factors. Within the provinces the cities became increasingly influential, and among the provinces the province of Holland became increasingly dominant (Micklinghoff, 1982). Nevertheless, for as much as two centuries the provinces were the constituent elements of Dutch government.

The period 1795–1848

In this period, the provinces were transformed into a unitary state – the 'Batavian Republic' (1795–1806) – which was subject to intermittent centralizing and decentralizing forces (Breunese, 1982). In 1795, the States-General rejected Stadholder William V and concluded peace with France. In 1798, the provinces were replaced by pure administrative districts, each headed by a commissioner who was comparable to the French prefect. Today's figure of the Queen's Commissioner (Commissaris van de Koningin) in a way originates from this office.

In 1801, the provinces regained their old borders and some of their former autonomy. The formation of the 'Kingdom of Holland' (1806) and its incorporation by France (1810) implied the re-establishment of the French centralized system, including the prefectorial structure. After the restoration of Dutch independence (1813), the framers of the new Constitution of 1814–15 feared the recuperation of the traditional provincial power. As a consequence, provinces were granted no more power than as agencies of the Ministry of the Interior.

The period 1848–1945

The historian and statesman Johan Rudolf Thorbecke (1798–1872), with his Constitution of 1848, designed the constitutional and legal framework of the contemporary Dutch 'decentralized unitary state' (Toonen, 1987, 1990b). The constitutional reform of 1848 reflected dissatisfaction with the former centralistic constitutional approach. The key conception became that of the bounded, or relative, autonomy of the component parts of the state. The Constitution of 1848 and the subsequent so-called organic legislation (the Provincial Government Act of 1850 and the Municipal Government Act of 1851) grant a general competence – autonomy – to provinces and municipalities; the governance and administration of their 'own household' is constitutionally 'left' to municipalities and provinces. Provincial supervision serves as a constitutional check to balance municipal autonomy; national government supervises provincial autonomy.

Next to their autonomous general competence – that is, the supervised right to legislative initiatives – the municipalities and provinces may constitutionally also be charged with delegated executive tasks in the context of national legislation. This legal arrangement will be referred to as (provincial or municipal) co-governance (*medebewind*).

Up until the present day, and despite many revisions, Thorbecke's design of the decentralized unitary state has established the constitutional framework for the Dutch province and its relations to the other state authorities. Within this constitutional framework of course many changes and developments have taken place since the middle of the last century.

In the second half of the last and the first half of this century, provinces played a relatively minor – but not necessarily unimportant – role in the Dutch governmental system. As today, municipalities acted as the main implementors of national legislation and policies. Also, in exercising their autonomy municipalities played the more active role. The province mainly developed its role of supervising authority for municipal legislation and finance. The province played a role in settling disputes among municipalities and within inter-municipal 'regional' co-operative arrangements . As far as policies are concerned , from the turn of the century onwards, the provinces got gradually involved in infrastructural activities with respect to roads, waterways, physical planning, public transport and public utilities (water, electricity).

The period after 1945
The post-war period shows a great deal of at least verbal attention to regional government. Already before the Second World War, many local government activities started to exceed the municipal scale. This process continued and, after the war, led to a series of varying proposals to 'fill the regional gap', that is, the functional meso between the municipal and provincial level of government. In this respect, the meso level has now become a long-standing issue in the Netherlands. In retrospect, the process of trying to reorganize the territorial structure of the Dutch intergovernmental system goes back as far as the late 1940s. The desirability of a territorial reorganization and enlargement of governmental units, especially around the bigger cities, was expressed even earlier, by the end of the 1920s. Later, in 1947, a governmental committee – the Koelma Committee – recommended a fourth layer of government between municipalities and provinces. These 'districts' were thought

to be necessary in order to be able to deal with the supra-local and regional problems which were considered to be the cause of many frictions within the intergovernmental system. The idea was rejected. In 1950, a law was enacted which extended the possibilities of intermunicipal co-operation as a way to deal with supra- and inter-local problems. All regulations about intermunicipal co-operation to be found within different laws were being brought together into one Joint Provisions Act.

During the 1960s, ideas about a separate governmental structure to deal with regional affairs started to regain popularity. In 1969, a governmental note was issued which proposed to extend the law on joint provisions of 1950. The law should enable municipalities to create regional authorities of a general-purpose character. In the course of this process and anticipating a future legally recognized status, some forms of general-purpose regional government bodies were installed at the level between municipalities and provinces. The best-known and best-developed regional council has been the Rijnmond Authority. This regional authority covered the area in the south-western part of the country, in the urbanized area of the Rotterdam region. The Rijnmond Authority was characterized by a representative body which was directly elected by the population of the Rijnmond area. Its main tasks have been in the areas of environmental control, public housing and physical planning.

In 1971, the idea of general-purpose regional government authorities was more or less incorporated into a proposal which would enable municipalities to co-operate on a general-purpose basis (as against a limited-purpose or functional character of co-operation, which was allowed for by the existing law on joint provisions). However, the proposal ran into strong parliamentary opposition. A fear of a 'fourth layer of government' and a resulting complexity of the structure of sub-national government played an important role in the debates. The proposal was withdrawn. The idea, however, that the 'rationalization' and 'democratization' of the system required a fundamental reorganization at the municipal level remained.

In 1974, the outcomes were published of an investigation which was set into motion as a result of the debates some years earlier. The Ministry of the Interior issued a document in which a territorial division of the Netherlands into forty-four socio-economic regions was proposed as the point of departure for reorganizing the structure and size of local governments. At present, nearly twenty years later, this division has resurfaced in the debate about the Dutch meso. But in the meantime, several other developments have occurred.

In 1975, after a change in government coalition, the national government proposals suddenly changed. Instead of a municipal reorganization, attention shifted to a provincial reorganization. The partition of the traditional provinces and the instalment of 37 and later 26 'new-style' provinces were proposed as the way to bridge the 'regional gap'. The tasks and authorities of these provinces should be extended. Provinces should become more active in actually carrying out government policies, even at the expense of municipalities.

Again, these plans gradually underwent several changes. Both the number of proposed provinces and their proposed tasks were reduced. In 1977, the number of 24 provinces was proposed. In 1978, the Minister of the Interior mentioned 17 provinces. In 1983, the idea of a provincial reorganization was dropped altogether. The solution to inter- and supra-municipal frictions was seen, again, in the co-operation of municipalities. Starting on 1 January 1985, a new Joint Provision Act was adopted by Parliament. Thus, the process of 'territorial reorganization' had come full circle.

As a consequence of the change in policy, the Rijnmond Authority and some other regional councils in other parts of the Netherlands were abolished. The main argument for abolition was that a 'fourth layer of government' would unnecessarily complicate decision-making processes and that the new (functionally oriented) Joint Provision Act would provide sufficient instruments to deal with the inter- and supra-municipal problems of scale.

The Rijnmond Authority resisted its abolition until the very last minute. The Province of South Holland and the Ministry of the Interior were the most outspoken protagonists against Rijnmond. The city of Rotterdam kept a 'low profile' in the debates. The municipal council of Rotterdam once even accepted a proposal in support of Rijnmond, but the municipal executive and its bureaucracy seemed very much in favour of the elevation of Rijnmond as a way to reduce the 'administrative density' in the region. They grasped their chance to eliminate some bureaucratic competitors in their immediate environment. The smaller cities around Rotterdam seemed to take the side of Rijnmond. Their main consideration was that Rijnmond played an important role in balancing the power of the city of Rotterdam in the region. Their efforts to maintain Rijnmond, however, did not make a very strong impression.

More generally, the Rijnmond case illustrates that the Dutch municipalities so far have been quite effective in occupying the local Dutch meso and in fighting off the threats which were brought against

Figure 2   *Intermunicipal co-operation areas: the national meso*

them by proposals to install a fourth layer of government or to strengthen the position of provinces at the meso level.

The local meso of the Netherlands: intermunicipal
co-operation
Under the Joint Provision Act of 1950 intermunicipal co-operation continued to increase. Some rudimentary forms of general-purpose co-operation have developed. The bulk of co-operative arrangements were functional in nature. Depending on how one defines a joint provision, the estimated numbers in the early 1980s varied from 1,250 to 2,000.

The new Joint Provisions Act of 1983 prescribes a more or less uniform administrative structure for all joint provisions. The aim was to tie the control of the co-operative arrangements more closely to the participating municipalities. The general and the daily boards of

Figure 3   *Euroregions: the European meso*

intermunicipal joint provision have to be recruited from municipal representatives. There are no direct elections.

The second purpose was to 'rationalize' the system. This desire was formulated in a legal requirement to 'concentrate' and 'integrate' different joint provisions within a certain area. The provinces had to identify different so-called 'co-operation areas'. These are intended to serve as devices to group and cluster (functional) joint provisions. Municipalities in principle are only allowed to enter or establish joint provisions with municipalities which belong to the same co-operation area'. Joint provisions among municipalities located within different co-operation areas are in principle not allowed any more.

By 1986 the provinces had organized their territories into 62 co-operation areas. This aggregate figure ranges from one co-operation area in the newly established province of Flevoland to 12 in the province of South Holland. The largest co-operation area contains

911,000 inhabitants, the smallest 42,000. The territory ranges from 1,539 sq km to 73 sq km. In terms of number of municipalities, the co-operation areas vary from 4 to 28 municipalities (Toonen, 1989: 412).

The multiple meso
The developments at the Dutch meso have thus led to a manifold structure. The different territorial demarcations are presented in Figures 1, 2 and 3. There is a distinction between the functional and the organizational or administrative meso. Figure 4 provides a schematic, graphic presentation. In terms of the existing administrative meso, the figure indicates that the province – the historical Dutch meso – is embedded in a network of organizations, representing the other two layers of government at the intermediate level. On the one hand, the national government departments have installed many deconcentrated field service agencies. These are inspectorates and consultants which mostly deal with municipalities and only indirectly with citizens, firms or other social institutions. They are characterized by varying and overlapping territorial jurisdictions above and beyond provincial borders. On the other hand, there are the municipal joint provisions or joint regulations: the current local Dutch meso. As indicated, the joint provisions at the end of the 1980s were clustered into sixty-two legally prescribed co-operation areas.

The dotted line in Figure 4 represents the functional Dutch meso in terms of a European definition. The European Dutch meso is located

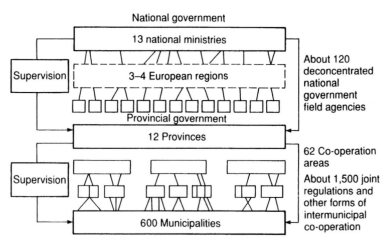

Figure 4   *The multiple meso of the Netherlands*

at the level somewhere between provinces and national government. As indicated, this European meso has so far no administrative form and organizational expression within the Dutch intergovernmental system, other than through the co-operation of provinces, particularly in the northern part (Groningen, Friesland, Drenthe) and the western part of the country (North Holland, South Holland, Utrecht).

The provinces: position, organization, functions and policies

The twelve Dutch provinces represent a pluralistic system with many differences in terms of size, culture, economics and politics. Some of this diversity is reflected in Table 1. The table shows some disparities which occasionally enter the national political arena and result in rather restricted regional economic conflicts. A striking phenomenon, for example, is that more than 40 per cent of the gross national product is produced in the two western provinces, North Holland and South Holland. For this reason they claim to be the economic heart of the country, demanding special attention. In the middle of the 1980s, the northern and southern provinces clearly were the economically weaker regions. In the second half of the decade the province of Limburg much improved its regional economic circumstances, leaving the rural northern part in a somewhat peripheral situation. More generally, it seems that recently the economic growth centres have been located more and more just outside the urbanized western parts of the country.

Provincial expenditures: relative size
As stated before, many observers consider the provinces to be of little importance in the overall administrative structure of the Netherlands. The reason for this is to be found in the relatively small share which provinces take out of the total of governmental activities. This is reflected in the share of provincial expenditures as a proportion of total public sector expenditures, illustrated by Tables 2 and 3. For an understanding of the proportion of provincial expenditures one may start with a look at the overall picture of public sector spending in the Netherlands (Table 2).

Public sector expenditures are more or less evenly distributed into social security payments and national government and sub-national government expenditures. The growth of public sector expenditures has largely been caused by the growth of social insurance payments. The expenditures of sub-national governments have undergone several changes over the past forty years and most recently have

Table 1   *Socio-economic figures by province in 1985*

Province	Relative size	Total area (sq km)	Total population (000s)	Inhabitants per sq km	Number of municipalities	Unemployment (%)[1]	Gross regional product[2] (million guilders)	(%)
Groningen	Small	2,607	1,110	426	50	23.4	29,254	7
Friesland	Small	3,788	909	240	31	20.0	11,472	3
Drenthe	Small	2,681	477	178	34	18.7	10,918	3
Overijssel	Medium	3,926	1,076	274	47	18.8	22,185	6
Gelderland	Large	5,128	1,785	348	87	18.4	30,395	8
Utrecht	Medium	1,396	981	703	48	14.2	22,959	6
North Holland	Large	2,935	2,542	866	81	14.3	65,942	17
South Holland	Large	3,363	3,649	1,085	129	14.5	86,685	23
Zeeland	Small	3,017	600	199	30	13.8	8,606	2
North Brabant	Large	5,106	2,175	426	131	18.6	47,563	13
Limburg	Medium	2,209	1,105	500	69	19.9	21,878	6
Flevoland	Medium	1,136	1,409	124	4	n.a.	n.a.	6
The Netherlands	—	37,291	15,886	426	741	16.9	368,860	100

[1] As percentage of the labour force.
[2] In market prices.

Source: CBS (Central Bureau of Statistics, The Hague), *Regional Statistical Handbook*, 1986

Table 2   *Public sector expenditure by type of authority, 1950–90*

	National government (% GNP)	Sub-national governments[1] (% GNP)	Social insurance (% GNP)	Total public expenditure (% GNP)
1950	17.5	10.0	4.0	31.5
1955	18.7	11.4	4.3	34.4
1960	14.0	13.6	8.3	35.9
1965	13.6	15.8	12.0	41.4
1970	14.0	17.7	16.5	48.2
1975	16.0	21.4	21.9	59.9
1980	19.0	20.2	24.1	63.3
1985	21.2	22.6	`22.9	66.7
1990	19.7	17.6	24.2	61.5

[1] Sub-national governmental expenditure is mainly municipal expenditure.

Source: Ministry of Finance, 1990

faced a relative decline due to retrenchment and cut-back policies.

Table 3 shows that sub-national expenditures are mainly municipal expenditures. It also highlights the fact that the past forty years show a gradual increase in provincial and intermunicipal expenditures relative to the bulk of municipal sub-national expenditures. Most of sub-national spending remains, however, municipal spending.

Public sector spending patterns reflect that the province in the Netherlands mainly performs co-ordinating, organizational and planning activities. Production and public service delivery mainly take place at the municipal level of government.

Table 3   *Absolute and relative expenditures of sub-national governments*

	Provinces (million guilders)	(%)	Joint provisions (million guilders)	(%)	Municipalities (million guilders)	(%)
1957	224	4	24	1	4,994	95
1960	263	4	34	1	5,839	95
1965	598	5	103	1	10,770	95
1971	1,383	6	714	4	19,622	90
1974	2,064	7	1,367	4	28,171	89
1980	3,021	5	3,973	6	58,750	89
1986	4,893	8	4,721	7	53,494	85

Provinces: legal structure
The Constitution requires that provincial authority is based upon law under the Provincial Government Act. The Constitution stipulates three preconditions (Monchy, 1976). First, the governance of their own household is to be 'left' to the provinces. This provincial autonomy can only be circumscribed negatively, as activities which are not regulated by higher authorities or required from provinces by these authorities. Second, provincial actions are subject to state supervision.[2] Third, provincial authorities can be required to partici- pate in the execution of national legislation. This so-called co- governance (*medebewind*) takes different forms.

It might imply the actual execution of national laws. In practice this role in the policy process is more often played by municipalities than by provinces. Provinces generally act as institutions of administrative appeal in the context of co-governance. Provinces traditionally play an important role in this area.

Co-governance also entails participation in policy-making through supplementary legislation or (delegated) co-ordination. There has been an important increase of provincial activity in this respect. In several policy areas, particularly in housing, physical planning, transport and environmental affairs, provinces are central planning and co-ordinating institutions.

Formal-legal organization   The general administrative structure of each province contains a provincial council (*provinciale staten*), a provincial executive (*gedeputeerde staten*) and a Queen's Com- missioner (Commissaris van de Koningin). In addition, each prov- ince has a (provincial) clerk who is responsible for the administrative organization. The provincial councils may delegate certain adminis- trative powers to provincial committees as a form of intra-provincial functional decentralization. Interest groups, professional experts and citizen associations can thus be incorporated into the provincial policy process.

The provincial council is directly elected and the highest formal authority within a province. The council decides, with a simple majority, about provincial legislation and the provincial budget. It formally governs the provincial household (autonomy). The council appoints from its own membership the provincial executive. Exter- nally, the provincial council elects the members of the First Chamber (Senate) at the national government level. The council installs water control boards (*waterschappen*) and delegated provincial (advisory) committees. It plays an important role in processes of restructuring the municipal government system, which usually means municipal amalgamation and scale enlargement.

The provincial executive is charged with the day-to-day management of provincial affairs. The executive is responsible for preparing and implementing provincial ordinances and the administration of provincial finance and property; and it governs, in a collegiate manner, the provincial administration. Externally, the executive is responsible for the supervision of water control boards, municipalities and intermunicipal joint provisions. It settles disputes among municipalities. The provincial executive appoints the chairpersons of provincial committees and acts as an independent administrative court of appeal for citizens. This is now changing under the impact of a reorganization of the Dutch judicial branch and EC regulations.

The most important provincial function is the supervision of municipalities. This supervision focuses on municipal finance and municipal regulations. The province may request the national government to suspend or annul municipal decisions which are considered to be in conflict with the law or the public interest. Municipalities are required by law to have a balanced budget. This principle is subject to supervision by the provinces.

The Queen's Commissioner has a twofold function which situates his or her role and functions somewhat outside the organizational 'pyramid' of the provincial administration. On the one hand, the commissioner represents central government. In this quality he or she, for example, visits municipalities at regular intervals and formally informs the Minister of Home Affairs of special findings and of municipal or provincial decisions he or she considers to be at odds with the law or the public interest. The commissioner plays an important role in the appointment of the mayor or burgomaster (*burgemeester*) for the municipalities within the province. The Queen's Commissioner is responsible for the maintenance of public order during crises and emergencies.

On the other hand, the office of the commissioner is an independent provincial institution. The emphasis in recent years has been on this side of the function. The commissioner chairs the provincial council and the provincial executive, in which he or she has a casting vote in case of a tie. He or she is the supreme supervisor of the administrative organization and an independent institution for appeal. The Queen's Commissioner represents the province in external affairs, like lobbying activities at the national level or promotional activities in foreign countries.

Provincial administration   Until recently, and although not legally prescribed, the traditional provincial tasks within all provinces have been rather uniformly organized into four divisions of the provincial administration. Activities in the area of physical and land-use

Table 4a *Number of persons employed by national, provincial and municipal government*

	National		Provincial		Municipal	
	(000s)	(%)	(000s)	(%)	(000s)	(%)
1975	136	39	15	4	195	57
1978	149	40	16	4	212	56
1980	155	39	17	4	223	57
1982	163	40	18	4	229	56
1984	162	39	19	5	233	56
1986	158	39	18	4	231	57

Source: CBS, *Statistical Yearbook of the Netherlands*, 1988

Table 4b *Personnel employed in public service, grouped by function, 1986*

	Provinces		Local government municipalities		Intermunicipal corporations	
	(000s)	(%)	(000s)	(%)	(000s)	(%)
Agriculture, fishing, forestry	—		0.1	0.04	—	
Mining, quarrying and manufacturing	—		21.2	8	49.9	70
Public utilities	3.3	18	16.7	7	5.0	7
Trade, hotels, cafés, restaurants and repair of consumer goods	—		0.2	0.08	0.0	0
Transport, storage and communication	0.4	3	12.5	5	0.2	0.3
Banking, insurance and other business service	—		3.8	2	0.3	0.4
Other services	14.5	79	197.3	78	16.2	22
Total	18.3	100	251.8	100	71.6	100

planning – generating regional development plans and supervising municipal land-use plans – are performed by the provincial planning authority (*provinciale planologische dienst*). The construction and maintenance of canals, highways and railways and the supervision of water control boards are taken care of by the provincial waterworks (*provinciale waterstaat*). The department of provincial works (*provinciale werken*) performs production activities at a provincial scale: for example, the production and supply of electricity. Finally, the provincial secretariat (*provinciale griffie*), which is headed by the provincial clerk as the formally highest civil servant, is responsible for the internal and external administrative tasks such as the supervision of municipalities and for administrative tasks in the context of, for example, municipal amalgamation and intermunicipal co-operation.

In recent years, this characteristic provincial organization has come under the pressure of several new tasks: environmental protection, regional socio-economic development, subsidizing hospitals and homes for the elderly, alcohol and drugs prevention, advising and planning secondary and special education and shared responsibility for organizing and reorganizing the Dutch local government system. These developments have recently led to a wave of provincial reorganization, so that the present administrative structure is less uniform than is described above. However, the different functions outlined still have to be performed by the provincial bureaucracy.

Table 4a provides an overview of numbers of people employed at the provincial level of government relative to the national and municipal levels. Table 4b provides some information on personnel employed for certain general employment categories within provinces, municipalities and intermunicipal joint provision. The data confirm that by far most of the people employed at the provincial level of government provide general administrative services. The tables also reflect that the actual production of governmental services at the meso level is conducted by intermunicipal joint provisions.

Provinces: political structure
Table 5 provides us with an overview of the number of positions within the different parts of the government structure of the different provinces: the council, the executive and the provincial civil service.

Elections for the provincial council are held every four years. The size of each council is legally prescribed and depends on the number of inhabitants of a province. Elections take place by proportional representation. Provincial elections are characterized by a relatively low voter turn-out. Table 6 presents the data for the years 1986 and 1987. These data are a bit skewed in that in the 1987 provincial elections also the majority position of the national government coalition in the First Chamber was at stake. This resulted in a somewhat higher turn-out than usual, but it still stayed well below the figures for the national and the municipal elections.

Table 5   *Size of provincial council, provincial executive and provincial administration*

	Political seats		Number of civil servants		
	Provincial Council	Provincial Executive	1970	1974	1982
Groningen	55	7	611	831	910
Friesland	55	7	462	545	823
Drenthe	51	6	355	389	505
Overijssel	63	6	638	685	873
Gelderland	71	7	608	735	964
Utrecht	59	6	448	556	934
North Holland	79	8	704	910	1,214
South Holland	83	8	1,205	1,652	1,887
Zeeland	47	6	295	334	451
North Brabant	79	7	552	767	960
Limburg	63	7	482	544	666
Total	705	75	6,560	7,548	9,086

Sources: VNG, 1975a, 1982

Table 6   *Voter turn-out as a percentage of the enfranchised*

Parliamentary elections		Provincial elections		Municipal elections	
Date	%	Date	%	Date	%
1982	81.0	1982	68.4	1982	68.3
1986	85.8	1987	66.3	1986	73.2
1989	80.3	1991	52.3	1990	62.3

Source: CBS (Central Bureau of Statistics)

Provincial politics usually does not get much attention in the mass media and is rather unknown among the general public. At elections there is a strong tendency to vote on the basis of national preferences and the stands of the (leaders of the) political parties in the national arena. Table 7 shows the results of two provincial elections and their consequences for the composition of the provincial executive.

The key event in the provincial political process is the coalition formation of the provincial executive after the elections. Until 1970, the composition of the executive simply reflected the distribution of seats in the provincial council. After 1970 it became the practice to try to reach a substantial policy programme agreement as a condition

Table 7 *Current party standing on meso representative and executive bodies, 1987 elections*

Seats in	Provincial council					Provincial executive				Queen's Commissioner
	PvdA	CDA	VVD	Other	Total	PvdA	CDA	VVD	Other	
Groningen	25	13	7	10	55	4	1	1	—	VVD
Friesland	22	19	6	8	55	4	3	—	—	VVD
Drenthe	24	13	9	5	51	4	1	1	—	PvdA
Overijssel	20	27	7	9	63	2	3	1	—	CDA
Flevoland	14	12	6	7	39	1	1	1	—	PvdA
Gelderland	24	27	11	13	75	3	3	1	—	VVD
Utrecht	16	19	11	13	59	2	2	2	—	CDA
North Holland	28	21	16	14	79	3	2	2	1	PvdA
South Holland	29	25	15	14	83	4	1	2	—	PvdA
Zeeland	14	15	8	10	47	2	2	2	—	CDA
North Brabant	24	36	10	9	79	3	4	1	—	CDA
Limburg	21	28	6	8	63	2	3	1	—	CDA
Total	261	255	112	120	748	34	26	15	1	12

VVD Volkspartij voor Vrijheid en Democratie (People's Party for Freedom and Democracy) – Conservatives
CDA Christen Democratisch Appel (Christian Democratic Appeal) – Christian Democrats
PvdA Partij van de Arbeid (Labour Party) – Social Democrats

for the co-operation of different political parties. Still, the outcomes of the coalition-building processes tend to reflect the consensual and accommodating character of Dutch politics in general and provincial politics in particular. Almost every provincial executive board has continued to be composed out of the three main Dutch political parties (PvdA, CDA and VVD).

Negotiators in the provincial government formation process usually strive for both policy programme agreement and a continued representation of the main political parties. The latter is seen as strategically useful for contacts with the national government agencies and Parliament in The Hague. As a consequence, the distribution of provincial executive seats tends to be rather stable, and very often does not reflect fluctuations in electoral support. Post-election reactions and adaptations are subtle and concentrate on the political weight of the portfolios for the different provincial executives and, for example, the number of seats and chairs in provincial committees. This so-called 'depoliticized politics' has also resulted in coalitions among the Social Democrats (PvdA) and the Conservatives (VVD), which thus far have proved to be impossible in national politics. Again, this illustrates the consensual nature of meso politics in the Netherlands.

Policy-making at the provincial level
The recent increase in the relative importance of, and attention to, substantive policy-making issues, as against the more procedural provincial orientation of the past, has so far not resulted in much political polarization. The provincial policy process is described as 'kind-hearted' and conflict-avoiding. The harmonious atmosphere is explained by the long tradition of monism instead of dualism in the relationship between the provincial council and the provincial executive, the lack of public interest in provincial politics, the emphasis on administrative tasks and the rather limited degree of discretion in provincial policy formation.

Within the provincial policy process the provincial executive, the civil servants and the political party specialists are the most important actors (Brasz and Haccou, 1982). As usual, political reality is somewhat different from what the formal representation of the provincial organization seems to suggest. The actual ranking in terms of power is: first, the provincial executive; second, the civil servants; and third, the provincial council. The provincial council formalizes and legitimizes the implementation of the provincial executive's policy. The council performs more or less a 'double-check' in provincial affairs; it supervises the provincial supervisors.

When, in addition to municipal supervision, provincial activities started to include more policy-making tasks, provincial councils started to make use of internal committees which consist of the policy specialists of the different political parties. Yet, in striving for more grip on the policy process, the provincial council – like any representative body – is hampered by constraints of time and information and by a lack of bureaucratic authority, which is in the hands of the provincial executive. Furthermore, provincial councils have been subject to a substantial fluctuation of membership. A strong display of specific interests is being observed. It is relatively easy for interest groups to have their representatives penetrate provincial councils. The workload is rather limited. In addition, the integrative forces of political parties and party-political discipline are less prevalent, since the lack of public interest results in a rather low-key role for political parties at the provincial level of government. Typically, provincial councils reflect an over-representation of national, and even more local, civil servants. Provincial council membership is a part-time job which is forbidden – not by law, but by the political parties themselves – to local, politically elected officials for fear of an accumulation of mandates. Thus the strange situation has emerged that local civil servants may 'fight against' their local political bosses by using a provincial political mandate.

The provincial executive takes the lead in provincial affairs. It governs in a collegiate manner. This amounts to a relatively strong concentration of experience, political support and bureaucratic authority within its confines. There are relatively few overt political conflicts among provincial executives. This might be partially explained by the common bureaucratic and technocratic, instead of party-political, background of many *gedeputeerden* (provincial executives). The provincial political culture of harmonious relation-ships and depoliticized politics does the rest. The provincial executive usually faces a hardly interested provincial electorate in combination with rather co-operative political parties.

The provincial civil service is generally considered to be relatively influential, especially in the non-secretariat sections. The provincial administration has shown a considerable growth in recent years as was shown in Table 5. The provincial bureaucracy has recently become subject to major reorganizations and budgetary cut-backs. Many of these reorganizations have striven for a more integrated organization, mainly by consolidating provincial secretariat sections and the executive units into one structure.

The Queen's Commissioner, finally, is studied even less than the other provincial branches. The Queen's Commissioner is independent of provincial organs in his or her role as representative of the Crown. In emergencies the commissioner is bestowed with far-reaching powers and his or her role as representative of the province has traditionally been ceremonial. Recently the Queen's Commissioner has become more and more involved in the policy process as initiator and co-ordinator, and as an active promoter of provincial interests. The commissioner has always played this latter role to a greater or lesser degree. Yet recently these international promotional and national lobbying activities on behalf of the province seem to have become more marked or are at least conducted much more publicly.

Provinces: meso functions and finances
The profile of the Dutch provinces as a form of meso government, is clearly dominated by their various intermediate tasks and functions: planning, conflict regulation, co-ordination, integration. We have already noted their supervisory role *vis-à-vis* water control boards and municipalities. In contrast, it is very difficult to produce an exhaustive but distinctive list of distributional meso-policy functions which are more or less predominantly executed by the provinces.

Traditionally, observers point to the hinging role which provinces play in many areas of government policy. Provinces play, for example, a rather pivotal role in the area of physical planning and public housing. They are the intermediate institution between the (macro) physical planning schemes and policies of the national government and the eventually legally binding municipal land-use plans. Provinces play a role in the transformation of national policies into local projects and of local spatial needs and preferences into national programmes. More generally, provinces fulfil important functions at the junction of the bottom-up aggregation, such as co-ordination and communication of local projects, proposals, demands, interests and information. A similar role is played in relation to the top-down flow of government authority, directions, policy proposals and financial resources. In many instances, this has resulted in assigning co-ordinative and planning tasks to provinces without granting real executive authority or additional administrative resources for effective implementation.

As far as substantial policy tasks are concerned, provinces traditionally play an important role in the area of public infrastructure and the provision of public utilities. Since the beginning of this century provinces have been involved in the area of (regional) traffic, transportation and roads and freeways. Provinces, together with water control boards, play an equally traditionally role in water management. More recently, provinces have started to play a somewhat more executive role in areas such as welfare and cultural affairs (protection of landscapes and historical sites). Environmental affairs, in particular in the areas of the cleaning up of polluted soil,

Table 8 *Current and capital expenditures of the provinces*

Functional division	1960 million guilders	1960 %	1974 million guilders	1974 %	1980 million guilders	1980 %	1985 million guilders	1985 %
General management	27.7	6.1	256.4	8.6	253	5.5	358	3.3
Public order	1.4	0.3	9.9	0.3	23	0.5	18	0.4
Traffic/transportation	160.3	35.4	905.6	30.5	1,804	39.0	2,059	19.1
Water control	160.3	35.4	905.6	30.5	109	2.3	111	1.0
Public health	20.2	4.5	181.7	6.1	392	8.5	631	5.9
Environmental affairs								
Education and culture	14.2	3.1	130.5	4.4	74	1.6	82	0.7
Recreation								
Economy/agriculture	25.4	5.6	479.1	16.1	744	16.1	591	5.5
Welfare	13.4	3.0	17.0	0.6	488	10.5	2,650	24.6
Housing/planning	4.1	0.9	61.3	2.1	114	2.5	350	3.2
General finance	25.9	5.7	22.5	0.8	622	13.5	3,909	36.3
Total	452.9	100	2,969.6	100	4,623	100	10,759	100

environmental regulation (granting of permits) and enforcement policies, have recently become rather crucial provincial tasks.

The relative importance of different provincial policy areas is represented by provincial expenditures in Table 8.

It is interesting to note that there are some more or less recent developments at the meso level which are not reflected in officially proclaimed government policy. The revision of the Provincial Government Act will mainly corroborate the traditional intermediary function of the province in contrast to the ideas current in the middle 1970s in favour of a more active and extensive role for the province. At the same time, however, there are several indications which point in the direction of a reinforcement of the role of the province at the meso-policy level of government. In the decentralization process, tasks, money and authority are often not transferred to the municipalities, but to the provinces. The area of urban renewal is one example. National government has transferred tasks and budgets to the larger municipalities. It has assigned the province the task of co-ordinating and funding activities of the smaller municipalities within their borders. Also, in the area of health care and care for the elderly, the provinces instead of the municipalities have been the preferred recipients for decentralized tasks. In the area of cultural affairs the national government has concluded several policy agreements (covenants) with several of the larger cities in the Netherlands by which the ministry transfers – under previously negotiated conditions – tasks, budgets and authority to those cities. In the more rural parts of the Netherlands the province acts as the contracting party for the ministry.

Sometimes national policy-makers are quite explicit in emphasizing that, due to their larger scale, provinces are in a better position than municipalities to act as a buffer and spread the consequences of national retrenchment policies among a large number of units within any policy area. More generally, national ministries seem to have a preference for the province over the municipality as the receiving agent in a decentralization process. The reason for this seems to vary from functional scale considerations to existing animosity between national ministries and municipal governments.

Whatever the reason, these types of developments in the different policy sectors might unintentionally result in a 'silent accumulation' of the tasks of the province at the meso level of government. At the same time, the official national government policy with respect to the provinces is merely to corroborate their traditional intermediary role and functions. It is still somewhat speculative and too early for a valid assessment of any such trend. This consideration should be kept in mind, however, when looking at Table 9. The table presents

Table 9 *Sources of provincial income*

Income category	1950	1955	1960	1965	1971	1976	1981	1986
General grants	24	26	26	28	25	28	31	16
Categorical grants	—	22	30	38	43	37	34	61
Share in national taxes	20	14	12	9	4	1	—	—
Provincial taxes	—	—	—	—	—	3	8	6
Other own means[1]	56	38	32	25	28	31	27	17
Total (relative %)	100	100	100	100	100	100	100	100
Total (in million guilders)	130	170	241	438	1,088	2,094	3,031	6,302

[1] Such as retributions, dividend, profits of provincial firms (utilities, etc.) and rent.
Source: CBS, *85 Year Statistics*, 1986

an overview of developments in the main sources of provincial income.

Table 9 represents a gradual process in which relatively fewer financial resources are allocated to provinces through the system of general revenue sharing. These are the general grants from the Provincial Fund, which is a centrally administered fund fed by a proportion of the nationally collected taxes. The Provincial Fund is set up by transferring 1 per cent of the national tax-yield. The money is divided among the provinces – essentially – by using fixed criteria:

● 42 per cent is divided in equal proportions;
● 35 per cent depends on the number of inhabitants of a province;
● 17 per cent is divided proportionally to the size of a province's land- and water-area;
● 6 per cent depends on the average length of canals and the general condition of the soil.

The allocation of general grants from the Provincial Fund has tended to be constant. Yet, the total budget doubled during the period. As a consequence, its share of total provincial revenues dropped from 31 per cent to 16 per cent.

The growth of the provincial budget is caused by the growth of specific grant allocation by national ministries. This allocation mechanism is commonly seen as a means by which national ministries tie subnational government to 'golden strings'. It is appropriate, however, also to interpret these grants as an expression of a, not necessarily always effective, form of joint policy-making which has been as beneficial for sub-national as for national government (Reitsma, 1983; Toonen, 1987).

The table also shows a typical characteristic of provincial finances in that a considerable, declining, but by Dutch standards relatively substantial, proportion of provincial income is generated by 'other own means'. This parameter reflects the traditional provincial role in public infrastructures and public utilities, such as water, gas and electricity production. In the past this has provided an important source of provincial income. Nowadays this source of provincial income is gradually being eliminated by the privatization policies of the national government with respect to provincial electricity companies and other provincially owned public utilities.

The main reason which accounts for the relative decline of general grants and other financial means is the increase of total provincial income. This increase is produced by the increase of the income from categorical or specific grants allocated to provinces for specific purposes by the various national ministries. It is precisely this increase in categorical grants which reflects the modest but nevertheless noticeable process of 'silent accumulation' of tasks at the historical meso – the province. It is all the more noticeable since it is a recent process and one which is not induced by any proclaimed national nor any official provincial policy to increase functions at this meso level of government. An explicit proposal to extend the role of the provinces in conducting substantial public policies would most probably be defeated by municipal resistance. A gradual process in which national ministries offload their former policy tasks to provinces instead of municipalities might do the job of extending the policy role of provinces at the meso. It is clear, however, that the recently renewed municipal interest in abolishing 'this superficial and unimportant layer of government' actually has to be explained by the growing importance of provinces in the 1980s. Locals can no longer afford to ignore the province, as they used to. Many would therefore prefer to get rid of it.

Reshuffling the meso?

The province is, as stated before, often presented as a relatively unimportant, 'stuffy' and otiose layer of government in the Netherlands. It is criticized for its procedural, formalistic and conflict-avoiding atittude and the lack of political courage to engage in the pressing administrative issues of these times, such as the current regional agglomeration problems. To this assessment is occasionally added the view that provinces may just as well be abolished. Despite such predictions it is more likely that the provinces are here to stay for the foreseeable future. They are under pressure, however, to adapt to the changing circumstances which the Dutch administrative system as a whole faces.

Intermediary functions
The condescending attitude with respect to the provinces is prompted by the restricted quantitative role which provinces play in overall administrative affairs. Yet, one should not overlook the qualitative, strategic role which provinces play at the meso level of the governmental system.

Recently, the State Secretary of the Ministry of Home Affairs reassured the provinces by asserting that they were valuable institutions. But she criticized them, among other things, for not implementing forcefully enough national government policy and guidelines with respect to the execution of the law on municipal joint provisions. As stated before, this law requires the 'rationalization' of intermunicipal co-operation by grouping and integrating municipal joint provisions into the different regional co-operation areas. Since it restricts local government discretion in choosing partners for co-operation, this requirement is not very popular among municipalities. Provinces should be criticized, according to the state secretary, since they had not taken the implementation of this central government directive in hand strongly enough (de Graaff-Nauta, 1990: 11).

The state secretary thus pointed out unintentionally a rather crucial function of provinces in the overall Dutch administrative system. Her criticism actually illustrates that the provinces act, and have acted in the past, as a buffer and broker in the relationship among different layers of government. Municipalities often complain about the way supervision at the provincial level is being exercised. Municipalities, however, thus far wisely prefer provincial supervision to direct central government supervision (VNG, 1982).

Under present conditions, supervisory structures in the different policy areas reflect the general structure of the decentralized unitary state, in which central–local relationships are largely indirect in nature and run through the province as an intermediary institution. This is reflected in empirical findings. By the beginning of the 1980s a total of 454 statutorily prescribed supervision relationships existed among the different layers of government. Out of these, 245 referred to national–provincial relationships, 197 to provincial–municipal relationships and only 12 to direct central–local relationship (BiZa, 1982). These indirect central–local relationships may at times be experienced by the participants as being rather cumbersome. But from a viewpoint of flexibility, adaptability and municipal autonomy, it seems preferable to a system of direct central supervision.

The intermediate role of the province may sometimes slow down the decision-making process, but at the same time it offers the opportunity to break through deadlocks and some typical central–local behaviour patterns. As an alternative to direct intervention, the intermediate role of provinces creates some bargaining arenas which help to 'soften' central control and 'relax' local resistance. In a plural system like the Netherlands, which is in need of consensual and joint policy-making, this is not a minor benefit.

It is a recognized role of provinces that – over and against prefectorial deconcentrated services – they have the advantage that the representative provincial structure provides an open 'democratic window' for the public exposure of the intermediate, reticulist and supervisory roles performed by institutions at the meso. This offers external legitimation of the governing sytem as a whole as well as reinforcing the credibility of the intermediate or broker activities performed at the meso among actors involved. At the same time, provincial intergovernmental 'diplomacy' is served and nourished by the absence of a highly politicized environment and associated publicity.

Supervision

The classical conception of provincial supervision within the overall structure of the Dutch decentralized unitary state was that of creating a veto position or blocking power *vis-à-vis* individual municipalities on behalf of the other municipalities within the province (Visser 1986: 112; Toonen, 1990b). Thus, provincial supervision was intended to serve the purpose of 'bottom-up' consensus or 'unity' building and conflict regulation among different municipalities as well as their component parts. From this perspective provincial supervision serves decentralist purposes. Local, intermunicipal and regional conflicts will where possible be contained within the confines of the provincial domain. Seen from this perspective, provincial supervision disaggregates and diffuses conflict and subdues the potentially 'upward-pushing' centralistic tendencies of regional competition and conflict. In this way provinces have served to protect and secure municipalities against the ever-present threat of the 'nationalization' of local decision-making.

Once established, supervisory authorities by definition achieve a degree of relative autonomy and discretion in the exercise of their supervision powers. They will also become the subject of others, such as national government agencies, which will try to use the powers of, in this case, provincial supervisors for their own particular ends and for purposes of central state control. In this context it is predictable that, both historically and regionally, a variety of supervisory practices, styles and approaches will develop.

Research reveals that provincial supervision strongly varies across different provinces. The style ranges from a rather rigid, hierarchical and authoritative 'tutelage' approach to an active counselling role in which provinces use their supervision authority to co-ordinate and assist (smaller) municipalities by bringing them together and stimulating co-operation. Provinces provide municipalities with expertise and experience which they would not have had on their own. The Council of Municipal Finance, for instance, attributes the generally healthy financial position of Dutch municipalities to the well-developed routine of provincial budgetary supervision (RGF, 1989). Not only the control, but also the financial expertise function plays a role in this respect.

Neither theoretically nor empirically is there any reason to interpret provincial supervision merely as a vehicle for hierarchical co-ordination and control. Overall, the strategic contribution of the intermediate role of Dutch provinces to creating a rather strong sub-national, municipal government system should not be underestimated. This is the case even if this role 'in the heat of the everyday encounter' is not always operationally acknowledged by municipalities, nor by provinces themselves. Strategically speaking and seen from the viewpoint of local autonomy, it would be wise for Dutch municipalities to think twice before they decide to support any proposal which would eliminate the province as a form of intermediate government between national ministries and municipal governments. Frustration over the formalistic way in which many provinces in the past have exercised supervisory powers, however, seems to blind many local officials to this basic 'constitutional' consideration.

Scale and the rise of the European meso
At the moment, the twelve provinces seem to be both too large and too small in relation to the roughly forty nationally distinguished socio-economic regions and the three to four Dutch 'Euroregions'. Thus, some functional 'gaps' exist at the meso, which may become the future provincial field of activity. Provinces can play a pivotal role in adapting the administrative system to changing functional-scale requirements. At the beginning of the 1990s, however, the urban agglomerations were the more active and entrepreneurial institutions at the Dutch meso. They are supported and encouraged by current developments in the national government spatial policy and physical planning.

The current national government policy is characterized by a spatial targeting approach, identifying a dozen regional urban centres, which will act in the future as the 'junctions' or 'nodal points' in European-oriented regional-economic, spatial, infrastructural and technological development policies. In other words, current national government policy more or less explicitly identifies 10 to 15 urban centres in the Netherlands as the entities at the meso level of government which are designated to link Dutch local and regional governments to international and in particular European developments.

The 'Europeanization' of Dutch governmental affairs thus induces the larger Dutch central cities to claim a more dominant position at the current local Dutch meso level: the urban agglomeration, which is situated on the scale between municipalities and provinces. Reform policy so far has mainly aimed at strengthening metropolitan government in the urban agglomerations around the bigger cities – notably Amsterdam, Rotterdam and The Hague – by introducing 're-gional councils' in those areas. In 1992, seven years after the abolition of the Rijnmond Authority, the municipalities in that region pro-posed to establish a 'province-free' regional council and administra-tively to split up the city of Rotterdam into smaller municipalities. This Europeanization changes definitions and introduces different considerations to the debate on what the local Dutch meso in an international perspective should contain. In the context of the cur-rent local meso in the Netherlands, the central city is perceived as the nucleus of the urban regional hierarchy. The interdependencies are defined in terms of a conglomerate of distinct municipalities which are bound together by a mutual dependence due to the fact that the urban region is characterized by a spatial differentiation and special-ization in terms of work, recreation and domestic life.

From an international perspective, the role and position of a central city will be defined differently. Dente (1990: 65) speaks of the 'capital city'. In this perspective the urban centre and problems and developments at the meso will be defined in terms of relationships which relate the urban city – and implicitly the surrounding regions – to a European, or for some cities even a global, network of co-operation and competition in a specialized area (as, for example, European or global financial, cultural, stock exchange, logistical or transportational centres). Whereas the first definition relates de-velopments at the meso to links of, say, Rotterdam to Capelle a/d Ijssel as one of the main Rotterdam suburbs, the second definition links Rotterdam, as the largest seaport in the world, to cities like Tokyo, New York, Seattle and Hamburg.

Not only the relevant linkages, but also the relevant mesos within the national context, are different according to which definition is adopted. If discussion is confined to, say, the private or social housing market of Rotterdam, it suffices to define the immediate surroundings as the relevant area. But as soon as one focuses on the 'capital city' function of Rotterdam in the area of international transport, then suddenly the relevant meso extends itself at least with linkages and interdependencies to, say, the Amsterdam area, if not the Antwerp region in Belgium and the Ruhr area in Germany. In any specific region, these different definitions of the relevant meso – differences which might not always be stated and of which the players in the field might even not always be aware – might cause tensions due to the drastically different outlook each definition offers of developments and issues at the meso level.

If the bigger cities define themselves in terms of their position within Europe rather than their position within the regional urban hierarchy, conflicts between such cities and the urban-region-oriented suburbs on their periphery are unavoidable. The definition of any given city as an 'urban regional centre', versus a justified or unjustified definition as a European 'capital city' in some functional area, is bound to create tensions even within the ranks of that city itself. All of this contributes to the dynamics of the current developments at the Dutch meso level.

An economically driven political focus on the urban agglomeration will create competition among the different urban centres within the country. Also, it will eventually make the government pay attention to the role and position of the non-urbanized rural areas of the Netherlands. The various urban agglomerations are distributed rather unevenly over the Dutch territory, creating different disparities and redistributional issues in different regions and provinces. The first signs of a political juxtaposition of urban affluence and development and rural poverty and decline may already be observed.

There is little doubt that a definition of the meso in European terms gains salience and will gradually impose itself on the Dutch administrative and intergovernmental system. In terms of scale, the historical meso – the province – is in the Netherlands much closer to any international or European meso than the current local Dutch 'urban agglomeration meso'. The only way in which Dutch municipalities can cast themselves in the European drama, according to this view, is, therefore, to eliminate or bypass the historical meso: the province.

Ironically, the activated urban agglomerations and their struggle for economic development might trigger a process in which the province might be required to become activated in its traditional capacity of an intermediate and balancing institution. In urban–rural conflicts provinces could become the balancing powers. Provinces might be well advised to leave the economic dimension of the

'Europeanization process' in the Netherlands predominantly to the urban centres. Instead, by capturing the redistributional, socio-economic, cultural and conflict-management and sustainability dimensions of the same process there is a chance that the province might finally become publicly and administratively acceptable as the main local meso. This will primarily require, however, that provinces succeed in developing institutional co-operative arrangements that transcend their current territorial boundaries. The emerging European meso within the Netherlands is in need of a flexible institutional expression and potential for flexible regionalization. In several cases this will require cross-national co-operation on the European continent, with Germany and Belgium, as well as across the North Sea, with the Scandinavian countries and Britain.

Conclusion

The European meso will unavoidably become a part of the local definition of the meso in the Netherlands. However, continued searches, struggles and conflict due to different definitions of the relevant mesos in the Dutch context cannot be averted. This is not to say that this is something inherently bad. On the contrary: it is a condition for progress. But it means, for example, that the traditional, more procedural and introvert historical meso with its 'lawyers' and 'technicians' – the province – has to face up to the challenge of the modern, more aggressive and extrovert metropolitan area governments and their 'public managers'. At the beginning of the 1990s, the long-standing struggle for the Dutch meso has entered another round. At stake is whether the province will manage, under the current conditions, to transform itself – to use Bagehot's famous phrase – from a dignified into an efficient part of the Constitution.

Notes

The author would like to thank Frank Hendriks and Nikol Hopman, graduate students of the joint Rotterdam/Leiden Programme in Public Administration, who have assisted in various stages of this project, and Jim Sharpe for his editorial help and advice.

1 It is thus hardly a coincidence that one of the more all-embracing monographs on the Dutch provinces, outside the domain of public law, has so far been published by foreigners: Hesse, 1990.

2 In the following ways: (a) repressive supervision – the Crown (national government) has the power to suspend or annul provincial measures if they are at odds with the law or the general interest; (b) preventive supervision – some decisions (for example, tax regulations) are subject to the Crown's approval; (c) the supervision of the Queen's Commissioner – he or she informs the provincial authorities and the

Minister of Home Affairs about issues he or she considers to be at odds with the law or the public interest.

Select further reading

Boone, J. H. (1972) 'De provincie', in Instituut voor Bestuurswetenschappen (IBW) (ed.), *Onderzoek naar de bestuurlijke organisatie*, Part 1: *Literatuurrapport*. Rijswijk.

Brasz, H. A. and Haccou, H. A. (1982) 'Politieke ruimte aan de provinciale top', *Bestuurswetenschappen*, 6, special issue, Provincies in een nieuwe rol.

Hesse, J. J. and Kleinfeld, R. R. (1990) *Die Provinzen im Politischen System der Niederlande*. Opladen.

Jagt, A. van der (ed.) (1983) 'Regionalisatie: van problematiek tot bestuurlijke vormgeving', *Bestuur in beweging*, 9.

Monchy, S. J. R. de (1976) *Handboek voor het Nederlands provincierecht*, 2nd edn, Zwolle.

Rieken, Baayens (ed.) (1984) *De provincie als bestuurlijk midden: evenwicht tussen rijk, provincie en gemeente*. Deventer.

Toonen, Th. A. J. (1987) *Denken over binnenlands bestuur: theorieën van de gedecentraliseerde eenheidsstaat bestuurskundig beschouwd*. The Hague.

Vereniging van Nederlandse Gemeenten (VNG) (1982) *Van verre vriend naar goede burr: een studie naar de veranderende positie van de provincie*, by C. H. Marle and E. Gijsen. The Hague.

Vereniging van Nederlandse Gemeenten (1984) 'Gemeenten: provincies en de nieuwe grondwet', *Bestuurswetenschappen*, 5.

Visser, B. L. W. (1986) *Toezicht in bestuurlijke rechtsverhoudingen*. Deventer.

Vonhoff, H. J. L. (1988) *De positie en de rol van de provincie*. The Hague.

References

BiZa (Ministerie van Binnenlandse Zaken) (1982) *Inventarisatie bestuursinstrumenten*. The Hague.

Blokland, J. (1987) 'Toekomst voor de provincie', *Ons Burgerschap*, special issue, Provinciale staten.

Boone, J. H. (1972) 'De provincie', in Instituut voor Bestuurswetenschappen (IBW) (ed.), *Onderzoek naar de bestuurlijke organisatie*, Part 1: *Literatuurrapport*. Rijswijk.

Brasz, H. A. and Haccou, H. A. (1982) 'Politieke ruimte aan de provinciale top', *Bestuurswetenschappen*, 6, special issue, Provincies in een nieuwe rol.

Breunese, J. N. (1982) 'Twee Nederlandse eeuwen provincie', *Bestuur: Maandblad voor Overheidskunde*, 7.

Commissie Montijn (1989) *Grote steden, grote kansen: rapport externe commissie grote steden beleid*. The Hague.

Daalder, H. and Irwin, G. A. (1989) *West European Politics*, 1, special issue, Politics in the Netherlands: how much change?

Dente, B. (1990) 'Metropolitan governance reconsidered, or how to avoid errors of the third type', *Governance: An International Journal of Policy and Administration*, 3 (1), January.

Geersing, J. (1987) 'Provinciale staten: het verleden', *Ons Burgerschap*, special issue, Provinciale staten.

Graaff Nauta, D. IJ. W. de (1990) 'Zal de provincie volwaardig bestuur blijven?' *Bestuurswetenschappen*, special issue, Provincie.

Hesse, J. J. (ed.) (1990) *Local Government and Urban Affairs in International Perspective*. Baden-Baden.

Hesse, J. J. and Kleinfeld, R. R. (1990) *Die Provinzen im politischen System der Niederlande*. Opladen.

Huisman, H. A. (1972) *De toekomst van de provincie: derde rapport in opdracht van het ministrie van BiZa*. The Hague.

Instituut voor Toegepaste Sociologie Nijmegen, vakgroep Planning en Beleid en vakgroep Planologie RU (1981) *Provinciale beleidsplanning, onderzoek naar de wenselijkheid en mogelijkheden*. Nijmegen/Utrecht.

Jagt, A. van der (ed.) (1983) 'Regionalisatie: van problematiek tot bestuurlijke vormgeving', *Bestuur in beweging*, 9.

Meer, J. van der (1989) *Wat beweegt de stad? een studie naar de stedelijke dynamiek in de Rotterdamse agglomeratie*. Rotterdam.

Micklinghoff, F. H. (1982) *Provinciale staten, geschiedenis bevoegdheden en organisatie*. The Hague.

Ministerie van VROM (1988) *Vierde nota over de ruimtelijke ordening, deel a: beleidsvoornemen op weg naar 2015*. The Hague.

Monchy, S. J. R. de (1976) *Handboek voor het Nederlands provincierecht*, 2nd edn. Zwolle.

Oomen, J. (1974) 'Provincie en provinciale staten', *Intermediair*, 13.

Raad voor de Gemeentefinancien (RGF) (1989) *Overzicht van de specifieke uitkeringen die voor gemeenten en provincies van belang zijn*. The Hague.

Raad voor het Binnenlands Bestuur (RBB) (1989a) *Tweede advies over plaats en functies van provincies*. The Hague.

Raad voor het Binnenlands Bestuur (1989b) *Advies over bestuur in grootstedelijke gebieden*. The Hague.

Reitsma, K. (1983) *Specifieke uitkeringen aan lagere overheden: gevolgen voor de grond-, water- en wegenbouw*. Amsterdam.

Rieken, Baayens (ed.) (1984) *De provincie als bestuurlijk midden: evenwicht tussen rijk, provincie en gemeente*. Deventer.

Ruiter, D. W. P. (ed.) (1982) 'Vertikaal machtsevenwicht in het binnenlands bestuur', *Bestuur in beweging*, 3.

Staatsen (1980) 'Bij 13 provincies horen 35 gewesten', *Binnenlands bestuur*, 5.

Toonen, Th. A. J. (1987) *Denken over binnenlands bestuur, theorieën van de gedecentraliseerde eenheidsstaat bestuurskundig beschouwd*. The Hague.

Toonen, Th. A. J. (1989) 'Bestuurlijke reorganisatie en intergemeentelijke samenwerking', in W. Derksen and A. F. A. Korsten (eds), *Lokaal bestuur in Nederland, inleiding in de gemeentekunde*, 2nd edn. Alphen a/d Rijn.

Toonen, Th. A. J. (1990a) 'Change in continuity: local government and urban affairs in the Netherlands', in J. J. Hesse (ed.), *Local Government and Urban Affairs in International Perspective*. Baden-Baden.

Toonen, Th. A. J. (1990b) 'The unitary state as a system of co-governance: the case of the Netherlands', *Public Administration*, 61 (3): 281–96.

Vereniging van Nederlandse Gemeenten (VNG) (1975a) *De staten gehoord*. The Hague.

Vereniging van Nederlandse Gemeenten (1975b) *Sterke gemeenten in nieuwe provincies*. The Hague.

Vereniging van Nederlandse Gemeenten (1979) *Gewesten onderweg, inventarisatie en analyse van feiten en meningen* (in opdracht van de Raad voor de Territoriale decentralisatie). The Hague.

Vereniging van Nederlandse Gemeenten (1982) *Van verre vriend naar goede buur, een studie naar de veranderende positie van de provincie*, by C. H. Marle and E. Gijsen. The Hague.

Vereniging van Nederlandse Gemeenten (1984) 'Gemeenten, provinces en de nieuwe grondwet', *Bestuurswetenschappen*, 5.

Vereniging van Nederlandse Gemeenten (1986) *De veranderende provincie: een momentopname*. The Hague.

Visser, B. L. W. (1986) *Toezicht in bestuurlijke rechtsverhoudingen*. Deventer.

Vonhoff, H. J. L. (1988) *De positie en de rol van de provincie*. The Hague.

6

Intermediate-Level Reforms and the Development of the Norwegian Welfare State

Tore Hansen

In 1987 Norwegian municipalities celebrated the 150th anniversary of the legislation establishing the modern system of Norwegian local government. Although the basic structure laid down in the 1837 legislation by and large has remained unchanged during these 150 years, primary as well as county municipalities have undergone substantial changes over this period. In the first place, the level of activity has increased far beyond what was even thinkable 150 years ago. In the second place, the local government units themselves have changed, first by dividing the original primary municipalities into smaller units and later on by a process of amalgamation into larger units. The process of changes and reforms has not, however, been a 'linear' and continuous one. Apart from certain more or less 'autonomous' changes during the first 100 years of local 'self-government', most changes and reforms have taken place during the past 40 years, as a consequence – and manifestation – of the development of the Norwegian welfare state. In fact, if we just consider the meso level of government, the reform period is even briefer; here the first major reform was introduced in 1964 when the urban municipalities were incorporated as members of the county municipalities, along with a change of the representative system of the county council.

By and large, one may distinguish between two major stages in the process of local government reforms in Norway. During the first stage, most attention was paid to changes in the primary municipalities – first by amalgamating them into larger units (implying a reduction in their numbers from 744 to 454) and secondly by providing them with several new tasks and responsibilities. The second stage – and for our purpose the most interesting one – concerns the reforms at the county level. In what follows I will discuss the background and the general objectives of the reforms. I then give an outline of the major steps in this reform process, not going into detail about the particular reforms. In the final part of the chapter some consequences of these reforms are considered.

Reform principles

The meso level of government in Norway would be equivalent to counties or county municipalities. Although there have been some attempts to establish other regional units or levels of government – for instance, in connection with physical and economic planning – most such attempts have not succeeded, and the tasks to be performed by such units have normally been given to the counties or county municipalities.

In certain respects the county has both remained the most stable level of local government and at the same time undergone the most fundamental changes during recent years. It has remained stable in the sense that the number of counties and the geographical areas of the individual counties have been only marginally changed since 1837. In fact, this applies as well to one of the basic elements in the administrative set-up of the counties, namely the county prefect. In contrast to this high degree of stability as regards the structure, the counties have during recent years experienced reforms and changes which probably are of far greater magnitude and significance than the reforms of the primary municipalities.

Norwegian local government is made up of a two-tier system, with 19 county municipalities and about 450 primary municipalities. Currently, the county and primary municipalities share the same status as fairly autonomous political units, performing separate as well as complementary functions. In this sense, both governmental levels act independently of each other, with no formal subordinate status of either unit. This has not, however, always been the case; it is only over the past fifteen years that the current system and the current relationships between the two levels of government have been established. Before considering this process of reforms, it is important to make a distinction between a county as a regional agency of central government and a county as a local government unit proper, with its own elected bodies, its own taxes and budget and a certain amount of local autonomy. In practice, these two major functions of the counties have been rather blurred, not least because the two 'branches' of the county used to share the same administrative bodies – with the prefect as the head of the administration of both 'branches'. The prefect even performed a more genuine political role as a member and chairperson of the executive committee of the county municipality.

The reforms introduced at the county level since 1964 may to a considerable extent be regarded as a process aiming at a more clear-cut separation of the functions performed by the counties as a regional state administration and the counties as autonomous local governments. At the same time, the reforms may be considered as attempts to get a better and more 'correct' accommodation of tasks, functions and financial burdens between central government, counties and the primary municipalities. In this sense the reforms have been developed in the point of intersection between the conflicting aims of preserving as much local autonomy as possible in the running of services and the need to secure the financial basis as well as conforming to national standards in the provision of local services. Although not being pure collective services in technical terms, local services are collective in the sense that people are supposed to have equal – as well as easy – access to such services wherever they live in the country. In this respect, the meso-level reforms may be viewed as a process aiming at striking a balance between three partly conflicting aims: first, to increase local autonomy in deciding on the types, levels and standards of service provision; second, to secure a basic level of national equality in the access to and consumption of public services; and third, to internalize externalities and secure fiscal equivalence in service provision.

It is, however, difficult to trace any clear-cut single principle or any general agreed-upon bundle of principles for the reform processes that have taken place at the regional or meso level in Norway during the past forty years. The reform process may – at least to an external observer – look like a rather random sequence of events not framed within a more comprehensive structure of objectives or intentions as to what the final arrangements may look like, or rather the ultimate purposes to be served by the individual reforms. In this sense, short-term pragmatic considerations, rather than long-term principal objectives, have guided the development of Norwegian local government reforms. This applies in particular to the reforms that have taken place at the meso level of government – despite the fact that these reforms generally implied far more fundamental changes as regards organizational structure and functions than the reforms of primary municipalities.

A first attempt to formulate some general objectives for the meso – or county – development was made at the beginning of the 1950s by a government committee on municipal amalgamations and annexations, which made some general comments on the appropriate size and structure of the county communes. The approach of the committee was functional, in the sense that it was concerned with the question of what the minimum population threshold would be in order to be able to maintain a certain range and level of service provision (*Innstilling II*, 1952). In fact, the committee was quite explicit in writing off the county municipalities as a 'breeeding place' for local democracy (Kjellberg and Mydske, 1987). Also the next government committee, which was mandated the task to review, and eventually revise, the geographical jurisdictions between counties, used mainly economic/functional arguments, based on such concepts as population thresholds, optimal size and scale economies, in justifying changes in the jurisdictional structure. Actually, the committee did not propose any changes in the current structure, arguing that larger geographical units would hamper efficient political/democratic control of service provision in the counties (*Innstilling*, 1965; Kjellberg and Mydske, 1987).

The most comprehensive effort to formulate a general framework and to draw up a set of basic principles for Norwegian local government reforms was made in the mid-1970s by a government committee on local government reform, a committee which later on was made into a permanent advisory board on local government affairs and reforms. In the committee's major report on 'objectives and guidelines' of local government reforms (NOU, 1974: 53), three basic goals of this process were formulated:

(a) decentralization;
(b) democratization;
(c) efficient administration.

Thus, the pure functional arguments forwarded by the two previous committees became of marginal importance to this new committee. As far as the counties were concerned, the report's major concern was with the political consolidation of the county municipalities.

This quite fundamental change of focus or concern may be attributable to two major developments which had been (and were) taking place during the time that had elapsed since the last committee issued its report on the structure of the counties in 1965. First – as I will return to later – urban districts became a part of the county communes from 1965, a change which also affected the system of representation at the county level. Secondly, the county municipalities had been given responsibility for the provision of what became their most important services at the end of the 1960s and the beginning of the 1970s, namely hospitals and general secondary education. In this respect, the committee's main concern was almost a residual one: of making the necessary adjustments in the political, administrative and not least financial structure of the counties according to the functional reforms that already had been taking place.

However, there is also a third factor that needs to be taken into account in order to understand this change of focus in the direction of democratic/decentralist values, namely the spread and growth of populist values (in particular left-wing populism) following in the wake of the Norwegian debate on EC membership. In fact, regionalism – meaning the need to develop new economic policies for backward areas in the coastal periphery of western and northern Norway – became a major argument for not entering the EC. Furthermore, the sense of an increasingly strong centralist bureaucratic 'iron cage', as a consequence of the general welfare state developments that had been taking place up to the time of the EC decision in 1972, and which was expected to grow even more as a consequence of EC membership, contributed to strengthen the pressures for increased local autonomy and popular participation in public decision-making. Altogether, the general political climate was in favour of this shift of focus from narrow economic/administrative considerations   towards   much   more   stress   on   decentralist/ participatory values.

If we look at the arguments put forward by the committee, they were particularly concerned with the need – as they defined it – to relieve the central government from several administrative burdens, and in particular tasks which could be performed more efficiently (however measured) by local authorities. Thus, the objective to decentralize was not guided by any clear theory about optimal distribution of functions between various governmental levels. Neither was it rooted in some version of democratic theory. The objective to decentralize was rather justified on the basis of what the committee regarded as increasing political and administrative 'overload' at the centre, although not fully subscribing to the kind of 'overload' arguments and their normative implications put forward by Rose and Peters (1978). Rather, from the committee's perspective decentralization might as well be regarded as an instrument for strengthening the capacity of planning and general policy-making at central level, and it did not necessarily reflect any genuine interest in giving local authorities more decision-making power. However, the committee also underlined that decentralization should not merely imply a transfer of administrative functions to local state agencies. In order to accomplish more efficient decisions – for example, in relation to popular needs and demands – decentralization should be accompanied by delegation of authority. In this respect, decentralization was regarded as a prerequisite for pursuing the second major objective, namely democratization.

Apart from a more generally expressed aim of improving the contact between ordinary citizens and public authorities, the objective of democratization was operationalized as one of strengthening the powers and autonomy of local elected bodies – in relation both to central government authorities and to administrative officials at local level. The committee was particularly concerned with the political organization at the regional level – that is, the county municipalities – and suggested a list of various measures in order to strengthen the political as well as the administrative leadership at this level. In a political and administrative sense, the counties were the least modernized political institutions, representing a mixture of administrative principles deriving from the period of the absolutist monarch (the prefectorial system) and political representative principles deriving from an early stage of Norwegian democratic development (the system of indirect elections and/or delegates to the county councils from individual municipalities). At the time the committee published its report on 'principles and objectives of local government reform', a major reform concerning the political organization of the county municipalities was already proposed – and in the process of being implemented – namely direct proportional elections to the county councils (NOU, 1972: 13). This reform was regarded as a fundamental step in the process of strengthening the autonomy of the county municipalities, as well as a basis for further political and administrative reforms at this governmental level. As I will return to· describe, direct proportional elections were not least regarded as a prerequisite for the creation of an independent political identity of the county, as a political unit in its own right.

One interesting aspect of the discussions in the report on principles of reforms is that taxation, or the right to direct taxation, is treated under the heading of 'democratization'. In a way the committee rephrased the old principle of 'no taxation without representation' into one in which any changes in the representation system were made dependent on taxation reforms, or rather: 'no representation without taxation'. This way of linking the system of representation with the tax system has of course to do with the way in which the old system worked, and stresses implicitly probably the most fundamental principle of the local government reforms advocated by the committee, namely that of autonomy in relation both to central authorities and not least to primary municipalities. The county municipalities should no longer function as a 'common municipality' or as a forum for intermunicipal co-operation, composed of delegates from the municipalities within the county jurisdiction. Nor did the committee want to give the counties the status of being a super-municipality in relation to primary municipalities. The objective was to make the counties autonomous political units in their own right – accountable only to the individual citizens or voters. From this perspective, direct elections were not sufficient as a means to make the county councils accountable to the citizens. Only by establishing a direct link between the right to vote and the burdens of taxation (which means mainly taxes on personal income), would the objective of making the county councils accountable to the citizens be accomplished.

A part of this 'package of principles' was the objective of separating the municipal part of the county administration from the state or prefectorial part of it, and also of developing the municipal administration into a fairly powerful instrument for the elected members of the county councils. In a sense this may seem to contradict the objectives of making the administrative system more efficient, and less bureaucratic. But again, the objective of administrative efficiency should be seen in the context of becoming independent of the rather rigid system of controls and decision-making procedures which had been the trademark of the prefectorial system. An autonomous administration would imply a weakening of yet another controlling link to the central authorities.

Thus, behind the headlines, principles and even 'slogans' used by this committee we may discern two, or three, distinct developments, all leading in the same direction for the county municipalities, namely that of increased autonomy. First, by changing the election and tax system, the counties would become autonomous in relation to the primary municipalities. Secondly, by changing the administrative system, the county municipalities achieved much more autonomy in relation to the state authorities. And finally, by the suggested tax reform, the county municipalities established direct linkages to the citizens. This process of increasing the autonomy will be returned to later in the chapter. Let me now consider the major reforms, as well as their outcomes, in more detail.

Major reforms

It may be useful to make a distinction between four types of reforms of the county municipalities:

(a) territorial;
(b) functional;
(c) representative;
(d) financial.

In this section I will give a fairly brief account – and assessment – of such reforms in Norway. Although the reforms may be categorized as suggested above, I have found it more useful to present and discuss the reforms in chronological order rather than to organize my discussion according to the suggested categorization. The reason for doing this is that the various types of reforms are closely linked to each other, as I hope will become evident in the discussion that follows. Thus, rather than treating the individual reforms as independent discrete events, I regard the whole post-war development of the county municipalities as a dynamic process, where each step in this process has served as a precondition for further steps.

As indicated previously, the geographical areas of the counties have by and large remained unaltered since the introduction of the Municipal Act in 1837. There is, however, one exception to this. Until 1964 only rural municipalities were members of the county communes, and the members of the county council were the mayors of these municipalities. Consequently, the county council functioned as an assembly of delegates from the rural districts. In 1964 this system was changed by making urban municipalities a part of the county council. At the same time the representative system was changed by the introduction of indirect elections where any member of the council of a primary municipality was made eligible for office on the county council. Furthermore, the arrangement that the prefect should be a member and chairperson of the executive committee of the county council was abolished. In this sense the county council and its executive committee became more politicized. But also in other respects the county council became more politicized. The previous representative system where only the mayors of the primary municipalities were represented on the county council often had the consequence that the council was composed of members from only one political party – making these councils highly unrepresentative in relation to the distribution of votes, and seats in the municipal councils, among the various political parties. The new system of indirect election was, of course, no guarantee of a more representative composition of the county councils, but in practice they became less unrepresentative than they had previously been.

The county councils became more politicized also in another sense of the term. The inclusion of urban municipalities provided the county council with more financial resources, via the system of the so-called repartition tax, while the major tasks remained the same. One may distinguish between three such major functions (Fevolden, 1979). In the first place the county municipalities were normally responsible for providing certain services which the individual primary municipalities were not able to provide – either for financial reasons or because of limited possibilities to internalize the benefits of this service provision. This would include services like hospitals, certain types of secondary schools and roads. Before the last reforms, and seen in relation to the other major tasks, these services were of limited importance. Secondly, the county councils were provided with the task of deciding on the distribution among the primary municipalities of the so-called tax equalization grants. This is, or was, a central government grant, representing no fiscal burdens to the county communes. In this respect, the county council functioned more as an arena for negotiations between the individual primary municipalities than as a budgetary authority in its own right. Thirdly, the county council was responsible for transferring, or redistributing, its own tax revenues to primary municipalities and other public and private authorities responsible for particular tasks. Approximately one-third of total expenditures consisted of such transfers. Again – as in the case of the distribution of tax equalization grants – this function was likely to create considerable conflict between the individual primary municipalities, a conflict which became even more intense as a consequence of the inclusion of urban areas as a part of the county municipality. This was not least due to the way in which the system of repartition tax operated, where the urban municipalities by and large paid proportionately more than other municipalities, due to their (assumed) better financial situation. In fact, although the rural municipalities were most opposed to the inclusion of towns and cities as members of the county municipalities, they probably benefited most from this inclusion.

These tasks and functions remained more or less unaltered until the end of the 1960s, when two major reforms were implemented. In 1969 the county municipalities were given responsibility for running all hospitals, apart from certain specialized hospitals serving the whole country and run by the state. The second reform was implemented in 1973 when the county councils were made responsible for all secondary education. In both cases, these tasks were made mandatory for the county municipalities, although the councils still may exert some discretion as to the level of activities (or coverage) and the way in which the provision of such services is to be organized, including the geographical location of hospitals and schools. In addition to these two functions, the county councils were also given certain new responsibilities in the area of cultural policy.

For all three areas, the central government established a system of specific grants – earmarked for these purposes, but not of a magnitude sufficient to cover the total expenses of these tasks.

Altogether, these new tasks implied an almost complete change of the role and functions of the county municipalities. This is illustrated by some figures on the financial growth of county municipalities. In 1945 county expenditures constituted approximately 10 per cent of total net expenditures for the municipal sector (primary and county municipalities). In 1973 this share had increased to 21 per cent, and it constituted 49 per cent of net local government expenditures in 1985. In 1985 the overall level of gross expenditures per capita for the counties was 13,000 Norwegian kroner, varying between the nineteen

Table 1 *Percentage distribution of total current expenditures, 1979 and 1983*

	1979	1983
Central administration	1.7	1.5
Education	18.1	15.9
Health	58.7	58.7
Social insurance	0.1	0.6
Culture	0.9	0.9
Development/roads	6.5	4.4
Enterprises	10.1	11.0
Other purposes	3.8	7.2
Total	99.9	100.2

counties from about 8,500 kroner in Vestfold to just above 18,000 kroner in Finnmark. In other words, at least financially, the county municipalities are now in the process of becoming as important as a service-providing institution as the primary municipalities. This is also clearly demonstrated by the increasing share of GNP controlled by county municipalities. While this share was 5 per cent in 1973, it increased to 7 per cent in 1985. Another way of looking at the financial consequences of these reforms is to consider the relative distribution of expenditures between various tasks. This is displayed in Table 1, which shows the percentage distribution of total current spending for various purposes in 1979 and 1983.

As is evident from these figures, more than 75 per cent of total current expenditures is appropriated for these new mandatory tasks. We also note that the more 'traditional' tasks of the county councils – related to physical development and roads – have increased in importance between 1979 and 1983. Of even more importance is that the very nature of the functions of the county municipalities has changed. While the most important function of the county councils before these functional reforms was to serve as a vehicle for financial transfers and redistributions in relation to the primary municipalities, they now provide services directly to the inhabitants. In other words, from being a kind of service institution for the primary municipalities, the counties have turned into becoming a direct service provider – alongside with and as a complement to the service provision performed by the primary municipalities. In this context it is interesting to note that the major service areas performed by the county municipalities are more exclusive and individually directed in terms of consumption than are municipal services. In this sense, the justification for strengthening the meso level of government is not solely related to the need to internalize externalities from local service provision. Rather, it is also a reflection and manifestation of the basic idea and aim that has governed local government reforms throughout the whole post-war period, namely to secure equal geographical access to basic welfare services throughout the country, in conjunction with ideas relating to economies of scale and minimum population thresholds. This is to suggest that the reforms at the county level have less to do with localist or decentralist values than with more 'centralist' ideas about welfare state development and social equality in the consumption of centrally determined public services, as well as financial efficiency in the provision of the services.

These changing functions contributed to call into question the very system of representation at the county council. The county council was no longer primarily accountable to the municipal councils, but as much (or even more) to the individual citizens of the county. In 1970 a government committee was appointed to consider the introduction of direct elections to the county councils. This question had been raised already at the end of the 1950s by the Minister of Municipal Affairs, but met considerable opposition particularly from representatives of rural municipalities. In 1970 the committee was not asked to consider *whether* direct elections should be introduced, but rather *how* such elections should be organized and how many members each of the eighteen county councils should have. The committee proposed a proportional election system similar to that used in ordinary municipal elections, but with the addition that one-sixth of the representatives should be elected on the basis of geographical criteria, in order to secure a 'just' representation across the various districts or primary municipalities within the county. However, the county at large was to constitute the constituency (NOU, 1972: 13). As regards the size of such councils, this varies according to number of inhabitants within each county: from between 25 and 35 councillors in counties with less than 100,000 inhabitants to between 63 and 85 councillors in counties with more than 300,000 inhabitants. This proposal was accepted and enacted by Parliament, and in 1975 the first direct election to the county councils took place.

One rather immediate effect of the introduction of direct election was a more 'just' political composition of the county councils. While the former system of indirect elections could imply that one single political party occupied all seats in the county council with only 50 per cent of the votes (on a county-wide basis) in the local election, the new election system served to strengthen the system of proportional representation, thereby making the county councils more 'representative' in relation to the election results. This is clearly

Table 2 *Differences in percentage of votes in elections and
percentage of councillors by political party, 1971 and 1975*

	County							
	Vestfold		Sogn/Fjordane		Møre/Romsdal		Troms	
Party	1971	1975	1971	1975	1971	1975	1971	1975
Socialist Left	−3.9	0.4	−1.3	−0.1	−2.5	0.8	−0.8	−0.1
Labour	2.9	−1.3	2.9	−1.1	−9.8	0.9	21.0	0.4
Liberals	1.4	0.7	−3.9	−0.9	3.0	0.8	−6.7	−0.2
Agrarian	3.7	−0.1	13.1	1.4	25.8	0.3	1.8	0.2
Christian	−0.5	0.6	−4.6	−0.8	−0.5	0.5	0.5	1.2
Conservative	−3.1	−0.1	−4.2	0.8	−5.1	−0.5	−5.2	0.2

Source: Andersen, 1988

demonstrated in Table 2, which shows the differences between the
proportion of votes in local elections and the proportions of
councillors of various political parties in the county councils for four
counties in 1971 and 1975.

As we can see from these figures, the gap between proportion of
votes and proportion of seats – which was considerable (by Norwegian standards) in most counties – was closed after the new
election system was introduced. In other words, the county councils
became more representative in political terms as a consequence of
the new system. In particular, the largest political parties (in the
individual counties) suffered most in terms of proportion of representatives on these councils. This has partly to do with changes in
territorial representation, which under the old system made for a
fairly heavy over-representation from smaller municipalities. Under
the old system, every municipality with less than 6,000 inhabitants
elected one representative to the county council. Moreover, municipalities with more than 6,000 inhabitants got one extra representative
per 6,000 inhabitants. There was, however, a fixed upper limit to how
many representatives one single (and large) municipality could elect,
namely one-third of all representatives on the council. Taking into
consideration that about one-third of the Norwegian primary municipalities had and have a population of less than 3,000 inhabitants, this
made for over-representation from the smaller rural municipalities.
According to Andersen (1988), the new election system also resulted
in a more representative composition of the county councils in
territorial terms, in relation to the population size of the individual
primary municipalities.

Table 3   *Percentage distribution of county councillors by political party and county, 1983 election*

County	Labour	Socialist	Agrarian	Christian Dem.	Liberal	Conservative	Progressive
Østfold	49	4	6	9	2	25	6
Akershus	34	7	5	5	6	35	8
Oslo	36	9	—	4	2	39	9
Hedmark	58	7	11	4	2	15	4
Oppland	55	4	15	5	4	15	4
Buskerud	45	4	7	5	4	29	5
Vestfold	36	4	4	7	4	36	9
Telemark	49	5	5	11	4	22	4
Aust-Agder	37	3	9	14	6	26	6
Vest-Agder	29	2	7	20	6	29	7
Rogaland	30	4	8	15	5	28	8
Hordaland	33	7	6	13	6	27	8
Sogn/Fjordane	33	5	18	13	8	21	3
Møre/Romsdal	30	4	11	17	12	20	6
Sør-Trøndelag	41	8	10	7	4	25	4
Nord-Trøndelag	42	4	22	7	9	13	2
Nordland	44	10	7	7	6	23	3
Troms	42	9	7	7	4	27	4
Finnmark	54	12	3	6	6	17	3

In Table 3 the relative composition of the county councils by political party after the 1983 election is reported. In order to simplify the presentation, I have grouped the smaller parties into the following two categories:

Socialists

● Socialist Left Party (SV)
● Workers' Communist Party (AKP)
● Norwegian Communist Party (NKP)

Liberals

● Liberal Party (V)
● Liberal People's Party (DLF)
● Others/local parties

I have put the Norwegian abbreviations of the name of the parties in parenthesis. Apart from these two groups, the following national political parties are today represented on most county councils: Labour Party, Conservative Party, Agrarian Party (now called the Centre Party, but I prefer its old name in order to indicate its links to the farming communities, which are still quite strong), Christian Democratic Party and Progressive Party (a right-wing neo-liberalistic party, like its Danish counterpart, whose chief ideologist and leader has been Mogens Glistrup).

As is evident from this table, with three exceptions, no one single party holds a majority of its own in any of the counties. The three exceptions are Hedmark, Oppland and Finnmark, where the Labour Party holds a fairly clear majority – though considerably narrower than it used to be under the old system in these three counties, which for many years have been termed 'the red counties'. In contrast, the Labour Party held a clear majority in nine of the counties in 1971, the last election before the reform – a majority which in only four of these counties was 'justified' on the background of the election results.

There is another aspect of this reform which is important to note, namely the fact that political fragmentation, in terms of the number of parties represented in the county councils, has increased as a consequence of the election reform. While the average number of political parties represented in the county councils was 5.2 in 1971, this figure increased to 7.6 after the 1983 election. This also indicates that the problems of forming stable political majorities within the individual counties have increased substantially. In this sense, the election reform did not just contribute to a more just representation, but also paved the way for increased political conflicts and instability.

The strong links between the county councils and the councils of the primary municipalities were not completely broken by the introduction of direct county elections. As late as in 1983, Mydske (1987) observed that altogether 74 per cent of all county councillors in Norway had previous experience as councillors in primary municipalities, and 25 per cent served as members of the two councils at the same time. However, only a small minority of the councillors with a background in primary municipalities viewed their own role as being that of a delegate from their local community. Rather, most of the county councillors had a 'county-wide perspective' on their work as councillors, although with a fairly strong identification with their own political party.

Despite the introduction of direct elections, not all links to the primary municipalities were broken. A major revenue source of the county councils was still the repartition tax – that is, a tax paid by the primary municipalities according to their fiscal abilities. Apart from being a revenue system which caused considerable conflict, relating to the assessment of fiscal abilities, the system was vulnerable to financial recession and cut-backs at the level of the primary municipalities. It was therefore decided to introduce direct taxation – which in Norway implies taxation of income and wealth – where the counties and primary municipalities were to share the same tax base. In practice, the county councils were 'given' a certain proportion of the total local tax rate, implying that they could charge a maximum of 8 per cent (changed to 7.5 per cent in 1979) of assessed taxable personal income. This right of direct taxation was introduced at the end of the first election period of the first directly elected county councils in 1978.

Through this revenue reform the county municipality achieved, at least formally, full independence from the primary municipalities, although the county councils were still composed of either members or former members of municipal councils. But what about the links to the 'state branch' of the counties, to the prefect and his or her administration? An immediate consequence of the introduction of direct elections to county councils was the establishment of administrative bodies of their own. Until 1964 the county municipalities had only two administrative bodies of their own: a treasury and an accountants' department. However, both agencies were subordinated to the county prefect. Between 1964 and 1975 another three administrative agencies were added, mainly as a consequence of the new responsibilities as regards health and secondary education, namely a chief officer for health and hospitals, an education agency and an agency for buildings and property management. The most important administrative change after 1975 was the establishment of the position of head of administration, taking over all municipal functions previously taken care of by the prefect. Furthermore, the prefect's planning department was transferred to the new county council administration. In addition, two more agencies – one in charge of communication and the other in charge of cultural affairs – were established in most county municipalities. By this process, the separation between the 'state branch' and the local government branch of the county was completed. What is interesting to observe is how closely these two processes of separation, from the primary municipalities and the county 'state branch', are linked. In fact, it is one and the same process, which made the county municipalities independent of the two other levels of government. Breaking the direct links between the county council and the individual municipalities may even be considered a precondition for separating the state functions from the municipal functions at the county level. This is not least due to the controlling functions – on behalf of the central government – which the prefect performs *vis-à-vis* the municipalities. Linking such functions to a directly elected county council would imply that this council achieved the position of a kind of super-municipality – a development which was feared among the primary municipalities in connection with the introduction of direct elections – and taxation. In order to avoid such a development, it was therefore necessary to separate the two branches of the county.

Apart from establishing an administrative staff of their own, the county municipalities have also become quite important employers. In 1987 the total number of person-years used in connection with service provision at the county level was almost 70,000, which corresponds to approximately 19 person-years per 1,000 inhabitants. This approximates to about 4 per cent of the total workforce. It should be noted that Oslo – due to its dual status as primary municipality and county municipality – is excluded from the figures. In Table 4 the distribution of person-years by service sector and by county is shown.

As is evident from these figures, social services and in particular health care (mainly hospitals) are the most labour-intensive activities at this governmental level. In relative terms, the proportion of employment going into this service sector is far higher than the sector's share of the total budget. On the other hand, the number of person-years within education (secondary) is surprisingly low compared to the proportion of total expenditures for education.

It is even more interesting to compare the various counties as regards the number of person-years. Again, the figures give clear evidence of the territorial equalization in service provision that has taken place in connection with the transfer of such tasks to the county municipalities. In fact, the highest number of person-years per 1,000 inhabitants is found in the most peripheral and least urbanized county of Finnmark, and Akershus in the Oslo region is found almost at the bottom of the list. To some extent, this is a reflection of scale economies in service provision, but it may also be interpreted as the result of the objective to increase universal access to such services. If we subscribe to this last interpretation, the table gives evidence of the important role which the county municipalities have played in the development of the Norwegian welfare state.

However, there is a third kind of dependency relationship which was not particularly affected by these reforms and changes, namely the relationship to central authorities. According to a recent survey (1986) more than 80 per cent of the county councillors considered their autonomy severely restricted by central laws and other regulations. This has, of course, to do with their mandatory obligations relating to the running of hospitals and secondary schools. But even more important is the nature of the system of state grants to the county municipalities. In 1983 altogether 45 per cent of total revenues came from state grants, of which more than 80 per cent of total state grants were earmarked for specific purposes. Apart from the reduced autonomy resulting from such an earmarking of the revenues, the grant system also hampered efficient resource allocation at the local level. As a last step (at least temporary) in the

Table 4   *Person-years per 1000 inhabitants, Norway, 1987*

County[1]	Central administration	Education	Social and health care	Church and culture	Technical sector	Business enterprises	Others	Total
Østfold	0.32	0.97	19.94	0.08	0.05	0.18	0.11	21.65
Akershus	0.20	0.79	12.52	0.08	0.06	0.49	0.07	14.22
Hedemark	0.52	1.14	19.63	0.06	0.01	0.58	0.35	22.28
Oppland	0.53	1.33	10.82	0.06	0.00	0.57	0.16	13.47
Buskerud	0.39	1.13	12.02	0.08	0.07	0.58	0.44	14.71
Vestfold	0.41	1.08	17.27	0.09	0.00	0.08	0.20	19.13
Telemark	0.56	0.82	17.98	0.12	0.05	0.07	0.19	19.79
Aust-Agder	0.45	1.43	15.95	0.12	0.24	0.07	0.07	18.33
Vest-Agder	0.29	0.71	14.26	0.09	0.12	0.10	0.19	15.74
Rogaland	0.26	1.01	12.67	0.05	0.04	0.02	0.03	14.09
Hordaland	0.25	0.80	17.95	0.06	0.05	0.03	1.47	20.61
Sogn/Fjordane	0.53	1.51	14.37	0.21	0.10	0.08	0.09	16.87
Møre/Romsdal	0.44	0.99	20.23	0.07	0.11	0.03	0.01	21.89
Sør-Trøndelag	0.44	1.15	18.63	0.05	0.09	0.04	1.50	21.89
Nord-Trøndelag	0.67	1.56	11.96	0.23	0.07	2.23	0.00	16.72
Nordland	0.55	1.86	13.36	0.14	0.06	0.09	0.92	16.97
Troms	0.51	1.85	18.21	0.13	0.14	0.04	1.17	22.06
Finnmark	1.12	1.78	20.47	0.32	0.16	0.27	0.52	24.64

[1] Oslo is excluded.

Table 5   *Relative distribution of revenues for county and primary municipalities in 1987 and 1988 (percentages)*[1]

Revenue source	Primary municipalities		County municipalities	
	1987	1988	1987	1988
Taxes	57	53	36	42
State grants	26	32	58	51
Fees and charges	10	10	4	5
Interest payments	3	3	1	2

[1] Since transfers between primary and county municipalities are not included here, the figures do not add up to 100 per cent.

Source: NOU, 1988: 38

reform process, the state grant system was reorganized from 1986 by merging all various specific grants into three larger sector-based block or general grants. Actually, the sector division of the grants is only used for calculating purposes, based on so-called fixed objective criteria. The actual transfer of the grant is made in the form of one cheque, not indicating how much each sector ought to receive of the total amount. In this way, another important regulating link to the central authorities was broken. To what extent this has made the county councils more autonomous is still to be seen. In Table 5 the relative distribution of revenue sources in 1987 and 1988 is reported. In the table I have included similar figures for the primary municipalities.

As we can see, the counties are still much more dependent on state grants than are primary municipalities. However, the figures indicate clearly that the two levels of government are in the process of moving in opposite directions as regards their dependency on externally determined revenues. While state grants take on increased importance for the primary muncipalities, the counties are becoming more 'self-sufficient' in terms of increased revenues from local taxes. These relative figures – although reflecting a real trend – are, however, somewhat deceiving, in the sense that the major cause of these changes lies in different expenditure growth at the two governmental levels. While total revenues from these sources grew by 18 per cent in the primary municipalities from 1987 to 1988, the counties experienced a *negative* growth, or a decrease, in total revenues by 9 per cent. This had its background in a transfer of certain tasks within the health sector from counties to primary municipalities. Regardless of this, the table testifies to a movement in the direction of a more autonomous status in financial terms for the counties.

Table 6   *Population, area and population density of Western European nations, 1984*

Country	Population (000s)	Area (000s sq km)	Density (inhabitants per sq km)
Norway	4,140	324	13
Denmark	5,112	43	119
Finland	4,882	337	14
Sweden	8,337	450	19
Belgium	9,877	31	324
France	54,935	547	100
Greece	9,896	132	75
Ireland	3,535	70	50
Italy	56,983	301	189
Netherlands	14,420	41	353
Portugal	10,164	92	110
Spain	38,717	505	77
Great Britain	55,624	244	228
Fed. Rep. Germany	61,181	249	246
Austria	7,552	84	90

Territory, access and externalities

In considering the territorial divisions of Norway into 19 counties and about 460 primary municipalities, it is important to keep in mind the geographical size of the country. In terms of area, Norway ranks as number five among Western European nations. At the same time it is almost at the bottom of the list as regards population size. This is clearly shown in Table 6.

As shown, Norway is the most sparsely populated country in Western Europe (with the exception of Iceland), with only 13 inhabitants per square kilometre, compared to a West European average of 96.

The figures in Table 6 should, however, be treated and read with caution. While the average population density in Norway is 13 inhabitants per square kilometre, 70 per cent of the population live in what may be termed densely populated settlements, which in addition to towns and cities also include small rural villages. By European standards Norway is probably still the least urbanized nation. In 1987 only 25 per cent of the population lived in cities with more than 100,000 inhabitants. By contrast, almost 40 per cent of the population of Denmark lived in such cities. Thus, despite a continuous and fairly rapid process of urbanization – particularly since 1945 when just 50 per cent of the population lived in densely populated areas – the Norwegian settlement pattern is still dominated by small towns and villages scattered over a fairly huge area. Furthermore, topographical features – such as high and steep mountains, deep fjords, narrow valleys, lakes and a long coastline with a considerable number of inhabited islands – have contributed to an insulation of the various settlements from each other. The geographical distances between the individual settlements have not just been long, but often also almost beyond the possibility of establishing a reasonably functioning communication network in terms of roads, bridges and railways. In this sense, the population-density figure for Norway reported in Table 6 is not just an arithmetical artefact, but reflects the actual Norwegian settlement pattern. It is interesting to note in this context the contrast between Norway and, say, Denmark. In area terms, Norway is 7.5 times larger than Denmark. In fact, the largest Norwegian county (Finnmark) is larger than Denmark. By contrast, the cultivated area in Denmark is three times as large as in Norway.

In order to interpret and understand the developments and reforms that have taken place at the county level in Norway, these facts about the size and the settlement pattern of the country are of central importance. To some extent they also help to explain why no fundamental territorial reforms have taken place at this level since local government legislation was introduced in 1837, although there has been some discussion as to the optimal territorial structure (*Innstilling*, 1965). Although the jurisdictional borders between the counties have their historical roots, it is – as I will suggest later in this section – difficult to see how more modern functional needs could be better attended to by changes in the current territorial divisions, apart from certain minor adjustments. This is, of course, not the same as suggesting that the current divisions represent an optimal solution in relation to functional needs. Rather, the jurisdictional divisions represent a compromise between at least three basic considerations as regards public service provision at this level, namely (a) scale economies, (b) universal access to services and (c) internalization of externalities.

As regards scale economies, this would call for larger units, not least in terms of population size. On the other hand, since the counties with the fewest inhabitants also tend to have the largest areas, any spatial extensions or amalgamations may well lead to diseconomies of scale judged from spatial considerations. Yet to subdivide the spatially largest counties would more probably than not have adverse effects in relation to scale economies from the perspective of population size. The figures in Table 7 are indicative of these problems.

Table 7   *Population, area and population density, counties, 1986*

County	Population (000s)	Area (sq km)	Density (inhabitants per sq km)
Østfold	235,813	4,183	60.6
Akershus	299,797	4,917	87.2
Oslo	449,221	454	1,054.0
Hedmark	186,305	27,388	7.1
Oppland	181,620	25,260	7.5
Buskerud	221,384	14,927	16.0
Vestfold	192,934	2,216	90.2
Telemark	162,595	15,315	11.5
Aust-Agder	95,475	9,212	11.3
Vest-Agder	141,284	7,280	20.7
Rogaland	326,611	9,141	38.2
Hordaland	402,343	15,634	26.9
Sogn/Fjordane	105,966	18,634	5.9
Møre/Romsdal	237,489	15,104	16.3
Sør-Trøndelag	247,354	18,831	13.9
Nord-Trøndelag	126,648	22,463	6.0
Nordland	241,048	38,327	6.6
Troms	146,595	25,954	5.8
Finnmark	74,690	48,637	1.6

As shown by these figures, the spatially smallest and most densely populated counties are found in the Oslo Fjord region (Østfold, Akershus, Oslo, Vestfold and partly in Buskerud). What is important to note, however, is that 10 of the 19 counties have a population of less than 200,000 and 7 of the counties have a population density of less than 8 inhabitants per square kilometre. The figures on density are indicative of the second problem, namely that of securing universal access to services. Probably the greatest obstacle in securing universal access to location-oriented services is that of geographical distance. Although there have been considerable improvements in the communication network and communication possibilities over the whole post-war period, distances still represent rather serious problems for easy access between various settlements and various locations of public as well as private services. Even within individual primary municipalities, geographical distance may represent a problem for access to various local services. For example, in 1986 about 25 per cent of the pupils in primary schools (which are run by the primary municipalities) needed public transport in order to get to the school on a daily basis, and this figure varied between 6 per cent in the city of Oslo to 41 per cent in the county of Troms. It should be added that all pupils are expected to attend the nearest school.

This points to a central dilemma in the provision of public location-oriented services on a universal basis in Norway, or at least in large parts of the country. In order to maximize access to the services, even the primary municipalities may be too large units in spatial terms. But at the same time they are too small in terms of population size to be able to maintain the services in an efficient manner, both financially and as regards the need to secure a certain level of quality in service provision. Also in this respect, the counties – far from being optimal units for the provision of such services – represent at least acceptable compromises in a trade-off between economies of scale and considerations relating to access to the services. What is interesting to observe is that this policy has to a considerable extent been successful in terms of accomplishing reasonably good access to public services in the various parts of the country. This is demonstrated not least by looking at the rate of attendance at secondary schools (which are run by the county municipalities) in various counties. See Table 8.

Table 8   *Proportion of pupils in secondary school half a year after finishing primary school (ninth grade), by county, 1974 and 1984*

County	1974	1984	Percentage change
Østfold	75.5	87.0	15
Akershus	82.8	87.7	6
Oslo	81.8	89.4	9
Hedmark	75.1	84.5	13
Oppland	72.6	90.3	24
Buskerud	75.7	86.4	14
Vestfold	74.1	92.2	24
Telemark	77.4	89.4	16
Aust-Agder	72.5	92.0	27
Vest-Agder	79.0	89.6	13
Rogaland	75.2	85.8	14
Hordaland	74.8	87.3	17
Sogn/Fjordane	72.0	90.0	25
Møre/Romsdal	69.5	86.9	25
Sør-Trøndelag	77.1	88.4	15
Nord-Trøndelag	69.5	90.7	31
Nordland	64.4	86.6	34
Troms	61.7	82.7	34
Finnmark	49.7	77.4	57
Total	74.1	87.6	18

Apart from showing a significant increase in the total proportion of pupils from primary schools moving on to secondary education during this decade, the most striking feature of this table is the equalization in access to such education on a geographical basis that has taken place. The relative increases in attendance rate are largest in those counties who were worst off in 1974, and these counties were also the least urbanized. If we compare the coefficients of variation (defined as the standard deviation divided by the mean), this dropped from 0.10 to 0.04 from 1974 to 1984. When we take into consideration the fact (which I will return to) that the responsibility for the provision of secondary education was given to the county municipalities in 1973, the achievement in terms of giving universal access – and thereby equalizing the actual receiving of such education – must be judged quite successful over this period. There may, of course, be qualitative differences among the counties as regards both the content of this education (such as number of subjects taught) and the teaching itself (competence of teachers and other pedagogic qualities); but what is important to stress is that the transfer of such responsibilities to the county municipalities in fact made secondary education an almost collective good on a country-wide basis. This was also achieved without having to make any alternations in the territorial divisions of the Norwegian counties. In interpreting these figures one should, however, be cautious not to make a direct causal inference between the transfer of responsibilities for secondary education to the county municipalities and the increase in access as well as increased geographical equality in secondary education. Central government has of course played a crucial role, not least in providing the necessary financial means for this development. On the other hand, it is doubtful whether other public authorities or institutions would have had any greater success in implementing this legislation than the county municipalities.

Let me now turn to the problems of internalizing the externalities of public service provision at the county level. As already suggested, each individual Norwegian county covers a rather large territory. As shown in Table 7, the average size of the counties is approximately 17,000 square kilometres. In comparison, the total area of the Netherlands is 41,000 square kilometres, or only twice as large as an average Norwegian county. As Table 7 shows, the size of the counties varies considerably – with Finnmark at the top with an area of more than 48,000 square kilometres and (ignoring Oslo) Vestfold at the bottom with an area of 2,200 square kilometres (which is actually smaller than the largest primary municipalities, such as Tromsø). If we in addition take account of the settlement pattern and the population densities, this implies that the problems of externalities –

Table 9   *Pupils in secondary school resident (a) outside the county and (b) inside the primary municipality of the location of school, 1985*

County	No. of pupils	(a) % resident outside county		(b) % resident in primary municipality
		Total	Regulated by legislation[1]	
Østfold	10,574	6.1	2.1	36
Akershus	17,664	6.9	3.3	56
Oslo	22,522	27.0	23.2	73
Hedmark	8,114	7.9	1.4	49
Oppland	9,582	11.1	6.4	49
Buskerud	10,917	13.8	6.5	48
Vestfold	9,827	8.0	2.9	34
Telemark	7,472	7.6	4.0	51
Aust-Agder	5,423	19.3	14.2	32
Vest-Agder	7,412	13.8	6.4	60
Rogaland	15,777	6.9	4.5	53
Hordaland	20,816	6.3	3.2	67
Sogn/Fjordane	5,459	7.4	3.5	44
Møre/Romsdal	11,976	3.2	2.4	53
Sør-Trøndelag	13,516	8.6	5.3	65
Nord-Trøndelag	8,065	9.6	4.6	56
Nordland	12,998	4.5	3.3	63
Troms	7,661	6.5	4.5	54
Finnmark	3,811	5.8	4.4	63

[1] Schools run by county municipalities.

linked to the catchment areas of the services – ought to be far more easy to handle in Norway than in most other European nations.

Although there may be severe problems in making an empirical assessment of the extent to which possible externalities have become internalized, some data concerning secondary education may again serve as an illustration. Table 9 presents the percentage of all pupils in secondary schools in each county who are resident in other counties. As is evident from this table, non-resident pupils comprise only a minor proportion of all pupils in secondary schools in most counties. This is particularly the case if we restrict our attention only to those schools regulated by the national legislation on secondary schools (which includes 92 per cent of all pupils). In fact, with two exceptions, the proportion of non-resident pupils does not exceed 6.5 per cent in any county. The two exceptions are Oslo and Aust-Agder. In the case of Oslo, the fairly high proportion of non-resident pupils is easily explained by the city's status as the nation's capital and as a regional centre, but also by the fact that Oslo is, in terms of area, the smallest Norwegian county. However, first and foremost the figure for Oslo is yet further evidence of the asymmetrical relationship between a central city and the surrounding region as far as the consumption of public services is concerned (Hansen, 1984; Sharpe and Newton, 1984).

It is far more difficult to interpret and explain the figure for Aust-Agder. Compared to other counties, there does not seem to be any obvious reason – such as topographical features or the settlement pattern – for this deviation. Furthermore, the density of secondary schools in this county is in fact lower than the average for all Norwegian counties, and the average size of each school is also below the national average. The most likely explanation may be that, as we observed in Table 8, Aust-Agder has a better coverage of secondary schools, in relation to its potential clientele, than all other counties with one exception. This may suggest a certain overcapacity on the 'supply' side, which gives the county authorities a possibility to 'sell' this surplus to residents in other counties. As the last column of this table also suggests, the school structure in this county is also fairly centralized in the larger towns and villages.

Apart from these two deviations, the figures suggest that the current county structure actually serves to internalize the externalities of the service provision. 'Spillovers' in the school sector are rather modest or marginal. It is in this context interesting to consider the last column of the table, which reports the percentage of pupils in secondary school who live in the same primary municipality as the one where their school is located. As shown by these figures, between 50 and 60 per cent of the pupils attend a secondary school located in their 'home-municipality', and the table also indicates a positive correlation between these figures and the size of area of the county (cf. Table 7). This goes some way towards explaining the high attendance rates reported in Table 8, and contributes also to stressing the importance of minimizing geographical distance in securing universal access to such services. What is as interesting in this context, is that the table suggests that the primary municipalities would be unable to supply such services on their own in sufficient amounts to meet the total demand. Although the number of such schools in each county exceeds the number of primary municipalities, secondary schools may be rather specialized, including general training for higher education (universities, etc.) and specialized vocational training. This degree of specialization and differentiation would most likely be impossible to maintain if the primary municipalities were responsible for running such schools.

Altogether, my discussion suggests the following tentative conclusions.

1 By transferring the responsibility for secondary education to county municipalities, one has achieved an equalization of such education opportunities across the whole country, while at the same time increasing the total capacity of the secondary school system, with a coverage rate in 1984 of about 90 per cent of all *potential* pupils. It is hardly likely that this proportion would increase much more, even if the supply was higher.

2 Externalities of such service provision have been reduced to a minimum, in the sense that more than 90 per cent of the pupils attending such schools are residents in the same jurisdiction as the one responsible for running the school which they attend. Further specialization may, however, lead to higher externalities.

3 By transferring the responsibility for secondary education to the county rather than the primary municipalities, it has been possible to achieve a certain degree of specialization and differentiation of curricula. In other words, also in qualitative terms, secondary education has improved on a nationwide basis after it became the responsibility of the county municipalities.

Having said this, it should again be stressed that I do not suggest any simple causal relationship between the development observed here and the transfer of responsibilities to, and the consolidation of, the county municipalities. One should also take care in not generalizing these tentative conclusions to other policy areas, such as the health sector. This applies in particular to the question of externalities, where both secondary education and the health sector are characterized by the possibility of applying mechanisms of exclusion in relation to potential consumers. Lack of empirical data on the pattern of consumption does not, however, permit any similar assessments of other policy sectors.

In my discussion here I have put special emphasis on spatial factors, such as size of area and population density. My major argument has been that in order to achieve a geographical (and thereby also a social) equalization in the access to and actual consumption of location-oriented services, a decentralized decision-making system is superior to a centralized system. In this sense, the consolidation and strengthening of the Norwegian county municipalities may be viewed as an attempt to collectivize public services in real terms. Judged from the data presented so far, this policy has been successful.

Conclusion

With its huge area and scattered settlement pattern, Norway may, at least on the surface, seem to be rather ungovernable. Furthermore, neither the primary municipalities nor the county municipalities have a population size which makes them self-sufficient in financial terms. Any geographical equalization in local public service provision is dependent on financial transfers from central government. Also national legislation has been crucial to the development of local service provision, not least at the county level. In this sense both county and primary municipalities may simply be regarded as implementing mechanisms for national policies. But what is striking about Norway is that the implementation of modern welfare state services and objectives (such as geographical equalization) has been achieved by means of a fairly simple political/administrative structure at the regional and local level: by a multi-purpose two-tier system of regional/local government and with no special-purpose authorities besides or at the top of this system. Actually, attempts at creating other regional units, such as in connection with economic and physical planning, have not succeeded. This contrasts with developments in other Western European countries, where a much more complex structure of regional government has emerged.

How to account for such differences? I have no simple answer to offer, and the explanation varies of course from one nation to another. One general suggestion may, however, be offered to account for such differences, and this relates to the settlement pattern and geographical features of a country. As suggested before, the sheer size of Norwegian counties and the scattered settlement pattern imply that externalities from public as well as private activities are being reduced to a minimum. Although the individual settlements are not self-sufficient in any sense, they are still fairly independent of each other. This also implies that problems of co-ordination in connection with public service provision – at least between various counties – are negligible. Typically, it is in the Oslo region, the most densely populated part of the country, that we have observed externalities of some magnitude in connection with secondary education. It is also in this region that there has been a need to establish special regional authorities – for example for transportation and planning – besides the county municipalities, to solve specific problems linked to the existence of externalities. This suggests the general hypothesis that the smaller the area of a country (and county), and the higher its population density, the more complex the regional governmental structure. This links to the more general suggestion that density in itself (of people, cars, industrial activities and so on) is a driving force behind the establishment of public/ collective regulations (to handle chaos). My data on Norway are of course insufficient to provide any test of these suggestions, but may serve as a starting point for further research into the development of the meso level of government.

Note

Data have been provided by the Norwegian Social Science Data Services.

Further reading and references

Andersen, T. (1988) 'Innføring av direkte valg til fylkestingene'. Thesis, Institute of Political Science, Oslo.
Fevolden, T. (1979) 'Fylkeskommunen – fra hjelpeorgan til selvstending forvaltningsnivå', in L. H. Skare (ed.), *Forvaltningen i samfunnet*. Oslo: Tanum-Norli.
Hansen, T. (1984) 'Urban hierarchies and municipal finances', *European Journal of Political Research*, 12.
Innstilling II fra Kommuneinndelingskomitéen (1952) Oslo: Ministry of Municipal Affairs.
Innstilling fra Fylkesinndelingskomitéen (1965) Oslo: Ministry of Municipal Affairs.
Kjellberg, F. and Mydske, P. K. (1987) *Om fylkeskommunens funksjon i norsk forvaltning*. Oslo: Institute of Political Science.
Mydske, P. K. (1987) *Fylkestingene i 1986*. Oslo: Institute of Political Science.
NOU (1972) *Valg til fylkesting*. Oslo: Norges Offentlige Utredninger.
NOU (1974) *Mål og retningslinjer for reformer i lokalforvaltningen*. Oslo: Norges Offentlige Utredninger.
NOU (1988) *Nye mål og retningslinjer for reformer i lokalforvaltningen*. Oslo: Norges Offentlige Utredninger.
Rose, R. and Peters, G. (1978) *Can Government Go Bankrupt?* London: Macmillan.
Sharpe, L. J. and Newton, K. (1984) *Does Politics Matter?* Oxford: Oxford University Press.

7
The Polish Palatinatus: Experiences and Prospects

Antoni Kukliński and Paweł Swianiewicz

An up-to-date analysis of the Polish meso[1] experience is extremely difficult due to the degree and velocity of change. The Polish meso is not an isolated phenomenon and it should be seen in a very broad context. It is also important to emphasize that, viewing the Polish meso historically, there have been periods of both progressive and regressive change and also periods of slow development, fictitious reform and stagnation. Therefore we have decided to make the chapter a short presentation of the three historical models and one contemporary model of the Polish meso.

The historical models are related to the period of

(a) the Polish–Lithuanian Commonwealth (1569–1795);
(b) the Second Republic of Poland (1918–39);
(c) the Third Republic of People's Poland (1944–89).

The recent experience of the Third Republic is very important, for in the year 1989 it changed its status profoundly. That experience is now over; it is also a closed historical chapter of the Polish meso. The main part of our chapter is an attempt to present a very general evaluation of the Polish meso of the Third Republic. The historical review is supplemented by a section presenting the actual experience of the Fourth Republic and predicting a meso adapted to the needs of that republic which is dedicated to parliamentary democracy and the market economy.

The meso: the experience of the Polish–Lithuanian Commonwealth, 1569–1795

The history of the Polish palatinatus[2] as a territorial unit goes back to the end of the thirteenth century when Poland was being unified after a period of division. But the fifteenth, sixteenth and seventeenth centuries are most important for the creation of meso institutions and their development. In 1569 the Sejm (national Parliament) of Lublin

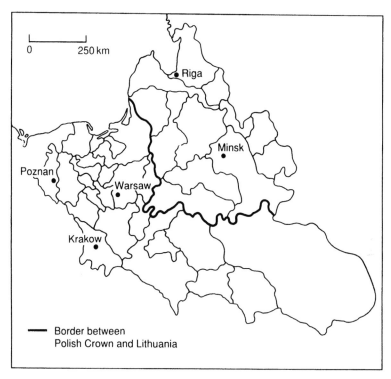

Figure 1 *The Polish palatinati in the sixteenth century*

fixed the territorial division of the Crown into 22 palatinati and the Grand Duchy of Lithuania into 10 palatinati (see Figure 1). That territorial division remained unchanged until the first partition of the Commonwealth in 1772.

The stability of the Polish–Lithuanian meso was an exceptional phenomenon in Europe of the sixteenth, seventeenth and eighteenth centuries. The palatinati (*województwa*) were relatively big regions representing strong territorial identities characteristic of the federal nature of the Commonwealth. The palatinus (*wojewoda*) was a member of the Senate and theoretically he was nominated by the king, but the dignity of the office derived from the fact that it was allocated to the members of powerful aristocratic or semi-aristocratic families dominating in the given region.

In the sixteenth century, the palatinus represented, *grosso modo*, the superior interests of the Commonwealth; but in the seventeenth and eighteenth centuries, palatinati were more and more dominated by the centrifugal forces leading to the disintegration of the

Commonwealth and to the destruction of the state. In the seventeenth and eighteenth centuries the palatinatus was much less a unit of state administration and more a unit of self-government of the gentry, guided or manipulated by the powerful local families and very often also by foreign influences.

In the last years of the Commonwealth, the Grand Parliament (Sejm Wielki) considered, *inter alia*, the establishment of a modern administration including a new status and a new role for the palatinatus. But the third partition of the Commonwealth (1795) closed this chapter of the Polish meso. To sum up, the meso of the First Commonwealth was an important institution within a relatively weak federal state, changing from the status of power in the sixteenth century to the status of annihilation at the end of the eighteenth century. Nevertheless the image of the palatinatus of the First Commonwealth is a significant element of the current Polish approach to the territorial organization of the state.

The meso of the Second Republic, 1918–39

The Second Republic emerged after a period of 'partitions', for in the nineteenth century the western and northern Polish regions belonged to Germany, while the central and eastern zones belonged to Russia and the south-eastern regions to Austria. Each segment was divided territorially on a different basis. The perpetuation of this variation after the creation of the Second Republic was criticized as a barrier to complete integration of the new Polish state; nevertheless changes in this structure were not introduced until 1938.

Following historical tradition, a network of 16 relatively big palatinati was created (see Figure 2) and they had a high status. An important role was allocated to the palatinus, who was nominated by the President of the state, and was predominantly a representative of the central government in the given region. He was also the head of the regional administration with strong supervisory powers in relation to local government. The palatinatus of Silesia had a special status and enjoyed a certain autonomy in relation to the central government.

To sum up, the meso of the Second Republic was an important institution within a centralistic state which changed from the model of parliamentary democracy of the early and middle 1920s to a semi-autocratic state in the 1930s.

The meso of the Third Republic, 1944–89

The experience of People's Poland is a closed chapter now, and therefore its meso may be viewed in a new historical perspective.[3] In

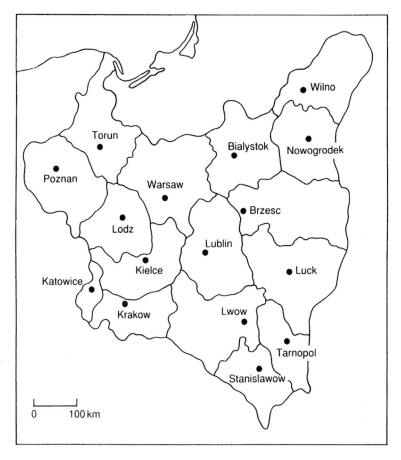

Figure 2   *The Polish palatinati under the Second Republic (1938)*

this new evaluation we will consider three stages in the evolution of the meso level during the Third Republic. We pay special attention to the last stage because of its strong implications for the present changes.

At the risk of oversimplifying it is possible to distinguish the three stages as follows:

1 the 'Polish' stage, 1944–50;
2 the 'Polish–Soviet' stage, 1950–75;
3 the 'Polish–Soviet–French' stage, 1975–89.

The first stage
The great political and territorial changes experienced by Poland in the middle 1940s did not destroy the continuity of the Polish tradition

Figure 3   *The Polish palatinati 1945–75*

in the territorial organization of the state. In the years 1944–50, the
meso of the Third Republic was a continuation of the institutional and
structural pattern established by the Second Republic. The palatinatus was a big region and its status was considerable (see Figure 3). The
distribution of competence between central, regional and local
government was also relatively clear. Such was also the distinction
drawn between government and self-government. The model of
territorial organization of the state was still Polish and close to Western
European traditions.

The second stage
In 1950, the Soviet pattern of territorial organization of the state was
introduced in Poland. The division of the country into palatinati,
counties and communes was left intact. This Polish spatial form was
however filled with institutions of the Soviet type, namely a system of

councils (*rady*) functioning according to the principle of 'democratic centralism'. The historical title of the palatinus (*wojewoda*) was eliminated and replaced by the chairman of the Council of the Province.

The introduction of this doctrine had to be secured by the Law Concerning Local Organs of the Homogeneous State Authority (Ustawa o terenowych organach jednolitej władzy państwowej), voted by Parliament on 20 March 1950. According to this law, local regional self-government and communal property were liquidated (article 32). Regional and local administration and their budgets were not separate from those of the state. The palatinatus was merely an administrative unit. Its ruling body had to represent the state authorities in the palatinatus and thus was supposed to be concerned with the interests of the whole state rather than of a particular region. Central authorities could abolish a local law or even dissolve a local or regional council if their decisions were in conflict with the policy of a state (art. 27, 28). We can also observe the centralization of functions in this period. Some of them were removed from the communal to the regional level and some from regional to the central level. All of these centralistic aims were hidden behind the façade of 'new speech'. At the beginning of the 1950 Act we can read that the Act was intended 'to deepen the democratic processes in the Polish People's Republic through the participation of the working class in the managing of the State and through the concentration of people's rule in local councils'.

The meso level was, however, 'repolonized' and rejuvenated following the 'Polish October' in the middle 1950s, but without any substantial change in the doctrinal base of the territorial organization of the state. *Inter alia*, the meso was strengthened by an imaginative network of regional planning offices which were, at that time, among the best in Europe. This positive evolution was stopped in the middle 1960s by negative transformations in the framework of the ruling Communist Party. The meso of the party which corresponded to the administrative meso was perceived to be dangerous for the central leadership. In order to destroy such federalistic tendencies in the party, Edward Gierek promoted a major reform of the meso during the period 1972–5.

The third stage
In 1975, when Western Europe was moving from a small to a big meso, the Gierek reform moved in the opposite direction, replacing the big 17 traditional palatinati by 49 small palatinati more or less the size of the French Napoleonic departments (see Figure 4). Also, the county – the intermediate level between the palatinatus and the

Figure 4   *The Polish palatinati after the 1975 reform*

commune – was abolished. This reform is now seen to have been very unsuccessful and it is claimed to have led, among other things, to

- the consolidation of many special divisions apart from the administrative divisions of the country;
- the fragmentation of urban regions that were economically homogeneous; the Warsaw agglomeration, for example, was divided into four palatinati: Warsaw, Skierniewice, Siedlce and Ostrolęka;
- the emergence of very weak palatinati on the periphery of these urban regions;
- the division of some historical regional communities; also, towns of similar size and level of development but different administrative status were included in one unit, which led to regional conflicts;
- a reinforcing of centralization processes, despite the fact that one of

the official aims was decentralization and making the administration more accessible to the people.

These problems will be examined in more detail later.

The basic functions of the palatinatus
The main difficulty in defining the role of the palatinatus in the Third
Republic is its unclear position in Poland's socio-political system. As
was mentioned above, for the greater part of the post-war period the
palatinatus was merely an administrative division. Its governing body
represented the state authorities in the palatinatus and thus was
supposed to be concerned with the interests of the whole state rather
than those of the particular region. This system was in conformity
with the Soviet 'homogeneous state authority' doctrine.

With the political reforms of the 1980s, attempts at decentralization and self-government were undertaken in both the economy and
the administration. However, the 1983 Act did not define clearly the
status of the palatinatus authorities. They appear to be both
self-government organs and organs of the state authority. This
resulted in the regional administration (and the chief of the
palatinatus especially) having an ambiguous role, being under both
the control of regional councils and the state administration. Yet it
was indispensable for the palatinatus to have an unequivocal position
in Poland's political system. Only then could the mode for performing specific functions be established. The list of functions of regional
authorities was very wide and at the same time inexact. Sometimes
the 1983 Act concerning local and regional self-government contra-
dicts other legal regulations (for example, contacts of regional and

Table 1   *Basic data on the size of palatinati*

	1938[1]	1970[2]	1986
Number of palatinati	17	22	49
Area (000s sq km)			
● average	22.9	14.2	6.4
● maximum	35.7	29.4	12.3
● minimum	0.2	0.2	1.5
Population (000s)			
● average	1,903	1,482	776
● maximum	3,126	3,695	3,917
● minimum	1,057	470	241

[1] Including Warsaw-agglomeration with special urban status.
[2] Including five agglomerations with special urban status.

local councils with enterprises located in their areas). Such ambiguity causes many problems and Sobczak maintains that 'in such conditions it is impossible to define the sphere of activity of regional and local councils' (1989: 18). One of the crucial defects is a failure to distinguish clearly the functions of regional and of local government. The Local Government Act confers on the regions the tasks of co-ordinating local government activity and economic, social and cultural activity of a wider than local scope (art. 13). In particular, the Act referred to decisions concerning enterprises of the state sector, transport enterprises, retail trade, road maintenance, schools, theatres, libraries, museums at the regional level and the health service. In 1988 a new Local Government Act established that the regional level would be responsible for environment protection, fire protection, problems of disasters, some problems concerning living conditions and problems resulting from particular parliamentary decisions. Obviously such tasks are not very precise, but some idea of the true role of the region can be derived from its administrative structure. This consists of the following departments:

- Budgetary-Economic,
- Financial,
- Trade and Services,
- Communal and Dwelling Economy,
- Communication and Means of Transport,
- Tourism and Sports,
- Culture and Arts,
- Environmental Protection,
- Architecture and Town Planning,
- Employment,
- Health Services and Social Care,
- Agriculture,
- Interior Affairs.

Although one of the aims of the 1980s reform of the political and economic system was the decentralization of the administration of the country, the autonomy of the palatinatus has remained rather limited. This seems to be true for both the political and economic systems. The most important manifestation, and cause, of this limited autonomy is the fact that the chief of the palatinatus (the palatinus) is nominated by the central government. Moreover the regional council can only refuse to grant him or her a vote of acceptance of the budget when his or her term of office ends. The most essential economic limitation is the financial position of the palatinatus. This will be discussed in detail later. The above-mentioned factors are specific, however, and centralization is implicit in the doctrine of the 'homogeneous state authority' which still governs the status of the region. The domination of the central authorities over the palatinatus is often reflected in the domination of the palatinatus over the local authorities.

The relationship between the various levels of the state authorities and administration has been changing rapidly over the last few years. This is due to numerous amendments to the law (first of all to the Regional and Local Self-Government Act, voted in 1983) and minor regulations as well as to changes in practices. The general trend has been to increase the autonomy of the lower levels, especially the autonomy of towns and communes from the respective palatinati.

However, research carried out in 1986 and 1987 indicated strong domination of the palatinatus authorities over the communes. According to Sobczak:

> the palatinatus organs influence the units of the lowest level by means of numerous legal instruments each of which is in conformity with the law, or at least on the borderline. . . . In practice, we are dealing with a sophisticated form of management which attempts to create the illusion that the organs of the lowest level are independent to a great extent. The phenomenon in question manifests itself first of all in the fields of investment planning and financing, where the local councils were supposed to be independent. (1989: 3)

Sobczak provides numerous examples of such influences. Directors of the departments of palatinatus offices often interfered in the work of local administration. The research carried out by Konieczny (1986) indicates that the control of the palatinatus over the local finances was also very firm. In many communes, the structure of budget expenditures was almost entirely imposed by the palatinatus office. According to information gathered from questionnaires, local administration officials often complained of the autocracy of palatinatus officials, being themselves reproached by the latter for passiveness and administrative misconduct (Grzeszczyk, 1988).

The financial dependence of towns and communes on regional authorities is derived not only from the scale of grants from the region but also from psychological factors. According to the latest research (Bartkowski et al., 1990), although only 19 per cent of respondents agree that there are direct interventions of the regional authorities in decision-making at the local level, at the same time 44 per cent maintain that regional authorities have determined the structure of the local budget, and only 30 per cent maintain that local authorities are fully independent concerning the local budget. These findings suggest that regional control of the localities is taken for granted by many local leaders. After many years of a centralist system they cannot imagine full independence.

The most important causes of the domination of the higher over the local level seem to be:

- The existence of the system of goods rationing related to the prevailing 'economy of shortages'. The allotment of deficit goods and materials frequently serves as a method of 'disciplining' local units.
- The distribution of grants for communes depends almost entirely on the subjective decisions of palatinatus officials (Swianiewicz, 1989a). What is more, only a part of the grant is distributed at the beginning of the year. The rest of the money becomes a subject for bargaining lasting sometimes for the greater part of the year. Its distribution was treated as a means of interference in local budget expenditures (Konieczny, 1988). Similar results were obtained by the so-called palatinatus share or precept on the local budget. Its existence as well as the extent of the share was often the result of purely subjective decisions. It was theoretically meant to equalize the situation of particular units and to intercept the 'surplus' revenues of the richer communes. Practice shows, however, that the share did not always depend on the financial situation of a commune. For example, in 1985 the Legnica palatinatus budget collected shares in all the units within the area of the palatinatus, even those with the smallest revenues (Swianiewicz, 1989a).

In fact all investments designated by towns and communes had to be included in regional plans for two reasons: first, lack of money among the local authorities; second, in towns and communes there was a lack of enterprises which could undertake such investments. The result is that fiscal and economic planning at the local level has been fictitious.

In recent years (1986) the expenditures of regional and local budgets have constituted about 35 per cent of the state budget (regional budgets were 23 per cent and municipal were 12 per cent).

There are four sources of the palatinatus revenue:

- Revenues from own sources.[4] This comprises different taxes, fees and charges. In 1986, revenues from own sources constituted about 35 per cent of the total revenues.
- Shares in the central budget, which constitute over 40 per cent of the total regional revenue. According to the regulation in force, they are included in the revenues from own sources. This designation has been contested by most specialists (Konieczny, 1988; Guzowska, 1988). The shares, expressed as a sum, were always included in the budget plan. If the real revenue, taken as a basis for calculating a share, exceeded the planned revenue considerably,

the surplus was taken by the central budget. If the situation was the reverse, the deficit was wiped out by means of grants. Therefore, attempts at increasing the revenues taken as a basis for calculating shares did not directly affect the financial situation of the palatinatus.

- Shares in the town and commune revenues. These did not exist in all palatinati and were significant in a few only, especially the Warsaw palatinatus. They consisted of taking the 'surplus' revenue from the richest towns and communes. In practice, however, they were frequently determined by discretionary decisions by the palatinatus, noted earlier.
- General and conditional taxes, which constitute about 25 per cent of the total revenue of the palatinatus.

The grant system is one of the major factors which limit the financial independence of the palatinatus. The 1983 Regional and Local Council Act stated that grants had to be fixed for five-year periods, but because of inflation it had to be amended frequently (Guzowska, 1988). As a result, the amount of the grant was still likely to be unknown in the period of planning at the palatinatus level. What is more, the criteria for fixing grants have been discretionary: the planned expenditures have been compared with the expected revenues, which has been far from an objective method of estimation. Very often the grant was finally fixed as a result of bargaining and informal pressure. What made the situation additionally anti-incentive was the permanent shortage of financial resources, which often resulted in grant reduction if revenues from own sources increased. Such a system gives preference to the units which keep to their expenditure plans but do not obtain the planned revenues from own sources. It should be noted that the same applies to the relationship between the palatinatus and the local budget.

Another serious drawback was the limited freedom of the palatinatus to plan its own expenditures. 'Numerous revenues and, first of all, expenditures have to be discussed in detail by the palatinatus with the Ministry of Finance as well as its particular departments. As a result of the discussions, certain financial decisions are often imposed on the palatinatus budget' (Konieczny, 1988: 106). This process was repeated, as we have noted, in the relationship between the palatinatus and the commune. Regional councils were also restricted by various budget norms and limits. For example, certain expenditures – such as those determined by food rates or fixed salaries paid from the budget – could not be exceeded. It seems that giving the palatinatus more freedom in this respect might be advantageous for the success of regional development policies. Obviously, the situation summarized

Table 2   *Data on palatinati in 1986*

Palatinatus	Area (sq km)	Population (000s)	National income	Revenues from own sources	Total expenditure
			in thousand złotys per capita		
Warsaw	3,788	2,431	7,115	34.9	37.7
Biała Podlaska	5,348	301	2,059	26.4	21.1
Białystok	10,055	679	3,423	25.2	24.8
Bielsko Biała	3,704	884	3,622	20.1	17.2
Bydgoszcz	10,349	1,096	3,040	20.1	21.9
Chełm	3,866	241	2,251	27.9	29.2
Ciechanów	6,362	422	2,185	20.0	20.3
Częstochowa	6,182	771	2,734	17.5	16.7
Elbląg	6,103	472	2,738	30.7	38.0
Gdańsk	7,394	1,419	3,973	19.2	16.9
Gorzów	8,484	490	2,835	28.6	30.1
Jelenia Góra	4,378	513	3,263	25.8	23.0
Kalisz	6,512	703	2,616	19.3	16.8
Katowice	6,650	3,917	4,293	17.7	16.4
Kielce	9,211	1,115	2,616	18.5	19.0
Konin	5,139	463	2,456	22.5	21.3
Koszalin	8,470	498	2,665	26.5	30.6
Kraków	3,254	1,216	3,385	33.1	32.8
Krosno	5,702	482	2,501	22.3	18.8
Legnica	4,037	502	4,206	33.5	31.5
Leszno	4,154	380	2,261	23.9	24.4
Lublin	6,792	997	3,089	22.8	20.4
Łomźa	6,684	342	2,105	23.4	23.1
Łódź	1,523	1,148	4,571	32.4	34.6
Nowy Sącz	5,576	679	1,987	20.8	16.0
Olsztyn	12,327	738	2,679	29.7	30.1
Opole	8,535	1,022	3,180	21.3	19.8
Ostrołęka	6,498	389	2,011	21.0	16.7
Piła	8,205	472	2,345	25.3	29.2
Piotrków	6,266	639	3,169	19.3	17.9
Płock	5,117	512	5,838	20.7	22.2
Poznań	8,151	1,316	3,629	27.4	20.7
Przemyśl	4,437	400	2,105	22.4	25.0
Radom	7,294	736	4,265	21.6	21.6
Rzeszów	4,397	703	3,430	20.4	18.4
Siedlce	8,499	703	2,119	14.5	15.1
Sieradz	4,869	642	2,338	22.6	20.4
Skierniewice	3,960	413	2,407	18.7	18.3
Słupsk	7,453	403	2,550	24.5	31.1
Suwałki	10,490	459	2,178	28.6	30.8
Szczecin	9,981	958	3,249	28.4	29.8
Tarnobrzeg	6,283	586	2,957	19.5	18.3
Tarnów	4,151	651	2,526	17.2	16.9
Toruń	5,348	649	2,971	19.2	22.5
Wałbrzych	4,168	739	2,860	23.2	21.1
Włocławek	4,402	428	2,383	21.9	18.9
Wrocław	6,287	1,121	3,938	29.7	32.1
Zamość	6,980	489	2,129	21.6	18.1
Zielona Góra	8,868	654	3,635	25.0	25.9

above was sharply differentiated in particular palatinati, but it is difficult to find a universal index of the differentiation. Revenues from own sources per capita and total budget expenditures per capita seem to be a good partial index, however.

Variations in key characteristics of the palatinati are considerable (see Table 2). Revenues from own sources (including shares in the central budget) per capita vary from 14,500 zlotys in the Siedlce palatinatus to 34,900 zlotys in the Warsaw palatinatus. Expenditures per capita vary from 15,100 zlotys in the Siedlce palatinatus to 38,000 zlotys in the Elblag palatinatus. There is a high correlation between the two rates (Pearson's correlation coefficient, 0.89), especially for the group with the highest revenues and expenditures. Slightly more differences occur in the group of 'poorer' palatinati. Some of the examples indicate the not always correct functioning of the system of grant distribution, which corresponds with the general remarks above. For example, revenues from own sources in the Nowy Sacz palatinatus are 20,800 zlotys per person (thirty-third place among the palatinati with regard to this rate), whereas expenditures amount to 16,000 zlotys (forty-eighth place). The difference seems to be due to relatively small grants from the central authorities and big grants for towns and communes.

The correlation between revenues from own sources per capita and the national income per capita is not very high, but statistically significant, the correlation coefficient being 0.3. This indicates that the relationship between the wealth of a palatinatus and its expenditure is not very close.

On the whole, 21 palatinati expenditures are lower by over 500 zlotys per capita than revenues from own sources. It is worth noting that this situation is more frequent in poor palatinati; among the first sixteen palatinati on the list of revenues from own sources per capita there are only 3 such palatinai, among the next 16 there are 9, and among the last 17 there are 10. The reason seems to be the fact that the towns and communes which need the biggest grants are usually those situated in the poorest palatinati. The system of grants from the central budget does not eliminate the phenomenon. This proves that in many cases the officially stated aim of grants distribution – equalization – has not been achieved.

Also interesting are changes of central grants for a particular palatinatus. In 1985 they varied from 2,000 zlotys per capita in Warsaw palatinatus, to 16,300 zlotys in Elblag palatinatus. Among 10 regions with the lowest grants, there were 5 with the biggest agglomerations, and 3 localized in south-eastern Poland. Among 10 with the highest grants, 8 were localized in western Poland, in the so-called 'Recovered Territories'. It is clearly evident that the relation between grants and the 'wealth' of a particular palatinatus was not very strong.

Between 1985 and 1987 the situation changed rapidly. In real terms the rate of change varied from 77 per cent in Elblag palatinatus to 211 per cent in Tarnów palatinatus. The biggest increase of grants occurred mainly in regions with the lowest grants per capita in 1985. The correlation coefficient between grants in 1985 and change in 1985–7 is 0.73. This relationship was transferred to regional grants for municipalities so that they increased mainly in those palatinati which received more grants from central level. Generally, in the 1985–7 period we can observe changes leading to a more rational distribution of grants. This does not mean, however, that the case for a general reform of the grants distribution system (so as to replace subjective with objective distribution criteria) is weakened.

Generally, there are two possible goals of the distribution of grants:

- *equalization*; and
- *efficiency* – that is, the satisfaction of only the minimal needs of every local unit and to give preference to municipalities with the highest own revenues (on the assumption that they are the most efficient ones, and that their influence on state development can be the most positive).

To sum up this section of the chapter: during almost forty years of the post-war history of Poland the official grant doctrine has been equalization. However, research indicates that neither this goal nor that of efficiency has been accomplished in Poland.

The influence of the palatinatus on regional planning and development

The basic barrier to the palatinatus's influencing the development of a region has its roots in the main development strategy of the Third Republic. One of the important features of this strategy may be called 'the domination of the sector over the region'. Another important barrier is an administrative one. It is commonly agreed that the forty-nine palatinati are too small, and that is the reason why regional authorities find it difficult to stimulate their development. The palatinatus authorities can direct the development of a region in a number of ways:

- by independent implementation of development plans (establishing enterprises, for example), which are mainly restricted by the fiscal situation; in practice, most economic investments are only initiated by the palatinatus, where their realization seems likely because of central support;

● by influencing the activity of the enterprises and individuals in the region (for example, location restrictions and other restrictions included in plans).

As a result of the 1975 administrative reform, there have been big changes in the regional planning system. The level and organization of regional planning in Poland in the 1960s have been considered by many experts to be among the best in Europe (Fisher, 1966). It is worth noting that the changes that occurred in the 1970s are usually judged differently in the 'new' and 'old' palatinati (Strembicka et al., 1988). The prevalent opinion in the 'old' palatinati is that the abolition of the mature county system brought about many unfortunate results. In planning, for example, there has been a substantial reduction in the number of planners. Prevalent opinion seems to suggest that this situation does not seem to apply in the 'new' palatinati, however.

According to the 1983 Local and Regional Self-Government Act the palatinatus was required to create one-year and five-year development plans. These plans were to be co-ordinated with the plans of state enterprises in a given region. In practice, enterprises were usually strong enough to pursue their goals even when the regional authority was against. Palatinati authorities had to take into consideration plans of enterprises as an independent variable. Generally, influence through plans were mainly restricted by:

● lack of integrated planning, including spatial and socio-economic plans;
● frequent non-implementation of plans (spatial plans especially).

It should also be mentioned that the reform launched in the 1980s dealt with the economy rather than the regional system. As a result, it consolidated the domination of the branch system over the regional (Gorzelak, 1987).

Palatinatus administration
Between 1975 and 1987, the number of people employed in state administration increased from 134,000 to 171,000 including the increase from 100,000 to 126,000 in regional and local administration (see Table 3). The fact that the latter was bigger than the average is due to a process of decentralization of administration. The only break in the process occurred in 1982 (centralization caused by martial law), when there was a decrease in the number of people employed in regional and local administration. In the traditionally strong palatinati (Poznań, Warsaw, Gdańsk and so on) the increase was much smaller than the average. The reason seems to be the

198 The rise of meso government

Table 3 *Structure of employment in the state administration*

	1975	1981	1982	1986	1987
Central level	33,494	35,006	43,186	49,466	45,463
Regional and local levels	100,309	100,349	88,886	127,861	125,756
Regional level	27,090	25,158	23,706	32,742	29,859
Local level	73,219	75,191	65,180	95,119	95,897

greater efficiency of administration in these regions, as well as the fact that it was the weak palatinati that attempted to strengthen their administration by means of employing more people. More than 50 per cent of palatinatus administration officials hold university degrees. For the managers the rate is much higher – for example, for department managers of palatinatus offices, 97.6 per cent. The level of education has recently been improving. There are, however, regional differences, which are mainly due to the availability of university education in the palatinati. Probably the most important feature of regional administration was its political dependence on the Communist Party. There was a high correlation between membership of the party, known as the Polish United Workers' Party (PUWP), and the post occupied, which is shown below (Grzeszczyk, 1988):

Percentage membership of PUWP
Department managers – 90.6
Assistant department managers – 76.6
Inspectors – 48.7
Section managers – 47.5

For the last few years the proportion of PUWP members has slowly declined. For department managers, for example, it was 96.7 per cent in 1978 and 90.6 in 1987. The decline was even faster for lower posts. In some palatinati, the proportion of PUWP members among department managers has declined by more than half. Differences between individual palatinati reflect differences in the selection procedures for managers. A more detailed presentation of the variation would require a more thorough study. From the data available at present, it can only be surmised that the Piotrków Trybunalski palatinatus was special in that there was an increase in the proportion of PUWP members at nearly all levels of the managerial class in the late 1980s. Obviously, the statistics provided can only give very general knowledge of the functioning of the palatinatus administration. As far as can be ascertained, there does not seem to be any coherent system of selecting the managers and other officials or methods for the improvement of their qualifications. Palatinatus administration officials receive only moderate salaries, and their posts are not very prestigious. There was, therefore, a high staff turnover rate. Only for the high managerial posts was an intentional system of selection applied, the criterion being mainly political.

Meso level and special divisions
One of the officially announced aims of the administrative division reform carried out in the 1970s was to bring government closer to the people. In order to achieve this, most of the powers of the former counties were taken over by the stronger communes. Smaller palatinati, with offices more available for the people, were created whose functions were to be more specific. In practice, the reform turned out to be Utopian: 'some competences belong to communes only formally. Communes are too weak to use these competences (because of lack of specialized staff, material and technical possibilities, etc.). Some decisions formally depend on the commune, but in fact are based on data collected in bigger towns – the former county capitals' (Pańko, 1982: 227).

The former counties still function as various kinds of districts. The situation is even worse than before, since a person who needs several matters dealt with often has to visit several towns where respective district offices are located. In many spheres, large supra-regional units have remained whose boundaries correspond more or less with the former palatinati. Sometimes there is no legal basis for creating such units, for there is a law stating that special divisions may be made only on the basis of separate Acts, but in many cases this condition is not fulfilled:

> The stability of old territorial structures can be also illustrated by the number of macro-regional boards (concerning different special divisions) located in particular cities. In the last of the 'old' palatinati capitals – Koszalin – 48 boards are located (out of 72), while in the first of the 'new' capitals – Toruń – only 26 are located. (Nierychło, 1989: 12)

The existence of the special divisions is nothing unusual, yet their increase in the late 1970s was more like an epidemic. Panko maintains that before 1975 the 'number of special divisions was about 20; after 1975 a lot of new divisions emerged, and now we can speak to about 200 special divisions' (1982: 118). An atlas issued by the Cabinet Office provides examples of 84 divisions in different branches of the economy where there are units of an inter-palatinatus nature. Obviously, their existence limits the influence of regional authorities in many fields of socio-economic life as well as the development of the functions in their charge.

Conclusion

To sum up, there were three fundamental weaknesses of the meso of the Third Republic:

1 Political weakness based on the fictitious elections of the regional councils and on the monoparty system.
2 Managerial weakness related to the constant intervention in the affairs of the regional administration by the apparatus of the party and by the central government.
3 Financial weakness generated by the strongly centralistic policies of the Ministry of Finance which never allowed regional or local financial autonomy to develop.

In short, the Third Republic was a soft version of the true socialist state but still dominated by the Communist Party. The meso level was an important but relatively weak link in the territorial organization of the soft socialist state. The weakness of that link was especially pronounced in the third stage. The relatively strong role of the meso was limited to the years 1944–50 and 1955–70.

The meso of the Fourth Republic

The year 1989 saw the transformation of the Polish People's Republic (Polska Rzeczpospolita Ludowa) into the Republic of Poland (Rzeczpospolita Polska), a state dedicated to parliamentary democracy and the market economy. A similarly rapid transformation has taken place at the meso level, characterized by the procedures that have taken place since the first half of 1990.

The first step was a set of parliamentary Acts establishing a new legal framework for territorial self-government in Poland and free local elections that were held in May 1990. A new Local Government Act was voted on 30 March 1990. It provides legal status for communes (art. 2) and communal property (art. 43), and introduces local administration and a local budget that is separate from the state's (art. 51). The Act also decrees that the supervision of municipalities shall be exercised only on the basis of conformity with the law (art. 85).   ·

The act on territorial self-government creates a new institution, the Provincial Assembly, at the meso level (palatinatus). This is a small Parliament whose members are elected by the council of the communes. This Sejmik has the following tasks:

(a) the evaluation of the activity of the communes;

(b) the dissemination of experiences in the field of self-government;

(c) mediation where there are conflicts among the communes;

(d) evaluation of the activity of the governmental administration of the palatinatus;

(e) the expression of opinions concerning important problems of the palatinatus;

(f) the formulation of motions to invalidate the decisions of the palatinatus which are in conflict with the law; and

(g) representation of communal interests in relation to governmental administration.

The tasks of the Sejmik are clearly related to two spheres of competence:

(a) the co-ordination of the self-governmental activities covering the area of the palatinatus; and

(b) the creation of a forum to establish the proper interrelation between self-governmental and governmental institutions acting in the area of the palatinatus.

Also in March 1990 the national Parliament voted a new Act concerning the governmental administration at the meso (palatinatus) level. According to this Act, the palatinatus is mainly an administrative unit. The palatinus (*wojewoda*) is a regional representative of government, nominated by the Prime Minister (art. 5). It is worth stressing that the process of replacing the old *nomenclatura* in the regional administration by new cadres representing new political and professional orientations is already under way. The Sejmik Samorządowy is only an advisory body for the palatinatus (art. 19), and supervision over the palatinatus is exercised not only on the basis of conformity with law, but also on the criterion of competence and harmony with the policy of the state (art. 42).

The transformation of the local administration along these lines was set in train after the local elections in May. The division of the country into forty-nine small palatinati will remain intact for a few years. So the new wine of democracy has been put into the old bottles of the territorial organization established in 1975. That is why the introduction of the self-government system at palatinatus level has been postponed until after the reforms just outlined. It proved impossible to introduce simultaneously a great structural reorganization of the country, and it is envisaged that this will take place in the middle 1990s. We will return to the system of grand palatinati in a moment.

The Institute of Space Economy of the University of Warsaw is preparing for the Prime Minister's Office an expert document concerning the meso level in Poland. The system of grand palatinati it will recommend will probably be, to some extent, similar to that abolished in 1975. However, the reform of the middle 1990s will be less dedicated to the traditions of the past than to the anticipation of the needs of the society and state in the twenty-first century. In this respect the new palatinatus in Poland should be seen not only as a Polish but also as a European palatinatus. It will be established in two stages:

- The first stage is what occurred in 1990, namely the new Acts of Parliament, free local elections, the establishment of the 'small Parliament' in the palatinatus and the reconstruction of (state) administration at the meso level.
- The second stage will take place in the middle 1990s and will comprise the reform of the territorial organization of the country, involving the elimination of the network of small palatinati and its replacement by a network of big palatinati.

There is a strong case, however, for bringing forward some changes scheduled for the second stage. Among these is the restitution of the counties which were abolished in 1975. This was first recommended by Kukliński (1989). However, such 'new' counties should not be identical with the old ones, so as not to disturb the present palatinati borders. It is worth stressing that most counties already exist in the form of the numerous 'special divisions'. According to a survey of local leaders (Bartkowski et al., 1990), about 60 per cent of them complain that the present administrative division is harmful for the development of the country. When asked about proposals for change, 40 per cent of local leaders mentioned the restitution of the counties and 25 per cent gave it first priority. The second most popular change was the unification of the special divisions, which was mentioned by 60 per cent of the sample and placed as a first priority by 6 per cent. It must be emphasized that these results provide further evidence of the popularity of recreating the county, since the unification of the special divisions is, to all intents and purposes, a form of county restitution.

Nowadays, the idea of recreating the counties as the lowest level of state territorial administration is officially accepted by government. The Act concerning Regional State Administration introduced the counties (*rejony*) as units the boundaries of which will be defined by government (art. 36). The chief of the county administration will be nominated by the palatinus (art. 38). The Institute of Regional Planning and Development of the University of Warsaw has prepared an expert document concerning the boundaries of these units. According to this document, about 200 'new counties' would be established; this is some one hundred less than the total of old counties, so the new units will be considerably bigger than the old.

Since May 1990 when this chapter was first written some important changes have occurred. There is not enough space to describe them in detail, but it is necessary to notice that most of the new elected local governments have not supported governmental plans to establish new *rejony*. Local leaders have perceived them as an attempt to limit their autonomy. This caused strong conflict in central–local relations which focused on two subjects: (a) local government protests against the idea and functions of the *rejony*; (b) conflicts about the demarcation of particular *rejony*. Despite this fact the government introduced new units in August 1990, agreeing to a substantial increase in their number, to about 250.

Summing up

It is clear now that the meso of the Fourth Republic will be an important institution in a number of respects:

- the *political*, in the sense that it will stimulate the creation and development of a new system of political parties;
- the *political-administrative* character of the regional organization of the government;
- the degree of *self-government*, since one of its tasks will be to evaluate and co-ordinate the activities of the communes;
- the *European* sense, for, as in Western Europe, the Polish palatinati, especially the big ones, will be in a position to participate directly in different European developments.

Appendix A: The most important Acts of Parliament related to the Polish meso

Ustawa z dn. 20 marca 1950 r. o terenowych organach jednolitej wladzy państwowej [March 20, 1950 Act about local organs of homogeneous state authority], Dz. U. 14, poz. 130.

Ustawa z dn. 25 stycznia 1958 r. o radach narodowych [January 25, 1958 Act about local councils].

Ustawa z dn. 28 maja 1975 r. o dwustopniowym podziale administracyjnym Państwa oraz o zmianie ustawy o radach narodowych [May 28, 1975 Act about two-level administrative division of the state and about changes in act about local councils], Dz. U. 26, poz. 139.

Ustawa z dn. 20 lipca 1983 r. o systemie rad narodowych i samorządzie terytorialnym [July 20, 1983 Act about system of local councils and local self-government], Dz. U. 41, poz. 185.

Ustawa z dn. 8 marca 1990 samorządzie terytorialnym [March 8, 1990 Local self-government Act], Dz. U. 16, poz. 195.

Ustawa z dn. 22 marca 1990 o terenowych organach rządowej administracji ogólnej [March 22, 1990 Act about territorial organs of state administration], Dz. U. 21, poz. 123.

Appendix B: The palatinatus in relation to the major political and social forces in Poland under the Third Republic

In this appendix three main forces will be considered. The first is the Communist Party (PUWP) which had real power in regional decision-making in the Third Republic. The second is the Solidarity movement (and 'its children') which emerged on the political scene in 1980 and which seems to be decisive nowadays. The third is the Catholic Church which has never aspired to be a leading force, but whose moderating role was often very important during the whole of the post-war period.

The palatinatus versus the political parties

The territorial structure of all the official parties in the Third Republic corresponded to the administrative borders. Therefore, the 1975 administrative division reform brought about a reform of the party machine. In many people's opinion it was one of the political aims of the reform to weaken the PUWP Regional Committees by breaking them, thus creating considerably smaller palatinati. A second aim was to remove certain spheres of activity from the Committees' control by means of special divisions (as we have seen) which were made independent of the formal administration. Up until the 1980s, decision-making at the regional level was in the hands of the PUWP but undoubtedly it had been losing its domination. Information gathered from questionnaires in towns and communes, however, indicates that by the end of 1988 it was still the most important pressure group (Swianiewicz, 1989b).

The palatinatus versus Solidarity

This section consists of two parts. In the first the regional structure of the trade union Solidarity in 1980–1 is discussed. The second part concentrates on the 'post-round-table' period, and the characteristics of the main political forces connected with the Solidarity movement.

Solidarity in the period 1980–1   Between 1980 and 1981, that is during its legal activity, the Solidarity movement was in fact a federation of regional unions. The choice of a territorial form of organization rather than one based on branches of production had its internal and external motives. The reason why branch sections were subordinate to regional structures was to pacify internal conflicts between representatives of individual trades. The external reason was to make it easier to exert pressure on the state administration.

The territorial division of Solidarity did not, however, correspond to Poland's administrative structure. At first, Solidarity units emerged spontaneously as a result of the creation of the so-called MKZs.[5] There were 65 MKZs altogether, 46 of which were situated in the capitals of the palatinati. The next step was the unification of some of the MKZs, which resulted in the emergence of 39 so-called 'regions' of very different sizes. In the Śląsko-Dąbrowski region, the largest one, the membership was over fifty times as big as in the smallest region.

According to the Solidarity Programme, regions were to 'correspond to administrative boundaries as far as possible. Division of palatinati should be avoided as it precludes influence on administrative authorities.' Some of the regions, like those of Mazowsze, Dolnoslaski, Malopolski or Srodkowowschodni, consisted of several palatinati. Others, like Bydgoszcz, Rzeszów, Toruń or Chełm, consisted of one particular palatinatus. There were also small regions, several in a single palatinatus, like Ziemia Sandomierska and Federacja Tarnobrzeska in the Tarnobrzeg palatinatus or Kędzierzyn-Koźle, Nysa and Opole in the Opole palatinatus.

Generally, Solidarity's regional units were of two kinds:

(a) *Cumulative regions* These are created around the largest cities and are much bigger than the area of a single palatinatus. It is interesting to note that in most cases, these regions adopted historical names of geographical regions instead of names originating from the capital cities of the palatinati, for example, Mazowsze, Małopolska, Dolny Śląsk.

(b) *Divided regions* The creation of regions and the delimitation of their boundaries involved numerous conflicts whose sources were twofold. Some of them arose from strong antagonism within the palatinatus which had been caused by an arbitrary delimitation of the boundaries of palatinati in 1975. One such conflict was that between Tarnobrzeg, Stalowa Wola and Sandomierz, which was a very sharp one. Unless a palatinatus was strongly influenced by a centre of supra-regional importance, it usually became divided into two or more small regions, like the Tarnobrzeg palatinatus for example. This was against the Solidarity Programme.

The other type of conflict arose from the fact that very often the capitals of the 'new' palatinati wanted to establish independent regions whereas other towns in those palatinati preferred to adhere to the 'old' borders. For example, the Legnica MKZ wanted to establish its own region while Glogów and Lubin, two towns in the Legnica palatinatus, wanted to join the Wroclaw palatinatus and to create a single large region, Dolny Śląsk (Lower Silesia). After a long dispute, the latter was chosen. Conflicts of this kind were very frequent during 1981 and Solidarity's national leaders usually opted for larger and stronger regions.

Between 1980 and 1981, Solidarity was a significant pressure group at the palatinatus level. Numerous conflicts of national importance originated in disputes between Solidarity and palatinatus authorities. For example, the so-called 'Bydgoszcz events', the most fierce conflict in Solidarity's history, started with Solidarity's demand for a special session of the Bydgoszcz Regional Council.

The history of the 1980–1 period indicates that the 'new' palatinati were especially liable to conflicts. This was due to the fact that policies were often 'brought in a briefcase'. In short they had little connection with the region (Jałowiecki, 1982). According to Holzer (1989), one of the most important achievements of Solidarity was that it undermined Warsaw's dominance over the rest of Poland, making the emancipation of the provinces possible. Regional pluralism was an important element of Solidarity's structure, even though it occasionally reduced the union's capability for effective action. The Mazowsze region, for example, was very influential, but not more than that of Gdansk. Also, the role of small regions in decision-making was unprecedented.

The period after the round-table negotiations (1989) After 'round-table talks' and the 1989 elections, the Solidarity movement takes at least three forms, first

as a trade union; secondly as a system of Citizens' Committees (*Komitety Obywatelski*) in particular towns, communes and palatinati; finally as a Citizens' Parliamentary Club (*Obywatelski Klub Parliamentarny*).

The Trade Union has its centre in Gdańsk. According to a number of Solidarity experts, Z. Romaszewski among them, great changes occurred in the regional dominance of Solidarity after the declaration of martial law in December 1981. Between 1980 and 1981, big cities like Warsaw or Wrocław, where a high percentage of the intelligentsia live, were dominant. At present, Solidarity is strongest in regions such as Belchatów or Stalowa Wola, where the percentage of workers is very high. This may have caused a change of Solidarity's territorial structure after its re-legalization. The disposition of the forces exerting pressure on palatinatus authorities may also be different. Today there is a tendency for the branch structure of the trade union wing of the movement to grow at the expense of the territorial structure.

The Citizens' Committee was created in 1988 as a political body before the round-table negotiations. Citizens' Committees chose candidates to parliament and organized campaigns before the elections in June 1989. Nowadays Citizens' Committees in particuiar municipalities are a leading force in the organization of local elections. This means that the Committees are much stronger than the trade union wing and better related to the governmental system. The Committees are not politically homogeneous and represent liberal as well as social-democratic ideology.

The Citizens' Parliamentary Club comprises 260 members. They are elected in particular palatinati, and the most important element among them are those elected to the Senate, which is composed of two deputies from each of the 47 palatinati plus the deputies from both the Warsaw and Kraków palatinati. The present status of the Senate is seen by many, including perhaps most Solidarity members, as petrifying the present system.

The palatinatus versus the Catholic Church

The present territorial organization of the Catholic Church in Poland is a result of a very long process which started as early as the tenth century, when the first dioceses were established. The most recent changes occurred with the creation of new dioceses in the so-called 'Recovered Territories' in the 1970s. It is worth noting that the capitals of those dioceses were at the same time the capitals of the respective palatinati. The only exception is the Gorzów diocese, which contains the capital city of Zielona Góra palatinatus. Obviously, the borders of the Polish diocese rarely correspond to administrative boundaries. What is more, in eastern Poland they do not correspond to the state border. The bishops in the towns of Bialystok, Drohiczyn and Lubaczow are Apostolic Administrators whose capitals are situated in the Soviet Union.

At present Poland is divided into 27 dioceses (Zdaniewicz, 1983), 23 of which have their seats in the capitals of palatinati. The only exceptions are Drohiczyn, Gniezno, Lubaczów and Pelplin. All the capitals of the 'old' palatinati except for Bydgoszcz, Rzeszow and Zielona Góra are bishops' seats.

In all there are 10 palatinati whose areas are divided between two dioceses. The areas of the Sieradz and Tarnobrzeg palatinati are divided among three dioceses; each of the areas of the Częstochowa, Piła and Pitorków palatinati are divided among four dioceses and the territories of the Katowice and Kalisz palatinati overlap into five dioceses. On the other hand each of the Przemyśl, Włocławek and Wrocław dioceses included four capitals of palatinati. The correspondence between the two structures was closer in pre-war Poland, where there was only one palatinatus, the

Pomeranian one, whose capital was not the seat of a diocese at the same time. Up till now the shape of the Katowice diocese has been identical with the pre-war Silesia palatinatus.

As the role of the Catholic Church in Poland's social and political life has been growing since the 1980s, the importance of the Church on the regional and local scale has increased accordingly. Obviously, the bishops' influence on decision-making is limited and mainly concerns decisions about location. However, consultation, negotiation and intervention at the palatinatus level are becoming more and more frequent. The influence seems to be greater in the palatinati whose capitals are also the bishops' seats.

Notes

1 One of the first problems in describing the Polish meso is a proper English name for the Polish *województwo*. In this chapter we use an old Latin term: *palatinatus*. This term was used commonly in Polish historical documents. In some other studies one can also find the term *voievodship*.

2 For more about the historical roots of the Polish palatinati, see, for example, Davis, 1982.

3 The analysis applies to the period from 22 July 1944 (the formal beginning of the Third Republic) until May 1990 (first post-war free local elections in Poland). Although a formal end of the Third Republic could be seen at the end of December 1989 (when the law changing the official name and emblem of state was accepted by Parliament), in fact we can observe the transition period from the 4 June 1989 elections, through to the change of central government the following September, to May 1990.

4 In this model 'own revenues' are not exactly 'own'. Revenues from own sources depend very strongly on central government; for example, rates of all 'local' and 'regional' taxes are fixed and changed at the central level. Also an introduction of new taxes (or liquidation of the old ones) is determined by the centre and not local or regional authorities.

5 MKZs were committees consisting of representatives of several or many plants, whose aim was to establish Solidarity in those plants.

Select further reading

Ash, T. G. (1983) *The Polish Revolution: Solidarity 1980–1981*. London: Cape.

Bennett, R. J. (ed.) (1989) *Territory and Administration in Europe*. London: Oxford University Press. See especially chapters by Bennett, Maurel and Ciechocinska.

Davis, N. (1982) *God's Playground: a History of Poland*. Vol I: *The Origins to 1975*. New York: Columbia University Press.

Fisher, J. (ed.) (1966) *City and Regional Planning in Poland*. Ithaca: Cornell University Press.

Gorzelak, G. (1987) *Local Poland Project: Aims and Methods*. Local Studies in Poland. Warsaw: Institute of Space Economy, University of Warsaw.

Lewis, P. (1989) 'Political authority and Party Secretaries in Poland 1975–1986', *Soviet and East European Studies*, 63.

208   The rise of meso government

References

Ash, T. G. (1983) *The Polish Revolution: Solidarity 1980–1981*. London: Cape.
Bartkowski, J., Kowalczyk, A. and Swianiewicz, P. (1990) *Strategie władz lokalnych*. Warsaw: University of Warsaw.
Davis, N. (1982) *God's Playground: a History of Poland*. Vol. I: *The Origins to 1975*. New York: Columbia University Press.
Denek, E. (1989) 'Władze terenowe stopnia wojewódzkiego i podstawowego w reformowanym systemie rad narodowych', in J. Wierzbicki (ed.), *Finanse gospodarki terenowej*. Warsaw: PWE.
Denek, E. and Wierzbicki, J. (1989) 'Problemy ekonomicznego i systemowego wyodrębnienia gospodarki terenowej', in J. Wierzbicki (ed.), *Finanse gospodarki terenowej*. Warsaw: PWE.
Fisher, J. (ed.) (1966) *City and Regional Planning in Poland*. Ithaca: Cornell University Press.
Ginsbert-Gebert, A. (1988) *Infrastruktura komunalna, jej stan i tendencje zmian w Polsce w latach 1950–2000*. Biuletyn KPZK PAN no. 140. Warsaw.
Gintowt-Jankowicz, M. (1989) 'Prawno-systemowe uwarunkowania finansów rad nardowych' in J. Wierzbicki (ed.), *Finanse gospodarki terenowej*. Warsaw: PWE.
Gorzelak, G. (1987) *Local Poland Project: Aims and Methods*. Local Studies in Poland. Warsaw: University of Warsaw.
Gorzelak, G. (1989) *Rozwój regionalny Polski w warunkach kryzysu i reformy*. Warsaw: University of Warsaw.
Grzeszczyk, T. (1988) 'Zatrudnienie w urzędach wojewódzkich', archiwum CPBP 09.8.
Guzowska, A. (1988) 'System finansów miasta, gminy i województwa', archiwum CPBP 09.8.
Holzer, J. (1989) 'Refleksje noworoczne', *Tygodnik Powszechny*, 4.
Jalowiecki, B. (1982) 'Regionalne oblicze kryzysu', in A. Jaroszyński and S. M. Komorowski (eds), *Gospodarka przestrzenna Polski i organizacja terytorialna kraju*. Warsaw: University of Warsaw.
Kalinowski, T. (1986) 'Organizacja przestrzenna regionu metropolitalnego Warszawy' (typescript).
Kokotkiewicz, I (1982) 'Podział administracyjny kraju na tle dawnego podziału administracyjnego, podziałów planistycznych i resortowych', in A. Jaroszyński and S. M. Komorowski (eds), *Gospodarka przestrzenna Polski i organizacja terytorialna kraju*. Warsaw: University of Warsaw.
Konieczny, W. (1986) 'Planowanie finansowe jako praktyczny instrument wpływu władz lokalnych na rozwój terenu', archiwum CPBP 09.8.
Konieczny, W. (1988) 'Formalnoprawne bariery gospodarowania finansami lokalnymi – pozadochodowe ograniczenia samodzielności rad narodowych', in K. Sobczak and Z. Niewiadomski (eds), *Strategia zmian systemu lokalnego*. Warsaw: University of Warsaw.
Kukliński, A. (1989) 'O gospodarce przestrzennej Polski' (typescript).
Leszczyńska, C. (1989) 'Województwo w II Rzeczypospolitej', archiwum CPBP 09.8.
Nierychło, A. (1989) 'Linie podziału', *Przegląd Tygodniowy*, 12 and 13.
Pańko, W. (1982) 'Porównawcza ocena dwóch modeli organizacji terytorialnej kraju', in A. Jaroszyński and S. M. Komorowski (eds), *Gospodarka przestrzenna Polski i organizacja terytorialna kraju*. Warsaw: University of Warsaw.
Problematyka organizacji terytorialnej kraju (1974) Biuletyn KPZK PAN no. 83. Warsaw.

'Program NSZZ Solidarność' (1981) *Tygodnik Solidarność*, 29.

'Program Solidarnośći' (1981) *Tygodnik Solidarność*, 22.

Raczkowska, A. (1989) 'Województwo w I Rzeczpospolitej', archiwum CPBP 09.8.

Regulski, J. (1989) 'Reforma gospodarcza w układzie terytorialnym', in J. Wierzbicki (ed.), *Finanse gospodarki terenowej*. Warsaw: PWE.

Siemiuta, K. (1981) 'Regiony – małe czy duze?', *Tygodnik Solidarność*, 13.

Sobczak, K. (1989) 'Nadzór nad władzami lokalnymi jako instytucja prawna wyznaczająca zakres ich samodzielności – synteza badań', archiwum CPBP 09.8.

Sobczak, K. and Szpringer, W. (1989) 'Funkcje województwa w systemie organizacji państwowej PRL', archiwum CPBP 09.8.

Sobczyk, J. (1981) 'Czas konfliktów', *Tygodnik Solidarność*, 13.

Strembicka, D., Korzeń, J., Tarczyński, J. and Lęska-Oleszak, T. (1988) 'Planowanie przestrzenne w systemie gospodarki terenowej', archiwum CPBP 09.8.

Swianiewicz, P. (1989a) *Społeczno-gospodarcza typologia miast i gmin w Polsce*. Warsaw: University of Warsaw.

Swianiewicz, P. (1989b) 'Local pressure groups in decision-making in Poland: new tendencies', in H. Baldersheim, R. Balme, T. N. Clark, V. Hoffman-Martinot and H. Magnusson (eds) *New Leaders, Parties and Groups: Comparative Tendencies in Local Leadership*. Bordeaux: Institut d'études politiques de Bordeaux.

Zdaniewicz, W. (1983) *Religion and Social Life*, Poznań: Pallotinum.

8

The Autonomous Communities as the Spanish Meso

Montserrat Cuchillo

It is already well known that the restoration of parliamemtary democracy and political pluralism in Spain was accompanied by a territorial redistribution of power which resulted in the establishment of seventeen Autonomous Communities (henceforth referred to as regions) vested with legislative and executive powers. Since their establishment, some regions have proceeded to partial reforms of their local government system, creating institutions oriented to

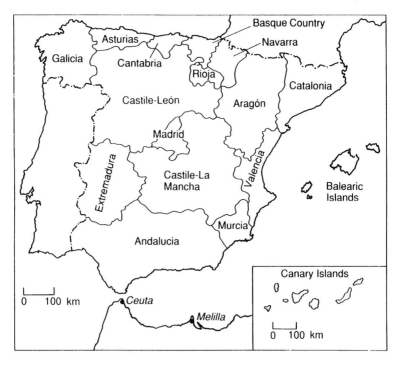

Figure 1   *The Autonomous Communities of Spain*

performing 'meso' functions within the regional structure. That is the case, for example, in Catalonia, where thirty-eight new elected bodies called *comarques* have been set up by the Catalan Local Government Act 1987. On the other hand, a variety of public authorities still exist between the regional and the national level for the performance of central government functions which may also be considered as another form of 'meso'. None the less, the impact on the Spanish system of the establishment of regional governments and the relevance of the political and administrative role assumed by them strongly suggest that regions are the most authentic institutional setting for considering recent developments in the meso level in Spain.

The Spanish meso experience could be considered to fall within the Southern European 'structural' category, since, as in Italy, meso developments have resulted in the establishment of elected regional governments all over the country with political and administrative powers and functions. As Cassese and Torchia (this volume) reveal, in Italy too, the long-standing tradition of a binary administrative system based on only two tiers of government and functional links between levels of government (central, regional and local) are still playing an important role in most parts of the country.

The Spanish regional system

The historical context

Even though Spain is one of the oldest political structures of Western Europe it may be said to be in chronic crisis over its national identity and, in parallel, involved in a continuing debate concerning the distribution of political power. Regional particularities – from the traditional Right – and federalism – from the liberal Left – confronted the conception of a single, or indivisible, nation and its corollary, the unitary nineteenth-century centralist state constructed by conservative liberalism (Carr, 1966; Brenan, 1967). The conflict between regional identity, on the one hand, and the organization of the state apparatus, on the other, characterized many of the civil struggles of the nineteenth and early twentieth centuries and they found their most tragic expression in the 1936–9 civil war.

The dictatorship of General Franco tried to stifle this conflict by increasing the centralized character of the state and also by refusing to accept any cultural or linguistic differences between the various Spanish regions. These repressive policies did not succeed in their task and regional particularism was an important element throughout in the political opposition to the regime (Carr and Fusi, 1979).

Table 1   *Autonomous Communities: key data*

Autonomous Community	Date of autonomy statute	Expenditure functions[2]				System of finance[3]	Regional taxes[5]	Senators in central Parliament[6]		Provinces (no.)	Municipalities (no.) (1986)	Other local tiers (potential)[7]
		Level	Education	Health	Police			Direct	Reg. parl.			
Andalucia	1981	H	D	D		C	LT	32	7	8	764	CO
Aragón	1982	L				C		12	2	3	727	CO
Asturias	1981	L				C-P		4	2	1	78	CO, MET
Balearic I.	1983	L				C		5	1	1	66	IC[8]
Canary I.	1982	H	D	E		C	OT	11	2	2	87	IC[8]
Cantabria	1981	L				C-P		4	1	1	102	CO
Castile-León	1983	L				C		36	3	9	2,248	CO
Castile-La Mancha	1982	L				C		20	2	5	916	CO
Catalonia	1979	H	D	D	D	C	GT, GS	16	6	4	940	CO[x], SM
Extremadura	1983	L				C		8	2	2	380	CO
Galicia	1981	H	D	E		C		16	3	4	312	CO, PA
Madrid	1983	L				C-P	GT, GS	4	5	1	178	SM
Murcia	1982	L				C-P		4	2	1	45	CO, MET
Rioja	1982	L				C-P		4	1	1	174	CO
Valencia	1982	H	D	D		C	GT, GS	12	4	3	536	CO, MET
Navarra	1982	H	D	D		S-P		4	1	1	265	—
Basque Country	1979	H	D	D	D	S	IS	12	3	3	236	SM
Ceuta and Melilla[1]	—	—	—	—	—	—	—	4	—	—	2	—
Spain	—	—	—	—	—	—	—	208	47	50	8,056	—

[1] Ceuta and Melilla are territories in Northern Africa.

[2] H = high; L = low; D = decentralized; E = expected in the near future. Regional police concurs with central police.

[3] C = common; S = special; P = provincial revenues.

[4] Formally, the Balearic Isles constitute one province, but provincial revenues are used to finance insular councils and not the regional government.

[5] LT = land tax; OT = oil tax; GT = gambling tax; GS = gambling surcharge; IS = income surcharge (levied on the Basque Country in 1984 only).

[6] Senators are elected by direct voting of people of each province, or by the regional parliaments.

[7] CO = counties; MET = metropolitan councils; PA = parishes; IC = insular councils; SM = supra-municipalities (not specified).

[8] These ties have already been created by the regional parliament.

Moreover, the 1960s and the beginning of the 1970s saw the development of a political and ideological process which put forward devolution, and the subsequent dismantling of the administrative apparatus, as a means of eradicating the authoritarian tendencies ingrained within the political system. It was also seen as a way both of establishing a model for economic development that would help combat the serious disparities between different areas of the Spanish territory, and of opening the way to radical social change (Hebbert and Alonso, 1982; Tamames and Clegg, 1984; Cuchillo and Vallés, 1988).

The 'transition' to democracy between General Franco's death in November 1975 and the promulgation of the Constitution in December 1978 should be understood as a period during which an agreement was reached between the Francoist sectors, conscious of the need for reform so as to preserve part of their power, and the sectors of the democratic opposition to Francoism, well aware of their organizing and mobilizing weakness as compared to the coercive institutions of the state appparatus. The problem posed by the existence of a number of regions with a linguistic, historical, cultural and social identity that was quite distinct from the rest of the state was one of the questions which were considered in this process of negotiations and consensus building. Out of these negotiations there emerged a set of agreements which led to the re-establishment of democratic institutions. Thus the accommodation of territorial differentiation was woven into the central fabric of the post-Franco Spanish state.

In a symbolic sense, then, the 1978 Constitution conceives the 'Spanish nation' as a group of 'nationalities' and regions with specific identities which differ in terms of language, cultural traditions and symbols of identity; and whereas Francoism had systematically ignored such differences and persecuted those who celebrated them, the new state would nurture them. In the new political-constitutional order, these particularist identities thus attain recognition and with it the right to self-government with a sphere of legislative and executive powers, and a series of representative institutions of their own. Such privileges, however, do not challenge or call into question 'the indissoluble unity of the Spanish nation, common and indivisible fatherland of all Spaniards'. This agreement is reflected in the Constitution (section 2) and later on in the seventeen Statutes of Autonomy establishing the regions and fixing their basic norms and institutions. In this sense, the historically dominant model of a unitary and highly centralized 'nation state' is abandoned, but so is the idea of a 'pluri-national federation' which some of the Left and regional nationalist political forces, the Socialist Party (PSOE) among them, had put forward in their initial projects and manifestos.[1]

The meso in the new constitutional system
The agreement regarding the territorial distribution of political and administrative power found its formal expression in a flexible formula which tried to give satisfaction to all of the different positions within the political spectrum, ranging from administrative decentralization to separatism. This accommodatory principle was reflected in the following aspects. First, the Constitution did not set out a predetermined map of the regions to be created. From a legal-constitutional point of view not all communities within the Spanish territory had necessarily to become part of a region and the acquisition of regional government had to take place through a process coming from 'below', that is, from the 'nationalities' and regions themselves. Second, the Constitution did not impose a specific model of devolution. The level of autonomy which could be reached by regions eventually constituted may range from so-called political autonomy, implying the assumption of legislative and executive powers, to so-called administrative autonomy, implying the assumption of merely executive powers. Finally, the Constitution did not establish a given set of powers and functions which were necessarily to be assumed by all regions. Once the above-mentioned choice had been made, the powers transferred to each region could vary widely, but within the range stated by the Constitution, and were enshrined in their respective statutes of autonomy.

The political agreement regarding the territorial distribution of power also involved the recognition of variations in the vigour of nationalistic feelings or the sense of singularity in different parts of the country. This recognition expressed itself both in the absence of a uniform method of being granted regional self-government, and in the imposition of transitory differences in the powers and functions which may be assumed by regions.[2] That is why distinctions are made between regions with initially full autonomous powers and regions with initially restricted powers, such as 'full autonomy' and 'deferred autonomy' regions, or 'high-level' and 'low-level' regions. Eventually all such distinctions may disappear (Entrena, 1981; Garcia de Enterria, 1982; Hebbert and Alonso, 1982).[3]

The distribution of powers and functions
As a result of leaving the initiative for the devolution processes to the regions, the Constitution simply states the framework within which each region will determine the powers and functions that it has decided to assume.

The constitutional framework is basically defined by four elements. First, a listing of the powers and functions liable to be devolved to regions and of those which are necessarily reserved to national institutions (sections 148 and 149.1 of the Constitution). Second, a 'residual clause' vesting all powers and functions not expressly assumed by regions in their Statutes of Autonomy to the central government (s. 149.3). Third, a provision allowing future adjustments, both widening and restraining regional autonomy, of the distribution of powers and functions enshrined by the Constitution (s. 150). Finally, the establishment of the Constitutional Court as the body responsible for the settlement of disputes between central and regional governments over their respective spheres of power and over the constitutionality of national and regional legislation (s. 161).

The distribution of powers between the centre and the region is as follows:

Powers which may be assumed by all regions (s. 148)*

- Organization of regional institutions.
- Supervision of local government within national regulations.
- Town and country planning and housing within national basic legislation.
- Public works of regional interest (within the region's territory).
- Regional roads and railways, private ports and airports.
- Agriculture and cattle-raising within national legislation.
- Implementation of national policies on environmental protection, forestry and freshwater fishing.
- Water supply and hydraulic works on regional waterways.
- Regional economic development within national economic polices and planning.
- Local commercial fairs, handicrafts and tourism.
- Regional museums, libraries, sports and cultural activities.
- Social welfare services and sanitary conditions.

* Where no specification of the functions is made, regions may assume legislative and executive powers.

Powers reserved to the central government (s. 149.1)*

- Basic conditions ensuring equal treatment for all Spaniards in the exercise of constitutional rights and duties.
- Nationality, immigration and foreign affairs.
- Defence, armed forces and administration of justice.
- Legislation on criminal, private[†] and commercial law, labour relations and copyrights and patents.
- Customs administration and foreign trade.

- Monetary system, foreign currency, holdings and exchange and basic rules of credit, banking and insurance.
- Economic planning and general rules of public finance.
- Basic conditions and co-ordination of health policy, national health service and superannuation services.
- Legislation on pharmaceuticals.
- Legal basis of public administration, including basic legislation on local government, civil servants and common administrative procedures.
- Sea fishing and basic legislation on environmental protection and forestry.
- Railways and roads of 'national interest'.
- Basic legislation on communications and traffic, post office, telephone, cable and radio.
- Public works of 'general interest'.
- Merchant shipping, coast protection, national and commercial ports and airports, air space and airways.
- Legislation on hydraulic resources and electricity and management of waterways covering more than one region.
- Basic regulation on mining and the production of energy.
- Basic regulation on the press, radio and TV.
- Public order and civil defence, though regions can create their own police forces with responsibility for some areas.
- Basic norms on education and co-ordination of scientific and technical research.
- Protection of the artistic, cultural and architectural patrimony and 'national' museums, archives and libraries.

* Where nothing is stated (for example, armed forces) national institutions retain all legislative and executive powers.

† Where a special private law system already existed, regions have the right to develop that legal system.

The institutional setting of regions

The Constitution assigned to the regions the establishment of their political institutions and the definition of their internal organization, except in the case of those regions having direct access to 'full autonomy'. These authorities were to be organized institutionally through a regional assembly or parliament, directly elected by the population, an executive council or regional government supported by a majority within the regional parliament and a president elected by the regional assembly. Other regions were free to organize themselves differently, establishing institutions similar, for example, to those set up in the Italian regions. But all regional governments have adhered to the above-mentioned system, with slight variations as regards the distribution of functions between the regional organs (Muñoz Machado, 1982–4; Font, 1985).

Considerable discretion was also granted in relation to the creation of regional administrative structures. Some debate took place during the constituent process about alternative models which sought to avoid the disadvantages of highly centralized and hierarchical administrative structures. None the less the regions have not gone a long way in their search for new formulas and for a number of reasons they have all set up administrative organizations which reproduce, with minor adjustments, the model still very much in force at the central level and inherited from the former regime (Viver Pi-Sunyer, 1981; Argullol, 1983; Bassols, 1984).[4]

Financial agreements
The constitutional provisions on the financing of regional governments declare that the power to tax is originally vested in the national Parliament, so that regions have to obtain fiscal powers through explicit devolution granted by an Act of Parliament. The constitutional provisions also state that regions have the right to finance their expenditure with their own taxes, ceded taxes, revenue sharing, grants and other revenues, and that an Intergovernmental Compensating Fund (FCI) will provide for the transfer of project grants to poor regions in order to redistribute resources among them.

The gradual development of the Constitution entailed the establishment of a provisional financing system set up in the Finance Act 1980 (Ley Orgánica de Financiación de las Comunidades Autónomas: LOFCA), which was to be substituted by a definitive system after a six-year period.[5] The provisional system did not envisage a substantial devolution of fiscal powers to the regions. It was based on the centralization of revenues, the decentralization of expenditure and the assumption by the central government of responsibility for covering the cost of services transferred to the regions. The definitive system would entail a devolution of fiscal powers and the assignment of funds to each region which would not be based on an assessment of the 'effective cost' of the services devolved, but on a number of parameters such as population size, personal income, fiscal effort in terms of income tax revenue and the number of provinces within each group.

The period for the provisional system ended without the political parties having arrived at an agreement about the system to be definitively established. In the absence of such agreement, another provisional system was set up to be implemented during a five-year period (1987–91). In the new transitional formula the assignment of funds was no longer related to the 'effective cost' of devolved responsibilities but, with certain adjustments, to the above-mentioned parameters. The central government is negotiating with the regions the financial system proposed at the end of 1991. The new arrangement, which does not envisage a substantial remodelling of the current one, entails the assignment of a global fixed sum meant to provide for equalization to be drawn by regions during 1992–4, the transfer of a percentage of the income tax (around 15 per cent) and delegation of the collection and management of VAT and of other nationally fixed minor taxes. Some regions have already signed a pre-agreement but others, such as Catalonia and the Canary Islands, are reluctant to accept the proposal and have recently qualified their approval to revision of the economic programme for adjustment to European economic policies (Plan de Convergencia, June 1992), which was elaborated by the government without previous consultations and has been unanimously rejected by political and economic actors. In any case, even though the new arrangement warrants wider financial autonomy, it could still be maintained that a system where tax capacity, fiscal effort and needs are reasonably measured and where regions control relevant taxable resources and assume a degree of fiscal responsibility has not yet been found (Castells, 1987a, 1987b; Solé-Vilanova, 1989, 1990; Colldeforns, 1992).

The setting up of the Spanish regions

The translation of the basic agreement from which the new Spanish system emerged may be divided into a 'prelude' and three stages (Cuchillo and Vallés, 1988).

The prelude or preliminary stage (1977–8) ended with the promulgation of the Constitution in December 1978. This period is characterized by the unavoidable ambiguity of the new system as the final negotiations on the Constitution were completed. However, due to intensive pressure coming from the most active nationalist political actors, some decentralizing measures were adopted. These resulted in the establishment of regional provisional bodies empowered to act as decentralized organs for the exercise of executive functions in fields such as public transport, regional highways and town and country planning.

The first stage (1979–81) This period was characterized by the complexity and difficulties of matching the democratization of the state and the implementation of the provisions on devolution. In this period the political reorganization expressed in the constitutional pact acquired a considerable impulse. The pressure was coming from the regional nationalist parties often backed by the Socialist and Communist parties and it offset the centralizing inertia of the governmental party (Unión del Centro Democrático, UCD), which was conditioned by its commitment to the economic and bureaucratic elites of the former regime who were intent on the preservation of a centralized political structure.

The enforcement of the measures on devolution resulted in the approval of the Statutes of Autonomy of the 'historical' regions (the Basque Country and Catalonia in December 1979 and Galicia in April 1981). None the less, the UCD adopted a number of measures oriented towards delaying and controlling the extension of similar processes to other parts of the country, thereby reversing the constitutional provisions which left the initiative to the 'regional' political actors. This strategy was clear in the long negotiations preceding the approval of the Statute of Autonomy for Galicia, and also in the definition of policies stating that any other communities willing to constitute themselves as regions in the future would have to accept ascription to 'second-class' or 'low-level' regional status. But following intensive political and popular pressure the central government had to abandon this position in Andalucia, which was granted 'full autonomic powers' in 1980 (Tamames and Clegg, 1984).

By the end of this period, with three regions already well established (the Basque Country, Catalonia and Andalucia) that were eager to fully exercise their powers, attention moved on to the definition of the scope and content of regional powers which were rather ambiguously stated in the Constitution. Open conflicts between central government and regional government ensued, which often required the intervention of the Constitutional Court to resolve them. Acting as a referee in such controversies, the court began to play a key role in the definition of central and regional powers, and it is a role it has maintained with obvious inconveniences and drawbacks for the working of the system (Muñoz Machado, 1981; Tomas y Valiente, 1985).

The second stage (1981–3)   This stage may be said to open with the failed coup in February 1981. The coup was the most spectacular element of a strategy designed to restrain the more dynamic aspects of the transition to democracy and it played an important role in the internal destruction of the party in power (UCD) in favour of a more conservative right-wing party (AP). This process, together with the rejection by the regional actors of the restrictive policies regarding devolution, led to the so-called 'Autonomic Agreement' between the UCD and the PSOE. This agreement found its legal expression in the Law for the Harmonization of the Devolution Process 1982 (LOAPA). The LOAPA provided for an indirect constitutional reform as regards the territorial distribution of power and for a homogenization of the devolution process. These measures were basically reflected in (a) simultaneity in the establishment of regions not yet constituted, (b) homogeneity of powers and functions liable to be assumed by the new regions and (c) recognition of central powers for the definition of criteria and guidelines to which all regional laws, regulations and activities must conform.

The LOAPA created a political row which gave way to the lodging of appeals with the Constitutional Court before it came into force. The court returned its ruling, in August 1983, striking down as unconstitutional the most restrictive sections regarding the distribution of central and regional powers. The court's decision resulted in the promulgation of the Law for the Devolution Process (LPA, 1983) and forced the PSOE, in power since October 1982, to revise its strategy on devolution. 'Full' powers were granted to Valencia, the Canary Islands and Navarra and extensive negotiations took place during the drafting of the Statutes of Autonomy of communities awaiting access to regional government. On the other hand, the 'Autonomic Agreement' did bear fruit, for by the spring of 1983 the whole of the Spanish territory was organized in regions. This was achieved despite resistance by some communities that did not wish to become regions or to become part of other regions. Moreover, all of the regions assumed fairly similar powers and functions. Thus the diversity envisaged by the constitutional provisions on devolution was narrowed down to the establishment of two broad categories of regions all over the country.

The third stage (1983 to date)   This period may be divided into three phases corresponding roughly to the successive mandates of the Socialist government. The first, which runs to the autumn of 1986, is characterized by a considerable quickening of pace of devolution as a result of the political stability derived from the electoral victory of the PSOE (October 1982) with an absolute majority. In a context in which there was a significant readjustment of the political forces and in which most of the senior posts in the central bureaucracy were filled with persons selected by the Socialist government, the PSOE had sufficient strength to implement its programme on devolution with little opposition, and to achieve a fundamental reconstruction of the former state apparatus (Cuchillo and Vallés, 1988; Tornos et al., 1988). Most of the 'basic' legislation reserved to the national Parliament was passed, thus providing for the adjustment of the legal basis of the system to the new democratic principles. The institutions of the seventeen regions existing within the country were set up, and with different degrees of intensity they all started to exercise their powers. The transfer of administrative services, facilities, personnel and resources necessary for the exercise of powers devolved to the regions also occurred at a relatively stable pace.

This stage is also characterized by the fact that even though the LOAPA was repealed, some of the ideas which inspired it, and some of the motives whereby it was passed, continue to influence the stance of the Socialist government. The 'Autonomic Agreement' (1981) was the result of a common conviction held by the conservative Right (UCD) and the Socialist Party. Its main premises were that the 'flexibility' of the provisions on devolution had to be narrowed down and translated into a better-defined and more specific model; also that the model to be adopted had to ensure the primacy of central institutions and the preservation of their role as supreme custodians of the general interest. At the same time it had to ensure that the regions were institutions capable of satisfying functional needs derived from upward mobility factors and of coping with popular pressures for decentralization and participation.

The Socialist Party has not succeeded in proposing an alternative model to that promoted by the LOAPA that is acceptable to regional and opposition parties. The absence of a basic consensus on devolution gives way to constant conflicts between the PSOE and the regional parties and between central and regional institutions. This friction is reflected, among other aspects, in the lack of agreement on the regional financing system and in the slowness with which services and administrative facilities regarding devolved functions are transferred to regional bodies. It is also apparent in the meagre remodelling of central administrative bodies, and in the endless lodging of appeals with the Constitutional Court both by central and by regional institutions.[6] Finally and most significantly, it is reflected in the fact that in the regional elections held in June 1987 some recently created conservative regionalist parties gained a certain amount of popular support in their regions which hitherto had not exhibited very strong regional movements, for example Aragon, Cantabria and the Balearic Islands (Rodriguez-Aguilera, 1988, 1989).

The second electoral victory of the PSOE in 1986 marks the beginning of a phase, which runs through its third electoral victory in 1989 until the remodelling of the executive in 1991, characterized by a rise in conflict between the centre and the regions and by the slow-down in the process of devolution and administrative reform. The gradual implementation of the provisions on devolution and the disagreement on the model to be attained require continuous negotiation between central government and regional governments and between central departments and their regional counterparts, in order to build the consensus needed to adopt any decision affecting centre–periphery relations (Muñoz Machado, 1982–4; Tornos et al., 1988, 1990).

The Socialist government retains the capacity to impose its options in case of a deadlock, but its dominance secured by three successive mandates with an absolute majority is undermined by two factors: first and in general terms, by the increased ability of regions to resist and obstruct central policies as a result of the expansion of their political and administrative powers. Second, in those parts of the country where regional governments are strong (that is, Catalonia, the Basque Country, Galicia, Valencia, Andalucia), central capacity is undermined by the revival of radical nationalism and regionalism and the subsequent systematic opposition to central initiatives. Such regional resistance is re-enforced as a result of disappointment with devolution and frustration by the continued dominance of the PSOE and the lack of any alternative either on the conservative Right or on the Socialist and Communist Left.[7] This stalemate may explain why a number of contentious issues pending since 1986 have not been resolved. Such issues include the establishment of a definitive regional financing system, the definition of the mechanisms whereby regions may participate in the drafting and negotiation of EC regulations and directives and assume a degree of responsibility for their implementation, and the revision of the Statutes of Autonomy of the eleven regions with until now 'deferred autonomy' status, which have put forward demands for full autonomy powers after completion of the five-year transitional period.[8]

The third electoral victory of the PSOE and, especially, the remodelling of the central executive in 1991, mark the beginning of a phase characterized by a change in the strategy on devolution. In the above-mentioned context, the narrow margin by which the Socialist government retains an absolute majority and the sharp rise of popular support for the right-wing conservative party (Partido Popular, PP, formerly called AP), nearly led to a global deadlock that forced the political actors to reconsider their positions. The new stance has been basically reflected, up till now, in three aspects. In the proposal of a financial arrangement, now being discussed, liable to be accepted by all regions, except those already granted a special financing system (the Basque Country and Navarra), in the near future. In the formulation of a new Autonomic Agreement, recently signed by the PSOE and PP, providing for a uniform expansion of the powers granted to the eleven regions with 'deferred autonomy' status, which shall most probably be translated into the legal revision of the eleven Statutes of Autonomy by the end of the 1992. Finally, in the sharp decrease in the lodging of appeals with the Constitutional Court, both by central and by regional parties and institutions. It

Table 2 *Autonomous Communities: general and economic data*

Autonomous Community	Population (1986)		Area		Income per capita (1985)[2]		Net migration[3] People (000s)		
	People	%	Sq km	%	US$	Mean: 100	1961–75	1976–80	1981–5
Andalucia	6,789,772	17.6	87,268	17.3	4.5	77.5	−1,041.6	−53.9	162.9
Aragón	1,184,295	3.1	47,669	9.4	6.6	112.4	−48.1	9.9	7.4
Asturias	1,112,186	2.9	10,565	2.1	6.5	111.9	−17.4	−4.0	−23.3
Balearic I.	680,933	1.8	5,014	1.0	8.2	140.3	−28.3	28.3	90.1
Canary I.	1,466,391	3.8	7,273	1.4	5.2	88.7	137.4	−39.6	108.9
Cantabria	522,664	1.4	5,289	1.0	6.3	108.5	−12.7	−1.9	0.6
Castile-León	2,582,327	6.7	94,147	18.6	5.8	100.0	−627.2	−25.4	−15.7
Castile-La Mancha	1,675,715	4.4	79,226	15.7	4.6	79.4	−904.6	−57.9	−15.8
Catalonia	5,978,638	15.5	31,930	6.3	6.7	114.4	947.1	39.2	−72.9
Extremadura	1,086,420	2.8	41,602	8.2	4.0	69.2	−494.1	−45.3	1.7
Galicia	2,844,472	7.4	29,434	5.8	5.0	86.5	−220.1	−12.7	−56.1
Madrid	4,780,572	12.4	7,995	1.6	6.8	116.2	996.7	31.9	8.6
Murcia	1,006,788	2.6	11,317	2.2	4.9	84.9	−109.1	17.4	18.9
Rioja	260,024	0.7	5,034	1.0	7.6	130.6	−14.9	4.6	3.3
Valencia	3,732,682	9.7	23,305	4.6	5.8	99.9	476.9	72.7	40.5
Navarra	515,900	1.3	10,421	2.1	7.0	120.3	15.8	4.8	−4.4
Basque Country	2,136,100	5.6	7,261	1.4	7.2	123.7	320.3	−40.8	−53.9
Ceuta and Melilla[1]	117,539	0.3	32	0.0	4.0	68.0	n.a.	n.a.	n.a.
Spain	38,473,418	100.0	504.782	100.0	5.8	100.0	−623.9	72.7	200.8

[1] Ceuta and Melilla are territories in Northern Africa.
[2] 1 US$ = 115 pesetas.
[3] The Spanish totals represent net migration with respect to foreign countries.
Sources: Instituto Nacional de Estadística and Ministerio de Economía y Hacienda.

could thus be considered that the momentum of the devolutionary process reached its peak by the autumn of 1986. From then onwards the problems encountered in the working of the new system came to the fore. These problems are difficult to solve due to the serious technical deficiencies of the complex political and administrative structure established. But they are basically difficult to solve because of there being neither an agreement on the model for the territorial distribution of power to be definitively adopted, as regions having assumed wider powers and functions insist on further devolution and in the future remodelling of the state structure into a federal system, while the national parties persist in the political options and policies reflected in the 'Autonomic Agreements' 1981 and 1992, nor a clear option that might provide impetus to the attainment of such agreement.

An attempt at evaluation

The dominant position of central government

Central institutions play a dominant role in the Spanish political system. But a relatively high degree of decentralization has been attained and central government no longer has the power of imposing its will on the regions without their consent.

The dominant position of national institutions is a logical consequence of the preservation of the unitary character of the state and of its constitutional status as the custodian of the 'general' interest. However, this dominance has been reflected in some ways that are considered unacceptable by regional and opposition parties and by some other sectors of the population. Among others, the following may be mentioned. There is, first, what is regarded as the over-expansive interpretation of the powers reserved to the national Parliament and to central government; second, the survival of a pervasive central administration; third, the establishment of a system for the assignment of funds to finance regional government which leaves the control of most resources and the decision on the distribution among regions to national institutions; finally, there is the assumption by central government of exclusive powers for international affairs and especially for relations with EC institutions.

Interpretation of national powers

The Constitution reserves very few matters to national institutions. In relation to most public functions the state is only responsible for the setting of the legal framework ('basic legislation', 'basic norms' or 'basis'). Regions have assumed legislative and executive powers exercisable within the basic framework. But the Constitutional Court in various Resolutions (STCs) has sustained a position in the definition of the respective scope of central and regional powers regarding these concurrent matters that has given way to an extremely wide and confusing interpretation of the powers retained by the state.

The court has maintained that regions did not have to wait for the establishment of the general framework to exercise their powers on concurrent matters and that when passed, national legislation had to leave a certain leeway for regions to make their own options in relation to these concurrent matters (STC2 and 14/1981, 98/1985). It has also maintained, though, that national powers consist not only in fixing the minimum common criteria to be respected by all regions but also (a) in formulating basic unitary policies (that is, in education or public health) through the definition of objectives, guidelines and principles to be followed by all regions, and (b) in defining these sectors or aspects of a given matter which are to be considered basic and may be pre-empted by the state.[9] These decisions can be stated both in formal Acts of the national Parliament and in statutory instruments and executive decisions of central government (STC 1/1981, 25/1983, 91/1985).

This interpretation generates great uncertainty – because regions may be obliged, at any time, to change and redefine their own policies in case they happen to become incompatible with a later policy defined by the national government, and because there is no way to know what is 'basic' at a given moment (Martin Mateo, 1981). The decision on that question, which is of an essentially political nature, is left to the Constitutional Court.[10] The assigning of a function which should belong to Parliament and the continuous lodging of appeals it entails are overloading the Constitutional Court and seriously hampering the working of the system (Garcia de Enterria, 1989; Tornos et al., 1988, 1990). It has to be noted, though, that recurring statements by the court's president urging the political resolution of central–regional conflicts, together with successive rulings restating the court's doctrine on the subject, have probably favoured the significant decrease in the lodging of appeals from nearly one hundred in 1989 to eleven in 1991.

Central administrative structures
The maintenance of an extensive central administration seems to be a direct consequence of the above-mentioned interpretation of national powers. But it is also derived from resistance to devolution by the central political actors and bureaucratic elites and from the diversity in the powers and functions devolved to different regions.

Resistance is demonstrated by the obstacles placed in the path of the transfer of services and facilities ascribed by the Constitution to the regions, and to the dismantling of central field services existing in the 43 remaining provinces and in the 7 uni-provincial regions. The functions performed by these peripheral offices are mainly related to public law and order, local government and finance. Their relationship with regional authorities is often strained as a result of the concurrence of competences, and also because these offices are viewed as direct successors to the authorities which under Franco were responsible for the political supervision and control of local communities (Salas, 1979; Argullol, 1987; Prats, 1988).[11]

The preservation of the central administrative structures is also a consequence of the constitutional provisions allowing regions to assume the powers and functions they desire within a predetermined range and establishing two categories of regions, at least for a provisional period. This has resulted in a degree of variation that prevents the dismantling of a number of central offices that should have become redundant in certain regions but which are still in full operation in other regions. None the less, it has to be stressed that a substantial reorganization would have been attained if the precepts contained in the LPA of 1983 had been enforced. These provided for the merging of sectoral central departments, the reduction of their executive competence and the assigning to central structures of planning, supervisory and informative functions. Instead, all state departments subsist; direct management survives; and planning, advisory and information offices have hardly been set up, or are clearly underdeveloped (Parada, 1990; Tornos et al., 1988, 1990).[12]

Financial arrangements
The financial system agreed in 1986 has not solved the problems of the provisional system set by the LOFCA. Central institutions continue to consider themselves as the 'owners' of all public resources and regions continue to be mere receivers of taxes and other revenues that they neither fix, regulate nor control. On the other hand, the parameters selected to calculate the assignment of funds and the weight given to each of them leave a wide field for negotiation. This entails a high degree of uncertainty and also a high potential for conflict, as final amounts are renegotiated every year and they depend more closely on the capacity of each region to negotiate with the government from a strong position than on its needs and fiscal effort. The financial system now being discussed is meant to solve some of these problems, but it still does not provide for a real decentralization of resources matching the legislative and executive powers which have been devolved to the regions.

The financial arrangements until now in force have impaired the fulfilment of three necessary objectives. First, the establishment of co-responsibility of regions in the use of public moneys: the lack of financial autonomy created by central control of all significant taxable resources makes regions in fact financially unaccountable to their electorate. Second, the establishment of a distribution formula for resources among the different levels of government (including the local level) which will enable them to perform the functions assigned by the Constitution: insufficiency of resources, together with the above-mentioned lack of fiscal co-responsibility, has resulted in poor performance and in an alarming indebtedness of most regions (and of some local authorities). Finally, the attainment of a degree of equalization between regions: deficiencies in the calculations of the different factors on which the distribution of resources is based have resulted in the transformation of the FCI, which was meant to compensate for inequalities between regions, into a grant assigned to all regions in order to finance their capital expenditure (Castells, 1987a, 1987b; Solé-Vilanova, 1989, 1990; Colldeforns, 1992).

Relations with EC institutions
International affairs and relations with the EC institutions is an especially contentious issue. The Spanish Constitution states that foreign affairs are reserved to the central government and that the powers so implied permit the centre to sign treaties affecting matters devolved to regions. Regions have not challenged this interpretation, but they have claimed the right to be informed of negotiations. They have also argued that they are entitled not only to be informed about but also to participate in the drafting of, and to be held responsible for, all EC regulations and directives dealing with matters pertaining to their constitutional powers.

The government has followed a restrictive course of action which excludes regions from the preparation and negotiation of EC regulations and also from their implementation (for example, in agriculture). It has also tried, unsuccessfully, to prevent regions (until now the Basque Country, Catalonia, Valencia and Andalucia) opening 'shadow' offices in Brussels and conducting informal negotiations with the EC. The regions resent this attitude, which excludes the possibility of playing a role which they foresaw in their Statutes of Autonomy and which is accepted by some European countries with what they see as comparable meso structures (such as Germany) (Morata, 1987). Some steps were taken in 1986 to reach an agreement on this subject. The agreement which has not been accepted by some regions, such as the Basque Country, states that central and regional bodies shall be responsible for the enforcement of EC regulations and policies that affect those functions which fall within their constitutional ambit. But it does not provide for regional participation in the drafting and negotiations of such regulations.

The role of regions
Statements about the role assumed by regions since their establishment which are valid for all of them are quite difficult to make due to the Spanish model of devolution with its capacity to permit a high degree of variation. Some generalizations, though, may be possible in relation to their performance as political and administrative bodies representing the interests of the regional communities.

Public participation   Regional institutions have not so far been able significantly to awaken public interest in regional policies and have only contributed marginally to bringing public affairs nearer to the citizens. For example, the degree of electoral participation is lower at the regional than at the national level, averaging 60 per cent in most regions as against 76.9 per cent in general elections. The percentage is lower (around 63 per cent) in the so-called 'special regions' (Catalonia, the Basque Country, Galicia and Andalucia), where regional elections are not held on the same day as local elections. But electoral turn-out is consistently decreasing all over the country, in regional as well as in national and local elections, to a record 54.9 per cent in the regional elections held in Catalonia in March 1992 (only surpassed by the European elections held in 1989, with 51.5 per cent of the total voting population). See Appendix for fuller details. One of the reasons accounting for this low turn-out record could be the constraints deriving from the proportional electoral system, where parties gaining less than 5 per cent of the total vote are excluded and seats are allocated according to Hondt's rule. The weak implantation of political parties in Spain and the mobility of the electorate do not fit well with a voting system which requires a comparatively high degree of political consciousness and stability. One suggested reform of the regional electoral system is open lists so as to enhance popular participation. But there is neither agreement nor clear evidence that this measure will improve turn-out (Rodriguez-Aguilera, 1988, 1989; Tornos et al., 1988).

Other factors accounting for weak participation and feeble interest in regional issues probably include the following. First, the dominance of national party politics at the regional level: this does not apply so much in those regions with a long-standing tradition (the Basque Country, Navarra and Catalonia), and in those regions where regional feelings have steadily risen since devolution (Andalucia and Valencia). The second reason for the lack of public interest is institutional. The working of regional parliaments, the nature of regional functions and the secrecy of regional institutions have all dampened popular interest. Most regional parliaments are organized on the national model, which restricts the political debate to a minimum. Regional policies are usually adopted in a highly secretive way. And regional functions are basically of an executive character, and although often contentious (for example, refuse disposal and treatment, territorial planning, environment) rarely raise issues as highly controversial as those occurring at the national level (such as participation in NATO, income taxes, abortion or public versus private education). Finally, the media and especially television are highly centralized, and they tend to ignore regional issues and focus public attention on national politics and national issues. Only where the regional media are being progressively developed, regional newspapers and television channels steadily expanding their coverage and audience, is this not the case (as in Valencia, Andalucia, Catalonia and the Basque Country).

The coincidence of the above-mentioned elements with the generalized decline of interest in politics (the so-called *desencanto*), as a result of both the almost obsessive moderation of democratic institutions and the 'high' popular expectations of the new political system, has had an immediate negative impact on public participation at the regional level (McDonough et al., 1986; Alvira-Martin and Garcia-Lopez, 1988). It has restrained the building up of involvement and interest on the part of the regional communities in regions with a weak sense of identity. It has also watered down initial willingness to participate even in those regions with a noticeable degree of politicization and relatively intense 'nationalist' feeling.

The regional institutional setting   The general lack of imagination in designing regional institutions has already been mentioned. Two developments deserve perhaps some further attention. Most regions have promoted a somewhat pathological expansion of their administrative structures such as the establishment of regional peripheral offices in each province (for example, Catalonia, Galicia and the Basque Country) and a widespread proliferation of 'quangos' and of all kinds of administrative bodies. The objective seems to have been to make regional institutions better known to the regional population and to legitimize and consolidate regions as public institutions (Bayona, 1987). Such strategies have helped some regions to assume a relevant and identifiable role in public life in a relatively short time. But the consequences are unnecessary duplication and overlapping of functions, inefficiency, waste of resources, improvisation and the establishment of regional institutions which are not patently more accessible and accountable to the citizens than central institutions.

It should be mentioned that regions have tended to follow central institutions in the selection and management of personnel. This mimicry is partly a response to restrictions imposed by national legislation and partly the regions' own choice. The bureaucratic model established during Francoist times, granting 'tenure' to administrative personnel, was finally preserved by the Constitution. This choice has hampered both the democratization and the decentralization of administrative structures.[13] Regions have had to fill many of their administrative posts with personnel formerly serving in peripheral offices of the central administration. The heterogeneity of training, methods of selection and regulation of their rights and duties, together with the already mentioned resistance of such personnel towards regional authorities, has been an important handicap in the management of regional staff. It has also led to an expansion of regional personnel as the regions effect control by creating a top cadre of their own appointees. Regions in turn have not profited from powers which allow them to modify slightly the national model when recruiting their own personnel. They have in general terms assigned posts to a generation which is not attached to the values of the former regime but to democratic values. But leaving aside considerations of increased administrative efficiency and following the stance of successive national governments, regions have opted for the advantages of reproducing and expanding the bureaucratic tenured model. This is a model which generates a high level of 'unconditional loyalty', based on the confidence that 'loyalty' will translate into the preservation of working conditions and privileges granted, and which enjoys wide popularity, as it entails a perception of governments as reliable employers at a time when the unemployment rate is approaching 15.5 per cent (Nieto, 1984; Parada, 1990).

Regional performance   The above-mentioned criticisms should not lead to the conclusion that regions have shown an overwhelming inability to fulfil their role and to meet the expectations they raised. Some regions enjoy a well-deserved degree of legitimacy and popular support which derives not only from their ability to satisfy 'nationalist' feelings and cultural and linguistic identities. They have also revealed a capacity to make policies in accordance with regional interests (for example, in territorial planning, environmental protection, public works and economic promotion); to improve public services (in education and public health); to show imagination in the development of certain activities in fields until now abandoned or forgotten by other public bodies (in social services, culture and sport, and services for the young and the elderly); and to promote a relative increase of popular participation in the conduct of public affairs through co-option in consultative and managing administrative bodies (in education, health and consumer protection). Some regions have also developed agricultural and micro-economic policies, despite central encroachment, which have contributed a considerable impulse to the regional economy (as in Navarra, Catalonia, Andalucia, Valencia, Galicia and the Canary Islands).[14]

It could be argued that these achievements would have been attained anyway, even without devolution, simply as a consequence of the democratization of Spanish institutions. But the fact is that it was the regions which made the changes. It may be that the closer connection these institutions have with the community accounts, at least in part, for such successes.

A final consideration is that the regions have tended to ascribe responsibility for any difficulties and drawbacks in the working of regional institutions and policies to resistance to devolution by central government and central bureaucratic elites. In this way the parties in power, especially in those 'nationalist' regions which are not controlled by the PSOE, have consolidated and expanded their support in the regional community. Often they claim lack of resources in comparison with national institutions and also that regional governments are 'victimized' by the central government. In a context in which centre–periphery relations are still unclear, clear popular support strengthens the regions and enables them to negotiate from a strong position and thus achieve a wider margin of autonomy. In some cases they have been able to have additional central services and facilities transferred to them, together with higher resources as well.

The position of local government

A wholesale reform of local government is still pending in Spain and the situation will probably remain unchanged in the near future. After the re-establishment of democratic institutions, proposals for structural reform of the local government system soon appeared unrealistic for reasons similar to those encountered in most Southern European countries. On the other hand, priority given to devolution and disagreement on the stance to be adopted in relation to local government delayed developments at the local level. Thus more than seven years went by after the promulgation of the Constitution before the basic legislation on local government was passed, even though in the meantime some measures were taken in order to solve the more pressing issues in relation to local autonomy and the relationship between local authorities and central and regional governments.

The Constitution enshrined the right of municipalities and provinces to 'manage autonomously the interests of their respective communities'. This autonomy is of an administrative nature, entailing the attribution of merely executive powers. But its working required a deep revision of local government legislation, because under the Francoist regime local authorities were subject to controls on their activities which were declared incompatible with local autonomy by the Constitutional Court (STC 2/1981). The Local Government Law 1985 (LBRL) established that local autonomy entailed the right of local authorities to participate in all matters of interest to them or affecting local communities. The actual definition of local powers was left to national and regional legislation regulating different sectors in which local authorities may be interested or affected. The solution was inspired by the German model, but it did not include any guarantees as regards the assignation of financial resources and the right to participate in the formulation of national and regional legislation affecting them (Muñoz Machado, 1982–4, 1988).[15]

The role of local authorities

Municipalities   According to the LBRL, municipalities are the basic local government units and they assume an essential role as primary institutions for popular participation in public affairs and for the provision of basic services. The fulfilment of this double role is, however, dubious, because over 86 per cent of the nearly 8,000 municipalities have less than 5,000 inhabitants and thus lack the necessary resources (Parejo Alfonso, 1986). Moreover, the character of the former regime, and the absence of any linking mechanism similar to the French *cumul des mandats*, has prevented municipalities from building up a degree of influence and support at the national and regional levels, thus enabling them to compensate, at least in part, for their deficiencies as functional units.[16]

Provinces   The Constitution states that provinces have a dual character. They are intermediate local authorities and they are also territorial divisions for the performance of national functions. Subsequent legislation added that provinces should also be territorial divisions for the enforcement of regional legislation and policies.

In contrast to the French *département* on which they were modelled, the Spanish provinces never developed powerful and efficient administrative structures. During the Francoist regime they were basically organizations exercising close political control of local communities (Garcia de Enterria, 1978). This is the reason why since the re-establishment of democracy provinces have been the most contentious local institution. Their position was protected by the Constitution after strenuous debate due to pressures coming from the most conservative political sectors. Except in uni-provincial regions, where by definition they no longer exist, successive governments have insisted on preserving provincial powers. This is especially the case today in regions where the Socialist Party is not in power at the regional level, but controls all or most provincial councils. Regions in their turn sustain different positions in relation to provincial institutions. Some are working closely with provinces and maintain satisfactory relations with them. In other regions, such as Catalonia, Castile-León or Valencia, institutional conflict between the region and the provincial councils derives from overlapping functions and mutually antagonistic policies. The situation is exacerbated by the absence of mechanisms whereby the regional government can impose its policies in the name of the primacy of the wider interest over the sectional and restricted provincial interest.[17]

The working of provinces as local authorities depends closely on national and regional regulation of specific functional sectors (Martin-Retortillo, 1991; Morell Ocaña, 1988). It is therefore difficult to assess their performance without looking in detail into regional provisions. But the data available suggest that they are far from fulfilling their role as an intermediate tier making up for the deficient working of the municipal level and providing advisory and technical support to municipalities (Nieto, 1991).

The role of provincial authorities as territorial divisions for the exercise of national and regional functions is still unclear. As a result of the 'Autonomic Agreement' (1981) and with the object of avoiding duplication and proliferation of administrative structures, provinces were designated by the LPA 1983 as the basic units for the implementation of national and regional policies. In order to weaken the links between central and local government, the LPA also established that central powers and functions could not be directly transferred to the provincial councils; rather, transfer had first to be made to the respective regional government. Subsequent developments, at both the central and the regional level, have partially ignored these provisions.

The Local Government Act 1985 modified the LPA 1983, allowing the central government to relate directly to the provinces, so that central departments may now skip the regional tier and build up alliances with provinces and indirectly through them with municipalities. Many regions have denounced the centralizing effect of this measure, whose impact on regional autonomy is still difficult to evaluate. None the less, some national Acts have recently attributed a number of executive functions to the provinces in matters such as public works, road maintenance and public health (Gomez-Ferrer, 1991). This has antagonized certain regions which promote different policies in the same fields or in closely connected areas such as environment protection or highways. As a result, a series of regional–provincial conflicts have arisen. Although some regions such as Aragón, Castile-La Mancha and Extremadura have permitted provincial organizations to exercise regional functions, many regions have ignored provinces and have set up their own service-delivery structures, thus demonstrating a total lack of confidence in provincial councils. In so doing they have blocked the proposals on administrative rationalization envisaged by the LPA and have contributed to the establishment of an extremely complex pattern of inter-governmental relationships.

Dual links of local government
The Constitution established a dual link between local government and other levels of government (Sanchez Morón, 1983). Initial interpretations of the Constitution considered that central control of local government would be restricted to the establishment of the basic local government framework. The subsequent expansive interpretation has resulted in the establishment of detailed central controls concerning the organization, composition and functions of local government and in the preservation of extensive links between central and local authorities (Cuchillo, 1987, 1990). Direct links with municipalities are unusual, except in the case of provincial capital cities, and depending on subject matter, they are channelled through the provincial local authorities or through the peripheral central offices established in the province.[18]

Regional legislation developing the LBRL 1985 varies widely according to the competences assumed in relation to local government and the degree of regional development. In general terms, though, and with some exceptions (such as Valencia and Andalucia), it may be termed unimaginative. Regions have tended to entrench their position as political institutions supervising local activities quite closely and somehow reproducing the old controlling role of central government but at the same time without being able to offer the same advantages as regards the granting of resources and political influence. Consequently the localities resent their regional government more than central government (Clegg, 1987; Prats, 1988).

Municipalities have closer links with regions than with central authorities, but proximity has not resulted in a significant improvement in co-operative relationships. Where regional–provincial relations are collaborative, links with municipalities are often channelled through the province. Where relations with the provinces are not fluid, the regions often follow the same tactics as central government, skipping the provincial tier and building up alliances with municipalities. A similar bypassing gambit is also sometimes followed towards the capital cities where they are controlled by an opposition party.[19]

Central–regional relations
The Spanish system is based on the assumption that the recognition of the right of the regions to devolution is not contrary to the preservation of the unitary character of the state or to the concept of central institutions as the custodians and promoters of the 'national' interest. It is also based on the assumption that central and regional governments stand on an equal footing, so that central government has no controlling powers over regions, except under exceptional conditions which require the prior intervention of the Second Chamber (s. 155). Conflicts between central and regional governments are referred to the Constitutional Court, which acts as a neutral arbiter.

Regions have not questioned the primacy of central government, but they have argued that central and regional powers and functions are perfectly well defined and separated and that central–regional relations should be determined on that basis (Molas, 1980). Initial rulings of the Constitutional Court seem to have backed this position. In one of its first decisions the court declared that national and regional (and local) interests, and the powers and functions necessary to fulfil them, were clearly separated and perfectly identifiable (STC 2/1981). Further developments proved these assumptions to be rather unrealistic, because of the evident interconnection of governmental functions resulting from the way in which powers and functions had been distributed between tiers. Current positions on the definition of central and regional powers have reconsidered the idea of separation and now stress the ideas of 'integration' and 'mutual collaboration'.

The Constitutional Court has subsequently tried to define the principles which should govern central–regional relations. It has done so through a number of statements on the role assigned to each level of government and on the means whereby they should accomplish those roles without impinging on their respective responsibilities. The court has stressed that regions are political institutions with a sphere of powers for which they are responsible and accountable to the regional electorate. Central–regional relations must be guided by a mutual respect for the respective spheres of powers and competences of the two levels and by the conviction that vital interests assigned to one constitute a limit to the exercise of powers by the other (STC 32/1983). The court has also declared that, even though some regions are responsible for regional interests, they belong to the state's structure and the whole of the Spanish community is affected by their decisions. Thus 'national' interests are pursued both by national and by regional institutions. Therefore, argues the court, the fulfilment of their role as promoters of the public welfare may only be attained through an integration of their activities with other levels of government (STC 71/1983). In the coverage of this common aim, central and regional governments are bound by a 'mutual duty' to collaborate that is not expressly stated in the Constitution but is implicit in the decentralized system it enshrines (STC 18/1982).

The sense of mutual confidence, collaboration and respect that the Constitutional Court has sought to establish has been undermined by early interpretations on key issues and an impatient desire on the part of regions to affirm themselves as political institutions in their own right, with a well-defined sphere of powers and functions. There has also been an atmosphere of distrust engendered by central eagerness to preserve its predominance during the first decade of democratic government.[20]

Co-operative and co-ordinating devices
Central–regional relations are channelled through a number of devices meant to provide for the co-operation of governmental levels and for the co-ordination of their activities. It should be noted that these devices are still very limited and that their working is made difficult not only by the above-mentioned factors but also by the variation in the extent of powers devolved to different regions and in the degree of political identity attained by regions in different parts of the country. Thus even if an atmosphere of mutual trust and respect prevailed, it would probably be quite difficult to arrive at a situation where co-ordination and co-operation developed on a regular basis without a certain degree of uniformity in the level of powers and competences being established for all Spanish regions.

As a logical consequence of the lack of uniformity, co-ordination and co-operation between central and regional governments have developed on a highly fragmented and casual basis. Such co-operation as there has been has not resulted in the definition of joint tasks and in joint planning and financing of certain functions as has happened in Germany and in Italy (Alberti, 1985, 1986; Hesse, 1990; Cassese and Torchia, this volume). Rather it has resulted in the establishment of a number of joint bodies usually with advisory and information functions. These are very often of a bilateral character and deal with a specific subject matter (for example, special education for the mentally retarded). Some of them, though, are of a multilateral character, such as the interdepartmental commissions made up of representatives of the central department responsible for a matter in which regions have assumed a number of powers and functions and of representatives of the regions. These commissions were established by the LPA 1983 and were supposed to hold monthly meetings. Other multilateral bodies have been set up for the negotiation and discussion of issues concerning closely related matters. In general terms, though, it could be said that very few of these joint bodies have met regularly and have succeeded in performing an active role in central–regional relations.

Finally, it should be noted that up till now regions have not established co-operative relationships as a group on a stable basis, both in functional terms and as regards the creation of a common front in negotiations with central government. The Constitution expressly allows the development of such relationships and a number of voices have already pointed out the advantages that may derive from such co-operation among regions and from the creation of a standing body similar to, for example, the conferences of regional presidents established in Italy (Cassese and Torchia, this volume).

Conclusions

In the analysis of the Spanish meso experience perhaps the first thing coming to the fore is the fact that a relatively high level of political and administrative decentralization has been attained in a remarkably short period. Given that this decentralizing process has taken place in concert with the democratization of the political and administrative structures, it could be considered that the construction of the so-called 'state of the autonomies' has been a major achievement.

This being said, it should also be stressed that a certain impasse has now been reached in the implementation of the provisions on devolution and that the system presents a number of serious dysfunctions. As has been mentioned, the consensus on devolution during the process which led to the promulgation of the Constitution entailed the sanction of a flexible model which allowed, over the years, for the establishment of a highly imprecise and undefined system. This vagueness permits successive reinterpretations and readaptations of the constitutional provisions and requires constant central–regional negotiation, and it is clearly reflected in the diversity of attitudes adopted by central and regional actors. In some instances they are jointly fixing priorities and working together in the implementation of policies, conscious of the impossibility of taking independent or separate courses of action. In other instances, however, regions tend to consider themselves as institutions working apart from, and often in the opposite direction to, central institutions, when not openly antagonizing them. The central government, in its turn, tends to view regions as institutions promoting particularized interests which do not really participate in the building of national interests or in the conduct of national or general affairs. On some contentious matters the government has often decided to 'penalize' regions or to retaliate against them, in doing so showing an astonishing lack of concern for regional problems and interests and a very peculiar sense of the 'state' and the role of the national institutions as supreme custodians of the 'general' interest.

The imprecision of the Constitution in intergovernmental relations has also permitted an interpretation of central and regional powers in relation to local government which has brought about the establishment of a very complex system of intergovernmental relationships, imposing intense interdependence between tiers. In a context in which the role assigned to each level is far from being patently defined and accepted by all functional links between governmental levels render the adoption and implementation of policies more difficult. Such difficulties are particularly important because they are occurring at a time when there is intense pressure for the modernization of political and administrative structures with a view to their adaptation to European standards.

When focusing on meso developments in Spain, it could be said that the former state apparatus has been 'dismembered', but without an alternative structure being set up. Moreover, the absence of an agreed model universally applied has resulted in the piecemeal implementation of devolution without any coherent notion as to overall objectives. Attempts at reducing this coherence have been dominated by a legal approach which seeks a mechanistic distribution of functions between central and regional institutions in the hope of avoiding institutional confrontation and of ensuring a 'smooth' functioning of the system. This approach has proved inadequate, and is beginning to be felt as such. Only a new consensus on devolution being tentatively sought nowadays will facilitate the building of that sense of mutual loyalty between national, regional and local actors on which the system should rest.

Appendix: Elections for Autonomous Communities with 'full' autonomic powers

Andalucian parliament (3 June 1990)

Party	% vote	Seats
PSOE	49.6	61
CP	22.1	27
IU–CA	12.6	11
PA	10.8	10
CDS	1.2	—
Others	3.7	—
Total turn-out	70.6	109

PSOE Partido Socialista Obrero Español (Socialist Workers' Party of Spain)
CP   Coalición Popular (PP) (Popular Coalition)
IU–CA Izquierda Unida – Comunistas de Andalucia (United Left – Communists of Andalucia)
PA   Partido Andalucista (Andalucian Party)
CDS   Centro Democrático y Social (ex-UCD) (Democratic and Social Centre Party)

Basque parliament (25 February 1984)

Party	% vote	Seats
PNV	41.8	32
PSE–PSOE	23.0	19
HB	14.6	11
CP	9.4	7
EE	8.0	6
Others	3.2	—
Total turn-out	68.4	75

PNV   Partido Nacionalista Vasco (Basque National Party)
PSE–PSOE Partido Socialista de Euzkadi–Partido Socialista Obrero Español (Basque Socialist Party – Socialist Workers' Party of Spain)
HB   Herri Batasuna (Independentist Party)
CP   Coalición Popular (AP) (Popular Coalition)
EE   Euzkadiko Ezkerra (Basque Left)

Basque parliament (30 November 1988)

Party	% vote	Seats
PNV	23.6	17
PSE–PSOE	22.0	19
HB	17.4	13
EA	15.8	13
EE	10.8	9
CP	4.8	2
CDS	3.5	2
Others	1.6	–
Total turn-out	71.0	75

Additional abbreviations:
EA   Euzko Alkartasuna (fraction of PNV)
CDS Centro Democrático y Social (ex-UCD) (Democratic and Social Centre Party)

Catalan parliament (29 May 1988)

Party	% vote	Seats
CiU	46.0	69
PSC	29.2	42
IC	7.8	9
AP	5.3	6
ERC	4.1	6
CDS	3.8	3
Others	3.8	—
Total turn-out	58.6	135

CiU Convergència i Unió (Convergence and Union)
PSC Partit dels Socialistes de Catalunya (PSOE) (Socialist Party of Catalonia)
IC   Izquierda Comunista (Communist Left)
AP   Alianza Popular (Popular Alliance)
ERC Esquerra Republicana de Catalunya (Left Independentist Party)
CDS Centro Democrático y Social (ex-UCD) (Democratic and Social Centre Party)

Catalan parliament (15 March 1992)

Party	% vote	Seats
CiU	49.75	71
PSC	24.75	39
IC	4.5	7
ERC	9.5	11
PP	6.25	7
CDS	0.25	—
A. Verda	0.6	—
Others	4.4	—
Total turn-out	54.89	135

Additional abbreviations:

PP   Partido Popular (ex-AP) (Popular Party)
A. Verda   Alianza Verda (Ecologist Party)

Galician parliament (24 February 1985)

Party	% vote	Seats
CP	41.1	34
PSdG–PSOE	28.8	22
CG	13.0	11
PSG–EG	5.7	3
BNG	4.2	1
Others	7.2	—
Total turn-out	57.4	71

CP   Coalición Popular (AP) (Popular Coalition)
PSdG–PSOE   Partido Socialista de Galicia – Partido Socialista Obrero Español
(Socialist Party of Galicia – Socialist Workers' Party of Spain)
CG   Coalición Gallega (fraction of AP) (Galician Coalition)
PSG–EG   Partido Socialista Gallego – Esquerra Gallege (Galician Socialist Party
– Galician Left)
PNG   Partido Nacionalista Gallego (Galician Nationalist Party)

Notes

1 The PSOE agreed to put aside federalist proposals in return for acceptance by the governmental party (Unión del Centro Democrático, UCD) of a proportional electoral system for Congress, instead of the majority system favoured by UCD, which was restricted to elections for the Second Chamber (Senate).

2 Thus only the regions following three of the five different processes respectively envisaged by the Constitution in sections 143, 144 and 151 and in the transitory dispositions numbers one and two, could have direct access to the full range of powers which may be devolved to regional governments.

3 The Constitution establishes that 'deferred autonomy' regions, also called 'second class' regions, may initiate the proceedings necessary to have access to full autonomy powers after a five-year transitional period. On the stance followed by 'deferred autonomy' regions as regards this expansion and on the government's response, see page 250 and note 8).

4 Among the reasons accounting for mimicry in the setting up of regional administrative systems the following deserve to be mentioned. First, the procedure imposed for the transfer of state services, facilities and personnel relating to matters devolved to regions: this was done sector by sector, preventing regions from organizing subject areas as a whole and forcing them, in a way, to reproduce the central administrative structures. Second, priority given by regional actors to the setting up of their political organization and to overcoming resistance and inertia to devolution from central political actors and bureaucratic elites.

5 The system set up by the LOFCA did not apply to the Basque Country and Navarra, endowed with an special financial rule granting them a number of privileges, set up in their 'Economic Agreement' (1980) with central government.

6 There were more than 400 central–regional conflicts pending in the Constitutional Court in 1989. In December of that year the central government made a proposal for the negotiated resolution of about 100 of these conflicts. The proposal was not accepted by regions and there are still 320 conflicts pending in the court today. But as stated on page 253, the lodging of appeals has significantly decreased in the last two years. See, *El País* 30.12.89 and 27.4.92.

7 Claims coming from regionalist and opposition parties, backed by certain regional sections of the PSOE, put forward in the Fall of 1987 have generated a passionate debate on 'auto-determination'. This debate gave way to proposals for the revision of the Constitution which were taken to the regional parliaments in the Basque Country and in Galicia (January and February 1990), and only the forceful criticism and implicit threats of retaliation on the part of the central government excluded the consideration of the proposals on the modification of the state structure in the Catalan, Valencian and Andalucian parliaments.

8 The government stated, in 1987, that it would not consider these demands until 1990. *El País*, 13.11.87. The deadlock situation arrived at by the end of 1990 promoted the initiation of the negotiations that led to the 'Autonomic Agreement' (February 1992). The draft proposed by the government included (a) the regional financing system, (b) the expansion of the powers granted to 'deferred autonomy' regions, and (c) the reorganization of the central bureaucracy. But rejection of the initial proposal by all opposition parties, restricted the agreement to the second issue and the signature of such agreement to the PSOE and the PP.

9 This possibility is accepted in Federal systems such as the United States and the Federal Republic of Germany, but as is well known, their Constitutions establish a number of safeguards and guarantees so that the States and the *Länder* may contest unordinate deprivations of their powers and functions.

10 The Court has nuanced its position restraining slightly the scope of central powers (STC 28/1988) but a change in its stance capable of settling central–regional conflict is unlikely, as only a political decision may provide for such a settling. The Constitutional Court has recently expressed its inability to solve central–regional conflicts on the scope of their respective powers in recent rulings (STC 99/1991, 22/1992) restating its doctrine and refusing to go into the details of what is and is not basic, with regard to such issues as the regulation of chicken breeding.

11 The preservation of central peripheral offices under the command of an agent of the central government (the Civil Governor) was highly controversial, as it meant the

preservation of one of the most centralist and authoritarian institutions of the Francoist regime. Their virtual disappearance in uni-provincial regions, where most of their functions are assumed by the Governmental Delegate created by the Constitution (section 154) is highly resented by regions such as the Basque Country, Catalonia and Valencia, which insist on receiving a similar treatment.

12 In Spring 1992 the PP formulated a proposal for the establishment of a single or unified administrative structure ('Administración Unica'). The formula, which was in fact centred on effective completion of the LPA 1983 provisions, included the suppression of some state departments such as Culture and Social Services, and the delegation of central executive powers to regional bureaucracies. The proposal, which opened a heated public debate and was taxatively refused by the PSOE, was indirectly backed by regional parties in Catalonia, Valencia and Andalucia, attracted by it but openly opposed to PP.

13 This choice was the result of intensive pressure coming from the most conservative sectors representing the administrative elites of the Francoist regime.

14 The official publications of regional governments, year by year, state a listing and economic evaluation of their activities which show substantive performance in a number of sectors.

15 The system for defining local autonomy was inspired by the German model. But contrary to the German system, which allows local lodging of appeals with the Constitutional Court against exclusion of their right to participate, the Spanish system explicitly excludes such possibility.

16 Thus, even though a general competence clause empowers municipalities to develop any activities they think fit in the interest of their communities, only those with a certain amount of resources are capable of developing the role assigned by the Constitution and by local legislation.

17 Confrontation with provincial councils is especially acute in Catalonia where provinces have consistently been viewed as offshoots of the central government and successive Catalan governments have tried, until now unsuccessfully, to get rid of them. 'Comarques' have already been established as intermediate local authorities, but the preservation of provinces has prevented their fulfilment of such a role.

18 The possibility of central government relating with municipalities through the peripheral central offices and through the provincial local authorities has been consistently criticized by regions on the basis of the unnecessary complexity of intergovernmental relations it entails.

19 Perhaps the most spectacular example of the policies is to be found in Catalonia where the regional government abolished the metropolitan local authority set up for Barcelona and its surrounding area with arguments about its deficiencies similar to those claimed by the British government when it abolished the Greater London Council.

20 In the last few years there is a move, in certain matters, from opposition and conflict towards negotiation and co-operation. This tendency shows out in the developments mentioned on pages 250 and 253, but as mentioned in note 6, there are still 320 pending conflicts between central and regional governments now lodged with the Constitutional Court.

Select further reading

Aja, E., Carrillo, M., Alberti, E. (1990) *Manual de Jurisprudencia Constitucional.* Madrid: Civitas.

Alonso Garcia, E. (1984) *La Interpretación de la Constitución.* Madrid: CEC.

244   *The rise of meso government*

Comentaris a l'Estatut d'Autonomia de Catalunya (1988) Barcelona: Ed. Generalitat de Catalunya.

La Constitución y las Fuentes del Derecho (1981) 3 vols. Madrid: CEC.

Els Governs a la Constitucio Espanyola i a les Comunitats Autonomes (1989) Barcelona: Ed. Diputacio de Barcelona.

Estudios sobre el Estatuto de Autonomia del País Vasco (1988) Vitoria: Ed. Gobierno Vasco.

Fernandez Rodriguez, T. R. (ed.) (1979) *Lecturas sobre la Constitucion Española.* 2 vols. Madrid: UNED.

Fernandez Rodriguez, T. R. (ed.) (1985) *La España de las Autonomias.* Madrid: IEAL.

Garcia de Enterria, E. (ed.) (1980) *La Distribución de Competencias Económicas entre el Poder Central y las Autonomias Territoriales en el Derecho Comparado y en la Constitución Española.* Madrid: Civitas.

Garcia de Enterria, E. (1982) 'La primacia normativa del Titulo VIII de la Constitución', *Revista Española de Derecho Administrativo,* 32.

Garcia de Enterria, E. (1983) *La Ejecución Autonómica de la Legislación del Estado.* Madrid: Civitas.

Garcia de Enterria, E. (ed.) (1985) *Estudios sobre Autonomias Territoriales.* Madrid: Civitas.

Garrido Falla, F. (ed.) (1980) *Comentarios a la Constitución.* Madrid: Civitas.

Gil Robles, J. M. (1986) *Control y Autonomias.* Madrid: Civitas.

Medhurst, K. (1973) *Government in Spain: the Administrative at Work.* Oxford: Pergamon.

Monreal, A. (1986) 'The new Spanish state structure', in M. Burgess (ed.), *Federalism and Federation in Western Europe.* London: Croom Helm.

Muñoz Machado, S. (1979) *Las Potestades Legislativas de las Comunidades Autónomas.* Madrid: Civitas.

La Organización Territorial del Estado (Comunidades Autonomas) (1984) 4 vols. Madrid: CEC.

Otto, I. de (1987) *Derecho Constitucional: Sistema de Fuentes.* Barcelona: Ariel.

Perez Moreno, A. (ed.) (1979) *Comunidades Autónomas.* 2 vols. Seville: Instituto Garcia Oviedo.

Predieri, E. and Garcia de Enterria, E. (eds) (1980) *La Constitución Española de 1978: un Estudio Sistemático.* Madrid: Civitas.

Vandelli, L. (1980) *La Constitución Española de 1978.* Madrid: Ed. Estudia Albornontiana.

References

Aja, E., Alberti, E., Font, T., Perulles, J., Tornos, J. (1985), *El Sistema Jurídico de las Comunidades Autónomas.* Madrid: Tecnos.

Alberti, E. (1985) 'Las relaciones entre el Estado y las Comunidades Autónomas', in Aja, E. et al., *El Sistema Jurídico de las Comunidades Autónomas.* Madrid: Tecnos.

Alberti, E. (1986) *Federalismo y Cooperación en la República Federal Alemana.* Madrid: CEC.

Alvira-Martin, F. & Garcia-Lopez, J. (1988) 'Los españoles y las Autonomias', *Papeles de Economia Espanola,* 34.

Argullol, E. (1983) 'Gobierno y administración de las Comunidades Autónomas:

referencia al Estatuto de Autonomia de Castilla-León', *Revista Vasca de Administración Pública*, 7.

Argullol, E. (1987) *L'Organitzacio Territorial de Catalunya*. Empuries: Barcelona.

Bassols, M. (1984) 'Los organos ejecutivos de las Comunidades Autonómas: Presidencia y Consejo de Gobierno', *Revista Española de Derecho Administrativo*, 40–42.

Bayona, A. (1987) 'The autonomous government of Catalonia', *Government and Policy*, 5.

Brenan, G. (1967) *The Spanish Cockpit*. Oxford: OUP.

Carr, R. (1966) *Spain, 1808–1939*. Oxford: Clarendon.

Carr, R. and Fusi, P. (1979) *Spain: From Dictatorship to Democracy*. London: Allen & Unwin.

Castells, A. (1987a) 'Financing regional government in Spain: main trends and a comparative perspective', *Government and Policy*, 5.

Castells, A. (1987b) 'Tendencies recents en la descentralitzacio del sector public', *Revista Económica de Banca Catalana*, 83.

Clegg, T. (1987) 'Spain', in E. C. Page and M. Goldsmith (eds), *Central and Local Government Relations*. London: Sage.

Colldeforns, M. (1992) *La Balanza Fiscal de Catalunya con la Administración del Estado*. Ariel: Barcelona.

Cuchillo, M. (1987) 'Las relaciones inter-administrativas', in *Comentarios a la Ley Reguladora de las Bases del Regimen Local*. Barcelona: CEUMT.

Cuchillo, M. (1990) 'L'organitzacio territorial de Catalunya: opcions i nivells de concrecio, in Deu anys de vigencia de l'Estatut d'Autonomia de Catalunya', *Autonomies*, 12.

Cuchillo, M. and Vallés, J. M. (1988) 'Decentralisation in Spain: a review', *European Journal of Political Research*, 16.

Entrena, R. (1981) 'Estado regional. Estado Autonómico y Estado Federal', in R. Entrena (ed.), *Estudi Juridic de l'Estatut d'Autonómia de Catalunya*. Barcelona: Ed. Universitat Barcelona.

Font, T. (1985) 'La organización administrativa de las Comunidades Autónomas', in Aja, E. et al., *El Sistema Jurídico de las Comunidades Autónomas*. Madrid: Tecnos.

Garcia de Enterria, E. (1978) *La Administracion Española*. Madrid: Alianza.

Garcia de Enterria, E. (1982) 'El ordenamiento estatal y los ordenamientos autonómicos', *Revista Española de Derecho Constitucional*, 5.

Garcia de Enterria, E. (1989) 'La Constitución y las Autonomias Territoriales', *Revista Española de Derecho Constitucional*, 25.

Gomez-Ferrer, R. (1991) 'Legislación basica en materia de regimen local: relación con las leyes de las Comunidades Autónomas', in R. Gomez-Ferrer (ed.), *La Provincia en el sistema constitucional*. Madrid: Civitas.

Hebbert, M. (1987) 'Regionalism: a reform concept and its application to Spain', *Government and Policy*, 5.

Hebbert, M. and Alonso, A. (1982) 'Regional planning in Spain and the transition to democracy', in R. Hudson and J. R. Lewis (eds), *Regional Planning in Europe*. London: Pion.

Hesse, H. J. (1990) 'Recent developments at the West German meso level', in R. Hudson and J. R. Lewis (eds), *Regional Planning in Europe*. London: Pion.

Martin Mateo, R. (1981) 'La jurisprudencia del Tribunal Constitucional sobre las potestades legislativas de las Comunidades Autónomas', *Revista Española de Derecho Administrativo*, 30.

Martin-Retortillo, S. (1991) 'El tema de la autonomia provincial: las diputaciones y el

246   *The rise of meso government*

proceso autonómico', in R. Gomez-Ferrer (ed.), *La Provincia en el Sistema Constitucional*. Madrid: Civitas.
McDonough, P., Barnes, S. H. and Lopez-Pina, A. (1986) 'The growth of democratic legitimacy in Spain', *American Political Science Review*, 80.
Molas, I. (1980) 'El control dels organs de l'Estat sobre les Comunitats Autonomes', *Administracio Publica*, 3.
Morata, F. (1987) *Autonomia Regional i Integracio Europea*. Barcelona: IEA.
Morell Ocaña, L. (1988) 'Las provincias', in S. Muñoz Machado (ed.), *Tratado de Derecho Municipal*. Madrid: Civitas.
Muñoz Machado, S. (1981) 'La jurisprudencia del tribunal constitucional sobre las potestades legislativas de las Comunidades Autónomas', *Revista Española de Derecho Constitucional*, 3.
Muñoz Machado, S. (1982–4) *Derecho Público de las Comunidades Autónomas*. 2 vols. Madrid: Civitas.
Muñoz Machado, S. (ed.) (1988) *Tratado de Derecho Municipal*. Madrid: Civitas.
Nieto, A. (1984) *La Organización del Desgobierno*. Barcelona: Ariel.
Nieto, A. (1991) 'Cooperación y asistencia', in R. Gomez-Ferrer (ed.), *La Provincia en el Sistema Constitucional*. Madrid: Civitas.
Parada, R. (1990) *Derecho Administrativo*. 3 vols. Vol. 2: *Organización y Empleo Público*. 2nd edn. Madrid: Marcial Pons.
Parejo Alfonso, L. (1986) 'La autonomia local', *Revista de Estudios de Administración Local*, 229.
Prats, J. (1988) 'La Comarca', in S. Muñoz Machado (ed.), *Tratado de Derecho Municipal*. Madrid: Civitas.
Rodriguez-Aguilera, C. (1988) 'Balance y transformaciones del sistema de partidos en España', *Revista Española de Investigaciones Sociológicas*, 42.
Rodriguez-Aguilera, C. (1989) 'Algunas hipotesis sobre la continuidad del sistema de partidos en España a finales de los años ochenta', paper presented to III Congreso de Sociologia Política, San Sebastian.
Salas, J. (1979) 'Hacia una reestructuración de la Administración Periferica del Estado', *Documentación Administrativa*, 182.
Sanchez Morón, M. (1983) 'Las Comunidades Autónomas y la estructura de la Administración Local', *Revista de Administración Pública*, 100–2.
Sharpe, L. J. (1987) Research outline for this publication, 'Modernizing Intergovernmental Relations in Western Europe'.
Solé-Vilanova, J. (1989) 'Spain: Developments in regional and local government' in R. J. Bennett (ed.), *Territory and Administration in Europe*. London: Pinter.
Solé-Vilanova, J. (1990) 'Regional and local finance in Spain: is fiscal responsibility the missing element?' in R. J. Bennett (ed.), *Decentralization, Local Government and Markets: Setting a Post-Welfare Agenda*. Oxford: OUP.
Tamames, R. and Clegg, T. (1984) 'Spain: regional autonomy and the democratic transition', in M. Hebbert and H. Machin (eds), *Regionalisation in France, Italy, and Spain*. London: LSE.
Tomas y Valiente, F. (1985) 'Tribunal constitucional de Espana', in *Tribunales Constitucionales Europeos y Autonomias Territoriales*. Madrid: CEC.
Tornos, J., Aja, E., Alberti, E. and Font, T. (1988) *Informe sobre las Autonomias*. Barcelona: Ed. Ajuntament Barcelona.
Tornos, J., Aja, E., Alberti, E. and Font, T. (1990) *Informe sobre las Autonomias II*. Barcelona: Ed. Ajuntament Barcelona.
Viver Pi-Sunyer, C. (1981) 'Naturalesa juridica, organitzacio i funcionament del Parlament de Catalunya', *Administracio Publica*, 4.

9

The United Kingdom: The Disjointed Meso

L. J. Sharpe

Before discussing the somewhat ambiguous and haphazard development of the British meso, it might be helpful to say a few words first about the British constitutional tradition. As is well known, the UK is unique among the major Western states in not having a written constitution. Instead it follows the convention of *parliamentary sovereignty* which means in effect that the legislature is the supreme constitutional arbiter and cannot be bound by any other sovereign except, in a formal sense, the European Community. But since the EC has no means of enforcing its own law the constraint is not absolute. Some statutes, those governing the life of Parliament and the franchise, for example, have the effect of entrenched law, but there is no legal impediment to Parliament abolishing them if it so wishes. All is potential flux and nothing is constitutionally sacred. Nowhere, perhaps, within British government is this more true than in relation to the meso in its various forms. Any account of the British meso thus necessarily lacks that degree of legal consistency and form which might normally be expected in relation to such an important part of the governmental system. In short, there is very little basic framework of law in which the institutions to be discussed can be located, or defined.

The second consequence of the parliamentary sovereignty principle which is relevant is that major institutional change in the public sector is always possible and at short notice. For not only are there no constitutional constraints of a kind found in other representative democracies, the concentration of power on Parliament – in effect the Cabinet – means that all of the institutions we are to discuss can be abolished (or changed) by a simple majority vote in the House of Commons and all may be subject to ministerial control and direction almost at will. The parliamentary sovereignty principle also means that in formal terms sub-national government has no legislative powers.

This extraordinary concentration of potential power at the centre of the British system must not be confused with the exercise of central control over the day-to-day operations of sub-national bodies. Such control may be as Draconian as the centre may try to enforce, but in the normal course of events the non-executant tradition of the British centre renders such control unlikely and extremely difficult.

In order to come to grips with this peculiar mixture of power and self-imposed indifference it is essential to recognize that the British political ethos draws a sharp distinction between central government and the state. Constraints on the centre therefore are not considered to be necessary, since any extension of its power is not seen as an automatic extension of state power which may threaten the individual or group. Indeed, increasing governmental power over subnational collectivities may be even defined as facilitating an *extension* of individual liberty. This is precisely the terms in which the considerable increase in central control over local government was defined during the 1980s. The central government was able to claim that it was extending its reach in order to set the people free from the depredations of their local government in exactly the same terms that, for example, it extended its control over trade unions, or turned some public corporations into private monopolies.

It is impossible to comprehend the importance of the centre within the central–local relationship without reference to the considerable prestige and status of the centre. The simple fact is that local government has a comparatively low status in British society, whereas the centre enjoys the opposite. If given the choice between local and central government on, say, questions of probity or technical capacity, the majority would probably favour the centre.

Precisely why this is so it is difficult to ascertain. It is partly to do with a British obsession with a status hierarchy in all things. Much more important is the extent to which the centre projects itself onto British life. It must be remembered that British central government has never failed. In the modern era apart from the conflict on Ireland in the early 1920s, there have been no revolutions, no foreign insurrections, no invasions. Nor has the centre ever faltered and there has been unbroken continuity. France, by contrast, has enjoyed five Republics, two monarchies, three Empires and Vichy during the modern era; the French *commune*, however, has been a haven of stability and continuity. Hence one major reason for the intense localism of French political life. The reverse is the case in the UK, where local government has been under almost constant structural review since the 1950s and some areas have been subjected to actual structural change three times over the period. British central government is also so *capable* because, when the winner always takes all, all is possible. There are very few parliamentary deals, never a 'house without windows' and, above all, no coalitions. The government can *always* deliver the goods (whatever the quality of those goods may be) and this generates an aura of dependability and respect that is extremely rare outside Scandinavia.

Given such an exalted status, the centre has no need to identify its service-providing capacity with the integrity of the state, so the executant role can be devolved at will and where necessary to quasi-government institutions. The state, in so far as it has any place in the British political psyche, is immanent in British society. Where the centre needs cohesive symbols it gets them from the monarchy. The state, then, is not required to have its sovereign status reflected in field services or tutelary institutions. It is precisely this freedom from any necessary enmeshment in non-central institutions which, together with the absence of clientelism and very limited pork-barrelling, gives the centre its independence from territorial politics. The centre's curious mixture of power and restraint has diverse historical origins no doubt, but two factors seem to stand out above the ruck. The first is the British imperial tradition epitomized by the old Colonial Office and India Office with their complements totalling about eighty or so higher civil servants, which until 1945 administered 'a fifth of the globe' in territorial terms. The second characteristic is the utilitarian ideology which, to all intents and purposes, had captured the UK by the late 1830s. The first – the imperial tradition – severely limits the centre's role so that it can concentrate on those aspects of the central tasks that are the most important and, above all else, does not get involved in executant activities. The second – the utilitarian ideology – automatically downgrades government in favour of the market, which lingers still not as an overt doctrine (except for the recent upsurge of Thatcherism) but as an historical inhibitor to the full acceptance of the state in activities which are the norm for most Western states. The remote-control mode of government that both characteristics helped to create was able to flourish and evolve because it prevailed in an extraordinarily stable and affluent polity.

The central government, then, has little interest in providing public services directly – that is, via hierarchical, centre-to-periphery service-delivery systems on the French or Italian model. That is a technical task, worthy no doubt, but more appropriate for lesser mortals than central decision-makers, who in relinquishing it do, to be sure, automatically enhance the autonomy of the executant agencies but most emphatically not from any conscious theory of local democracy. The centre, then, rarely 'gets its boots muddy', unless for some reason the executant process attains political salience. This strong government but *sans* the state ethos – what may be called '*laissez-faire* collectivism' (Sharpe, 1985: 92) – has been termed the 'dual polity' (Bulpitt, 1983). One of its consequences is

that the centre usually uses three different types of executant
service-delivery agency: *public corporations* for public services
operating in the market; *local government*, for non-market public
services; and *quangos* for public services that are non-market, but for
various reasons are thought to be best kept out of politics. These
three agencies are usually left to their own devices while the centre
keeps a firm grip on the key higher management modes of finance,
standards, major policy and legislation.

This apparent paradox of almost unlimited potential power of the
centre but in practice its horizontal insulation from the sub-national
system meant that local government enjoyed high levels of operational autonomy. Hence, historically, Britain's reputation as the
home of 'local self-government'. The paradox lies at the heart of
British central and sub-national relations and it means that the centre
is both more dominant *and* less dominant than in most Western
states. With such inconsistency about a fundamental set of relationships the temptation is to attempt to resolve it by claiming a greater
degree of congruity than actually exists between the quotidian and
the long-term, either in terms of the centre being dominant in all
things (Ashford, 1982) or in terms of the centre, caught in the toils of
a 'differentiated polity', being not dominant at all (Rhodes, 1988).

Regrettably for the tidy-minded, incongruity persists, although it is
certainly true that there is less than there used to be because the
centre has become increasingly reluctant to let local government go
its own way in some day-to-day operational matters, for two reasons.
The first has been the increasingly national political salience of some
major local government services. From about the early 1950s
onwards no centre could afford politically to follow the insulated dual
polity mode any longer, because local government functions, such
as the provision of housing and education, were sources of inter-
party conflict to the extent that general elections might be won or
lost over policies towards them. The second reason why the centre
has been increasingly willing to intervene in what was hitherto for it
a *terra incognita* is simply the rising burden on the central exchequer
of grants to the localities. In 1920 local taxes (Rates) in England and
Wales were in excess of three times greater than central grants as
sources of local expenditure, but by 1940 a dramatic reversal had
evolved and governmental grants exceeded local tax revenue for the
first time. By 1958 grants exceeded rates by £15.3 million and by
1975 by £420.4 million (Foster et al., 1980: 150–1), or by 63.1 per
cent of local authority (Rate- and grant-borne) expenditure (Stewart, 1984: 5). As this charge on the central exchequer rose, so the
central Treasury was drawn into the local government arena,
seeking to control and reduce what had ceased to be seen as an

element buried in departmental expenditure and in aggregate came to be seen by the Treasury as the single biggest call on national expenditure. But more significantly, it was a call over which it could not exercise its normal direct control functions as it did over departmental spending; it was expenditure, moreover, occurring in a local world about which it knew nothing. The need to control this mysterious but apparently insatiable cuckoo in the nest was intensified by the acceleration of local expenditure growth during the 1960s. Control came to be seen as absolutely imperative following the world trade recession beginning in the early 1970s which affected the UK particularly sharply and entailed recourse to the International Monetary Fund.

The central control aim has been strongly reinforced by the successive Conservative governments since 1979, and some indication of the capacity of the centre to use its potential power in the operational as well as the constitutional sense can be shown by its success in cutting its grant contribution to local government between 1979 and 1989 by £6 billion, or 18 per cent in real terms (*Reform of Direct Taxation*, 1990: 86). However, the Conservative 'war on local government' since 1979 has gone well beyond the need to control local expenditure growth and has involved its wider policy aim of dismantling local government as such in favour of market substitutes.

The dual polity characteristic of British central–local relations must be seen in relation to another system characteristic and this is the assumption that all politics can be subsumed within a *two-party system*, that is, a system where the representative process is rigidly confined to the two main actors: government and opposition. This form of duality has implications for every nook and cranny of the system, but it has very special relevance for the meso since it automatically undermines the territorial dimension of the democratic process by seeking to transform all conflict into two non-spatial, nationwide and often abstract uniformities. The concept of territorially determined collective interests that may cut across vertical differentiation, like class or status, or income group is thus profoundly alien to the system. Both Scottish and Welsh nationalism (and local community interests, for that matter) have, of course, to be tolerated but they can never be adequately accommodated. The curiously *ad hoc* and completely pragmatic creation of the three Offices for Scotland, Wales and Northern Ireland over the past 100 years, which we will discuss later, is an example of the attempt to cope with an indelibly territorial problem that leaves the parliamentary supremacy principle, but also the anti-territorial dualism of the political process, largely unscathed.

Another example of this anti-territorial tradition is the notion of local government as having no legal status other than that of a service agency (*ultra vires*), for it is based on the assumption that local government has no democratic legitimacy, since the individual's democratic rights are deemed to have one, and only one, eminently national focus. The notion of the individual having communal democratic rights as well as his or her rights as an individual is thus only weakly recognized. The central government and the individual confront each other in the national representative process with the lines of accountability running from the former to the latter unimpeded by any intervening institution. It is almost as if the parliamentary sovereignty principle had abolished geography. It follows that the kind of territorial issues and pressures that we are to discuss are particularly difficult to describe and, of course, resolve.

The last system characteristic that is relevant to a discussion of the meso experience in the UK is the almost obsessive predominance that is always given to *production* efficiency in any discussion of designing sub-national structures. That is say, the dominant consideration is always in terms of designing institutions in order to enhance their capacity to produce services at least cost, and to professionally defined norms, and only very rarely with consumption efficiency, that is, how the particular service-delivery system might be designed so as to meet the preferences of the consumer of the particular service. A Thatcher devotee could, however, argue that enhancing consumer efficiency by transforming public monopolies into private monopolies was a major objective of Conservative policy from 1979. Be that as it may, the whole post-war history of sub-national institutional innovation illustrates that there has been a production-efficiency obsession best exemplified by the uni-functional 'one big national corporation' model that was applied in the nationalization of, for example, the electricity, gas, coal and railway industries (Sharpe, 1982). It is even more evident in the long debate about local government reform which was conducted in strongly production-efficiency terms and culminated in 1972 and 1973 Acts that gave the UK possibly the largest local government units in the world (Sharpe, 1978b).

The production-efficiency imperative is also reflected to some extent in the decision to create a separate institutional structure for the National Health Service (NHS) rather than allowing it to remain in local hands where it had largely been before nationalization. Similar considerations apply to the transfer of water supply (plus river control, main drainage and sewage) from local government to the Regional Water Authorities (RWAs) in 1973. The transfer of London Transport, the polytechnics, the colleges of further education and the seven metropolitan governments out of local government into a central limbo in the 1980s also reflects to some extent the production-efficiency imperative.

The key aspect of this production-efficiency emphasis is that it tends to equate such efficiency with unit-functional delivery systems and that delivery form slots neatly into the anti-territorial style of British representative politics already alluded to. It also means that the essentially general, multi-purpose nature of local government seems to have become more threatened when modes of service delivery are under discussion. Provided central government exercises overall control and is accountable to Parliament for the service, all is deemed to be well. The service is thus insulated from territorial politics and service-delivery structures and service content can then be designed largely on professionally defined technical criteria. In short, the uni-functional delivery system that forms part of neither the central government nor local government, but is firmly under the control of the former, incorporates almost all of the key characteristics of the British sub-national ethos we have outlined so far – whether it be the parliamentary sovereignty principle, the centre's unlimited capacity for fundamental structural change, the weakness of the territorial dimension or the heavy emphasis on production efficiency.

So much for system characteristics. The main focus of this chapter is the meso proper in Britain, and its major institutional expression is the *county*, which forms the upper tier of the local government system. In Scotland the equivalent level is called a *region*. The UK, then, falls within what may be called the Northern European 'functional' category of states in the sense that the relationship between the centre and the localities is predominantly on an indirect function-by-function basis, there being very few central field services, no prefect and no *tutelle*. However, there are other institutions and tendencies which also form part of the meso since their existence has influenced both the persistence of the meso proper, and the possibility of an alternative meso. These other forms of meso, both manifest and potential, may be called the *quasi-meso* – and their main component falls more appropriately with the Southern European 'regional' category. The UK, then, presents a kind of hybrid or disjointed meso picture. We will deal first with the various institutions and events that go to make up the quasi-meso.

The quasi-meso

Regional planning

The first aspect of the quasi-meso may be considered very briefly and has its origins in regional economic planning. For about two decades

Figure 1   *Regions of the United Kingdom*

from 1964 there was a system of regional planning institutions comprising nominated representative councils and boards of civil servants loosely modelled on the French regional planning system for each of the eight English regions and one each for Scotland and Wales (see Figure 1). The latter were always the more powerful institutions, with perhaps a more clear-cut mandate, and have survived and prospered. Some observers saw these regional bodies as a kind of embryonic meso government on the Southern pattern and their creation not only stimulated a regional consciousness of sorts but also promoted debates, as it did in France and Italy, about regional government being a vehicle for promoting popular participation, the modernization of the economy and an antidote to over-centralization (Hogwood and Keating, 1982). Following the collapse of the National Plan in 1967 these regional institutions slowly atrophied in England and were finally abolished there in the early 1980s. The English regions live on partly as standard areas for the collection of official statistics and partly for the purposes of administering land-use planning and cognate services. There are also deconcentrated offices of the central departments as the regional level. The 1960s regional structure warrants mention now because its creation did lay the foundations for a regional meso. In Wales and especially Scotland the regional planning idea had more important consequences, reinforcing the tendency, already taking shape with the rise of the nationalists, to assume both regions to be discrete economic entities; thus by the 1970s the 'Welsh economy' and the 'Scottish economy' became accepted and unquestioned concepts in political discourse. In England the planning regions live on in a political and non-administrative sense in that they usually form the basis, if not always the precise boundaries, for proposals for regional government – devolution – an aspect of the meso to which we now turn. In assessing the importance of the regional planning input to the evolution of the meso in the UK it is important to emphasize that although, as we have just noted, the regional bodies were invested by some with additional roles, including democratization and modernization, there was no public disruption that gave these additional roles a special importance and led to the creation of fully fledged regional governments. In short, there was nothing remotely like the French *événements* during the late 1960s, or the 'hot autumn' in Italy. The regional bodies for the majority remain in England stubbornly part of the history of planning and they diminished in public salience almost from the time they were created, except as reform proposals.

Devolution
The second aspect of the quasi-meso is again largely a tale of unfulfilled hopes and forms part of a century-old demand for what is now called 'devolution' but was formerly known as 'Home Rule' (Bogdanor, 1979). It usually involves the creation of elected governments for the so-called 'Celtic periphery' of Scotland and Wales. Northern Ireland is no longer included, for although it did have its own elected government, since the late 1960s a reverse process has been occurring in the province, as we shall see.

Increasingly of late, devolution also includes proposals for the creation of regional governments for the eight English planning regions. An attempt at devolution for the Celtic periphery was made by the Labour government in the late 1970s, when after a long battle with its own backbenchers two Acts were passed creating elected assemblies for Scotland and Wales. The Acts were never promulgated by the Labour government because results from referendums that were required to be held in Scotland and Wales (a concession to the said backbenchers) did not meet specific turn-out conditions. The decision of the Labour government to stick so closely to the letter of the statute deeply upset the Scottish Nationalist Party, since, it argued, a numerical majority of those voting in the referendum had in fact favoured a Scottish assembly. They therefore moved a motion of no confidence in the Commons which the government lost by one vote. This result precipitated a general election which the Conservatives under Mrs Thatcher won. Both Devolution Acts were rescinded by the new Conservative government in 1979.[1]

This episode requires further comment since it illustrates precisely the unitariness of the British political tradition and its anti-territorial bias. It is almost inconceivable under any other Western system that a party like the Labour Party, itself already ineffably the party of the periphery in terms of its support at the polls, would put its position as the governing party at risk over what was after all little more than the creation of a glorified county council for Scotland. But such is the dominance of the unitary tradition and the fear of decentralization that the Labour government made no attempt to reconcile its erstwhile partners in the Commons, the nationalist parties which alone kept the government in power, by waiving the turn-out conditions. More significant still, outside Scottish nationalist circles there have been no critics of the decision not to waive the condition but instead face an extremely risky vote of confidence, least of all in the Labour Party itself, despite the fact that the party has remained out of power ever since losing the 1979 vote of confidence.

It seemed that after 1979 the devolution issue had died as the onset of Thatcherism directed political attention from territorial issues. However, there are very clear indications that in Scotland at least it has become, by the 1990s, a major political issue. In 1988, for example, the Scottish National Party (SNP), for which devolution is the most important issue, won a spectacular victory at the by-election in the former Labour Party stronghold of Govan in Glasgow. The renewed importance of the devolution issue has also been reflected in opinion polls which showed throughout the late 1980s a growing majority of the Scottish population favouring devolution for Scotland along the lines of the 1978 Act. In the spring of 1989 a *Glasgow*

Herald poll showed some 57 per cent of those interviewed to be in favour not just of devolution, but of *independence* for Scotland. It should perhaps be emphasized, however, that it was a special kind of independence which meant a separate Scotland remaining in the EC (*Observer*, 1989). This was the formula promoted by the SNP in its Govan victory and in doing so the party sharply reversed its position from being strongly anti-EC. This switch may have been critical for its success at the by-election since it seems to have reassured marginal SNP supporters, 'the consumption nationalists' (Sharpe, 1988), who may fear the economic consequences of complete independence; but at the same time it carried connotations of internationalism and modernity to balance the inevitably backward-looking character of the Scottish nationalist appeal. Nevertheless, the SNP victory did demonstrate the strength of decentralist support in Scotland. Any lingering doubts on that score were banished in the spring of 1990 when a MORI opinion poll showed that the percentage of Scots favouring some form of constitutional change entailing increased autonomy for Scotland had reached 78 per cent. Nor does the devolution issue seem to be merely a reflection of party allegiance (so that a pro-devolution stance could be dismissed as mere anti-Conservatism), for the same poll revealed that 57 per cent of the Scottish *Conservative* supporters support devolution of some kind. Indeed, such is the extent of the support for devolution that some commentators have asserted that the devolution debate in Scotland is 'no longer between Unionist and Nationalist, but between constitutional nationalism and separatist nationalism' (*New Statesman and Society*, 1990).

Of equal significance for the momentum of the devolutionary upsurge of the late 1980s in Scotland was the meeting in March 1989 of a Scottish Constitutional Convention which was attended by all the opposition parties except, curiously enough, the SNP. The convention also included representatives from most Scottish local governments and from the churches. The convention was the culmination of a long process of co-operation among groups which did not usually co-operate, forming the 'Campaign for a Scottish Assembly' which set out the case for devolution in the publication *A Claim of Right for Scotland*, published in July 1988 (*Towards a Scottish Parliament*, 1990). It must be noted that despite the apparent importance of the devolution movement in Scotland that these events reflect, the SNP did not prosper at the 1992 general election when it lost one seat. Moreover, the Conservative Party which fought on an anti-devolutionary platform gained two seats.

A longer-term factor strongly influencing the devolutionary upsurge in the late 1980s was the result of the 1987 general election which left the national majority party – the Conservatives – with less than a seventh of Scottish seats (11 out of 72). The disparity between this and the national result (over a 100-seat majority in the Commons) immediately posed the questions of the legitimacy of all subsequent government actions pertaining to Scotland that did not seem to command majority support in Scotland. The legitimacy question was underlined by the fact that the Conservative Party had to draft Conservative MPs sitting for English seats on to the special House of Commons Scottish legislative committees in order to achieve a majority. The extreme unpopularity of some legislation forced through in this fashion, such as the poll tax and the dismantling of local community control of secondary education, further inflamed the legitimacy issue.

In formal constitutional terms, there is no basis for questioning the centre's legitimacy on such grounds, since Scotland is just as much an integral part of the British state as, the South-East region which, with its huge Conservative majority, would be equally short of majority-party MPs if Labour was in power nationally. Here we enter one of the many ambiguities of the British Constitution and its shadowy character, for Scotland in reality is more than a territorial segment of the UK; it is a former state which entered into a voluntary union of the two Crowns in the seventeenth century and completed the fusion by the Treaty of Union in 1707. Scotland has retained crucial symbols of its distinctiveness ever since, such as its separate legal system, a separate educational system, a separate established church, a separate local government system (hence the special legislative committees in the Commons already alluded to), different bank-notes, the Scottish Office (which we will come to in a moment) and its preferential treatment in the allocation of Common seats, at present amounting to 23 per cent more than it would be if the English ratio of votes to seats were followed.

Scotland's distinctiveness is also powerfully symbolized by extra-constitutional privileges, what may be called 'unobtrusive de-volution' (Sharpe, 1985: 2), which elsewhere are the emblems of nation states, such as acceptance internationally of Scottish sports teams complete with their own national flag, regalia and national anthem. Given such a distinctive status, it is clear that Scotland is not simply another territorial segment of the UK like an English region, but already enjoys a special political status which sometimes goes well beyond that conferred on a constituent state in a federal system, however self-consciously distinctive it may be. Neither Bavaria nor Texas, for example, has its own banknotes, nor can they field their own sports teams on the international stage against other nation states. The legitimacy issue and with it the devolution issue as a whole, then, cannot be brushed aside on formal constitutional grounds, or as disguised anti-Conservatism.

A major constitutional problem will almost certainly confront a Scottish devolution move that entails granting legislative powers to a Scottish assembly. Briefly it asks the question, if there is a separate assembly legislating for Scotland, why should Scottish MPs vote on English legislation when English MPs are excluded from voting on Scottish legislation? Greater point is given to this question when account is taken of the 23 per cent extra seats that Scotland enjoys in the House of Commons already noted. If this dilemma is ignored, thus creating a further special legislative privilege for Scotland, it will be extremely difficult to retain the special seat allocation as well. The Northern Ireland precedent will no doubt also be cited, for the Province, when it had its own Assembly, had *fewer* Commons seats per capita than the English average. The price of devolution, then, is likely to be paid· over the long run: that is, under a Conservative government in the future (which unlike Labour would not be dependent on Scottish seats for a majority in the Commons) the harmonization of the ratio of seats to votes for the whole of the UK. Since Wales, another Labour stronghold, also has more seats per capita than England, the effect of such harmonization could be a loss to the Labour Party of some of its safest seats, possibly of the order of a dozen. Only Wales compares with Scotland in terms of the extent to which devolved government is likely. However, it seems that a Welsh assembly following the 1979 precedent would be considerably weaker than its Scottish counterpart, in recognition of the lower support for it in the Principality (Kellas, 1991: 95). The reason for Scottish and Welsh exceptionalism on the devolution issue is simply that there is no popular demand for it elsewhere. In Northern Ireland, which enjoys distinctive political and governmental charac- teristics that rival those of Scotland, all parts of the political spectrum prefer direct rule from Whitehall (which in effect gives them the least territorial autonomy of any part of the UK) to any other alternative that would be likely to command the support of either of the religious communities, Protestant and Catholic. In England there never has been any deeply rooted political support for regional government, for it cannot be emphasized too strongly that the UK politico- administrative tradition is profoundly unitary, and nowhere is it more unitary than in England (Bogdanor, 1979: ch. 1).

The combination of the parliamentary sovereignty principle and the popularly assumed role of the central government as the legitimate custodian of both the national interest and individual interests, as against what are seen as the possibly illegitimate and sectional interests of the localities, powerfully reinforces this unitary tradition. Whatever the impact of a government's policies on sub-national government, and whatever the doubts which may arise about central policies which in other democracies would be regarded as constitutional issues, once Parliament has pronounced a favourable verdict on such policies they become law. There is no second bite at the cherry, for the House of Lords dare not thwart the First Chamber on a major issue, and the courts always defer on such key decisions to the executive under the parliamentary sovereignty principle. The war on local government that was systematically and successfully waged by the three Thatcher administrations over the 1980s is merely the most dramatic example of the ascendency of the centre and the deep thickets of ambiguity that surround the relative autonomy of the sub-national level within the British system. The fact that the centralist tradition is nowhere stronger than in the English trunk of the country is important if only because over 85 per cent of the population live there. It has been a unified kingdom for almost a thousand years, and although divided more recently into regions at various times for administrative purposes, and latterly, as we have noted, for planning, none of the English regions command anything remotely like the degree of popular allegiance to be found in either Scotland or Wales. Moreover, the country has been industrialized for two centuries, so that it has a uniformity of culture that probably has no parallel on such a scale anywhere else in Europe.

In Wales, the nationalist movement seems to be weaker than it was during its peak in the early 1970s, but the demand for a Welsh assembly has increased from less than a quarter of the electorate at the referendum in 1979 to almost a half (48 per cent) in a poll held in 1989 by BBC Wales. Ten per cent were against and 22 per cent would not bother to vote in a referendum on the issue (*Guardian*, 1989). Some of the dissatisfaction in the Principality making for devolutionary pressure, which is firmly rooted in the language issue, has probably been assuaged by a policy applied by the central government of 'unobtrusive devolution', such as the creation of a Welsh-speaking TV channel which relays twenty-eight hours of Welsh-only programmes per week; the creation of the Select Committee on Welsh Affairs in the Commons; the enhanced status of the Welsh language established under the Welsh Language Act of 1967 as an official language both in schools (where children can be educated wholly in Welsh if the numbers warrant it) and in the courts. Bilingual road signs have also been introduced, and state aid has been made available to sustain a Welsh national opera company, a symphony orchestra and infrastructural redevelopment in Cardiff, the Welsh capital, to match its status. The same privilege of fielding national sports teams complete with flag and anthem that applies for Scotland also applies for Wales (Sharpe, 1985).

The Offices

So much for the devolution aspect of the quasi-meso. We now come to another of its features, the so-called Offices. The UK is somewhat unusual for a large Western state in that it has no comprehensive and uniform level of deconcentrated territorial administration between local and central government, not even in a residual form as in Scandinavia. All intermediate administration is therefore either asymmetrical or confined to uni-functional service-delivery systems. The UK's asymmetrical administrative meso takes the form of the three Offices, which are formally deconcentrated levels of central general government in Scotland, Wales and Northern Ireland, and they constitute a feature of the British sub-national system that has loose parallels with a Napoleonic system.

The reason for discussing the three Offices is not to claim that they form part of a meso government in the accepted sense of the term, but simply because it would be impossible to understand why British meso development has been confined to the upper tier of the local government system if the quasi-meso is ignored. In other words, had the Offices not existed, the pressure for a fully fledged meso system at the regional level on the French or Italian pattern would probably have been considerably greater, certainly in Scotland and Wales. It would perhaps be an exaggeration to say that the Offices' collective existence actually ruled out the possibility of a uniform regional meso for the reasons already given, but their existence certainly made it very much easier to withstand, for example, pressure for such a meso during the 1960s and 1970s. Indeed, the Offices have their origin precisely in political pressures for decentralization in the sense that the Scottish Office, the first to be created, was a direct product of the Home Rule movement of the 1880s (Kellas, 1976: 28). Although the Welsh Office did not begin to achieve fully fledged status until the 1960s, the growth of Welsh devolutionary pressure later strongly aided the process.

It is unlikely that Stormont, the quasi-federal system of government in Northern Ireland, could have been abolished so easily in 1972 if there had not been the model of the Office to take its place. The two forms of the British quasi-meso to be discussed – the three Offices and the regionalized NHS – are, then, essential to any adequate understanding of why the British meso experience has taken the form that it has.

It must be emphasized at the outset that all three Offices are integral parts of British central government. Like all such deconcentrated forms, each Office is under the control of a common general superior, a secretary of state. He or she is a member of the House of Commons and sits in the Cabinet. Seven features of the Offices need to be noted. The first is that the Northern Ireland Office is distinctly different from the other two Offices in a number of respects. In the first place, it is much more a form of direct government from London in which public-order and counter-terrorist policy dominates. The Northern Ireland Secretary is more powerful on his or her home patch than either of his counterparts and comes closest to being a Prime Minister for his region (Bell, 1987: 191). In running the Office and formulating policy the secretary of state, also unlike the Scottish and Welsh counterparts, may or may not be supported by Northern Ireland MPs, all of whom belong to parties that are exclusive to the Province (the national parties were until 1990 banned from operating in the Province) and therefore will never have any particular allegiance to him or her. He or she will not sit for a Northern Ireland seat and his or her role is much more that of being 'a special voice for the territory at the centre of government in London' (Hogwood, 1982: 3). Moreover, the Northern Ireland Office is the most recent in the sense that up to 1972 Northern Ireland had its own directly elected, bicameral representative institutions (Stormont) and its own government exercising a wide degree of autonomy over internal affairs.

Central intervention in Northern Ireland's internal affairs was, until serious civil unrest began in 1968, virtually unknown. In 1972, as a result of the worsening secretarian conflict in the Province, and the unwillingness of the Northern Ireland government to relinquish its control of public order to the centre, Stormont was peremptorily abolished. This action cannot be bettered as exemplifying the extraordinary power of central government already alluded to and it occurred remarkably swiftly – that is, as a result of a simple, albeit well-supported, majority in the Commons. In early 1974 a much weaker 'power-sharing' executive replaced Stormont, which was not based on the majority principle, but gave access to power to the minority Catholic parties. For this reason it was very unpopular with the Protestant majority (Protestants outnumber Catholics by about two to one), which mounted a national strike against it on the grounds that sacrificing such an integral part of the democratic process as the majority principle constituted an unacceptable diminution of their rights. As a result it never functioned, collapsing in May 1974. Thereafter, a new Northern Ireland Office took over the reins of power in the Province on a temporary basis, and in 1982 an elected body was revived in the form of the Northern Ireland Assembly. Unlike Stormont, it was merely consultative and deliberative, and again, had its executive been created, it would have followed the power-sharing or non-majority principle. The aim was to enhance its status and powers over time by means of 'rolling devolution'. It was, however, even less popular than its predecessor, and the assembly was dissolved in June 1986.

The Northern Ireland experience is thus the reverse of what has been occurring elsewhere in Europe, since there has been a *decline* in the autonomy of the peripheral ethnically distinctive region, indeed a transformation from meso government to meso administration (Rose, 1982). The explanation for this apparent paradox is that the majority in the peripheral region want *closer* ties with the British core in order to protect their peripheral distinctiveness against what they fear may be submergence not by that core, but by an adjacent state, the Irish Republic, whose Constitution contains two clauses laying claim to the Province. Such Protestant fears are sharpened by the attitudes of the Catholic minority in Northern Ireland, a small majority of whom do not recognize the United Kingdom as their country but do recognize the Irish Republic. In a 1990 survey, some 56 per cent of Northern Irish Catholics favoured Northern Ireland joining the Irish Republic (Jowell et al., 1990). The Northern Ireland Office is also different because the Province is still in the grip of an incipient civil war, with strong overtones of irredentism, that has led, via the Northern Ireland Agreement with the Irish Republic, to the secretary having direct formal links with a foreign state. Moreover, the Northern Ireland Office is less integrated than its counterparts because its bureaucracy continues to operate outside the direct ambit of the secretary of state so as to facilitate the transfer to a representative system should that ever become possible (Bell, 1987).

The second aspect of the Office form of the quasi-meso to be noted is that no Office embraces all central government functions in its respective area, since some central departments operate a centre-to-periphery implementation hierarchy that is independent of and very much bigger that that of the respective Office. Essentially, both the Scottish and Welsh Offices perform a representative rather than a functional role in Westminster in the sense that their main task is to defend their area's interests and to gain more central resources. Also, the functional range of each Office differs. The largest and the most highly developed is the Scottish Office, which is over 100 years old and, unlike the Welsh Office, covers not only the health service in Scotland but law and order, the police and prisons (Keating and Midwinter, 1983: ch. 2).

The third aspect of the Offices to be emphasized is this pre-eminence of the Scottish Office, and above all, its secretary. The Scottish Secretary's predominance in London is mainly due to Scotland's separate legal, educational and local government systems, which entail special arrangements in the House of Commons that enhance the role of the Office and the secretary of state, and include the Scottish Grand Committee, two Scottish standing committees and a select committee that together handle most Scottish legislation and debate Scottish affairs. The role of Scottish MPs has also been enhanced with the expansion of Scottish institutions at the centre. As a symbolic gesture, the Grand Committee meets from time to time in the former Royal High School in Edinburgh, which was originally designated to be home of the proposed Scottish Assembly in the aborted Scotland Act of the late 1970s.

The Welsh MPs have a Grand Committee and a Select Committee on Welsh Affairs (Jones and Wilford, 1986), but neither carries the same weight as its Scottish counterpart, since Wales is much more institutionally uniform with England. It must be emphasized, too, that Scotland is by far the largest of the three territorial segments covered by Offices, having a population of approximately 5 million as compared with 2.8 million in Wales and 1.5 million in Northern Ireland. This difference is reflected in the staffing levels of the Scottish and Welsh Offices, the former having about four times the number of staff as the latter (Kellas and Madgwick, 1982: 9).

The fourth aspect of the Offices to be noted is the unusual nature of the post of secretary of state, who holds a unique position in British politics in the sense that, the Prime Minister apart, he or she is the only member of the executive who has a territorial rather than a functional base. In both Scotland and Wales, but particularly in Scotland, the secretary becomes an important *regional* political figure. This prominence is particularly marked when the Labour Party is in power nationally, because it usually holds many more seats than other parties in both regions and has held the majority of Scottish seats for over thirty years. The secretary is thus able to command special status within the government and within the parliamentary party. The Conservative Party, by contrast, is particularly weak in both Scotland and Wales. Following the 1992 general election, the Conservatives hold only 11 of the 72 Scottish seats and a mere 6 of the 38 Welsh seats. As Table 1 reveals, the 50 per cent of the three southern regional electorates (South-East, South-West and East Anglia) voted Conservative in 1987 but less than a quarter did so in Scotland.

The Labour Party is correspondingly strong in the periphery. Except for 1966, it has not won 50 per cent of the English seats since 1957. There has been a more spasmodic decline in the Conservative vote in Wales, but since 1979 the party has had difficulty finding a Secretary of State for Wales who sits for a Welsh seat. The present (1992) Secretary of State for Wales, for example, although of Welsh origin, sits for an English constituency, as did his predecessor.

Table 1   *Conservative vote by region, 1987 general election*

Region	Conservative vote (%)
London[1]	46.4
Rest of South-East	55.8
South-West	50.5
East Anglia	52.0
East Midlands	48.6
West Midlands	45.6
Yorks and Humberside	37.5
North-West	38.0
North	32.0
Wales	29.5
Scotland	24.0

[1] London is not a designated region but forms part of the standard South-East region.

Source: Independent, 13.6.87

As a member of the Cabinet, the secretary of state is able to give his or her region what may be a crucial advantage in bargaining with the Treasury over government expenditure, although his advantage is less evident for Northern Ireland and has to some extent been modified since the mid-1960s by rivalry between the Welsh and Scottish Offices and perhaps a more watchful Treasury. Though by no means all the differences in expenditure shown therein are attributable to the existence of the Offices, Table 2 shows that per capita expenditure is appreciably higher in Northern Ireland and Scotland than England, even allowing for needs factors. The figures in Table 2 refer to 1979, but later statistics (for 1986–7) suggest that Scotland at least has maintained its position: 'for every £100 of government spending in England in 1986/87, Scotland received £122.

Table 2   *Public expenditure by region for six main services, c. 1979*

	England	Scotland	Wales	Northern Ireland
(A) Per capita expenditure	100	122	106	135
(B) Relative needs	100	116	109	131
(A)–(B)		+6	−3	+4

Source: 1982: 22

In health the comparative figures were £97 in England and £122 in Scotland' (Dickson, 1988: 361). In 1987–8 Scotland had 23.8 per cent higher identifiable public expenditure per head than the UK averages and Wales 9.6 per cent (Kellas, 1991: 96).

Midwinter and Keating state that Scottish expenditure has been consistently higher than the UK average by about 20 per cent overall and very much higher in housing and agriculture. The allocation process, presided over by the Treasury, is both shrouded in secrecy and very complex, but they explain this difference as being attributable in part to the fact that originally the formula (the Goschen formula) for allocation was based on Scotland's proportion of the UK population in the 1890s (Keating and Widwinter, 1983: ch. 10). That proportion has declined, and the formula, now the Barnett formula, has changed; but the *base* budget, derived from Goschen, remains intact and thus so does the skew in Scotland's favour (Heald, 1983).

Direct expenditure is not the only form of governmentally determined redistribution, and an exhaustive account of its total effect regionally could very well reveal that the direct expenditure advantage enjoyed by Scotland is more than balanced by, for example, the massive subsidy entailed in governmental revenue figures in the form of tax relief granted to home-owners repaying mortages, which in 1990 was estimated to be in excess of £7 billion annually (*Guardian*, 1990). As Table 3 reveals, only 45 per cent of the Scottish population are home-owners compared with a 67 per cent average for the English regions and 68 per cent for the most affluent English region, the South-East. Similarly the South-East can be said to enjoy another extra 'hidden' governmental subsidy, as Table 3 again reveals, since the percentage of 16-year-old children staying on at school for the region is almost 70 whereas for Scotland it is 48.6 per cent.

One important aspect of all three Offices, and especially the Scottish, is the vigour with which they have pursued economic development and regeneration as compared with the English regions. Such policies have been undertaken, however, not by the Office directly but by development agencies (the successor to the regional planning board system mentioned earlier) in each region which enjoy relatively high levels of autonomy from their respective Offices and from Whitehall. Each has, as a consequence, acquired an identity and reputation of its own, especially the Scottish Development Agency, renamed Scottish Enterprises in 1990, which sometimes seems to rival the Scottish Office itself. Indeed, Scotland has the privilege of a second agency, the older Highlands and Islands Development Board, which covers the north-western part of Scotland and the adjacent islands.

Table 3 *Selected indicators of economic standards by region, 1987–9*

Indicator	South-East	West Midlands	East Anglia	South-West	East Midlands	Wales	North-West	Yorkshire & Humberside	North	Scotland	Northern Ireland
Average weekly household income (£)	338.6	241.7	256.8	273.7	241.3	227.5	245.8	232.8	220.1	234.2	224.8
Average household expenditure (£)	232.7	177.6	200.2	203.1	179.5	177.2	186.3	172.3	164.4	172.8	199.7
Gross value added manufacturing (£m)	25,031	10,429	3,102	6,020	7,523	4,529	11,376	8,003	5,093	7,085	1,549
Percentage of households owning 2 cars	23	17	17	22	16	16	16	13	11	11	14
Unemployment rate (%)	3.9	6.7	4.4	4.5	6.2	7.8	8.4	7.7	10.0	9.3	15.1
Infant mortality (per 000 live births)	8.6	10.2	6.9	9.5	10.0	7.6	9.3	9.3	8.4	8.2	8.7
Percentage of 16-year-olds staying on at school	69.9	19.5	7.3	14.7	15.4	13.1	23.5	18.3	11.3	48.6	NA
Percentage of housing owner-occupied	68.0	66.0	68.0	72.0	69.0	69.0	67.0	64.0	58.0	45.0	58.0

Source: Regional Trends 25 (HMSO, London, 1990)

The fifth aspect of the Offices to be noted is their relationship with local government. In Northern Ireland the local government system is very attenuated, and comprises twenty-six district councils which are responsible for minor functions; most of the services provided by local government in Scotland and England are provided by the Northern Ireland Office through quangos. The total of Northern Ireland local government annual expenditure is only about £150 million. This is because normal local government was abolished in the 1970s due to gerrymandering and religious discrimination (in public housing allocation, for example) by Protestant majorities within some local authorities. In Scotland and Wales, the respective Offices tend to have a closer relationship with local government and local pressure groups than Whitehall has with English local bodies (Kellas and Madgwick, 1982: 11). Since the Offices themselves are part of the periphery in relation to London departments, and in particular the Treasury, a sense of identity between local government and the Offices also builds up, so that the Office can intercede on behalf of a locality in conflict with Whitehall (Keating and Carter, 1987). This common front towards London is perhaps reinforced by the fact that most of the senior civil servants at the headquarters of each Office – St Andrew's House (Edinburgh) and Cathays Park (Cardiff) – tend to be, respectively, of Scottish or Welsh birth. In short, senior civil servants of the two Offices develop a dual relationship to their respective territorial area – reflectors of its interests to the centre as well as instruments of central control – that has its closest parallel to that of a prefect and his staff in a Napoleonic system (Machin, 1977).

The sixth feature of the Offices to be noted is their ambiguous and complex status. For example, they are both a form of deconcentration *and* a form of decentralization. It is also easy to exaggerate their importance. As we have noted, they form only a small part of non-local government in their respective areas, and the proportion of the total of civil servants in Scotland and Wales employed by the Offices is, respectively, 18 per cent and 6 per cent (Parry, 1981). They are a peculiar type of hybrid in the sense that, though formally a form of administrative deconcentration, they have a politician and Cabinet minister at their head. But he or she is a relatively junior Cabinet minister and does not sit on any of the most important Cabinet committees. They are also indubitably part of the national administration, and just as subject to Treasury control as any other department within central government (Hood and Dunsire, 1981: ch. 11). Yet is would be false to see the major departments of the three Offices as simply offshoots of their Whitehall counterparts, for they are formally wholly responsible for their functions within their territory. As Keating and Midwinter describe this complicated and ambiguous relationship:

> the relations between the Scottish Office and the UK departments are similar to the relationships amongst government departments generally. What distinguishes the Scottish Office, though (and also the Welsh and Northern Ireland Offices), is that it is responsible, within Scotland, for the same functions as are exercised, for the rest of Britain or for England alone, by the main 'functional' departments. This raises the question of where the policy input to these functions comes from and the extent to which the Scottish Office 'makes' its own, or simply administers policy made elsewhere. (Keating and Midwinter, 1983: 19)

Keating and Midwinter's answer to their own question is that for all-UK policy the UK departments take the lead, whereas the Scottish department takes the lead for purely Scottish policy. Vertical links between Office departments and the English department in Whitehall are also usually considerably stronger than horizontal links between departments within each Office. In fact, the Scottish Office itself was created originally, among other purposes, to bring some uniformity with central practices to what was at the time a highly fragmented jumble of Scottish institutions. The harmonization process was not completed until 1929 (Hanham, 1969: 61), and this date also marks the transfer of the Office from London to Edinburgh. But, equally, there can be no doubt that the special character of each segment of the national territory that each Office administers profoundly affects its own character and procedures and very sharply distinguishes each Office from the UK structure in London. Scotland has, for example, its separate legal, education and local government systems, plus the very special problems of the Highlands and Islands. It also acts as a kind of laboratory for testing certain types of legislation before they are launched on the country as a whole (Parry, 1987). The Welsh Office lacks a rich regional institutional substructure like Scotland and is remarkably English in its character, for despite the importance of the language issue, the Office has little direct interest in it (Thomas, 1987).

The seventh and final aspect to be noted is what difference do the three Offices make? In other words, how much real autonomy do they exercise? We have already noted the considerable difference between per capita public expenditure in Scotland and Wales as compared with the UK average. In addition, it must be emphasized that once an Office has received its block grant from the centre, the secretary of state does have considerable freedom to decide priorities within the block (Kellas, 1991: 96). But in relation to other aspects of policy-making within each Office it is extremely difficult to generalize, simply because of the relative absence of studies of the Welsh and

Northern Ireland Offices that confront the question. Keating and Midwinter suggest that, for the Scottish Office, the kind of issue involved is often crucial in determining the extent of autonomy. If the policy has no cross-border spill-overs with the rest of the UK – that is, if the policy area is rooted in Scotland's separate legal system, or its local government – high levels of autonomy are permitted. Similarly, where by convention Scotland is recognized as having a special tradition, leeway is again possible. Other lesser factors making for higher autonomy are, first, the greater salience of the issue in Scotland as compared with elsewhere – for example, fisheries policy; second, when the Labour Party is in power nationally, as we have already noted, the Secretary of State is a more powerful political figure and can use that power if he or she so wishes to enhance Office autonomy (Keating and Midwinter, 1983: 20–3).

We now turn to the other example of the quasi-meso: the uni-functional regional administration of health – the National Health Service in England and Wales.

The National Health Service
The regional bodies of the NHS present a fairly complex picture (Levitt, 1976; Haywood and Alaszewki, 1980; Haywood and Elock, 1982). There has been a regional level in the administration of the NHS since its inception in 1948, when the then Labour government decided that if the main aims of nationalization of health were to be fulfilled the system could not be left with, or transferred to, local government. Before 1948, health care was provided charitably, or by the market, or by local authorities. In 1948 the new nationalized system absorbed most of these forms and redivided health care into three parts: community health services provided by local authorities; family practitioners, dentists and so on administered by executive councils; and the hospitals, which were the responsibility of individual hospital management committees operating under fourteen Regional Hospital Boards. The areas covered by each board were each based on a medical school (that is, the medical faculty of a university), and the minister appointed to the board people nominated by local authorities and other bodies with an interest in health matters. Their main function was to satisfy themselves about the arrangements made about hospital management and the provision of services which displayed significant economies of scale, such as blood collecting, architectural services and in-service training. Later Regional Boards concerned themselves with the overseeing of hospital management, and by the 1960s they had become very important in implementing the hospital building programme. Yet below the level of the region the NHS was still split into three parts, each run by

different authorities and each based on different areas, two parts of which, community health and the family practitioner service, were separate from the regions. By the late 1960s such lack of coherence in what was supposed to be an integrated system was becoming less and less tolerable. In the discussion prior to the reorganization in 1973, the main argument was that there were unexploited service externalities. The separation of hospital and community services was also criticized in that it fragmented provision for childbirth and mental illness. A major problem was also perceived in the division of general practice from hospital medicine. These problems were first raised by the Guillebaud Committee in their report of 1956, but this concluded that despite them it was better to leave the NHS structure unchanged. By the 1960s, however, medical opinion was moving towards a view that the service should be integrated under Area Health Authorities, which would cover an area larger than the hospital boards but smaller than the existing regions. A second source of dissatisfaction was the apparent inability of the unified system to fulfil one of its principal aims, that of distributing medical care and resources equally between regions. A third perceived weakness of the system was the apparently ineluctable growth in the cost of the service. Greater managerial control was discerned as being the only way of curbing such growth.

The 1973 Act abolished the existing structure, but the fourteen regions were retained with changed boundaries. These new regional authorities, however, were made responsible for drawing up a long-term resource plan. Below the regions the more localized Area Health Authorities (AHAs) were created; these broadly corresponded to areas of local authorities and were the major policy-making part of the new structure. Underneath them were district management teams responsible for particular groups of hospitals within the area.

The large expectations invested in the 1973 reorganization were not fulfilled. The structure was too complex for coherent planning and power became too dispersed. The number of tiers also confused and clogged policy-making. AHAs also came to be seen as being too large, and instead of promoting co-ordination and efficiency they encouraged a new and costly bureaucratic tier. When the Conservative government came to power in 1979 it abolished the AHAs under the 1980 Health Service Act and replaced them with District Health Authorities. These were smaller, being based on a single general hospital, and they came into existence in 1982. While this appears to be a return to the old pre-1973 structure, one of the effects of the 1982 change has been to perpetuate the regions, the one continuous element in the service since its inception. In short, the regional structure has proved its worth as an appropriate level for the provision of hospital services.

In conclusion, the critical aspect of the NHS that requires emphasis is its sheer importance. Renowned as the ninth largest organization in the world, it absorbs over 7 per cent of the GDP, 13 per cent of all public sector expenditure and no less than 4 per cent of the national workforce. Yet in democratic accountability terms it exists in a semi-limbo, for it is not a formal part of the central administration and has only a very tangential relationship to local democratic government. One reason for this anomaly is the non-executant tradition of British central government we have alluded to earlier. Only for transfers (pensions, income maintenance, unemployment pay and so on) is there a centre-to-periphery service-delivery hierarchy; otherwise the centre relies, as we have noted, on different types of service-delivery agency: local government, public corporation or quango. In the same spirit the central bureaucracy has always sought to distance itself from the NHS in order to avoid the rough-and-tumble of often bitter conflicts and constant resource wrangles and also to reduce its own management load; it might even be said that it consistently seeks to avoid, if it can, the management of the NHS in the conventional sense altogether.

In the normal course of events the NHS would be part of local government, since it provides a non-market social service, the normal role of the British local government. But there have always been three fundamental reasons why this did not happen. The first is the strength of the production-efficiency tradition noted earlier and made ever stronger by the relatively higher status of the medical profession. Precisely because medicine deals with life-or-death issues, professionally defined objectives were all the stronger. So in most of the debates on the various reform proposals over the years popular participation, accountability and access have always taken a back seat to professionally defined objectives, which were assumed to be synonymous with consumption efficiency. In short, with the possible exception of the debate following the Green Paper of the late 1960s, democratic issues have usually been ignored, except in so far as the Community Health Councils, which are supposed to voice the consumer viewpoint, perform that role. But most observers seem to be agreed that the councils are largely ineffective (Hoggs, 1990). Radical changes in the NHS implemented in the early 1990s designed to 'marketize' it will curtail even further the formal accountability of the service to the public and abolish the last fugitive links with the local democratic process.

The second reason for not transferring the NHS to local government is the sheer cost of the NHS. This high cost factor posed severe problems since local government was restricted to a property tax, an income-inelastic form of revenue source peculiarly susceptible to inertia in an inflationary or growth situation, and thus local government could not possibly have coped without the centre footing almost all of the bill. The Treasury has always made it clear that it would never countenance local government control. The third objection to local government control of the NHS was made by the doctors and especially the specialist hospitals consultants. They dislike the idea of local government control intensely, whereas they do like the kind of professional freedom that arises from being in an administratively ambiguous and politically remote position between centre and locality. They enjoy what Richard Titmuss has termed a kind of 'syndicalist' status.

It may be that the meso as a governmental form of this type does offer special attractions for certain public sector technocrats, especially for those specialisms where professional autonomy is particular valued, as it most assuredly is in medicine. It provides such specialists, in short, with a form of 'decisional space' or 'opportunity space' (Hogwood and Keating, 1982: 68) to exploit on behalf of an increasingly technologically dynamic and therefore especially costly service. Also, the uni-functional meso like the NHS will have additional attractions for specialists because it is relatively free from direct political intervention. It is also free from the competition for resources and prestige of rival public services that is the consequence for all public services entrapped in the discipline of general government. These very important characteristics of this type of meso have been noted and emphasized by Gray (Gray, 1985) in relation to the now privatized Regional Water Authorities, by Saunders (Saunders, 1985) in relation to the NHS and the RWAs and by Hogwood (Hogwood, 1982).

The true meso: the counties

We now come to the British meso proper: the county councils in England and Wales and the regions in Scotland. Before 1974 the county as a unit of local government was universal in the whole of the UK and also in the Republic of Ireland. There is no county in Northern Ireland.

With counties in Hintze's terms as the 'higher level' of local government (Page, 1990: 48), the British sub-national governmental system comes closer, as we have noted, to the Northern European 'functional' meso type than to the regional model of Southern Europe. One reason for this, but only one, is the pre-existence of the county as a directly elected, powerful, traditional upper tier of local government having a status equal to that of the largest city and enjoying a salience altogether different from the French *départemental* council or the Spanish *diputación*. Because of its scale and territorial extent, the county has been able to cope with many of the pressures on the local government system in the post-war period derived from alleged mainly functional scale limitations, increased population mobility and increasing service externalities. The existence of a quasi-meso comprising the asymmetrical Offices together with the regional arrangements for the NHS has, as we have argued earlier, probably further inhibited the emergence of a uniform regional meso on, say, the Italian or French pattern. The same may be equally true of the county.

One major problem confronting any attempt to provide an adequate account of the modern county is the scarcity of systematic studies. With very few exceptions research has focused on British urban local government.[2] The position is no better for the Scottish region, with one or two exceptions (Page and Midwinter, 1980; Dawson, 1981; Midwinter, 1985). So the following account of the Anglo-Welsh county will have to be highly generalized, although a debt must be acknowledged to a recent compendium (Young, 1989). The counties, like most British political institutions, are not the product of conscious design; still less do they reflect any logical theory of local government or service-delivery rationality. They are pre-eminently, as Lee has emphasized, 'the creatures of political convenience' (Lee, 1990: 21). They vary considerably in scale, for in both England and Scotland (where the new, very much enlarged counties were renamed regions in 1975) most have their origins in early medieval times; originally some were even kingdoms, such as Sussex (South Saxons) and Essex (East Saxons). Counties are, in fact, the last survivors of the Saxon four-tier hierarchy of local government of which they were the most senior, the other levels being *hides*, *tithings* and *hundreds* (Stanyer, 1989b: 25). Like all comparable territorial units they do not usually command automatic public allegiance in the way that finite urban settlements such as cities and villages do. On the other hand, they are considerably older than most of their continental counterparts and were not imposed as a central state administrative convenience. Many of the English counties do command a traditional sense of loyalty that is reinforced by time-honoured institutions rooted in each county. To some extent that allegiance may have strengthened with the decline in the sense of locality (Stanyer, 1989a: 266). The county in England and Wales is usually, too, the territorial unit for organizing a wide range of recreational, cultural and other activities and this link further reinforces the importance of the county in public consciousness and the sense of identity felt towards it. Nowhere is this more the case than in the eighteen first-class cricketing counties which provide the premier cricket teams in the country. Until the cost-cutting regimental amalgamations of the 1960s, almost every county (including some of the pre-1975 Scottish counties) also either had its own named army regiment with its own headquarters barracks situated in the county, or shared a regiment with a neighbouring county.

Until relatively recently, another strength of the English and Welsh county as a territorial, and to some degree political, entity was the extent to which a segment of the aristocracy who lived within the county's boundaries, and together with the rural-dwelling upper middle class – the gentry – provided as social leaders the dominant cadre on the county council (Lee, 1963). This link with the social elite gave county government a status that most urban government lacked. It also lent it a certain style, which by the late twentieth century is now very attentuated. This style has been identified by Hintze as being characteristic of county government in the European 'peripheral state' thus: 'Administration was conducted in an old-world patriarchical style with the comfortable nonchalance which is the hallmark of an uncontrolled aristocratic self-government and which provides a striking contrast with the sharpness and bustle of continental administrative authorities' (Page, 1990: 48).

It is this quasi-aristocratic heritage which in part accounts for the counties' reputation as being the most civilized level of local government that was detached from both the hurly-burly of the traditionally party-dominated urban government and from the 'shopocracy' of the small town. County policy, so this view claims, was decided largely 'on its merits' by, if not aristocrats, then at least gentlemen. Until the big reform of 1973 such a view was still plausible especially for the very rural counties where 'Independents' (that is, non-party councillors) dominated. But the incorporation of the urban county boroughs into the counties in that year introduced party politics as a major element in county government. Before 1973 rarely more than five counties ever had a Labour majority and they were far exceeded by the 'Independent' counties. In 1966, 38 out of the 55 counties described themselves as being 'non-party' (Stewart, 1989: 103), although this proportion is probably inflated because some counties exaggerated the extent of their non-partisanship (Game and Leach, 1989). After 1973, the Independent proportion of the aggregate number of seats in English and Welsh counties fell from 40 to 14 per cent, and only five counties (Cornwall, Dyfed, Gwynedd, Powys and Isle of Wight) returned an Independent majority (Gyford, 1976: 62). By 1989 in three of the five that majority had disappeared. The Independents were after 1973 under a two-way squeeze (which had begun much earlier): first, from the Conservative Party, which demanded that all true anti-Labour voices should join them and, secondly, from its party rivals Labour and the Liberals which had now become major competitors overnight with the incorporation of the old county boroughs. By the 1990s in a 'normal' election year, Labour can control at least a quarter of the English and Welsh counties and the majority of the Scottish regions (see Appendix).

The Independent non-party characteristics of so much of county government up to the changes of the 1970s provides a rare parallel with continental local politics. The aristocratic thread which declined much earlier provides another echo of continental practices, for it gave the county a direct link with the House of Lords. Thirdly, the chairmanship of the county sometimes took on a dynastic aspect, which is also a characteristic of *notable* politics on the Continent. Thus the fifth Marquess of Bath as chairman of Wiltshire County Council succeeded his father, who had been chairman for 18 years, in 1906 and remained as chairman for the next 40 years. A similar dynastic system operated in a number of other counties, including on Oxfordshire County Council, where the Duke of Macclesfield's family held sway continuously up until the early 1970s.

These similarities with foreign practices must not be overdrawn. For the most part county politics was always much more like the rest of British local politics than any other system. Above all it was always practically bereft of clientelism. Party politics may not have been so important in the past as it is now, but, nevertheless, the motor which drove and still drives county politics and local English politics in general is policy execution rather than influence, power-broking or favours. The county administration no less than most British local government is in comparative terms a veritable redoubt of Weberian administrative practice. Given the virtual absence (the Offices apart) of territorial pork-barrelling, so, too, is the central administration. This is one of the direct consequences of being essentially the non-executant arm of the implementation process. If the centre does not itself build roads, dams, bridges, harbours, universities or hospitals, it is very much more difficult to subject it to pressures as to their location. The equal absence of clientelism among MPs plus the strict codes of probity and neutrality in the central civil service together reinforce that insulation of centre and locality from each other which was noted earlier.

One reason for the predominance of the gentry in the counties before 1975, in addition to the Independent tradition, was the probably concomitant high level of uncontested seats in county council elections which usually exceeded in aggregate those contested. In 1958, a not untypical election year, the number of uncontested seats was no less than 63 per cent overall and in only one county – London (London County Council) – were all the seats contested (Sharpe, 1962: 21). Another characteristic that is linked to the elitist style of the politics of the pre-reform counties was the aldermanic system whereby a proportion of the council were indirectly elected by the council itself. It was very rare for an alderman not to be re-elected if he or she wished to remain on the council, so that a kind of self-perpetuating oligarchy tended to predominate in many counties. The aldermanic system was abolished in the reforms of the 1970s.

It is important to emphasize that to some extent the county also remains an important sub-national territorial unit of organization in England and Wales by default because popular allegiance to the city rarely gets translated into political power to the extent that it does in other Western states. In a very real sense, English politics and government lack not only a regional dimension but an urban one too. Thus England's extraordinary political unitariness again reveals itself. Explaining adequately why English cities in what is one of the most urbanized countries in Europe fail to 'punch their weight', to use a boxing term, takes us outside the central focus of this chapter. The complete absence, however, of an institutionalized executive and especially a unitary executive – German *Bürgermeister* or French mayor – is certainly a vital factor, since it would concentrate urban power and give it continuity. Equally, a unitary executive would focus and symbolize popular city allegiance. Both consequences would strengthen the cities to the detriment of the counties by creating blocks of territorial power which could not be ignored either by the central government or by the national party. City leaders, or 'bosses', do emerge from time to time, but the power and status they achieve are usually exaggerated by the media and have to be created by the individual local politician in question despite the absence of institutional reinforcement, and they therefore also die or retire with them.

The dominance of *national* issues in party politics throughout most of local government would also have to be taken into account in any explanation of the political weakness of cities, for it tends to reinforce the conception of local parties as first and foremost hand-maidens in the task of achieving a parliamentary majority and not as defenders of collective local interests. The centralization of the media also takes its toll in undermining the importance of local politics. Over 95 per cent of the English and Welsh public read only a national morning newspaper published in London; the radio is equally centralized, and the television even more so.

The point of this digression into the extraordinary weakness of English big cities in political and administrative terms is to emphasize that, although the county's importance as a political and social entity varies considerably, and in no county – not even Yorkshire – does it command even the Welsh sense of popular identity, it has, none the less, no real rivals, and in many cities there is dual allegiance to city *and* county. It is of some interest in this connection that the big city which does have a marked sense of common identity – Liverpool – is also possibly the most cut off in every sense from its 'parent' county, Lancashire.

The English county, it must be emphasized, although its salience varies markedly up and down the country, is also still very much more important politically than the regions, the weakness of which also enhances the position of the county and therefore warrants another short digression from the main theme – especially so since, as we have noted, they will almost certainly form the basis of a regional meso if created. In some areas such as the East Midlands region, the North-West or the South-East, it is doubtful whether the region exists in popular consciousness. There is also the prior problem as to where the regional boundaries are to be drawn; for although the old planning regions of the 1960s have now become accepted for administrative purposes, there remain a number of critical problems about their popular acceptability for democratic government. As Hogwood has emphasized: 'The most striking feature of the English regions in terms of their role in British government is a complete absence of a coherent definition of their boundaries, their size or even of the concept of region' (Hogwood, 1982: 2; Hogwood and Lindley, 1982). To put the matter in a nutshell, whereas both Scotland and Wales (since the county of Monmouth and the Berwick-on-Tweed problems were resolved) now have immutable political boundaries,[3] none of the English regions enjoys such boundary security.

The second problem arising from the creation of English regional government concerns the South-East region, which not only embraces no less than 46 per cent of the English population, but also has a GDP per head that is almost 25 per cent higher than the English mean (and a staggering 59 per cent higher than Northern Ireland's). See Table 3 for further evidence of the South-East's comparative affluence. It would be very much a cuckoo in the nest and, moreover, have an absolutely impregnable Conservative majority.

To return to the main thread of our discussion, it must also be emphasized that the British county/region, like its Norwegian, Swedish and Danish counterparts, is considerably more important in a functional and financial sense than its nearest equivalent such as the

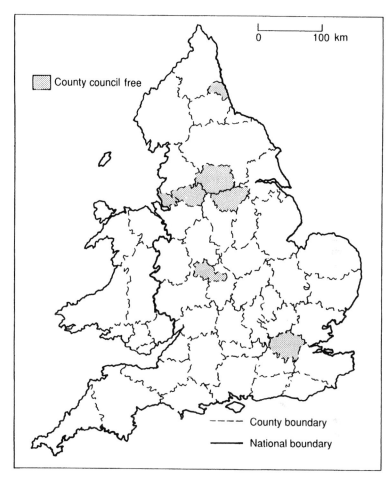

Figure 2 *The counties of England and Wales*

French *département*. It is also more important in these two senses
than either the Italian or French regional authorities. As a revamped
traditional institution it may lack the *cachet* of its Southern European
counterparts, and especially the status that is accorded, for example,
the first generation of Spanish Autonomous Communities; nevertheless the British county/region is a meso in the full sense of the term.
Under the *ultra vires* rule it does not enjoy any formal legislative
powers, however.

As a unit of democratic local government, the county began life in
1889 when it inherited some functions from its non-elected predecessor, the Justices of the Peace, who were central government

appointees before 1889 and provided a range of services including asylums, the Poor Law and, earlier, prisons (Redlich and Hirst, 1958). The existing traditional 51 counties (38 English and 13 Welsh) were increased in number by splitting up the larger ones (Sussex, Lincolnshire and Suffolk, for example) to give a new total of 61 'administrative counties'. In the early 1960s, a series of piecemeal changes reduced the total to 58. The major reform of 1973 reduced this figure to 53, but since this total included 9 entirely new counties the extent of consolidation in 1973 was greater than the total suggests.

The administrative county attracted functions steadily throughout the first fifty years of its existence, but it was not until after the Second World War that what may be called the 'upward functional mobility' factor began to take real effect. That is to say, existing functions such as secondary education and vocational training were transferred from the lower-tier local authorities to the counties in order to overcome growing externality problems and to reap alleged economies of scale. The county also acquired new major public functions such as planning, further education and a wide range of social services.

The 1972 (1973 in Scotland) Act accelerated the process of upward functional mobility by incorporating the areas of the biggest cities – the county boroughs in England and the counties of cities (of which there were four) in Scotland. Both had hitherto been entirely independent of the counties (cf. the German *kreisfreie Städte*), but following reorganization they were demoted to district status and lost all of their major functions except housing to the county or region. It should be emphasized that the county's survival and enhanced status arising from the 1972 changes reflected not simply a vindication of the county's appropriateness as a local government, but also two other aspects of its position within the local government system as a whole. The first was that the 1972 Act was the final resolution of what had been up to the mid-1920s a threat to the urbanized counties arising from the fact that as cities within their boundaries reached a certain population size they could become independent county boroughs. Alternatively the county boroughs could, with central approval, extend their boundaries to incorporate burgeoning suburbs at the expense of the county.

The second feature of the 1972 Act was that in shifting power away from the cities to the counties or regions the Conservatives, on balance, probably furthered their own party interests at the local level. The 1972–3 changes also entailed the consolidation of the existing smaller counties, especially in Scotland. The somewhat remote Scottish island groups of the Shetlands, Orkneys and Western

Isles are in effect regions but they also perform the functions of the districts (see Figures 1 and 2). In England, nine entirely new counties centred on major cities were also created in 1972, six of which were designated metropolitan counties covering largely continuously urban areas. The metropolitan counties had fewer powers than the rest of the other (shire) counties.

The Welsh county changes were more drastic than in England in the sense that they were reduced from 13 to 8. This disguises the true extent of change, however, since one of the old counties – Glamorgan – was split into three new counties as what can only be described as a gerrymander to enhance the fortunes of the Conservative Party, which in Wales was much less strong in rural areas than in England, because of coal-mining. If we leave out the element of gerrymander, the number of Welsh counties was more than halved. The effect of the 1972 and 1973 changes were as follows:

Before		*After*	
England and Wales:		Shire counties (including	
Administrative counties	58	Scilly Isles)	48
Scotland:		Metropolitan counties	
Administrative counties	33	(abolished in 1986)	6
		Regions (and islands)	12

In 1986 the metropolitan counties together with the Greater London Council (a special authority covering approximately the continuously built-up area of London) were abolished. There are thus seven 'county-free' areas in England, namely Greater London, Greater Birmingham, Greater Manchester, Greater Liverpool, West Yorkshire, South Yorkshire and Tyneside (see Figure 2).

The functions of the county in England and Wales are as follows:

Education (primary, secondary)
Social services
Libraries
Museums and art galleries

Reserve housing and town development

Major land-use planning control
Strategic plan (structure plan)
Local plans (special)
County parks
Footpaths and bridleways
Caravan sites
Smallholdings

Highways
Transport planning
Traffic management
Parking
Public transport
Road safety
Street lighting

Foods and drugs
Weights and measures
Consumer protection

Land drainage
Refuse disposal
Health education

Police, either administered directly by the county or by a board
jointly with neighbouring counties

Fire

The functions of the Scottish regions are very similar to those of the
English and Welsh counties. The main exception is that the regions
have water supply and main drainage, but do not have refuse disposal
or libraries. Their planning powers also exceed those of English
counties, and police powers are usually not shared with other
regions, most regions having their own force.

In comparative terms, the English and Welsh counties are
populous, the average population being 686,000. They range from
110,000 in Powys to over 1.5 million in Hampshire (see Figure 2). As
the major unit of local government, they are also considerable public
spenders and the average county expenditure for 1986–7 was almost
£319 million. By far the highest proportion of their expenditure – 61
per cent – is absorbed by education, which includes all forms, from
pre-school play groups to special universities called polytechnics (up
to 1989). The other big-spending services are the social services (10.3
per cent on average), police (8.6 per cent) and fire (3.0 per cent). In
aggregate, the English and Welsh counties absorbed in 1986 some
57.32 per cent of total local government expenditure, which was
derived principally from two sources, the Rates (local taxes on
property) and central grants, mainly block (based on needs) but also
some specific (that is hypothecated). In 1991, the local tax system was
changed and the rates were replaced by the Council Tax and the
counties derive their local income from this source and from fees and
charges. A striking difference exists in the ratio of grants to local
taxes between English and Welsh counties, as Table 4 reveals.

Table 4   *English and Welsh counties: statistical profile, 1986*

Population	Average: 686,000		
	Range: 110,600 to 1,544,000		
Area	Average: 303,487 ha		
Expenditure			
	Total average:	£231,914 million	
	Total range:	£61,641 to £639,768 million	
			%
	Proportion	Education	61.0
		Social services	10.3
		Police	8.6
		Total local government	57.3
		Total public sector	7.4
Revenue[1]			
	% Local taxes (rates)	England	60.2
		Wales	37.9
	% Central grants	England	38.7
		Wales	61.6

[1] Excludes fees and grants.

Whereas the rates in 1986–7 provided English counties with just over 60 per cent of their expenditure, for Welsh counties rates provided only a mere 38 per cent of expenditure. The tendency for Welsh counties to receive more central grant than their English counterparts has been explored by Sharpe and Newton. Over the period 1960–73 they found that, in per capita terms and allowing for special 'needs' factors that are built into the system, grants to Welsh counties were between a third and a fifth greater than grants to English counties. One consequence of these higher grants if not their cause is that Welsh counties spend more. In 1973 the Welsh counties as a group spent more on all nine of the major services and this expenditure difference cannot be accounted for by 'needs' or ecological differences (Sharpe and Newton, 1984: ch. 8). Perhaps we see in the greater generosity of the centre towards the Welsh counties yet another manifestation of unobtrusive devolution noted earlier.

The statistical profile for Scottish regions is broadly similar to that for their English and Welsh counterparts, as Table 5 reveals.

Table 5   *Scottish regions: statistical profile, 1983–4*[1]

Population	Average: 566,333		
	Range: 99,938 to 2,431,101		
Area	Average: 806,681.4 ha		
Expenditure			
	Total average:	£395,565 million	
			%
	Proportion	Education	44.3
		Road and transport	10.9
		Social services	9.0
		Police	8.6
		Total Scottish local government	78.9
		Total Scottish government	48.0
Revenue (1986)			
			%
		Local taxes (rates)	45.4
		Central grants	51.6

[1] Excluding the three island authorities of Orkneys, Shetland and the Western Isles.

The districts

It is important to remember that since the modern county was created as a unit of government it has always formed part – albeit usually the most important part – of a highly complex system of partnership with the second-tier local government units within each county's area (Stanyer, 1976). The second-tier authorities have varied a great deal in their scale and powers, but have always remained in some sort of relationship with the county council in terms of service delivery, ranging from mandatory co-operation in some services to concurrent equality in others to complete independence for the rest. Since the 1973 reform there has been a uniform system of districts. Some observers have likened the interrelationships between county and district to a federal system (Stanyer, 1967: ch. 5). An indication of the relative importance of the two levels can be gauged from the fact that in 1986–7 the English counties spent (less fees and charges) £419.51 per capita whereas the districts spent £59.91. In 1986–7 the counties employed 35.74 full-time and part-time staff per 1,000 of population whereas the districts employed 7.97. Table 6 gives a comparison of per capita expenditure between the two levels for shared services.

Table 6 *Comparison of £ per capita expenditure for shared services, English counties and districts, 1987–8*

	Functions						
	1	2	3	4	5	6	7
County	0.42	0.76	0.33	1.54	6.54	0.99	0.91
District	2.32	1.76	7.08	3.96	7.52	2.27	14.66

1 Museums, galleries and theatres (1986–7)
2 Economic development and promotion
3 Environmental health
4 Land-use planning
5 Libraries (1986–7)
6 Concessionary fares for public transport
7 Recreation (net cost)

Source: *Local Government Comparative Statistics*, 1988

This county–district relationship in England and Wales is, then, complex and each county has tended to evolve an inimitable pattern that best suits its particular circumstances, such as its sheer territorial extent (as in Devon, Lincolnshire or North Yorkshire), or the scale of the districts, especially where they were formerly county boroughs, that is, were formerly independent (Alexander, 1982: ch. 4). This last consideration has been particularly important in relation to the powers, such as highways, that were transferred from the county boroughs to the counties. The aim was to soften the blow to the ex-county boroughs, so an agency relationship was established whereby the new district acted as an agent for the county. Many of these agency schemes have been sources of acrimony between the two levels, since the district wished to retain them but the county has often sought to end them (Lee et al., 1974: ch. 6). There are no agency arrangements of this kind in Scotland (Stodart, 1981: 12).

Another form of interrelationship occurs mainly in England and Wales for those services where the two types of authority continue to operate the same service, but in their own separate institutions, such as libraries, museums and art galleries. The most difficult relationship between county and district occurs where the service is split between the two tiers, that is, where they share concurrently in the actual provision of a single function. This kind of sharing occurs in land-use planning, where the county produces the master or structure plan, but the district is responsible for the non-strategic local plan in its area. The district also handles most of the planning applications and therefore exercises considerable control over the actual implementation of the structure plan. Until 1980 this was an obvious source of conflict with the county, which when it disapproved of the district's decision was able to countermand it by means of 'call-in' powers. The 1980 Planning Act was designed to overcome some of these problems but tensions between the two tiers remain. In 1988 the larger districts in England and Wales launched a campaign (which was stimulated by the government's abolition of the metropolitan counties) to abolish all the counties and thus make them, the districts, the sole repository of local government power (*Closer to the People*, 1987). Such a proposal is not as improbable as it may appear, since the districts are by international standards very large local government units, whether the measure be one of population, area or resources. The districts *average* over 120,000 population, and only eleven districts have less than 40,000.

In the 1970s some of the districts mounted a similar campaign entitled 'Organic Change' that was somewhat less ambitious since it sought merely to restore to the nine largest former English county boroughs some of their original powers. The Labour government at the time was sympathetic and produced a White Paper supporting organic change in 1979 (Department of the Environment, 1979). A similar plea was made by six of the larger districts in Scotland, but nothing ensued from either proposal, because of the change of government in that year.

The abolition of the metropolitan counties may have heightened the dissatisfaction among some of the larger districts, since they are aware that the metropolitan districts in the former metropolitan county areas are now to all intents and purposes like former county boroughs, that is, independent all-purpose authorities, but with joint boards for some metropolitan-wide functions. The same is true of the thirty-two London boroughs in the former Greater London Council (GLC) area, especially since the abolition of the Inner London Education Authority. Giving the rest of the districts comparable powers and abolishing the shire counties can thus be defined as a form of harmonization.

Another source of dissatisfaction with the present county system, and perhaps with the regions in Scotland as well (Stodart, 1981: ch. 4), arises from the fact that the nine entirely new English counties created in 1973 have not commanded much popular support, and nor have the amalgamations that took place at the same time. The old county may still persist in everyday discourse and, more crucially, may be accepted by the Post Office as a place name in designated addresses. The most celebrated example of this 'ghost county' phenomenon is Middlesex, which was abolished under an earlier reorganization of London government of the early 1960s. Not only does Middlesex persist as an officially recognized address, it still has a first-class cricket team and many other sports teams. Hostility to the new counties is possibly strongest towards the entirely new counties and especially Humberside in northern England. It is of some significance that in 1989 the central government minister responsible for local government instructed the Boundary Commission – the official body for surveying local government boundaries – to look at the possibility of abolishing Humberside (*Planning*, 1989: 11). This move seems to have signalled the beginning of a major review of the English and Welsh counties which may have been precipitated by a pamphlet published by the Adam Smith Institute, a body which has been very influential with the Conservative government. Entitled *Wiser Counsels*, it advocates the wholesale reorganization of local government, involving the abolition of the county councils so as to create a single-tier system with a population range of 40,000 to 60,000 (*Wiser Counsels*, 1989: 49) – that is, smaller even than the present districts. At all events, by the spring of 1991, the Conservative government announced a plan to move to single-tier local government in England. Which of the existing two levels, county or district, would prevail would vary in different parts of the country, and in a few areas both tiers would be retained (*Structure of Local Government in England*, 1991). However, a note of caution must be struck, since the counties do have a special place among the traditional elite of the Conservative Party, partly for their long-standing historical associations already noted, but also because the party usually commands a majority in more counties than any other party (see Appendix). Any Conservative government proposing the abolition of counties wholesale could face serious intra-party revolt.

In Scotland the position of the county equivalent, the region, may be even more precarious than in England and Wales for a number of reasons. In the first place, because all the factors that may lead to the abolition of the English counties apply, but in addition the regional boundaries bear even less relationship to the former counties so may command less public support. Secondly, in proportion to the total Scottish population, the Scottish regions tend to be bigger than the English and Welsh counties, and so are more remote. Strathclyde, the largest Scottish region, accounts for almost a half of the total Scottish population and would be a very serious rival to an all-Scotland assembly. That may have been deliberately intended when the regions were created in order to weaken the case for a Scottish assembly. If so, it could have the reverse effect and it is hardly surprising that the most ardent of the devolutionary parties – the SNP and the Liberal Democrats – have both long advocated the abolition of the regions, and even the Conservatives decided to set up a party committee in 1988 to review the possibility of abolishing the Scottish regions.

Clearly the counties are under threat whichever party controls the centre. Two further factors, on the other hand, suggest that the traditional (that is, not the new creations of the 1970s) English counties, at least, may survive over the long term. The first is what may be called the counties' functional appropriateness, which is apparent in the tendency to upward functional mobility, already noted. That is to say, the county may not be the optimum area for any one function in terms of economies of scale, externalities or population movement, but it comes closest to kind of average optimality and is certainly far less remote and better comprehended than even the smallest region would be. It also commands more popular allegiance than the regions. As Stanyer has noted, since the birth of the county council as a unit of local government, they 'almost immediately established themselves as viable and vital elements in the local government system and grew in importance relative to other local authorities in every decade after 1889' (Stanyer, 1989b: 7). Also, the absence, emphasized earlier, of any strong sense of regional consciousness in many of the regions of England would leave a serious political vacuum if the counties were abolished. It seems possible, then, that the county may survive at least in England for the foreseeable future. As Owen has emphasized: 'The county has fought off a number of challenges in the past and prospered. There are strong territorial, political and institutional factors supporting the continuation of county governance' (Owen, 1989: 62).

Conclusions

The UK in meso terms is something of a hybrid. Its meso – the county/region – is clearly an example of the Northern European sub-national model. Yet at the same time the UK lacks the ethnic and linguistic homogeneity of other Northern European states and so it has also developed a kind of Southern European regional meso dimension to its sub-national politics. However, the impetus to devolution has yet to take concrete form but probably has a greater chance of becoming a reality in the near future, at least in Scotland and Wales, than at any time since the aborted devolution legislation in the late 1970s.

The vicissitudes of the devolution element of the British meso experience cannot be divorced from the existence of the three Offices of the so-called Celtic fringe. Together they comprise the great *ad hoc* compromise in the evolution of British territorial politics that has enabled the central state to accommodate sub-national difference while at the same time retaining the parliamentary sovereignty principle intact and its main concomitant tradition, the all-accommodating two-party system.

Another peculiarity of the British sub-national tradition that has shaped the evolution of the meso is the strong emphasis given to production-efficiency rather than consumption efficiency in public service delivery. One of the consequences of this tendency is the extraordinarily large population size of British local government units (Sharpe,1978b), which has in turn weakened the case for a regional meso. Equally, the production-efficiency obsession has strongly influenced the tendency for major public services such as the NHS, Regional Water Authorities, polytechnics, colleges of further education and London Transport, which might otherwise be candidates for a regional meso, to be hived off into an agency or market limbo relatively free from the direct control of central government and wholly divorced from local democratic institutions.

The UK is also unusual among Western European states in being apparently immune from conscious attempts to decentralize the modern state in general terms as a form of democratization. Quite the contrary, any discussion of the current state of the British meso must take into account the extraordinary and probably unique process of centralization that has taken place over the past ten years, apparently with public acquiescence if not outright approval. So the British county, or its equivalent the Scottish region, although still important in functional terms, could not be described as enjoying a new and dynamic lease of life along the lines, say, of the Danish or Norwegian county. In fact, the county has been losing powers over recent years in planning (to the districts), in education by the loss of the polytechnics and the colleges of further education, and the creation of 'opting-out' procedures that allow secondary schools to be run by parental management boards independently of local government. It would be premature to assume that the counties are on their way out, however. They are an ancient institution that have survived other crises and, moreover, grown in importance in the process.

In assessing the working of the meso in Britain and in particular the probably unique process of centralization over the last decade, a number of other special features of the British sub-national tradition are relevant. The first is that the potential power of the centre over the localities derived from the parliamentary sovereignty principle does not mean that the centre is normally intent on taking over the executant role. It follows that the authentic British meso, the county/region, like its counterpart in all non-Napoleonic systems, enjoys relatively high levels of autonomy in operational matters. The significance of the central–local relationship in the UK is the centre's capacity for the rapid assertion of its power over the localities and non-central institutions if it so wishes, such as abolishing the GLC and the six metropolitan counties, creating and then privatizing the Regional Water Authorities, abolishing Stormont and the quasi-privatization of the NHS.

The second characteristic of the system which bears on the future of the meso is the overwhelming unitariness of British political culture, especially in the great trunk of England, which works against all forms of territorial politics. This anti-territorial dimension is doubtless partly derived from the extraordinary continuity and stability of the British state – a continuity that has not been broken for four and a half centuries. Equally, too, the extent of cultural homogenization of British society following two hundred years of industrialization must also be taken into account in identifying the components of the anti-territorial bias. Finally, some recognition would need to be given to the relatively low status of sub-national government, to what one observer has called the centre's 'culture of disdain' for it (Greenwood, 1982: 72). This disdain must be contrasted with the comparatively high status of central government in British society. That high status is hard to exaggerate and the central government has thus been able to dispense with the burden of the positive state, for political unity is thought of as being immanent in society. Since government is always seen in general terms as being a threat to individual freedom, non-governmental institutions are always preferred, in theory at least, despite massive governmental growth. This tradition of *laissez-faire* collectivism has meant that the centre has considerable power but is not required to exercise it in a systematic fashion. Rather, it enjoys a special role as the exclusive guardian of the public interest against local sectionalism but, more surprisingly, it is also seen as the guardian of individual interests, interests that are rarely seen as having a territorial dimension.

If the emergence of the meso all over Western Europe betokens an important decentralist shift within the democratic nation state, it may be said without exaggeration that such a shift is least apparent in the UK.

Appendix: Political data

English and Welsh county councils, 1989

Party control	No. of councils	% of councils
Conservative	19	40.4
Labour	13	27.7
Liberal Democrat	1	2.1
Independent	2	4.2
No overall control	12	25.6

Election turn-out: 41.6 per cent.

Average size of councils: 74 seats (ranges from 60 to 100).

Area system of voting: each seat represents a geographical area called a ward, elected under the first-past-the-post system.

Election cycle: the whole council is elected every four years.

Scottish regions, 1986

Party control	No. of councils
Conservative	—
Labour	4
No overall control	5

Election turn-out: 45.6 per cent.

Average size of councils: 50 seats (ranges from 23 to 103).

Area system of voting: each seat represents a geographical area called a ward, elected under first-past-the-post system.

Election cycle: the whole council is elected every four years.

Notes

The author wishes to thank Michael Keating and John Stewart for their extremely helpful advice and suggestions.

1 The rebellion of Labour backbenchers may have been more apparent than real, for it seems likely that the string of limiting amendments to the devolution bills and perhaps the 40 per cent rule in particular had their origins in 10 Downing Street. The Labour Party leadership had no more enthusiasm for devolution than its back-benchers, but it had to promote the two bills in order to retain the support of the Liberals and the nationalists and thus stay in power.

2 If we exclude the many studies of the old London County Council, which was wholly urban and a very special case anyway, the rare exceptions to the city-centred approach to local government research, for England and Wales at least, are as follows: Samson, J. R., *Delegation of Services within Counties*, London: Institute of Municipal

Treasurers Association, 1952; Cohen, E. W., *Autonomy and Delegation in County Government*, London: Royal Institute of Public Administration, 1953; Keith-Lucas, B. 'The government of the county in England', *Western Political Quarterly*, 9 (1), 1956; Richards, P. G., *Delegation in Local Government*, London: Allen & Unwin, 1956; Lee, J. M., *Social Leaders and Public Persons*, London: Oxford University Press, 1963; Stanyer, Jeffrey, *County Government in England and Wales*, London: Routledge, 1967; Lee, J. M. et al., *The Scope of Local Initiative: A Study of Cheshire County Council*, London: Martin Robertson, 1974; Mansfield, J. D. (ed.), *The History of Lancashire County Council 1889–1974*, Oxford: Martin Robertson, 1977; Leach, S. and Moore, N., 'County–district relations in shire and metropolitan counties in the field of town and country planning', *Planning and Politics*, 3(7), 1979; Moore, N. and Leach, S., 'An interaction approach to county/district relationship', *Policy and Politics*, 7 (3), 1979; Karran, T., 'Borough politics and county government', *Policy and Politics*, 10 (3), 1982; McKeown, P., 'County councils and economic development in the early 1980s', *Local Government Studies*, 4 (13), 1987; Stanyer, Jeffrey, 'Assessing the Local Government Act, 1888', *Local Government Studies*, November/December 1989; Gyford, John, 'County government and Labour politics in Essex, 1930–1965', *Local Government Studies*, November/December 1989; Owen, Jonathan, 'Defending the county', *Local Government Studies*, November/December 1989; Lee, J. M., 'County government since 1889', *Local Government Studies*, January/February 1990.

Since the advent of significant third-party victories at county council elections in the mid-1980s, a new literature on the counties sprang up, among which may be noted: Blowers, A., 'The politics of uncertainty: the consequences of minority rule in an English county', *Local Government Studies*, 1 (14), 1987; Leach, S. and Stewart, J., *The Hung Counties*, Birmingham: Institute of Local Government Studies, 1986; Clements, Roger, 'Three-party politics in a new county', *Local Government Studies*, November/December 1989; Barlow, John, 'The politics of the budgeting process in Lancashire County Council', *Local Government Studies*, November/December 1989.

3 Some might argue that the Shetlands' distaste for Scottish nationalism still leaves a little mutability in the Scottish boundary. Certainly any Edinburgh-based Scottish Assembly will have to tread carefully in relation to the Shetlands. It has always been one of the more intriguing aspects of modern Scottish nationalism, steeped as it tends to be in a small-town ethos and given its unstinting awareness of London's indifference to Scottish issues, that it has been somewhat lax about Scotland's own periphery.

Select further reading

Bogdanor, V. (1979) *Devolution*. Oxford: Oxford University Press.

Bulpitt, J. (1983) *Territory and Power in the United Kingdom*. Manchester: Manchester University Press.

Gyford, J. (1976) *Local Politics in Britain*. London: Croom Helm.

Hogwood, B. C. and Keating, M. (eds) (1982) *Regional Government in England*. Oxford: Clarendon Press.

Levitt, R. (1976) *The Reorganized National Health Service*. London: Croom Helm.

Madgwick, P. and Rose, R. (eds) (1982) *The Territorial Dimension in UK Politics*. London: Macmillan.

Rhodes, R. (1988) *Beyond Westminster and Whitehall*. London: Unwin-Hyman.

Richards, Peter, G. (1980) *The New Local Government System*, 4th edn. London: Allen and Unwin.

Young, K. (ed.) (1989) *New Directions for County Government*. London: Association of County Councils.

References

Alexander, Alan (1982) *The Politics of Local Government in the United Kingdom*. London: Longman.

Ashford, Douglas (1982) *British Dogmatism and French Pragmatism*. London: Allen & Unwin.

Bell, P. (1987) 'Direct rule in Northern Ireland', in Richard Rose (ed.), *Ministers and Ministries*. Oxford: Clarendon.

Bogdanor, Vernon (1979) *Devolution*. Oxford: Oxford University Press.

Bulpitt, Jim (1983) *Territory and Power in the United Kingdom*. Manchester: Manchester University Press.

Closer to the People (1987) London: Association of District Councils.

Dawson, A. H. (1981) 'The idea of the region: the 1975 reorganization of Scottish local government', *Public Administration*, 59 (1).

Department of the Environment (1979) *Organic Change in Local Government*. London: HMSO, Cmnd 7457.

Dickson, A. D. R. (1988) 'The peculiarities of the Scottish', *Political Quarterly*, 59 (3).

Foster, C. D., Jackman, R. A. and Perlman, M. (1980) *Local Government Finance in a Unitary State*. London: Allen & Unwin.

Game, S. and Leach, S. (1989) 'The county councillor in 1889 and 1989', in Ken Young (ed.), *New Directions for County Government*. London: Association of County Councils.

Gray, C. (1985) 'Analysing the regional level', *Public Administration Bulletin*, 49.

Greenwood, R. (1982) 'Pressure from Whitehall', in R. Rose and E. Page (eds), *Fiscal Stress in Cities*. London: Cambridge University Press.

Guardian (1989) 19 January.

Guardian (1990) 31 December.

Gyford, John (1976) *Local Politics in Britain*. London: Croom Helm.

Hanham, H. (1969) 'The development of the Scottish Office', in J. H. Wolfe (ed.), *Government and Nationalism in Scotland*. Edinburgh: Edinburgh University Press.

Haywood, S. C. and Alaszewski, A. (1980) *Crisis in the NHS*. London: Croom Helm.

Haywood, S. C. and Elcock, H. J. (1982) 'Regional health authorities: regional government or central agencies?' in B. C. Hogwood and M. Keating (eds), *Regional Government in England*. Oxford: Clarendon.

Heald, D. (1983) *Public Expenditure*. Oxford: Martin Robertson.

Hoggs. C. (1990) 'Community health councils', in H. Deakin and A. Wright (eds), *Consuming Public Services*. London: Routledge.

Hogwood, B C. (1982) 'Introduction', B. C. Hogwood and M. Keating (eds), *Regional Government in England*. Oxford: Clarendon.

Hogwood, B. C. and Keating, M. (eds) (1982) *Regional Government in England*. Oxford: Clarendon.

Hogwood, B. C. and Lindley, P. D. (1982) 'Variations in regional boundaries' in B. C. Hogwood and M. Keating (eds), *Regional Government in England*. Oxford: Clarendon.

Hood, C. and Dunsire, A. (1981) *Bureaumetrics*. Farnborough: Gower.

Jones, J. B. and Wilford, J. (1986) *Parliament and Territoriality*. Cardiff: University of Wales Press.

Jowell, R. and Airey, C. (eds) (1990) *British Social Attitudes Survey, 7th Report.* Aldershot: Gower.

Keating, M. and Carter, C. (1987) 'Policymaking and the Scottish Office: the designation of Cumbernauld New Town', *Public Administration*, 65 (4).

Keating, M. and Midwinter, A. (1983) *The Government of Scotland.* Edinburgh: Mainstream.

Kellas, James G. (1976) *The Scottish Political System.* Cambridge: Cambridge University Press.

Kellas, James G. (1991) 'The Scottish and Welsh Offices as territorial managers', *Regional Politics and Policy*, 1 (1).

Kellas, James and Madgwick, Peter (1982) 'Territorial ministries: the Scottish and Welsh Offices', in Peter Madgwick and Richard Rose (eds), *The Territorial Dimension in United Kingdom Politics.* London: Macmillan.

Lee, J. M. (1963) *Social Leaders and Public Persons.* London: Oxford University Press.

Lee, J. M. (1990) 'County government since 1889', *Local Government Studies*, January/February.

Lee, J. M., Wood, B., Solomon, B. W. and Walters, P. (1974) *The Scope of Local Initiative: A Study of Cheshire County Council.* London: Martin Robertson.

Levitt, R. (1976) *The Reorganized National Health Service.* London: Croom Helm.

Local Government Comparative Statistics (1988) London: Chartered Institute of Public Finances and Accountancy.

Machin, Howard (1977) *The Prefect in French Public Administration.* London: Croom Helm.

Madgwick, Peter and Rose, Richard (eds) (1982) *The Territorial Dimension in UK Politics.* London: Macmillan.

Midwinter, Arthur (1985) 'Local government in Strathclyde, in J. Butt and G. Gordon (eds), *Changing Horizons.* Edinburgh: Scottish Academic Press.

New Statesman and Society (1990) 9 March.

Observer magazine (1989) 23 April.

Owen, Jonathan (1989) 'Defending the county', *Local Government Studies*, November/December.

Page, Edward (1990) 'The political origins of self-government and bureaucracy', *Political Studies*, 38 (1).

Page, Edward and Midwinter, Arthur (1980) 'Remoteness, efficiency, cost and the reorganization of Scottish local government', *Public Administration*, 30 (2).

Parry, R. (1981) 'Territory and public employment: a general model and British evidence', *Journal of Public Policy*, 1 (2).

Parry, Richard (1987) 'The centralization of the Scottish Office', in Richard Rose (ed.), *Ministers and Ministries.* Oxford: Clarendon.

Planning (1989) 24 March.

Redlich, Josef and Hirst, F. W. (1958) *The History of Local Government in England*, ed. B. Keith-Lucas. London: Macmillan.

The Reform of Direction Taxation: Report of the Taxation Review Committee (1990) London: Fabian Society.

Rhodes, R. A. W. (1988) *Beyond Westminster and Whitehall.* London: Unwin-Hyman.

Rose, Richard (1982) 'Is the United Kingdom a state? Northern Ireland as a test case', in Peter Madgwick and Richard Rose (eds), *The Territorial Dimension in United Kingdom Politics.* London: Macmillan.

Saunders, Peter (1985) 'The forgotten dimension of centre–local relations: theorizing the regional state', *Government and Policy*, 3.

Sharpe, L. J. (1962) *A Metropolis Votes.* London: London School of Economics.

Sharpe, L. J. (1978a) 'Modernizing the localities', in J. Lagroye ad V. Wright (eds), *Local Government in Britain and France*. London: Allen & Unwin.

Sharpe, L. J. (1978b) 'Reforming the grass roots; an alternative analysis', in D. Butler and A. H. Halsey (eds), *Politics and Policy*. London: Macmillan.

Sharpe, L. J. (1982) 'The Labour Party and the geography of inequality', in D. Kavanagh (ed.), *The Politics of the Labour Party*. London: Allen & Unwin.

Sharpe, L. J. (1985) 'Devolution and Celtic nationalism in the UK', *West European Politics*, 8 (3).

Sharpe, L. J. (1988) 'Local government reorganization: general theory and UK practice', in Bruno Dente and F. Kjellberg (eds), *The Dynamics of Institutional Change: Local Government Reorganization in Western Democracies*. London: Sage.

Sharpe, L. J. (1989) 'Fragmentation and territoriality in the European state system', *International Political Science Review*, 10 (3).

Sharpe, L. J. and Newton, K. (1984) *Does Politics Matter?*. Oxford: Clarendon.

Stanyer, Jeffrey (1967) *County Government in England and Wales*. London: Routledge.

Stanyer, Jeffrey (1976) *Understanding Local Government*. London: Martin Robertson.

Stanyer, Jeffrey (1989a) 'Assessing the Local Government Act, 1888', *Local Government Studies*, November/December.

Stanyer, Jeffrey (1989b) *A Hundred Years of County Government*. Exeter: Devon County Council.

Stewart, J. D. (1984) 'The future of local democracy', *Local Government Studies*, March/April.

Stewart, J. (1989) 'In search of county government', in Ken Young (ed.), *New Directions for County Government*. London: Association of County Councils.

Stodart (1981) *Report of the Committee of Inquiry into Local Government in Scotland*. Edinburgh: HMSO, Cmnd 8115.

The Structure of Local Government in England (1991) London: Department of the Environment Review Team.

Thomas, Ian C. (1987) 'Giving direction to the Welsh Office', in Richard Rose (ed.), *Ministers and Ministries*. Oxford: Clarendon.

Towards a Scottish Parliament: Consultation Document and Report to the Scottish People (1990) Edinburgh: Scottish Constitutional Convention.

Wiser Counsels (1989) London: Adam Smith Institute.

Young, Ken (ed.) (1989) *New Directions for County Government*. London: Association of County Councils.

10

The Continental Meso: Regions in the European Community

Michael Keating

Europeanism and regionalism

European integration and regional devolution have presented twin challenges to the Western European nation state. At first sight these may appear contradictory forces, the one aiming at larger-scale government and centralization, the other at disaggregation. In practice, their relationship is more complex, at times conflicting, at others linked in efforts to circumvent the nation state. Indeed, each itself is composed of a complex of strands.

European integration was based on an economic logic, a political logic and a theory linking the two. Economically, integration was justified in terms of free trade theory and comparative advantage, the assumed economies of large-scale operation and the need for Europe to compete in a world of large trading blocks. Politically, the first imperative was to prevent war and secure the conditions of Franco-German *rapprochement*; to secure the position of small nations in the new world order; and to overcome the legacy of nationalism. Idealists dreamed of a united states of Europe organized on federal lines. The theory linking economic and political logic was that of functionalism, the idea that increasing exchange in the economic and social spheres would be mutually reinforcing so that functional cross-linkages would lead to a decrease in national identity and the forging of a new European identity as the underpinning of new political institutions.

Regionalism was a response both to the needs of national states and to external pressures upon them (Keating, 1988). Unitary states committed to indicative planning came to realize the need for a spatial articulation of this in the form of regional policies and plans. They also accepted to a greater or lesser degree the need to promote dialogue at the intermediate level and gain the collaboration of local governments, with their land-use and service responsibilities, and of regional economic elites in the promotion of development strategies;

hence the establishment of consultative regional planning mechanisms in a number of European countries in the 1960s. These themselves became an object of political contestation and in Italy and, later, France grew into an elected tier of government. In Spain, the paranoia of the Franco regime about regionalism prevented even modest steps towards regional planning, while in Britain regionalists failed in their efforts to follow the Italian and French path.

Regionalism was also promoted in Europe as a response to re-assertions of cultural and historical identity. The Belgian state has progressively decentralized to become a federal system, while in Spain recognition of the demands of Catalonia and the Basque Country was a priority after the end of the Franco regime. In Britain, increasing pressures from Scottish and Welsh nationalism led to the abortive devolution proposals of 1975–9. Regionalism has also been a response to pressure for democratization, most notably in Spain but also in previously centralized democracies where the legitimacy of pluralism and diversity is now recognized. Germany is a case apart, because of its history as well as its status as the only federation within the European Community. There federalism represented a reassertion of old traditions as well as a measure pursued at the insistence of the Allies to prevent the resurgence of centralized dictatorship. Germany's cultural homogeneity, the absence of separatist movements and the practice of co-operative federalism have made decentralization here a means of strengthening the state rather than a threat to its integrity.

The development of the Community itself has affected the development of regionalism, first through the effects of economic integration. The progressive opening of the European market carries the danger of a homogenization of space, as historic territories are forced into the same relationship with the global market. Indeed, some critics see European integration as the latest phase in a process by which states, in the service of capitalist industrialism, have eroded traditional societies and cultures and broken down self-reliant communities.

In the peripheral regions of Europe, there are fears that the integrated market will accentuate the advantages of the 'golden triangle', the central part of the Community, and increase the existing economic disparities. These are already large, with a GDP per head ratio of 2.1:1 between Denmark and Portugal, compared with a maximum of 1.5:1 among American states (André et al., 1989). Peripheral regions with low output and unfavourable economic structures are in need of substantial long-term development assistance (Keeble et al., 1988). In some regions dependence on a single industry has meant vulnerability to Community-inspired rationaliz-ation. The free market is one of the bases of the Community, and national and regional protectionism, together with subsidies, are in principle outlawed. Yet the impact of the Community's own Common Agricultural Policy has served to increase regional dispa-rities (Strijker and de Veer, 1988), while deregulation of transport and telecommunications, by eliminating cross-subsidization, may damage remote peripheries (Fullarton and Gillespie, 1988). Con-cerns about the spatial impact of economic integration together with the weakening of national regional policies have sparked off a series of territorially based oppositions to European integration (Lan-kowsky, 1993), focused on the extension of the global market and the centralization of political power in Brussels. National governments and existing territorial elites, which were able to handle previous manifestations of regional discontent through protectionism, selec-tive subsidy, marginal redistribution and various types of pork-barrel, find themselves unable now to respond because of Com-munity restrictions. So crises in steel, viticulture, textiles or fishing take on both regional and Community dimensions and, while sometimes allowing national governments to deflect local anger, create a source of opposition to European integration.

Political dynamics

The development of the European Community and of regionalism creates the possibility of a new political dynamic around the triangular relationship of Europe–state–region. Such a dynamic can indeed be observed but it has taken a long time to develop and varies in importance across the Community. For the first thirty years of the Community's existence, nation states showed a remarkable resili-ency and an ability to use both European integration and regionalism to strengthen rather than weaken their authority. European inte-gration was reduced to a neo-functionalist logic, based on elite collaboration focused on the Council of Ministers. The supra-national elements of the Community were downgraded in favour of intergovernmental bargaining. A doctrine of the Community as 'foreign affairs' was adopted which gave national governments wide powers to enforce Community policy even in areas formally devolved to sub-national levels. It is striking, indeed, that states have largely avoided changing their constitutions to recognize the permanence of the Community. Even where states have undertaken constitutional revisions or changes in the structure of territorial government, they have not taken the opportunity formally to incorporate the European dimension. This is true, notably, of Spain, Italy, France and Belgium.

The response to the pressures of peripheral nationalism, too, was framed in a way calculated to strengthen the central state, by defusing separatism while treating autonomy as exceptional, confining it to specific regions and so warding off pressures to federalize the state. This was the Italian strategy after the war, when the special status regions were established, and the British response to Scotland and Wales in the 1970s. In Spain, there were attempts to confine regional autonomy to the 'historic nationalities' in Catalonia, Galicia and the Basque Country, while France conceded special status to Corsica. When deployed more generally, regionalism was, as far as possible, treated as an administrative matter. Even where, as in Italy and France, the state conceded elected regional governments, devolution took a functional form with regions tied in closely to national programmes and political autonomy de-emphasized. At the same time, the European and regional levels were convenient places to off-load policies considered too expensive or politically onerous for national governments, like agricultural support and retrenchment or the adjustment of regions to structural economic change. The example most pertinent to our theme is the development of the common regional policy.

Community regional policies

The Commission like other exponents of European unity has believed that a vigorous anti-disparity policy is an essential concomitant to the building of Europe. Such a policy can speed the process of restructuring while enhancing the legitimacy of the EC in the regions where support is most problematic. The Treaty of Rome established the European Social Fund (ESF) in order to deal with the employment consequences of industrial change, notably through training. In 1972, it was reformed to tie in more closely with the needs of sectoral and industrial restructuring, with priority regions receiving at least 50 per cent (but in the event about 80 per cent) of the funds. The European Regional Development Fund (ERDF) was established in 1975 partly as compensation to Britain which, following its accession in 1973, stood to lose heavily through other Community mechanisms. In principle, it was a centrally administered fund to award grants to public or private organizations in depressed or underdeveloped regions for industrial infrastructure investment.

In practice the structural funds, and in particular the ERDF, were caught up in intergovernmental conflict over control and power. Despite repeated attempts by the Commission to turn it into the instrument of a genuine regional policy (Mawson et al., 1985), all national governments applied the 'non-additionality' rule under which EC contributions were regarded as reimbursement for national spending on the projects in question. National quotas for ERDF funds, although progressively relaxed, supported this interpretation. The result was that the political presentation of Community regional policies bore very little relation to the reality, producing an extraordinary world of make-believe. In Britain, for example, all ERDF moneys were regarded as compensation for spending items already planned and in many cases completed, yet the need to sustain support for EC membership in the periphery, where it was consistently weak, dictated that Europe should receive credit. So the Scottish Office would proudly announce that such-and-such a firm had just been granted an ERDF award as evidence of the benefits of Community membership for Scotland, though the award in question had long been paid and spent under *national* regional policy, the ERDF money going to repay the Treasury. In the case of awards to local governments, European spending had to be accommodated within existing capital expenditure limits, though there was a small saving on loan charges. The most dishonest treatment of all was given to the 'rebates' received in the early 1980s on Britain's budget contributions. Although it was stipulated that these should go to investment projects in the regions, all the money was retained in the Treasury in London and signs placed on existing central government projects such as the A9 road and the Kessock Bridge announcing that these were the recipients of the funds. Press releases made the same claims. In France, by contrast, support for the Community was not a problem and the central government was able to corner structural fund moneys for its own purposes while giving no publicity to their existence (Mény, 1985).

The Commission has consistently tried to regain control over the structural funds and to make them the instruments of a genuine regional policy. In this it has had the support of regional governments and interest groups. The sheer administrative complexity of the matter and the relatively small size of the Commission bureaucracy, however, have ruled out direct administration. Instead, the Commission has tried to move towards a programmatic approach based on regional development plans which it will finance according to Community priorities. A 1984 reform relaxed the system of national quotas by expressing them as a range rather than a fixed amount. Member states would have to produce worthy projects to obtain the maximum. Projects themselves would have to form part of regional development programmes, some of which would be recognized as of special Community interest (Mawson et al., 1985). This did have one effect, in that the requirements for ERDF claims were the main reason why the British government retained a system of regional development grants in the mid-1980s. Development programmes for Britain, however, retained their fairy-tale character. At one stage, the British government submitted the entire capital programme of the Scottish Office as a 'regional development programme'. Other programmes were hastily assembled clippings of existing documents.

The Commission also sought to control its development funds through a series of 'integrated' operations, including the Integrated Development Operations (IDOs) for Belfast and Naples and smaller-scale efforts for other cities. Given the limits on the structural funds and national additionality rules, these have generated a great deal more publicity than hard cash. A consultants' report for Glasgow admitted that there is 'no new EC budget specifically for an IDO: benefits lie in increasing the effectiveness of existing funds, in increased priority accorded to applications and higher rates of grant, and in the unquantifiable gains following from a closer relationship with the Community' (Roger Tym, 1984). This did not stop them talking of a £500 million 'forward programme' for five years, a figure derived from thin air and largely by assembling various elements of expenditure which would occur in any case. Not surprisingly, this figure gained the headlines and has surfaced again since. There have also been Integrated Mediterranean Programmes which have permitted some flexibility in the use of funds.

The accession of Greece, Spain and Portugal greatly widened the extent of regional disparities in the Community and the commitment to the internal market by the end of 1992 posed new fears for the fate of the peripheral regions and the prospects of opposition from them. As part of the commitment to the internal market, therefore, a doubling of the size of the structural funds was agreed upon and a new regulation devised for their administration. Again, the Commission's aim has been to make the funds a genuine instrument of Community policy, to target them effectively and to involve regional interests themselves in their disbursal. The new ERDF regulation limits support to regions designated according to Community-wide criteria. This has required the elaboration of the Community's own data base and comparative indices of economic problems. The Community distinguishes three levels of territory or NUTS ('nomenclature of territorial units for statistics'). Luxembourg, Denmark and Ireland are themselves regarded as level 1 and 2 units. Elsewhere, units are formed from regional and local government divisions and their groupings. The divisions are given in Table 1.

Regional problems are now measured by a 'synthetic index' including GDP per head of population and per person employed, unemployment and the jobs required for anticipated population expansion. The new regional development fund regulation is based

Table 1   *Nomenclature of territorial units for statistics (NUTS)*

	NUTS 1	NUTS 2	NUTS 3
Belgium	Regions	Provinces	*Arrondissements*
Denmark	—	—	*Amter*
Fed. Rep. Germany	*Länder*	*Regierungsbezirke*	*Kreise*
Greece	NUTS 2 groupings	Development regions	*Nomoi*
Spain	NUTS 2 groupings	Autonomous Communities	Provinces
France	ZEAT (*Zones étendus d'aménagement du territoire*)	Regions	*Départements*
Ireland	—	—	Planning regions
Italy	NUTS 2 groupings	Regions	Provinces
Luxembourg	—	—	—
Netherlands	*Landsdelen*	Provinces	COROP–*regios*
Portugal	NUTS 2 groupings	NUTS 3 groupings	Groupings of *concelhos*
UK	Standard regions	NUTS 3 groupings	Counties, Scottish regions

Source: Commission of the European Communities, 1987

on this and emphasizes the needs of local enterprise and partnership. Global grants will be made on the basis of development plans to regionally based managing organizations designated by agreement between the member state and the Commission. These will have to be based in the regions concerned, to have a public mission and to involve local social and economic actors. Early evidence indicates that traditionally centralized states such as Britain, France, Spain and Italy have continued to administer those funds in a centralized manner. Decentralized states such as Germany and Belgium have given a larger role to sub-national authorities. National quotas are still informally recognized.

The new system shifts resources into the less developed areas of Southern Europe and Ireland. Small amounts of funding were retained for declining industrial regions, to keep the northern countries on side. Regional funds remain small in relation to the overall Community budget. In 1988, structural funds comprised 16.9 per cent of the budget, of which 8 per cent was for the ERDF. By 1992, structural funds accounted for 25.4 per cent of the budget. Poorer countries, led by Spain, have bargained progress towards political and monetary union against increases in structural fund support but still tried to maintain control of the funds at national level. So, instead of a large expansion of regional aid, the Maastricht summit produced a new inter-state cohesion fund. While Commission officials calculated that achieving regional convergence would require a tripling of the main regional expenditure by 2010, Germany was complaining at the size of the existing bill.

Institutional linkages

Regions and regional policy have thus become an object of contestation among regional, national and European elites. Despite the tendency of national states to defend their autonomy in the face of European and sub-national challenges, there has been a gradual process of change. The Community and, in some states, regions have strengthened their power and new patterns of institutional linkages have emerged tying Europe to the regions. It is too simple to see this in purely in terms of 'direct access' to Brussels by regions. Preponderant power remains in the hands of national governments acting through the Council of Ministers and European Council and there is no question of circumventing on these major policy issues. There is a common interest on the part of the Regional Policy Directorate of the Commission and regions in promoting contact and exchange to improve their information flow and encourage the emergence of a more European framework for discussion. The Competition Directorate, on the other hand, has opposed moves towards a stronger industrial or regional policy. The European Parliament, also seeking to expand its influence against national governments and the Commission, is a natural ally of the regions and has pressed both the Commission and the Council of Ministers to give more recognition to regional governments in the policy process. Given the varying national traditions and constitutional arrangements in the twelve countries, a variety of patterns has emerged.

In a complex intergovernmental network such as the triangular relationships emerging in the European Community, regions require both a degree of local autonomy and access to and influence over levels. Autonomy permits an area of independent action in response to regional demands as well as supporting a politics in which these can be formulated. Yet autonomy itself does not provide influence at the higher levels to which power has retreated. Indeed, it may diminish it as regional elites are politically isolated and contained. Systems in which devolution of power is organized strictly on functional lines may similarly serve to contain regional governments while not preventing national governments, under the foreign affairs doctrine, from using the Community as a pretext to encroach on regional matters.

Access and influence without autonomy are represented in the United Kingdom. There are no autonomous governments for the peripheral nations of Scotland and Wales. Instead, these are governed by territorially differentiated departments of the national administration which have the additional responsibility of acting as lobbyists for Scottish and Welsh interests in London (Midwinter, Keating and Mitchell, 1991). As part of the national administration, they are able to influence the British negotiating position in the Community. On matters affecting Scotland, for example, there will be a Scottish minister in the British negotiating team and occasionally, notably for fisheries matters, the Scottish minister will take the lead. In turn, the Scottish Office tries to ensure that the Scottish interests concerned are behind it. While this style of insider influence has proved quite effective on some issues, however, its weight should not be exaggerated. The influence of the Scottish Office in British government has been declining in recent years and since 1979 its ministers have become less and less representative of Scottish opinion. There is also a constant suspicion that, where trade-offs have to made among policies, the Scots and Welsh are liable to lose out. In France, the tradition of accumulation of mandates provides another form of intergovernmental influence within a unitary state. There is a degree of territorial autonomy but the powers and resources of the regions are restricted and, despite the reforms of the 1980s, there is relatively little functional differentiation between them and central government. The very centralization of the French state, however, has generated its own forms of territorial power. Mayors of large cities and presidents of departmental and regional councils will sit in the national and European parliaments and, in some cases, be ministers in the national government. This provides a territorial input to national policy-making, including policy-making on European matters. The design and implementation of many development initiatives, too, require a complex negotiation with territorially based elites.

Autonomy without access is illustrated in the Italian and Spanish cases. In Spain, as Cuchillo (this volume) notes, there is no formal mechanisms for involving the regions in Community matters and the state has jealously guarded its prerogatives. Similarly in Italy, the centre has retained control of Community matters even where these involve matters of regional jurisdiction. On the other hand, the institution of the State–Regions Conference indicates that Italy may be moving in the direction of co-operative federalism, with formal functional division becoming less important and intergovernmental exchange taking place over a broad range of issues. In both Spain and Italy, regional governments have complained about being forced to implement Community directives in devolved areas but have reluctantly complied.

The combination of autonomy and influence is best represented in the German system of co-operative federalism. This provides for *Länder* influence in national policy and thence Community policy through the Bundesrat and other devices. The *Länder* are able to participate in the German delegation in various community forums. This includes representation on EC committees and the team backing the representative to the Council of Ministers. In addition, the *Länderbeobachter*, a civil servant appointed by the *Länder* collectively, is responsible for collecting information about Community matters and can attend the Council of Ministers as a non-speaking member of the German delegation, can join the preparatory meetings for the Council held in the Ministry of Economic Affairs and receives the orders of the German delegation to the Committee of Parliament of Permanent Representatives (Gerstenlauer, 1985). After the passage of the Single European Act, the role of the Bundesrat in EC affairs was further strengthened. Given the German tradition of co-operative federalism and consensus politics, this permits a considerable degree of influence to be exercised.

While co-operative federalism allows for a regional input into Community policy it tends to be marked, in Germany as in other federations, by executive dominance. There is therefore a danger that its spread might exacerbate the 'democratic deficit' of the developing Community and increase tensions unless the Parliament strengthens its capacity for territorial representation. Systems of election to the European Parliament continue to differ among member states and not all have a territorial basis. Denmark, Greece, Luxembourg and the Netherlands have national list systems. France also has a national list system of election but the parties make sure that their lists have a balanced regional representation to the extent of including the territorial designation of each candidate in the publicity. Elsewhere, candidates are elected on constituency and regional bases and have explicit territorial mandates. The Parliament, struggling to assert itself against the Commission and national governments and parliaments, has on occasion shown itself sympathetic to the similar plight of regional governments. This attitude may also owe something to the influence within the Parliament of regional and local *notables* and especially those French *notables* who continue to hold local office. Several prominent French politicians, forced by the law on accumulation of mandates to surrender an elective office, have given up their national parliamentary mandate, choosing to retain their local and European ones. In 1988, having succeeded in persuading the Commission to establish a Consultative Council of Regional and Local Authorities, the Parliament pleaded for a charter of regionalization for member states, providing for democratic election, adequate powers and finance, autonomy and the participation of regions in defining the negotiating positions of member states in Community institutions (Chauvet, 1989). Of course, this remains a non-binding recommendation adopted neither by the Commission nor by the member governments.

Several regions and local governments have sought direct links with the Community by opening offices in Brussels. Although there has been some opposition from national governments, this practice has spread, and now includes all ten West German *Länder* and West Berlin (in nine offices), four Spanish regions (each with its own office), six French regions and two departments (in four offices) and four British local authorities (each with its own office) (Serignan, 1989). The main value of such offices is the ability to monitor developments in the Commission so as to be ready to put pressure on national governments to respond, and to inform regions about the availability of various Community funds. In addition, there has been a sharp increase in the number of visits to Brussels by regional and local delegations, for information and to try to expedite specific dossiers. There is, however, no question of individual regions negotiating directly with the Community or acting in opposition to their national governments. Commission officials welcome visits but point out that under the rules and procedures they are powerless to provide extra funds to individual regions.

More important politically are the various regional lobby and consultative groups. The Commission is traditionally more receptive to transnational interest groups and there are several organizations which aspire to this role. The International Union of Local Authorities and the Council of Communes and Regions of Europe are both wider in scope than the Community and have been closely associated with the Council of Europe, which they persuaded to establish a Permanent Conference of Local and Regional Authorities in 1957. In 1986, they opened a joint office to deal with the EC (Chauvet, 1989). In 1985, the Council (later Assembly) of European Regions was launched, with 107 members including eleven Swiss cantons and Austrian *Länder*. The establishment of formal rights of consultation with the Community owed a great deal to the pressure of the European Parliament, which, in the course of the reforms of the Community regional fund, stressed the need for greater involvement of regions themselves. In 1988, the Commission finally established a Consultative Council of Regional and Local Authorities with consultative rights over the formulation and implementation of regional policies as well as the regional implications of other Community policies. Its forty-two members are appointed by the Commission on the joint nomination of the Assembly of European Regions, the International Union of Local Authorities and the Council of Regions and Communes of Europe (Chauvet, 1989). The Maastricht treaty provided for a stronger, but still consultative, council of regions.

Other regional organizations seeking to influence policy-making in Brussels are the Conference of Peripheral Maritime Regions, the Association of European Frontier Regions, the Working Group of Traditional Industrial Regions and three Alpine groups. In addition, the development of the Community has encouraged the formation of a number of transnational frontier organizations. There is thus a great deal of activity in the region–Europe link. The difficulty lies in picking out the significant dialogue amid the surrounding noise. The Commission encourages lobbying by non-national groups as a source of information and a strengthening of the *communautaire* spirit. Sometimes this has aroused national jealousies, as in the case of the French Economic and Social Council which complained about the establishment of the Consultative Council of Regional and Local Authorities which merely created expectations and encouraged demands among which the national government would have to choose (Conseil Economique et Social, 1989). Yet the Commission has a fairly small bureaucracy and could not sustain continuous direct links with all regional authorities. One reason why national governments themselves have consolidated local governments is the difficulty of control in an excessively complex system. Nor is the Commission in a position to monitor the detailed administration of its own policies. While it can and does use regional governments as a resource, its main links are necessarily with member states. In those cases where regions have established links with Brussels, as in the German instance, these are not a means of bypassing national governments, which remain the key actors in policy-making, but a device to reinforce national-level lobbying (Anderson, 1990).

Beyond 1992

The programme to complete the internal market by the end of 1992 and proposals for monetary and political union will have major implications for the position of regions within the Community. The internal market and monetary union will tend to increase territorial disparities while reducing national governments' ability to protect vulnerable sectors and regions. A 1990 report for the Commission warns that the old industrial regions of northern Britain, north-west France and the Basque County could suffer severely (*Observer*, 14.1.90). This in turn is likely to spawn coalitions of regional defence such as were seen in several European countries in the 1970s. The expansion of the regional development funds will provide help in economic restructuring but, if the experience of national regional policies is a precedent, may raise expectations by more than the capacity to satisfy them. The opening of the European market, together with the strengthening of decentralist trends in politics, is also increasing territorial competition for mobile investment on a European scale, to the advantage of the regions best equipped to receive it. National governments are less and less able to control this. Nor would they wish to do so, since attempts at diversionary policy are likely to drive investment to other states. As the spatial economy restructures, large costs are imposed on communities in terms of job losses, migration and social stress. Indeed, it is at the local and regional level that the conflict between the economic conception of Europe based on market liberalism and the social conception based on solidarity and welfare is most acutely felt.

Regions differ markedly in the extent to which they are able to compete in this new environment and to manage the social consequences of change, in terms both of their natural endowments and their institutional structures. In Germany, there is a well-established regional level which is linked closely to national politics and which has been increasingly active in economic development including infrastructure planning, research and development and technology transfer (Esser, 1989). Germany and Belgium, indeed, are the only member states to have a level of government corresponding to the Community NUTS 1 level. In France, Italy and Spain, regional governments are less well endowed but there is evidence that some regional governments are learning more about mounting effective development policies. In France regions remain too small and arbitrarily drawn for the purposes of European competition, and decentralization has sparked off a great deal of competition among cities and departments within regions for mobile investment, to the detriment of the region as a whole. Since 1988, there have been moves to rationalize the spatial development effort through strengthened national urban policies and a relaunching of regional planning contracts, but radical proposals for redrawing regional boundaries are likely to meet the fate of earlier attempts to consolidate local government. In Britain, the absence of regional government was identified by the Commission report as a hindrance to progress. The pre-elected Conservative Government remains opposed to regional devolution.

Integration also carried implications for the character of politics within specific territories. In parts of Southern Europe, where class and territorial opposition to the internal market coincide, new movements of social protest can be anticipated, focused on the Community, as happened in the original Mediterranean members in the 1970s. Similar developments may occur in declining industrial areas of Northern Europe, though their target may depend on the content of national and Community policy. In Scotland where class and territorial oppositions combined to produce widespread rejection of the Community in the 1970s, matters changed as both Labour and nationalists saw Europe as a way of circumventing the centralist and market-oriented policies of the Thatcher government. The support of territorially based labour movements for the European project will hinge on the importance given to the social dimension.

Political integration has more radical implications for the territorial configuration of European states. A politically unified Europe, transcending the limitations of existing states, provides a new context in which problems, insoluble in the national context, may find solutions. German unification is the most prominent example but it also applies to other territorial issues. Some observers have hoped that the growing irrelevance of national borders might solve the Irish question, though the basis of that conflict in community struggles within Northern Ireland makes this unlikely. European unity has, however, given a new meaning to peripheral nationalist movements, which by campaigning for independence within Europe can discard the separatist label and, indeed, appear more cosmopolitan than their opponents within the existing states. Community membership has supplied a political and economic support system for small states since 1958 and may do so for more. The Scottish National Party has now adopted a policy of independence in Europe, reminiscent of an earlier phase when late-nineteenth-century nationalists called for independence within the Empire. Basque nationalists stress a similar message. In Catalonia, attitudes are more ambiguous. Nationalism there has historically been caught between regional assertiveness and a continued commitment to the Spanish state. The dominant Convergència i Unió (CiU) continues this theme, seeing the Community as a way of reconciling its European and Spanish missions. It is in Belgium that this process has gone furthest. The existence of the Community has allowed the dismantling of large parts of the central state itself in favour of the regions and autonomous communities. The constitutional provision allowing the latter to make international agreements in cultural matters has given them some independent scope in the Community. In other fields, the absence of national ministries has meant that regional representatives are the only Belgian presence in the Council of Ministers and meetings of officials.

There is a certain logic to these developments. In Scotland, Catalonia, the Basque County and other peripheries, membership of the 'national state' has always been somewhat contingent. In the absence of the deep-seated and exclusive national loyalty which French governments were able, with some success, to impose, Scots, Catalans and Basques preserved dual loyalties, favouring inclusion in the wider state when it coincided with class or other interests and was not unduly oppressive. The state also provided physical protection and economic support through trade policies, tariffs and subsidies. With military tensions relaxed in Europe and control over the key economic decisions moving to the Community level, this function is less important.

The more critical problem concerns the practicalities of the demand for independence within Europe. There is at present no provision for territories to secede from national states and rejoin the Community as independent members. It is difficult to envisage the Community refusing membership to a Scotland which had gained independence with the consent of the United Kingdom Parliament, since refusal would amount to expulsion; but the governments of Spain, France, Belgium and Italy would hardly welcome the precedent. The vision of all nation states breaking up into a 'Europe of the regions' remains strictly Utopian. Instead, there is likely to be increasing institutional differentiation within a wider European state order which itself is in rapid evolution. Some states will remain united and homogeneous. Others may tolerate degrees of autonomy coming close to separatism. Others may succeed in rationalizing their internal structures and stabilizing the relationship between state and region with the broader Community. It is very possible that the Community itself will divide into a core of integrated members and an outer circle of more loosely associated states. The opening of the Community to Eastern Europe will create yet further patterns. The future of the European state order is an issue too broad for this chapter, but what seems certain is that the clarity and logic of the nineteenth-century nation-state ideal or even the Community of nation states will give way to a new, and also older, picture of territorial differentiation and complexity.

Further reading and references

Anderson, J. (1990) 'Skeptical reflections of a "Europe of the regions"': Britain, West Germany and the European Regional Development Fund'. Paper to the American Political Science Association annual meeting, San Francisco.

André, C., Drevet, J.-F. and Landaburu, E. (1989) 'Regional consequences of the internal market', *Contemporary European Affairs*, 1 (1–2): 205–14.

Chauvet, J.-P. (1989) 'Participation des collectivités territoriales aux décisions européenes. Le rôle des lobbies locaux et régionaux', *Après-demain*, 314–15: 9–12.

Commission of the European Communities (1987) *The Regions of the European Community: Third Periodic Report on the Social Situation and Development of the Regions of the European Community*. Luxembourg.

Conseil Economique et Social (1989) Report on meeting of 25 and 26 April 1989, *Journal officiel de la république française*, 12, 26 May.

Esser, J. (1989) 'Does industrial policy matter? *Land* governments in research and technology policy in Germany', in C. Crouch and D. Marquand (eds), *The New Centralism*. Oxford: Blackwell.

Fullarton, B. and Gillespie, A. (1988) 'Transport and telecommunications', in W. Molle and R. Cappelin (eds), *Regional Impact of Community Policies in Europe*. Aldershot: Gower.

Gerstenlauer, H.-G. (1985) 'German *Länder* in the European Community', in M. Keating and B. Jones (eds), *Regions in the European Community*. Oxford: Clarendon.

Keating, M. (1988) *State and Regional Nationalism: Territorial Politics and the European State*. Hemel Hempstead: Harvester Wheatsheaf.

Keeble, D., Offord, J. and Walker, S. (1988) *Peripheral Regions in a Community of Twelve Member States*. Luxembourg: Commission of the European Communities.

Lankowsky, C. (ed.) (1993) *Europe's Emerging Identity: Regional Integration vs Opposition Movements in the European Community*. Boulder, CO: Lynne Rienner.

Mawson, J., Martins, M. R. and Gibney, J. (1985) 'The development of the European Community regional policy', in M. Keating and B. Jones (eds), *Regions in the European Community*. Oxford: Clarendon.

Mény, Y. (1985) 'French regions in the European Community', M. Keating and B. Jones (eds), *Regions in the European Community*. Oxford: Clarendon.

Midwinter, A., Keating, M. and Mitchell, J. (1991) *Politics and Public Policy in Scotland*. London: Macmillan.

Molle, W. and Cappelin, R. (1988) 'The co-ordination problem in theory and policy', in W. Molle and R. Cappelin (eds), *Regional Impact of Community Policies in Europe*. Aldershot: Gower.

Roger Tym (1984) *Integrated Development Operation for Strathclyde. Final Report. Preparatory Study*. London: Roger Tym & Partners.

Serignan, M. (1989) 'L'Evolution des relations entre la CEE et les collectivités territoriales' *Après-demain*, 314–15: 4–7.

Strijker, D. and de Veer, J. (1988) 'Agriculture', in W. Molle and R. Cappelin (eds), *Regional Impact of Community Policies in Europe*. Aldershot: Gower.

Appendix: Meso Government in Denmark and Sweden

Tore Hansen

The Norwegian model of meso-level government, described and discussed in Chapter 7, may to a considerable extent be viewed as an example of a common Scandinavian model, applying to all Scandinavian countries. This is, at least, the case if the definition is limited to Denmark, Sweden and Norway. Finland represents a completely different case, where there is no formal intermediate level of government between state and primary municipalities, and where regional tasks are dealt with by voluntary associations of primary municipalities or by regional state agencies.

Although the Danish and Swedish cases come quite close to the Norwegian one, there are certain differences which it may be useful to point out. In fact, while Denmark and Norway have quite similar meso-level systems, the Swedish model is slightly deviant. In this appendix I will provide some summary information about the Danish and Swedish systems, not going into any details about developments and reforms. I will also refrain from any lengthy discussion of possible causes of dissimilarities observed across the three nations.

Denmark

During the late 1960s and early 1970s the Danish regional administration was reorganized by moving several tasks and powers from the regional state authorities (*amt* – headed by the prefect, or *amtmanden*) to the county municipalities (*amtskommunene*). As in Norway, the leading principle of Danish local government reform has been to secure local political control over regional service provision. Furthermore, a central aim has been to abolish special service agencies in favour of multi-functional authorities both at local and at regional level. Even if this principle of 'unity administration' has not been accomplished completely (exceptions include the police and labour market authorities, which are still run by regional state agencies), most regional service provision is under the control of county councils. As far as the prefect is concerned, his or her primary function today is to conduct legal control over decisions made by primary municipalities. In addition, the prefect has certain minor tasks of a more juridical character, related to issues concerning private law.

Denmark is divided into fourteen county communes (*amtskommuner*). Each county commune is headed by a county council, consisting of between 13 and 31 elected members; the exact size is determined by the county council. The members of the county councils are elected directly for a term of four years. As in Norway, county council elections are co-ordinated with elections to municipal councils, and the composition of the councils is based on the principle of proportional representation.

Among the members of the council, a mayor (*amtborgermester*) is elected, a position which is a full-time job. Apart from being chairperson of the council – having major responsibility for preparing the agenda for council meetings and conducting control over the implementation of decisions – the mayor also acts as head of the administration. In addition, the mayor is chairperson of the finance committee, which acts as the central co-ordinating unit for all county council activities.

Apart from the finance committee, there are four mandatory standing committees composed of members of the county council: one on hospitals, one on social welfare and public health, one on building and construction and a committee in charge of culture and education.

This list of mandatory committees also indicates the major functions served by the county councils. Hospitals constitute the most resource-demanding function of the counties. However, it is not as dominating in financial terms as in Norway, or in Sweden, to which I will return. Apart from certain specialized hospitals which are run by central government, all Danish hospitals – somatic as well as psychiatric – are owned and run by the county communes. In addition, the counties have an administrative responsibility for sick pensions/pay; but as far as other social welfare services are concerned, the responsibility of the county councils is mainly restricted to planning and supervision *vis-à-vis* primary municipalities.

This planning and supervisory function also applies to the education sector and the cultural sector, but with certain exceptions. County councils may run secondary schools, and some of the regional theatres, regional orchestras and certain museums are run by the county councils.

Finally, the county councils are also in charge of some road construction and the planning and co-ordination of transportation facilities, as well as various tasks relating to the physical infrastructure of local communities, such as water supply and sewage systems. However, most important within such fields is the responsibility for comprehensive physical planning and planning control, including supervision of physical plans and developments in primary municipalities.

The relative importance of the various functions is illustrated in Table 1.

Table 1   *Gross current expenditures by sector/ function, Danish county councils, 1987*

Sector/function	% of total expenditures
Administration/planning	4.4
Urban development/housing	0.5
Roads	2.5
Education/culture	11.6
Hospitals	43.6
Social welfare	30.8
other	6.6
Total	100.0
Sum – million Danish kroner	48,619.0

To these figures one should add expenditures for investments, which brings total county council spending in 1987 up to 53,219 million Danish kroner. As a proportion of GNP this equals 7.7 per cent, while the total local government sector consumes just above 36 per cent of GNP, a proportion which is considerably higher than that observed for Norway.

As far as revenues are concerned, the county councils draw them from three major sources: direct taxes (primarily income taxes), general grants from the state, and fees and charges. The remaining revenues are made up of loans, interest, and some other minor sources. Table 2 shows the relative distribution of revenues in 1987 from these sources.

As is evident from these figures, taxes constitute the most important revenue source. As indicated, the major share of tax revenues comes from income taxation, as in Norway, but about 10 per cent of total taxes are property taxes. Compared to the Norwegian situation it is interesting to note the rather modest importance of state grants. While state grants were the most important revenue source for Norwegian county councils – constituting more than half of

Table 2 *Relative distribution of revenues, Danish county councils, 1987*

Revenue source	% of total revenues
Taxes	54.3
State grants	21.0
Fees/charges	19.3
Other	5.4
Total	100.0

total revenues – Danish county councils receive just above one-fifth of their revenues from the state. Furthermore, fees and charges constitute a similar proportion of total revenues. This means, by adding taxes and fees and charges, that altogether 75 per cent of total revenues come from local sources. This indicates the degree to which Danish county councils enjoy independence from central government, a degree of financial autonomy which is clearly greater than that observed in the Norwegian case.

Sweden

Developments in and reforms of Swedish meso government over the past two decades bear a strong resemblance to those observed in Denmark and Norway. A major aim of the Swedish reforms has been to achieve a more clear-cut separation of functions between regional state authorities (*länsstyrelsen*) and the county councils (*landsting*). In contrast to the two other Scandinavian countries, Sweden has not succeeded in its efforts to achieve a radical redistribution of functions and a clear-cut separation of powers between these two authorities. Rather, according to a reform in 1971 it was decided to introduce a representative unit to head the regional state authorities – where the county councils appoint 14 of the 15 members of this board in each county. The last member is the regional prefect (*landshøvding*), who is appointed by the central government. He or she acts as chairperson of the board, in addition to his or her functions as head of the regional state administration.

Even if the regional state authorities (*länsstyrelsen*) still are in charge of some important functions, the most important level – at least from a political point of view – is the county council. There are altogether twenty-three county communes in Sweden. Each county commune is headed by a council consisting of at least thirty-one members who are directly elected every third year. The county council elections are co-ordinated with elections to primary munici-palities and Parliament (the same election day). The actual number of representatives is decided on the basis of the population size of the county. The composition of the county council is based on pro-portional representation.

Among the council members a chairperson/mayor and vice-chairperson/vice-mayor is elected to serve for one year. In addition, an executive committee is elected by and among the members of the county council with a three-year term of service. The committee's chairperson is directly elected by the council, and he or she cannot at the same time hold the position of chairperson of the council. However, in reality, the position of chairperson of the executive committee is much closer to that of the chairperson of the county councils in Denmark and Norway than are the functions of the chairperson of the county council. The executive committee has the responsibility to implement decisions made by the council and is in charge of the administration of tasks to be handled by the county council. In addition, the committee performs supervisory functions *vis-à-vis* other special committees appointed by the council. None of these special committees are mandatory; it is up to the county council to decide whether to establish such committees or not, but if established they are subordinated to the executive committee.

The most important, and dominating, function of the Swedish county communes is the provision of health services. More than two-thirds of total expenditures are appropriated for such purposes. This includes the responsibility for hospitals as well as non-institu-tional health services. The county communes are also responsible for certain social welfare services, such as rehabilitation and aid to disabled people. The county councils also run certain secondary/ vocational schools, such as social work, nursing and basic education in agriculture and forestry. In addition, the county communes perform certain other tasks related to industrial development, planning and communication, as well as cultural policy.

The relative financial importance of the various services is displayed in Table 3.

As is evident from these figures, Swedish county councils are to a lesser degree than their other Scandinavian counterparts multi-functional institutions. Hospitals and health care account for the lion's share of the council budget, while none of the other sectors/ functions exceed 4 per cent of total spending. The category 'other' is, howeʋer, an exception, accounting for almost 13 per cent of the total budget. This category comprises several minor tasks, in addition to finance expenditures, which include debt servicing.

Even if the proportions appropriated to various sectors – with the

Table 3 *Gross expenditures by sector/function,
Swedish county communes, 1987*

Sector/function	% of total expenditures
Administration	3.0
Health	74.5
Education	3.8
Social welfare	1.3
Communication	3.8
Culture	0.8
Other	12.8
Total	100.0
Sum – million Swedish kroner	102,600.0

exception of health – seem small and insignificant the actual amounts
are not. Altogether county councils consume more than 10 per cent
of GNP, with health services alone accounting for 7.5 per cent of
GNP. Thus, the remaining services account for more than 2.5 per
cent, which is not much lower than the comparative figures observed
in Denmark and Norway. It should also be added that several
initiatives have been made over recent years to strengthen county
council activities within other areas than health, in particular with
respect to labour market policies.

The revenue system of Swedish county councils is quite similar to
those observed for Denmark and Norway, with direct taxes the most
important revenues source. In 1987 the tax rate amounted to an
average of 12.35 per cent, while the average tax rate for primary
municipalities was 17.11 per cent. Since the available data on county
council revenues do not permit a similar breakdown into major
categories as those presented for Denmark and Norway, only the
figure for taxes as a proportion of total revenues is presented. In 1987
taxes constituted 60 per cent of total county council revenues, which
is a higher proportion than in the two other countries. In this sense
Swedish county councils may seem to enjoy a higher degree of
financial autonomy than county councils in Denmark and Norway.
On the other hand, revenues from fees and charges are of minor
importance in Sweden; a rough estimate of this proportion indicates
that such revenues only amount to about 5 per cent of the total. This
implies that revenues from central government sources are of
considerable importance for Swedish county councils, although not
as important as in Norway.

Conclusion

By and large it seems justified to talk about a specific Scandinavian model of meso-level government. The three countries dealt with here display several similar features, and as far as the general institutional arrangements are concerned one may even talk about blueprints. Also the reform processes over recent years display very strong similarities. The common features of the systems may be summarized as follows:

(a) All countries have established a two-tier system of government, where regional and local-level political authorities (counties and primary municipalities) enjoy a fair amount of autonomy from central government.

(b) At the regional level reforms have moved in the direction of a clear-cut separation of tasks and powers between regional state authorities and the county councils.

(c) In all three nations a system of direct elections to the county councils – based on proportional representation – has been established.

(d) The county councils serve as multi-functional institutions.

(e) The functions of the county councils are by and large the same in the three nations, with health services/hospitals as the dominating function in each country – and county.

(f) None of the county councils serves as a super-municipality *vis-à-vis* lower levels of government. The county councils are political units in their own right.

(g) The basic structure of the revenue system is the same in the three countries, with local income tax the most important revenue source.

(h) As far as developmental features are concerned, the county councils within each nation have grown in importance, and seem set to continue to do so.

Index

Page references in *italics* indicate tables and figures.